MUSSOLINI'S ARMY
IN THE FRENCH RIVIERA

THE HISTORY OF MILITARY OCCUPATION

Edited by John Laband and Ian F W Beckett

MUSSOLINI'S ARMY IN THE FRENCH RIVIERA

Italy's Occupation of France

EMANUELE SICA

UNIVERSITY OF ILLINOIS PRESS

Urbana, Chicago, and Springfield

Library of Congress Cataloging-in-Publication Data
Names: Sica, Emanuele, 1975–
Title: Mussolini's army in the French Riviera : Italy's occupation of France /
    Emanuele Sica.
Description: Urbana : University of Illinois Press, 2016. | Series: The history
    of military occupation | Includes bibliographical references and index.
Identifiers: LCCN 2015024289 | ISBN 9780252039850 (hardcover : acid-free
    paper) | ISBN 9780252097966 (e-book)
Subjects: LCSH: France—History—Italian occupation, 1942–1943. | World
    War, 1939–1945—France—Riviera. | Italy. Esercito—History—World
    War, 1939–1945. | World War, 1939–1945—Social aspects—France—
    Riviera. | Riviera (France)—History, Military—20th century. | Riviera
    (France)—Social conditions—20th century. | BISAC: HISTORY / Military /
    World War II. | HISTORY / Europe / Italy. | HISTORY / Europe / France.
Classification: LCC D802.F8 S483 2016 | DDC 944.9/40816—DC23 LC record
    available at http://lccn.loc.gov/2015024289

CONTENTS

Acknowledgments   vii

Abbreviations   ix

Chronology of the Italian Occupation
of Southeastern France   xi

Maps   xvii

PART I: THE LATIN SISTERS AND THE COMING
OF THE SECOND WORLD WAR

Introduction   3

1   Countdown to War   15

PART II: THE ARMISTICE PERIOD:
JUNE 1940–NOVEMBER 1942

2   The Italian Armistice Commission with France (CIAF)   27

3   Italian Irredentism and French Patriotism
in the Côte d'Azur   42

4   A Prelude to Full Occupation   55

PART III: THE ITALIAN OCCUPATION OF SOUTHEASTERN
FRANCE: NOVEMBER 1942–SEPTEMBER 1943

5   The November 1942 Invasion   77

6   The Italians Settle In   91

7   Life under the Occupation   115

8 Military Repression, Civilian Resistance 127

9 Collaboration and Accommodation 151

10 The Italian Jewish Policy in France 162

11 Drawing the Curtain on the Occupation 174

Conclusion 183

Notes 191

Bibliography 257

Index 269

Photographs follow pages 24 and 150.

ACKNOWLEDGMENTS

As much as a research project and the writing of a book is often a solitary journey, many individuals were instrumental in helping me complete the task.

My friend and colleague Lynne Taylor had a lasting influence on my research and gave me the skill and passion to become a historian. Roger Sarty has also provided me with a love for military history and the impact of culture on warfare.

Series editors John Laband and Ian F W Beckett provided me with invaluable guidance and encouragement. Everyone at the University of Illinois Press has been extremely helpful in coaching me through the publishing process, but a special mention should be made to acquisitions editor Daniel Nasset, who strongly believed in the feasibility of the project, and to project manager Tad Ringo for smoothing the angles in the last steps of the process. Jill R. Hughes has been a kind and very effective editor, carefully polishing my manuscript from imperfections and inconsistencies. Her work has been invaluable and is a reminder that book editors are a crucial part of the printing industry. I should not fail to mention the fundamental role played by the anonymous reviewers of my manuscript. Your criticisms enabled me to significantly better the book.

My colleagues and friends at the University of Waterloo, Queen's University, and the Royal Military College of Canada have proven supportive and offered important advice for my research. Suzanne Langlois and Valerie Deacon also helped me at different stages of my career, and their support should be acknowledged. A heartfelt thank-you as well to my students in Waterloo and my officer cadets in Kingston, who remind me how enjoyable it is to teach and study history.

Many persons in the archives deserve my praise: Fabrice Ospedale of the Archives Départementales des Alpes-Maritimes, Nicola Cappellano, Alessandro Gionfrida of the Archivio dell'Ufficio Storico dello Stato Maggiore dell'Esercito, Stefania Ruggeri of the Archivio Storico Diplomatico del Ministero degli Affari Esteri, Valérie Renoux of the Archives Municipales de Menton, and the personnel of the Archivio Centrale dello Stato. For the fruitful discussions, sometimes around glasses of wine and espressos, I would like to thank in particular my Italian colleagues Nicola Labanca, Filippo Focardi, and Amedeo Osti Guerrazzi. Their works have been very inspirational.

I owe a great debt of gratitude to my family and friends. Elio Pesso supported in many ways my stay in Nice and graciously shared his knowledge and wisdom about the history of the French Riviera. My wife's family enthusiastically supported my research and gave me welcome company in times of loneliness. My own family backed me unconditionally in my peregrinations around the world. In particular, my father, Mario, who influenced my career in many ways, read my manuscript, correcting some glaring mistakes and providing insightful comments to my research. I am deeply grateful to my mother, Odette, for teaching me French and instilling my love of reading at a very young age. Finally, my wife, Elena, has never failed to support me in my career, and my book is truly her accomplishment as much as it is mine. Along with our two cats, Nymeria and Platone, she provided solid and heartwarming companionship far from our *Patria*.

This book is dedicated to my grandfathers, Giovanni Sica and Vittorio Cecchetto, who fought as Italian soldiers during the First and Second World Wars.

ABBREVIATIONS

ACS	Archivio Centrale dello Stato
ADAHP	Archives Départementales des Alpes-de-Haute-Provence
ADAM	Archives Départementales des Alpes-Maritimes
ASMAE	Archivio Storico Diplomatico del Ministero degli Affari Esteri
AUSSME	Archivio dell'Ufficio Storico dello Stato Maggiore dell'Esercito
CGQJ	Commissariat General aux Questions Juives (Office for Jewish Affairs)
CIAF	Commissione Italiana per l'Armistizio con la Francia (Italian Armistice Commission with France)
CTA	Franco-German Armistice Commission
DECSA	Delegazione Esercito Controllo Scacchiere Alpino (Army Delegation for the Control of the Alpine Front)
EFTF	Emanuele Filiberto Testa di Ferro (Italian army division)
GaF	Guardia alla Frontiera
GAN	Gruppi d'Azione Nizzarda (Nice Action Groups)
LFC	Légion Française des Combattants
LVF	Légion des Volontaires Français contre le Bolchevisme
MINCULPOP	Ministero della Cultura Popolare (Ministry of Popular Culture)
MUR	Mouvements Unis de la Résistance (Unified Movements of the Resistance)
NAP	*nucleo antiparacadutisti* (anti-paratrooper units)

ObW	Oberbefehlshaber West (German Army Command in the West)
OVRA	Organizzazione per la Vigilanza e la Repressione dell'Antifascismo (Organization for Vigilance and Repression of Anti-Fascism)
PCI	Partito Comunista Italiano (Italian Communist Party)
PNF	Partito Nazionale Fascista (Italian Fascist Party)
PPF	Parti Populaire Français
SBM	Société des Bains de Mers et des Étrangers
SIM	Servizio Informazioni Militare
SHAT	Service Historique de l'Armée de Terre
SMG	Stato Maggiore Italiano (Italian General Staff), also known as *Comando Supremo*
SMRE	Stato Maggiore dell'Esercito (Italian General Staff Army), also known as *Superesercito*
SOL	Service d'Ordre Légionnaire
STO	Service du Travail Obligatoire

CHRONOLOGY OF THE ITALIAN OCCUPATION OF SOUTHEASTERN FRANCE

Nineteenth Century

24 March 1860: Treaty of Turin; Duchy of Savoy and County of Nice annexed by France

1860s onward: Massive Italian emigration in France, especially the Côte d'Azur

1939

22 May: Pact of Steel—military alliance between Germany, Italy, and Japan

1940

10 May: Beginning of German offensive strike in France

10 June: Mussolini's speech at Palazzo Venezia: war declaration to France and England; wave of arrests of suspected Italian Fascists and irredentists in France, later sent to internment camps in southern France

14 June: German troops enter Paris

15 June: Italian emigrants invited to sign a declaration of loyalty in local police stations

22 June: Signature of the Franco-German Armistice at Compiègne

21–24 June: Battle of the Alps, the Italian invasion of France, minimal Italian advance in French territory.

24 June: Franco-Italian Armistice of Villa Incisa; Italian military occupation of Menton and a small strip of land along the border; creation of the CIAF (Italian Armistice Commission with France)

July: Implementation of CIAF bureaus in the free zone

17 July: Vichy law restricting access to civil service employment only to French citizens with French father

22 July: Vichy law announcing the revision of post-1927 naturalizations, impacting among others Jewish and Italian emigrants

30 July: Mussolini's "Proclamation Concerning the Administration and the Judicial Organization of the Occupied Territories," creation of the Italian-occupied zone

29 August: Creation of the Légion Française des Combattants (LFC)

September: Rationing system introduced in both zones

3 October: Publication of Vichy's Statut des Juifs (Jewish Statute) forbidding Jews to hold high-ranking public offices or comparable positions in media or teaching

18 October: Jews forbidden to own and manage enterprises and excluded from the army and professional occupations

28 October: Italian invasion of Greece

5 November: Creation of Amministrazione dei Territori Occupati (Administration of Occupied Territories Bureau), supervising the civil commissar in the Italian-occupied zone

1941

4 February: Creation of the Delegati per l'Assistenza ed il Rimpatrio (Delegates for the Assistance and Repatriation), in charge of repatriating Italian emigrants and of protecting their interests

April: Rationing system already malfunctioning in the Côte d'Azur

6 April: Italian state decree stating that those living in the Italian-occupied zone with Italian descent would be considered fully Italian and thus possibly enlisted in the Regio Esercito

28 April: Giornata D'Azione Nizzarda, irredentist meeting in Savona headed by Ezio Garibaldi

May: Beginning of the Axis occupation of the Balkans (Greece and Yugoslavia)

11 May: Joan of Arc's saint day celebrated across the free zone, especially in Nice

9 October: Visit to Nice of Pétain's deputy Darlan

12 December: Birth of the Service d'Ordre Légionnaire (SOL), especially strong in the Alpes-Maritimes department due to the influence of Joseph Darnand

1942

January: Nomination of Ambassador Gino Buti as "political plenipotentiary" in Paris and Count Vittorio Zoppi as consul general to Vichy;
merging of the military branches of Resistance groups in the Armée
Secrète organization

February: Creation of the Ufficio Assistenza per il Rimpatrio dei Mentonaschi (Office for the Repatriation of the Mentonese Population)

April-May: First rumors of an impellent Italian invasion of the Côte d'Azur

Summer: Offices of collaborationist groups in the Côte d'Azur bombed
by the Resistance

June: *La Relève*, Vichy calls for volunteers to work in Germany to be bartered for French prisoners of war but with minimal success

16 June: Collaborationist militants pillage the synagogue in Nice

4 July: Deal between the head of the German police in France, SS Carl
Oberg, and the secretary-general in charge of the French police, René
Bousquet, to dispose of the foreign Jewish population on French soil

16 July: *Rafle du Vél d'Hiver* (Vel d'Hiver Roundup)—twelve thousand
Jews rounded up with the help of the French police and later shipped to
extermination camps

26 August: Five hundred Jews in Nice rounded up and sent to Drancy

27 October: The French mayor of Menton, Jean Durandy, resigns under
increasing pressure from the Italian authorities

8 November: British-American invasion of Algeria and Morocco (Operation Torch)

11 November: Italian army units (Fourth Army) cross the border and invade the Côte d'Azur

12 November: Arrests of Italian *fuoriusciti* and French nationalists in Nice

20 November: Fourth Army General Vercellino's directive on the occupation policy

27 November: Fourth Army order to disarm all French military units and
secure all French army depots

30 December: Fourth Army directive stating that no Jew in the Italian occupation zone should be interned by Vichy authorities

1943

Winter: Italian units fighting in Russia suffer heavy losses after the Battle
of Stalingrad; foreign Jews flock in the Italian-occupied zone as rumors
of a safe haven spread like wildfire

January: Internal Resistance in the former free zone consolidates into the Mouvements Unis de la Résistance (MUR) under the guidance of Henry Frenay. Beginning of bombing attacks or sabotage against railway tracks and telephone lines

1 January: Delegates for the Assistance and Repatriation officially upgraded to the role of Italian consuls

10 January: Occupied territory divided in two zones: the combat zone around the coastline and the rear zone, encompassing the more inland areas

28 January: Vercellino's directive that local commanders can resort to collective sanctions in case of attacks on Italian troops

February: Creation of the Comité d'Aide aux Réfugiés (Refugees Aid Committee, later known as the Comité Dubouchage) to help rescue and protect foreign Jews

16 February: Start of the Vichy force labor program, the Service du Travail Obligatoire

March-April: Massive strikes in northern Italy as rationing and bombing increase

Spring: Food distribution in the Côte d'Azur collapses; black market thrives; creation of three internment camps in Sospel, Embrun, and Modane

1 April: CIAF military bureaus (army, navy, and air force) become integrated into the Fourth Army's administration; CIAF officials now subordinated to military commanders

26 April: Prefet of the Alpes-Maritimes, Marcel Ribière, resigns; replaced on 11 May by Jean Chaigneau

27 April: Curfew enforced in the combat zone; three Italian officers gunned down in downtown Nice, one killed

First week of May: Guido Lospinoso, general police inspector, arrives in Nice to solve the Jewish problem; no change in Italian Jewish policy

6 May: Massive roundup of civilians in Nice

11–16 May: Several bombing attacks on Italian troops in Nice, Cannes, and Marseille

13 May: Axis troops surrender in Tunisia; North Africa entirely under Allied control

June-July: Arrests of Italian Communist Resistance and French Armée Secrète leaders

5 June: Italian informers Giuseppe and Serafina Moraglia gunned down by *fuoriusciti*

10 July: Allied invasion of Sicily (Operation Husky)

20 July: Bombing attack on Davico restaurant in Nice; one soldier dead

and four seriously injured, among them Nino Lamboglia, an irredentist university professor

26 July: Mussolini dismissed as prime minister by King Vittorio Emanuel III and arrested

27 July: Jean Médecin, mayor of Nice, resigns

Late July: Gradual disengagement of Italian units from France to shore up the Italian coastline

17 August: *Bando Vercellino* (Vercellino Proclamation)—death penalty for a variety of crimes (sabotage, harming Italian soldiers, etc.)

3 September: Italian armistice signed with the Allies

8 September: Armistice publicly announced via radio broadcasts; exodus of the Jews of Saint-Martin-Vésubie, escorted across the border by Italian soldiers

12 September: Fourth Army officially disbanded

1944

Summer: Violent reprisals in the Côte d'Azur against collaborationists and Italian irredentists; beginning of the *Épuration légale* (legal purge)

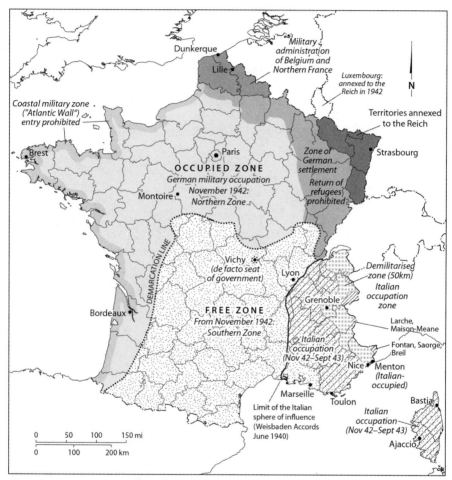

Map 1. Occupied France, 1940–1944.

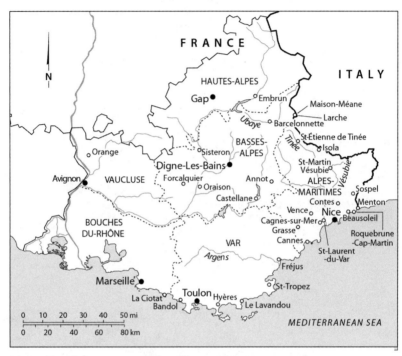

Map 2. French Provence and Côte d'Azur, 1940–1943.

Map 3. Close-up of the County of Nice and the Franco-Italian border.

PART I
THE LATIN SISTERS
AND THE COMING
OF THE SECOND WORLD WAR

INTRODUCTION

France and Italy had had a rocky but continuous relationship since the middle of the eighteenth century. France, under the guidance of the autocratic ruler Napoleon III, nephew of the more famous Napoleon Bonaparte, was instrumental in the birth of the modern Italian state by helping the kingdom of Piedmont-Sardinia secure a win against the Austrian Empire in 1859. As a token of gratitude, Vittorio Emanuele II, the king of Piedmont-Sardinia and the future first ruler of modern Italy, decided to hand over Nice and the Savoy territory to France. The relationship between Italy and France, the two Latin Sisters, however, soured during the last quarter of the century. The Scramble for Africa, referring to the greedy colonization of the "Dark Continent," quickly turned to the advantage of more established states such as Great Britain and France, which had started their colonization earlier in the century. The Italians resented especially the 1881 French *coup de force* in Tunisia, a territory with thousands of Italian settlers, which catapulted the former Ottoman province into the growing French colonial empire. Frustrated with its efforts at expansion into Africa, Italy signed the Triple Alliance with Germany and Austria-Hungary, a defensive pact to counter the French influence in Western Europe and Africa and Russian expansionism in the Balkans. However, the Triple Alliance rested on shaky grounds, as the *Irredentisti*, the Italian nationalists, vehemently advocated, on historical or ethnical principles, for the return of territories that were still under Austrian rule, such as the Trentino Alto-Adige (South Tyrol) region, Dalmatia, and the city of Trieste.[1]

In the meantime, the relationship between the Italians and French dramatically improved at the turn of the century. Italy also sought a degree of stability in the Mediterranean area that no country but France could guarantee. In January 1902 the French and Italian governments signed an accord settling their disagreements over several African territories and outlining their respective spheres of influence. This newly cordial relationship between the Latin Sisters was sealed by a triumphal Parisian *tournée* of the king of Italy, Vittorio Emanuele III, in October 1903.

The First World War and the postwar years were the apex of the entente between Italy and France. Italy adopted from the start a wary neutral stance, bargaining the country's eventual help in the upcoming war with an Austrian promise of handing over part of the "unredeemed" lands. Austrian officials, however, would not budge, fearful that later in the war other nationalities within the Austro-Hungarian Empire would ask for more political autonomy, which could tear apart the fragile fabric of the last multiethnic empire in Europe. Meanwhile, thousands of Italian migrants had flowed into recruitment offices to join the French army. The resulting Légion Garibaldienne, led by a grandson of Giuseppe Garibaldi, fought valiantly on the Argonne front in the winter of 1914 but lost more than one-fourth of its forces.[2] Their bravery provided considerable fuel for the interventionist propaganda in Italy, secretly funded by the British and French embassies in Rome, which advocated for Italy's immediate allegiance to the Triple Entente (Great Britain, France, and Russia.)

Italy joined the war in May 1915, ultimately persuaded by the Allied promises of territorial compensation (Trentino, Trieste, and Dalmatia among others) in return for its war effort. At once, newspapers and journals from both sides of the Alps initiated a campaign to stress the Latin character of the two countries, as the cradle of modern civilization, cast against the Teutonic barbaric hordes.[3] From the first offensives in the summer of 1915 to the end of the war, the Italians would be bogged down in the trenches, ghastly mirroring the deadly stalemate that pitted the Anglo-French armies against the Germans on the Western Front.

Common enemies eventually reinforced the bond between France and Italy as armies pooled their energies to counter the Central Powers' offensive strikes. Indeed, in reciprocation for the French and British divisions sent to reinforce the Austro-Italian front after the rout of Caporetto in October 1917,[4] the Italians sent a full army corps of fifty thousand Italian soldiers to shore up the Marne front. This unit doggedly resisted nineteen German assaults, which were part of the Second Battle of the Marne, at the appalling cost of eleven thousand casualties.[5] Its valor was officially recognized by the commander of the Fifth Army, Gen. Henry Berthelot, whose communiqué rhetorically insisted that "the Latin blood jointly shed on French soil, as the one spilled on the sunny fields of Italy, will more deeply bond the alliance between the two Sister States and the indestructible friendship of two great nations."[6]

Italy and France had slowly drifted apart after the end of the First World War. At the 1919 Paris Peace Conference, thanks in part to botched diplomacy from its delegation, Italy had been handed Trentino Alto-Adige and Trieste but had failed to secure Istria and Dalmatia. Thus, nationalist propagandists vehemently protested, fueling the myth of the *Vittoria Mutilata* (Mutilated Victory). In part capitalizing on the frustration of the Italian imperial dreams, Benito Mussolini came to power in October 1922. In a few years he and his cronies instituted a totalitarian dictatorship, the Fascist regime, based on a radical form of ultranationalism and tainted by extreme xenophobia and imperialistic tendencies. Indeed, as aptly demonstrated by Davide Rodogno and H. James Burgwyn, the Duce and his military advisors endeavored to create an empire over territories bordering the Mediterranean Sea, such as Greece, Dalmatia, the County of Nice, Tunisia, and Corsica, by the means of territorial conquests carried out by the Italian army, just as the columns of Roman legionaries had done two thousand years earlier.[7]

Italy's interests in southeastern France, Corsica, and Tunisia set the Fascists on a collision course with the French. The French colony Tunisia, for instance, was deemed paramount to Italian expansion in the Mediterranean area, because Italian control of the Tunisian and Sicilian coasts would strategically cut the Mediterranean Sea in half. The push to North Africa was also an important part of the affirmation on the international stage that Italy was willing to fight to get what the Fascists thought was a "place in the sun." In a speech delivered by Count Galeazzo Ciano to the Italian parliament on 30 November 1938, the Italian foreign minister, while broadly outlining the Italian strategy, boomed, "We will defend, with inflexible steadfastness, the interests and natural aspirations of the Italian nation," and the deputies roared in response, "Tunisia, Djibouti, Corsica, Nizza."[8]

Arguably, the disenchantment with France went along with rapprochement with Nazi Germany. After Adolf Hitler's rise to power, and with the quick Nazification of German politics and society, Germany became France's natural ally both on ideological grounds and on shared goals in international policy. After all, both powers dismissed the Versailles system as a relic of the past that was choking both Fascist and Nazi expansionist policies, and both ideologies understood that only violence and its manifestation on international politics, war, would ultimately be the means to forge new empires. Smoothed by the nomination of Galeazzo Ciano, Mussolini's son-in-law, as foreign minister, a common expansionist vision ultimately led to the signing of a friendship treaty between Italy and Germany in October 1936, establishing the nefarious Rome-Berlin Axis. The rapprochement between the two dictatorships was favored by their joint assistance of the Spanish Nationalists of Gen. Francisco Franco in the Spanish Civil War (1936–1939) and definitely sealed with the Pact of Steel on 22 May 1939.[9] Thus, when the Second World War erupted, French-Italian relations were at their nadir as the two countries prepared for a possible war at their common Alpine border, a suspicion proven by the forced expropriation campaign in the Alps in 1936, avowedly aimed at strengthening the Italian line of Alpine fortifications.[10] The war, indeed, would inflame the Alps in June 1940.

Italian soldiers were again marching in France, no longer as allies and trusted friends as in the First World War, but as enemies and dangerous occupiers. The Italian army, following an offensive strike on 21–24 June 1940, occupied a strip of land along the Italian-French border, with one significant French town, Menton. This military occupation was the prelude to a full-scale invasion in November 1942, which brought the *Regio Esercito,* the Italian Royal Army, in the Côte d'Azur and Provence regions up to the Rhône in the west and the Savoy in the north. More than 150,000 soldiers were deployed for ten months, until the Italian armistice with the Allies in September 1943.

The nature of the Italian occupation in France was ambivalent and quite different from the other important Italian military occupation during the war, that of the Balkans. For a long time after the war, the myth of the *Italiani Brava Gente* (Italian Goodfellows) thrived in postwar Italy. The myth goes, "The Italian soldier is essentially good-natured, firmly attached to family values, even a bit of a 'mummy's boy' [*mammone*]; as such, he is incapable of performing violence against the defenseless ones, he eschews reprisals, he does not yield to the overwhelming brutalities of war."[11] However, research in recent years had uncovered war crimes committed by the Italians, the consequences of not only being embroiled in a fratricidal war between local ethnic groups—namely, the Serbs and the Croats—that the Italians were unable to control, but also of ineffective strategy owing to a lack of means, a deep-seated friction between Italian officials and military commanders, and poor judgment in dealing with the local population.[12] At fault was the overall poor Italian counterinsurgency campaign in former Yugoslavia, a product of the deficient military training of both officers and soldiers, as well as an embedded racism in the Regio Esercito, which cast the Slavic populations as barbaric and primitive.[13] The infamous Circular 3 C issued in March 1942 by the head of the Italian army in former Yugoslavia, Gen. Mario Roatta, left little ambiguity as to the intention of Italian commanders. Unit leaders were given permission to raze villages whose populations were suspected of helping partisans. Male inhabitants of these villages were to be considered *favoreggiatori* (abettors) and, as such, to be executed while the remaining population—women, old people, and children—were to be deported to concentration camps.[14]

None of the inescapable spiral of partisan bombings and the Regio Esercito's ruthless reprisals ever happened under the Mediterranean sun. No massacres or wanton razing of villages marred the ten months of the occupation of the Côte d'Azur. The Italian policy was relatively moderate in its use of repression and instead sought to win over the local population through accommodations that lessened the impact of the occupation. Moreover, the Italian army effectively shielded those Jews who had fled to the Italian occupation zone from both the Nazi and the Vichy regimes' anti-Semitic policies, a unique case in Axis-occupied Europe. The attitude of the Italian army in France depended less on its supposedly good-hearted nature as on the conflation of two important differences between the two occupations: the contingency of war and the cultural and ethnic proximity between occupiers and occupied.

First of all, Italian commanders changed their approach to occupations of foreign territories according to the evolution of war. When Italian troops occupied the French strip of land in June 1940 and the Balkans in spring 1941, the Axis side was in firm control of Continental Europe; the United States had still not entered the war; and Russia was a formal, albeit erstwhile, ally of the Nazi regime. Thus, Italian commanders in former Yugoslavia and Greece exuded confidence in their reports, even after partisan bands began actively fighting back the Italian occupation. Italian commanders and civilian authorities could hardly hide their enthusiasm for the "New Mediterranean Order" headed by the Duce. On the contrary, the Italian occupation of France in November 1942 happened as the Russian victories on the eastern front and the awakening of the American colossus turned the tide of war to the advantage of the Allied side. The situation looked especially stark for the Italians, as the landing of Anglo-American units in North Africa exposed the Italian peninsula to possible Allied landings. The occupation of the French Mediterranean shoreline represented a strain in an already overstretched Italian defensive array at a time when the army's morale had considerably plummeted with the Axis setbacks on the eastern front and in North Africa. Fear and tiredness then became palpable in Fourth Army commanders' reports in glaring contrast with the bravado of the Second Army in former Yugoslavia.

Upon occupying southeastern France in November 1942, Italian commanders realized that an uncompromising approach to the occupation of France would only radicalize the internal situation in France at a time when the inherent weaknesses of the Italian army would not permit it to deal successfully with both an Allied invasion and a French uprising. To this end, the officers of the Fourth Army were given precise instructions to restrain native Italian separatist groups from fomenting the French populace with irredentist propaganda.

Aside from the contingency of war, the Italian occupation in southeastern France was shaped by the cultural and ethnic proximity between occupiers and occupied. Italy and France had enjoyed a steady flow of people and goods since the Middle Ages. The French border with the Italian peninsula, until the twentieth century little more than a mere line on dusty maps, was crossed back and forth by Italian migrants in search of a better life. These travels in turn cemented a common culture as migrants settled permanently in France starting from the late nineteenth century. French, Provençal, and Italian traditions did not evolve in parallel, but intermeshed together in a variety of ways, be it through idiom, the way of dressing, or the way of cooking. By the beginning of the Second World War, more than one-quarter of the population of the French departments bordering Italy were either Italians or of Italian heritage while the Italians in France peaked at more than one million.[15] As is often the case with massive immigration of one ethnicity into a given country, the integration process was far from being smooth, with latent xenophobia occasionally erupting in racial riots. However, over the years, Italian immigrants generally had been accepted by the local population.[16]

The overarching paradigm of a deep-seated Italian-French cultural intermixing in the Mediterranean part of France is central to understanding the attitude of the occupying Italian army from 1940 to 1943. Upon the occupation in November 1942, the Italian community in France largely acted as mediators between the local population and Italian soldiers, notwithstanding a visible Fascist minority that incessantly stirred the irredentist pot. Italian commanders, on the other hand, were loath to implement harsher rules against a population with such strong cultural and ethnic ties with the Italians. Contrary to the Balkans, where locals were generally considered at best barbarians or feral beasts to be tamed,[17] the Italians often sympathized with the local population. With little language barrier, misunderstandings, which in a war zone could rapidly aggravate to major confrontations, were kept to a minimum. If nothing else, the Fascist state experienced an inferiority complex with regard to the French. After all, the significant Italian minority all over France, particularly in the Côte d'Azur, was a constant reminder that Italy had been the poorer of the two Latin Sisters. Fascist propaganda, therefore, could hardly picture the occupation as the harbinger of an evolved civilization as had been the case in Africa and in the Balkans.

The Italian military occupation of southeastern France is analyzed in this book at three different levels, each involving a triangular relationship.[18] At a more general level the occupation is gauged with the lens of "historical sociology, whose comparative nature would allow the researchers to break out of the limitations of the national framework."[19] Thus, this study makes references to the triangular comparison of the Italian occupation of France to the German occupation of France and to the Italian occupation of the Balkans, the first sharing in common the same occupied population and state, the latter sharing the same occupiers: the Italian army. The subjects of comparison are both the occupiers' policy and their differences and similarities and the occupied society's reactions.

Additionally, this work examines "the structural effects of occupation on the occupied society's environment and living conditions."[20] Particular importance is given to the triangular and rocky relationship between the representatives of the French state, especially the prefects and mayors, with the Italian military authorities, the officers of Italian units deployed on French soil, and Italian civilian authorities who were officially dispatched by Rome to supervise the implementation of the Franco-Italian armistice and to secretly prepare for the annexation of the occupied territories. Relationships were tense as each side fought to keep their prerogatives. This situation stemmed first of all from the vagueness of the international laws of war, which, while sanctioning the passage of "the authority of the legitimate power . . . in the hands of the occupant," gave him the onus not only of law and order but also of abiding to the laws of antebellum France.[21] Furthermore, the French resented the fact that, contrary to the Germans, the Italians were acting as conquerors even though their army had barely made it through the Alps. Vichy prefects and Italian commanders thus locked horns over many sovereignty issues, never failing to delegitimize each other's authority in the eyes of the local populace. Adding further fuel to the tensions, the Italian side was also divided between military authorities, who believed in a strategically realist approach meant to defuse any possible insurrection of the French populace, and the more political approach of the Italian civilian personnel, moved by the nationalist belief of a prospective annexation of the Côte d'Azur as part of the aggrandizement of the nascent Fascist Mediterranean empire.

Finally, at a grassroots level, this book explores the "face-to-face interaction between occupiers and occupied people,"[22] understanding that this was a two-way relationship shaped by both groups' habits, culture, prejudices, and tensions. As in the case of other military occupations, people living in the Italian-occupied area of France were not only passive spectators impacted by the events but also actors who could shape the occupation, ranging from open or covert resistance, to foreign military rule, to "opportunist or political accommodations" as a way to further one's political, economic, and personal interests by collaborating with the occupying power.[23]

The interplay between civilians and soldiers was certainly favored by the cultural proximity. Speaking a similar language, or in some cases a common one, along with shared cultural roots, such as the Catholic faith, not only minimized the risks of faux pas or misunderstandings, which could erupt in serious incidents in the stressful atmosphere of a military occupation, but also favored a cordial cohabitation. It appears that in many cases Italian soldiers were eager to establish contacts with the local populace, whether out of boredom, curiosity, or self-interest. This laxity in discipline—though at times reprimanded, with little result, by the Italian commanders—was certainly the direct consequence of the Italian prolonged war effort on homesick and tired soldiers. The gorgeous scenario of the French Riviera, with its breathtaking landscape of palm trees against a backdrop of deep blue sea, conjured in the Italian soldiers' minds images of their homeland. Sunbathing on the shore of the Mediterranean Sea, the Italian *fante* (infantrymen) could not help but remark how the French Riviera bore a strong resemblance to many regions in Italy. In a way, with his sloppy attire and unruly attitude, the Italian soldier was recasting himself as a civilian, stripping off his uniform both metaphorically and in some cases even in real life. The French Riviera was therefore a mixed blessing: while providing a well-needed respite for units that in some cases had been confronted to deadly insurgencies in the Balkans or to an uncompromising total war in Russia, its beauty heightened the soldiers' melancholy toward their *Patria*. Embalmed in the warm weather of the Mediterranean region, soldiers idled and enjoyed themselves, as the front line seemed so far away.

Nevertheless, bombing attacks and ambushes were a powerful reminder that the Côte d'Azur was still a war zone. Military occupations are always a trauma for the local population, and in that respect the Italian occupation of France was no different. Local inhabitants were confronted with new constraints such as curfews and evacuations, which made their lives more miserable than they already were, while food shortages, the black market, and theft became even more widespread. In addition, the Italians inflicted random arrests and roundups, creating an atmosphere of constant tension. The population's frustration was heightened by the belief that the occupation was not legitimate, in that the Italians had not won the war against

the French army, and by the fear that the invaded territory would be annexed. However, the impact was less than one would think. Soldiers who
were lacking discipline and morale and whose main desire was to get back
home increasingly reverted to civilian behavior by quickly adapting to local
conditions, befriending the population, and actively participating in bartering and black-marketeering. Indeed, a widespread laxity within the Italian
ranks, tied to the evolution of a war that for the Italians had brought few
laurels of victory, along with the cultural proximity to the Italian population, could ultimately explain the moderate nature of the occupation.

This book follows a chronological and thematic approach. In the first
chapter, the study begins by focusing on the eve of the Second World War,
as the Italian Fascist regime embarked on a collision course against the
French Third Republic over the question of the irredentist territories such
as the County of Nice and colonies such as Tunisia. However, the Italian
armed forces were not in line with Mussolini's brazen threats, a truism demonstrated in the disastrous Battle of the Alps in June 1940. The campaign,
which lasted four days, resulted in a meager booty (the medium-size town
of Menton and a few pastures) for the Duce at the cost of envenoming the
relations between French and Italians.

Chapter 2 introduces an important actor in the story, the Commissione
di Armistizio con la Francia (Italian Armistice Commission with France),
or CIAF. The CIAF was officially invested with the task of ensuring that the
clauses of the Franco-Italian armistice were not infringed by the new French
state, the Vichy regime. More important, its officials in France proclaimed
themselves as paladins of the Italian community of the French Riviera. Their
welfare campaign, far from being moved on humanitarian grounds, was
promoted to impinge on French internal affairs with the avowed secret task
of spearheading a future Italian annexation of the French Riviera.

Chapter 3 focuses on Italian irredentist groups in the French Riviera.
Lobbying on both sides of the border, these separatists advocated for the
incorporation of the County of Nice into the new Fascist empire. In spite
of being united by a common goal, CIAF officials despised the irredentists,
whom they dismissed as uncouth, uneducated, lower-class individuals who,
with their brazen style, were attracting too much attention from French
authorities.

The fourth chapter explores the small area occupied by the Italian army
since June 1940. The city of Menton, in particular, became the primary
locus of the Italianization campaign, which mirrored the Germanization
efforts carried out in Alsace-Lorraine. The unofficial annexation of the area
soon became controversial as Italian military authorities, who considered

Menton part of a war zone whose security superseded the reconstruction of the city, clashed with the Italian civil servants who endeavored to make Menton a city model of the new Fascist region. However, in light of embezzlements and limited funding, by the end of the occupation the city was only a husk of its former self. Concurrently with the failure of Menton, the Italians enjoyed better success in the Alpine border villages, where soldiers and rural inhabitants quickly established a symbiotic relationship to ward off the chilly mountainous weather. This part of the occupation underlined the easiness of striking relationships if the occupation were unloaded of its political message.

The full occupation of southeastern France is introduced in the fifth chapter with a look at how the Axis invasion of the *zone libre* (free zone) shored up the Mediterranean coastline in the event of an Allied landing. The deployment of 150,000 soldiers was chaotic because of faulty logistics, but it occurred without major incidents, as the French population, following the advice emanating from Vichy, refrained from intervening aside from a few episodes of passive resistance.

With the sixth chapter comes an analysis of the occupation policy of the Italian army and its commanders' intent to enforce their own rules without resorting to indiscriminate violence or blind repression for fear of sparking an internal revolt, which could have proved problematic for a overstretched army. This firm yet modest policy encountered the opposition of embattled Vichy officials, who were desperate to keep the tatters of French sovereignty, as well as CIAF officials, who resented the intrusion of military officers with little interest in an annexationist agenda. At a grassroots level the discipline of Regio Esercito units was nosediving. The soldiers, with their shoddy appearance, casual demeanor, and incessant relationship with the local populace, especially its feminine side, were increasingly behaving like civilians.

The seventh chapter approaches the occupation with a bottom-up view of the daily interaction between occupiers and occupied as the Italians and French battled over the most precious resource in the French Riviera: food. Even though the impact of 150,000 hungry mouths in a dysfunctional rationing system is not to be underestimated, the Italian soldier, with his black-market deals, cheap scams, and outrageous thefts, blended perfectly with the shady atmosphere of the Côte d'Azur.

In chapter 8 the book moves chronologically in addressing the events of the summer of 1943, when in light of the escalation in attacks by local French Resistance fighters, the Italian repressive apparatus stepped up its campaign, alternating massive dragnets and more targeted arrests. This most controversial period of the occupation underlined the desperation of an army that was more intent on examining what happened in the Italian peninsula than cohesively fighting the Resistance—once again to the avowed irritation of CIAF officials, for an excessively "soft" policy was evident in the scathing reports sent to Rome.

Chapter 9 explores the concept of "collaboration" in the Italian occupation, underlining the range of opportunities for unscrupulous and desperate individuals to better their interests. Yet evidence shows that, as in other parts of France, the majority of the "collaborators" were not ideologically motivated and that their real motivations still remain unfathomable.

Chapter 10 narrates the Italian Jewish policy in France. Arguably the most famous aspect of the Italian occupation, foreign Jews found a marvelous sanctuary in the Italian occupation area. Thanks to the organizational skill and powerful networking of an Italian Jewish banker, Angelo Mordechai Donati, and the effective complicity of Italian military and civilian authorities alike, thousands of Jews found a needed respite from the unrelenting hunting of both Gestapo and Vichy chasers. The idyllic scenario was abruptly ended by the disintegration of the Italian army in September 1943, a consequence of the botched negotiations between the Allies and the Italian military government following the sacking of Mussolini on 25 July 1943. As explained in the concluding chapter of the book, chapter 11, Italian army commanders in the French Riviera, caught completely unaware by the armistice declaration on 8 September, had to make a hasty and disorganized retreat, with entire units ending up captured by the Germans. This frantic period unceremoniously ended the Italian military occupation in France during the Second World War.

CHAPTER 1

COUNTDOWN TO WAR

Banging the Drums of War

The Pact of Steel, signed on 22 May 1939, virtually tied the destiny of Italy to that of the Nazi dictator, and the Secret Supplementary Protocols undeniably forecasted an alliance in the eventuality of a war. Ciano, however, had received instructions from Mussolini to be adamant with the Germans that no war should be started before 1942.[1]

Mussolini's wary stance stemmed from the realization that in the summer of 1939, Italy and its armed forces were anything but prepared for war. The country lacked the raw materials, such as coal and oil, that were urgently needed for the operation of the Italian navy, which, ironically, was the only armed service capable of securing the routes to fuel extraction sites. Italy's economy had lagged behind the other Great Powers since the nineteenth century, a trend that was continuing in the first half of the twentieth century.[2] Industrial development was further hindered by the government's resort to autarchic plans. Because of the lack of necessary resources, the result was disastrous. Severe protectionism undermined Italy's preparation for war, as Italian war industries were not compelled to innovate owing to the lack of competition from foreign companies. Italian heavy industries production was propped up artificially by state-induced demand.[3] The country's financial assets were also depleted, as the regime had squandered hard currency reserves to fund the war in Ethiopia (1935–1936) and the intervention in the Spanish Civil War (1936–1939).

In fact, Italy's chief of general staff from 1927 to 1940, Marshal Pietro Badoglio, was nothing more than a ceremonial figure who had no role whatsoever in the making of strategy. Until the advent of Field Marshal Ugo Cavallero in December 1940 and his reforms of 1941, the chief of the armed forces' general staff did not even have staff of his own.[4] The Duce encouraged this divided and ineffective command structure. He refused to implement any interservice joint command, because he feared that the possible accretion of power it might entail ultimately could challenge his rule.[5] Mussolini's "divide and conquer" strategy was helped by long-standing rivalries between the different services. No service would have ever wanted to submit to the decisions of an integrated command.[6]

The inadequacy of Italy's preparation for war was effectively summarized in a report submitted by Badoglio to Mussolini on 1 November 1939. General Badoglio informed Mussolini that of the sixty-three divisions formally in existence, only ten were fit to go to war, twenty-two were no more than pawns on a battle map, and the remaining divisions were either lacking crucial military equipment, such as uniforms or ammunition, or were far below strength in terms of both numbers and firepower.[7] Given this and the dearth of raw materials plaguing the Italian economy, the Italian army of 1939 was incapable of sustaining even a limited war. Notwithstanding his hope that the Italian army would eventually be the standard-bearer for the new Fascist Italian race, Mussolini himself knew that his bellicose rhetoric could only momentarily sweep under the rug the inherent weaknesses of the Italian army.[8]

Small wonder, then, that a few days after the start of the German invasion of Poland, Mussolini opted for a third way, a policy of "non-belligerence." In truth, "non-belligerence" was more about procrastination than any effort to maintain an equal distance from both the Allies and the Axis as was purported. The unequivocal stance of the Fascist regime regarding its German counterpart was encapsulated in a letter Mussolini sent to Hitler on 5 January 1940. The Duce tried again to dissuade the Fuehrer from launching any major campaigns until 1942, but at the same time he reiterated Italy's willingness to remain loyal to its ideological partner. Mussolini's plea to delay a prospective major Axis offensive should not be viewed as part of a mediating strategy. Quite obviously, he wanted to delay Italy's entry into the war until the very end in order to allow the navy, the air force, and the army time to modernize.[9] The devastating blow the German panzer divisions inflicted on Poland in September 1939 could not have failed to impress the Duce and persuade him that Italy would soon have to join the fray. In his 31 March memorandum the Duce openly advocated Italy's entry into the conflict, with the goal of breaking the politico-military encirclement in the Mediterranean Sea. This "March to the Ocean" would be achieved through the annexations of the County of Nice, Corsica, and some French colonies (Algeria, Tunisia, and Djibouti).[10] Shortly thereafter the stunning German

victories in Scandinavia and France definitely persuaded the Duce that siding with the Nazi regime was betting on the winning horse.

In May 1940 the world watched with a mix of awe and fear the astounding
advance of the panzer divisions in France.[11] In less than six weeks the German
"lightning war" had pulverized the French army, whose soldiers joined the
massive civilian exodus to the south of France. Increasingly anxious about
being denied a share of the spoils if Italy did not join the fray before the fast-
approaching French capitulation, Mussolini ordered his troops to prepare for
an immediate invasion of France across the Alps.[12] To this end he persuaded
his skeptical generals to wage war by predicting that the forthcoming conflict
would last a few months at most and would thus be over before the strains
on the Italian military machine overwhelmed it.[13] Mussolini's tirades against
Britain and France in the famous speech broadcast over radio waves from
the Palazzo Venezia's balcony in Rome on 10 June 1940 ended all illusions of
appeasement. The Duce harangued the crowd, booming that "a great people
is truly such if it considers its own commitments as sacred and does not
evade the supreme trials which determine the course of history," then adding, "A nation of 45 million is not really free without access to the ocean."
By opposing the German and Italian "fertile and young nations" against the
French and British "sterile and aging nations," Mussolini officially switched
Italy from a policy of "non-belligerence" to one of "parallel war." On that
day, Italy declared war on France.[14]

Both the 31 March memorandum and the Palazzo Venezia tirade forcefully asserted Italian irredentist claims on French territories that were long-
standing. Since the inception of his regime, Mussolini had aspirations for
territorial expansion as he sought to annex French or Slavic provinces that
were considered culturally part of Italy, such as Corsica, Dalmatia, Savoy,
and the County of Nice. The cession of the Savoy territories in 1860 had
never been completely accepted by nationalists, especially by those in the
highest echelons of the state. After all, Italian school manuals in the 1860s
still claimed the County of Nice as Italian territory "under French domina-
tion."[15] With the rise of Mussolini, these territorial claims were made openly
by local Fascist groups organized in Fasci all'Estero (Fascist Organizations
Abroad).[16] For instance, the Fasci in the Alpes-Maritimes grew steadily until
the late 1930s, largely due to support obtained through the efficient network
of Italian state offices and organizations. Not only did the Alpes-Maritimes
department now boast a consulate in Nice; two vice consulates, in Cannes
and Menton; and four consular offices in other cities, but it also had seven
Case d'Italia (Houses of Italy) in Vence, Grasse, Menton, Beausoleil, Saint-
Laurent-du-Var, Cannes, and most importantly, Nice.[17] To be sure, through

its consulates, especially those in Nice and Marseille, the Italian state funded a plethora of organizations on French soil, from children's Balilla and Avanguardisti to recreational and leisure activities for adults (such as the Opera Nazionale Dopolavoro[18]). In order to instill a sense of belonging to the Patria in the younger generations, bigger cities saw the creation of Italian schools where children were taught the economic, cultural, and religious history of the Italian peninsula from a Fascist perspective.

In the interwar years, southern France had become the main battleground between Fascist and anti-Fascist groups, the *fuoriusciti* (literally, "the ones who went outside"), who created a wide network of workers' cooperatives, friendly societies, and Italian unions, often affiliated with parallel French organizations. Italian fuoriusciti organized attacks and intimidations on Italian pro-Fascist events.[19] Conversely, the Italian secret police, the OVRA,[20] along with the military secret police, the SIM,[21] infiltrated agents provocateurs into the communist and socialist organizations, while the SIM itself was instrumental in the murder of two well-known socialist figures, the Rosselli brothers, Carlo and Nello, in Bagnoles-de-l'Orne on 9 June 1937.

The significance of this political feud should not be exaggerated. Leftist political militants accounted for only 2 percent of the active Italian population in France and were highly dispersed among different groups ranging from the moderate Giustizia e Libertà to the revolutionary communists.[22] Fascist organizations, as much as the anti-Fascist ones, remained marginal compared to a total population of Italians in France, naturalized immigrants included, of nearly one million people, plus another million second- and third-generation Italians. Most of the immigrants, fearful of possible consequences for their jobs, shied away from any form of political activism. To embrace socialist or communist ideas as much as to support Fascist organizations was, at best, frowned upon by French employers and, at worst, to be openly condemned by Italian officials in France. Most of the immigrants were content to remain apolitical. In addition, what might have seemed to a casual observer to be excessive Fascist zeal might have been mere deference to local notables or even an easy way to further one's own interests, be it obtaining a passport, a job, or goods.[23] In addition, boundaries between economic and political emigration could be very hazy. Some Italians crossed the border to flee from poverty and from political repression at the same time.[24]

Apolitical and militant Italian emigrants alike dreaded the coming of a Franco-Italian conflict, since the "enemy within" myth had spread many years before the German or Italian divisions. In the late 1930s, as war loomed ominously over Europe, foreign immigrants on French soil saw their rights threatened by new legislature passed by the government of Édouard Daladier. Two law decrees passed on 2 and 14 May 1938 gave French security forces new sweeping powers to crack down on illegal immigration.[25] Prefects' prerogatives were further extended during the *drôle de guerre* (Phoney War) in 1939 as they were granted the power to expel or intern "individuals who posed a threat to national defense and to public security."[26] A top-secret dispatch from Albert Sarraut, minister of the interior, made clear the extent of their new authority: "This decree . . . put in your hands a formidable weapon . . . a wartime law, implemented for the duration of the war . . . as long as the war will force us to face exceptional circumstances, which, both internally and externally, threaten the national safety."[27] It was a serious abrogation of the basic tenets of the Declaration of the Rights of Man and of the Citizen, paving the way for the repressive Vichy laws to come. Until June 1940 this exceptional decree was directed against only leftist activists such as the Italian fuoriusciti, as Fascist militants enjoyed immunity thanks to the frantic search by the French government for an entente with Mussolini's regime.[28] The respite was brief, however. As the rumors of an impending Italian attack intensified, the Ministry of the Interior issued a secret directive on 14 May 1940 that instructed the prefects to immediately "neutralize [Italians who were] notoriously Francophobe or *simply suspects*" upon the opening of the hostilities with Italy.[29]

In order to weed out the hostile minority from the majority of Italians, who remained friendly to their host country, and to accelerate the conscription of the latter, French authorities, in the wake of Mussolini's declaration of war, immediately plastered every town and village with posters urging Italian residents between the ages of seventeen and sixty to report to the local police by 15 June 1940. In police stations, Italian citizens were invited to file a declaration of loyalty, which could entail an eventual tour of duty in the French army. The response was overwhelming: in Nice alone more than 5,000 emigrants flocked to police stations in the first three days.[30] In the Grasse region 1,532 signed the declaration, with only 6 people refusing.[31] This kind of enthusiastic response was not confined to the Alpes-Maritimes. In the district of Digne-les-Bains, the capital of the Basses-Alpes, more than 500 emigrants, the vast majority of the Italian male population, lined up to sign the oath.[32]

The results could give one the impression of the Italian population's unanimously siding, with a few exceptions, with their host country, to the point of embracing its fight against their or their ancestors' original country. After all, many Italians wanted to show their gratitude to a nation that had granted them political asylum, economic prosperity, and a chance to build a family. Some of them had even seen their children conscripted into the French army. A more careful examination, however, reveals a more nuanced picture. More than a few Italians probably filed for service out of fear of possible retaliation from the French state or population if they refused. Some were quick to grasp that serving in the French army would speed up their naturalization process.[33] A few, in bad faith, committed themselves to France only to change sides later with the arrival of the Italian occupation force.[34] Finally, a minority simply failed to report to the police stations. If some of them, in good faith, were not aware of the authorities' injunction—and that was particularly true in the most remote inland areas, where communication was difficult—some of those living in towns deliberately refused to heed the order. Some of these emigrants refused to sign not out of loyalty to Mussolini's regime, but out of fear of the dreadful prospect of having to face relatives and friends who had been conscripted into the Italian army. Needless to say, the French bureaucracy eyed these recalcitrant emigrants with considerable suspicion and automatically tagged them as Fascist militants.

French authorities did not wait for the deadline to begin their arrests. Massive roundups of suspected Fascist militants were carried out at the same time as the placards were posted. Starting in the afternoon on 10 June, policemen were hastily dispatched to arrest known suspect Italians. This category encompassed any Italian working in or volunteering for the Italian state (namely, in consulates and in the embassy) or for Italian-state endorsed organizations such as the Società Dante Alighieri and Italian schools, with the significant exclusion of the few Italians who had diplomatic or consular status.[35] Men were handcuffed, sometimes in front of their family, and taken away. A few were even beaten by overzealous policemen or openly ridiculed in the streets by hostile crowds. In fact, it was quite miraculous that no one was killed in the frenzied atmosphere that followed the start of the Italian offensive strike through the Alps that began on 21 June 1940. The French population was furious about Italy's attack on France, contemptuously christened "*un coup de poignard dans le dos*" (a stab in the back). The figure of the traitorous Italian, by nature a turncoat imbued with Machiavellian traits, prone to betraying his old friends for selfish reasons, reemerged with a vengeance.

All of those who were arrested in the Côte d'Azur were first held in the Beziers (Languedoc) bullfighting arena, staying there for one full week in appalling conditions. Eventually all of these prisoners were herded into different internment camps, among them Vernet (Ariège) and Saint-Cyprien (Pyrénées-Orientales).[36] Both camps antedated the roundups of Italians and had been run since their inception by the French army's Garde Mobile.[37] Prior to the arrival of the Italians, the camps had housed a heterogeneous population ranging from convicts with nonpolitical criminal records to German and Austrian citizens who had escaped the Nazi regime, foreign communists—namely, those who fought with the International Brigades—and Spanish militants fleeing after the end of the Spanish Civil War.[38] Thus, in an ironic twist of fate, Fascist militants ended up imprisoned with their hated compatriots, the fuoriusciti. One's political allegiance made no difference anyway; all of them endured incredible hardship. In Vernet prisoners slept in crude shacks with no illumination. The lucky ones were given a little hay to build makeshift mattresses; the less fortunate slept on wooden planks. The food was tasteless at best and spoiled in the worst cases. No cutlery or dishes were provided, so the prisoners had to eat with their hands from discarded tins unearthed from the garbage heaps. As one resident explained, "As regards food, accommodation and hygiene, Vernet was even below the level of a Nazi concentration camp."[39] Prisoners in Saint-Cyprien, most of them Italians from the southern France departments, did not fare any better. The Saint-Cyprien camp was twenty-five kilometers from Perpignan on the shores of the Mediterranean Sea. This condition exposed the prisoners to quite inclement and changeable weather. The combined effect of sand and wind not only reduced the prisoners' clothes to tatters but also encouraged skin diseases.[40] Prisoners slept in the damp sand with a minimal layer of hay as insulation. Food rations, consisting of sticky rice, a few vegetables of dubious quality, and a fetid soup, were minimal. Lice were so widespread they became the most frequent source of conversation among prisoners.[41] Nevertheless, what remained engraved in the collective memory of the Vernet and Saint-Cyprien prisoners was first and foremost their arbitrary mistreatment by the French military jailers. Italians and prisoners of other nationalities alike were constantly humiliated with insults, slaps with leather crops, and occasional beatings, sometimes resulting in hospitalization. Furthermore, the camp guards allegedly profited from a flourishing black market in the camp.

Italian nationals who were deemed hostile to the republic's interests were not the only ones shipped to southwestern France; French civilians living near the Italian-French border were also hastily evacuated on 10 June 1940. Upon hearing the Duce's speech, Gen. René Olry, the commander of the Armée des Alpes—the French formation that since October 1939 had the responsibility of guarding the Alpine border—gave instructions to blow up bridges and railways by midnight, using fifty-three tons of explosives, in order to bar access routes to France. These orders were carried out with such thoroughness and speed that many French civilians living in rural areas near the Italian border in Savoy and in the Alpes-Maritimes were cut off in their own retreat.[42] The overzealousness of the military engineers coupled with the sluggish bureaucracy of French local authorities helps explain why most of the escaping civilians brought very little luggage, as no warning had been issued. Food supplies and cattle were left behind.

The city of Menton, a mere three kilometers away from the Franco-Italian border, was also completely evacuated on the evening of 3 June, under the code name "Exécutez Mandrin." More than thirteen thousand people, with minimal luggage, were transferred in convoys of buses and trucks at first to Cannes and Antibes and, after a few days, on 7 June, farther west in the Pyrénées-Orientales department.[43] As in the rural areas, the evacuation was fraught with problems. Local French officials who were responsible for protecting both public and private goods, such as policemen and firefighters, were also forcefully evacuated by the French army and the local gendarmerie. In order to persuade the skeptical dwellers to leave almost all of their belongings, the municipal officials in charge of the civilians' departure stressed that the Alpine Maginot Line would thwart any Italian strike and that in the meantime French soldiers would guard the houses against any possible wrongdoing.[44]

Chaotic evacuations were unfortunately a trademark of the French war against Germany and the ensuing defeat. Already in September 1939, in the wake of the declaration of war against Germany, French authorities had forcefully displaced six hundred thousand Alsatians and Lorrainers from the border regions and created a ten- to fifteen-kilometer buffer zone.[45] The sudden order of evacuation was made both to facilitate the operations of French army units in case of a German invasion and to spare French civilians the horrors of a military occupation as in 1914. However laudable these intentions were, they certainly became a cruel joke in the eyes of French refugees a few months later when German tanks blazingly advanced into France. All in all, an estimated five million French people become refugees in their own nation, bitterly angry about their generals and politicians, the former blamed for the military defeat, the latter lambasted for their utter inability to lead at a time of modern France's worst national drama.[46]

The Battle of the Alps

The honor of the French army in the summer of 1940 was at least partially saved by the Armée des Alpes in the Battle of the Alps,[47] which between 21 and 24 June 1940 pitted three hundred thousand Italian soldiers and fewer than one hundred thousand French on the Alpine border ridge.[48] Even with their numerical deficiency, the French had strategic advantages that proved crucial to repel the Italian invasion. The geographical features of the Alps clearly favored defense over attack, with the High Alps creating a formidable strategic barrier with their steep mountainsides and ravines.[49] This natural barrier was compounded by a network of concrete fortifications on the Alpine crests that dominated the entire mountain range, the Ligne Maginot Alpine.[50] Finally, French troops benefited from the *section éclaireur-skieurs* (ski-scout platoons), or SES, whose hit-and-run tactics remained a constant thorn in the side of advancing Italian columns for the entire campaign.[51]

Perhaps the French army's best asset in the Alps was its unflinching morale. Many French elite units recruited local men, who not only knew every nook and cranny in the Alpine border but also were motivated by their desire to defend their families and properties from an Italian invasion. Indeed, in light of Marshal Philippe Pétain's address on 17 June, in which he urged French soldiers to stop fighting, the Italian belief that the Armée des Alpes was disbanding proved fatally wrong.[52] As a local commander optimistically put it, "A strong resistance cannot be anticipated, owing to the shaken morale of French Army units."[53] These rumors spread like wildfire among the lower ranks: Italian officers were already joking with their soldiers about behaving themselves with the French girls,[54] while the Italian General Staff wrongly estimated that the German push toward Lyon would compel the French High Command to dismantle their Alpine garrisons.[55] Thus, the Italian units ascended the mountain range in orderly columns and taking few precautions. Their purpose was to occupy as much French territory as possible before the armistice was signed. The Italian troops were heading toward certain doom.

On 21 June the bewildered Italian troops were overwhelmed by a barrage of machine-gun and rifle fire, mortar, and artillery shells. The Italians, bogged down in the snow and taken by surprise, were easy targets for French marksmen perched above. SES squads repeatedly ambushed units on the winding mule trails.[56] Because of inclement weather conditions, Italian artillery, essential to counter the French fortified positions, could not be towed up to the summits. In fact, the Italians' inability to overcome fortified obstacles was probably the major operational reason for their poor performance in the Battle of the Alps. The stormy Alpine weather was probably the best ally the French had. Apart from nullifying any possible threats from the sky, heavy snowfalls slowed the Italian progress to a snail's pace and disrupted the logistics of the Regio Esercito.

From 22 to 24 June the battle raged along the whole Alpine border. On the northern half of the front, Italian troops were bogged down by the combination of fierce French resistance and extreme weather, to the point that by the time of the armistice they had penetrated only four kilometers into French territory. In the south, units of the Regio Esercito enjoyed more clement weather and were less hindered by terrain. Therefore, in the Alpes-Maritimes the Italian army was able to score some minor successes. On 23 June units from the Cosseria Division, shielded by the foggy night, entered Menton. After furious street combat, the French withdrew from the "City of Lemons," except for the one impregnable fortified casemate at Saint-Louis Bridge.[57]

The occupation of Menton was the only success of any significance for the Italians, and for a steep price. Official Italian casualties reached 631 dead and 616 missing; the French had suffered only 37 dead. To make matters worse, the Italians had to soften their demands at the negotiating table. Worried that the Italian territorial claims would derail negotiations with the French delegation, Hitler pressured Mussolini to put on hold, at least for the time being, his wildest dream of occupying French territory stretching from the Alps to the Rhône, along with Corsica and Tunisia. On 21 June, Mussolini and his general staff agreed to limit the military occupation of the territories to those conquered in the offensive strike.[58]

The importance of the Battle of the Alps should not be underestimated; the Italian army's appalling performance in the Alps set the tone for their disastrous campaign in the Second World War. The army's prestige was considerably tarnished by not having been able to defeat the Armée des Alpes. Even if the invasion through the Alps was objectively a difficult task at a tactical level due to the jagged peaks and the dreadful weather conditions, the comparison with the blazing push of the German army in northern France was unforgiving. Moreover, the botched offensive strike severely undermined the morale of the Italian soldiers as well as their trust in their cadres and in the decisions of the Duce. Finally, the Italian setback fueled French contempt for the Italians. The Italians had tried to shamelessly exploit the state of extreme exhaustion in the French army with the *coup de poignard dans le dos* and, in the eyes of the French population, had been justly punished for their treacherous move. In fact, this odium for the Regio Esercito would be confirmed in the first months of the occupation after November 1942.

Alpine troops and their mules before the Battle of the Alps (summer 1940). (Archivio dell'Ufficio Storico dello Stato Maggiore dell'Esercito)

Italian soldiers (probably Cosseria Division) fighting in Menton, 23 June 1940. (Archivio dell'Ufficio Storico dello Stato Maggiore dell'Esercito)

Wounded soldiers removed from the front line during the Battle of the Alps. Note the inclement weather. (Archivio dell'Ufficio Storico dello Stato Maggiore dell'Esercito)

Italian soldiers at the border between Italy and France (Colle della Maddalena), presumably after the Battle of the Alps. (Archivio dell'Ufficio Storico dello Stato Maggiore dell'Esercito)

Italian officers chatting with French (Chasseur des Alps) officer. (Archivio dell'Ufficio Storico dello Stato Maggiore dell'Esercito)

Signpost somewhere along the Italian-French border: "For us, Fascist militants, the borders, all borders, are sacred: they should not to be argued about, they should be defended!" (Mussolini). (Archivio dell'Ufficio Storico dello Stato Maggiore dell'Esercito)

Italian troops, near the border, no date (note the 91/38 Carcano rifles). (Archivio dell'Ufficio Storico dello Stato Maggiore dell'Esercito)

Italian soldier and child in Menton. (Archives Municipales de Menton, 7Fi0064)

Menton under Italian occupation: Italian shops and desolate streets. (Archives Municipales de Menton, 7Fi0072)

Menton City Hall with the Italian flag. (Archives Municipales de Menton, 7Fi0024)

PART II

THE ARMISTICE PERIOD:

JUNE 1940–NOVEMBER 1942

CHAPTER 2

THE ITALIAN ARMISTICE COMMISSION WITH FRANCE (CIAF)

The Armistice and the CIAF

The French military catastrophe in May 1940 and the subsequent disintegration of the French state ushered in important political consequences that would reverberate throughout the years of the occupation. The Third Republic, widely blamed for the recent woes, was quickly replaced by an authoritarian regime headed by a widely revered hero of the First World War, Marshal Philippe Pétain. The Vichy regime, thus named for the thermal city hosting the new regime's institutions, quickly established a collaborationist agenda with Germany, a strategy that was widely espoused by both Pétain and his prime minister, Pierre Laval. Moreover, Vichy officials sought to reform internal politics and society in an effort to distance themselves from the reviled Third Republic and its liberal ideas. The new ideological program, the Révolution Nationale (National Revolution), emphasized an ultraconservative program in which one's duties toward the society trumped individual rights. Particular emphasis was placed on a traditionalist view of family, religion, hard work, and order, symbolized by the "return to the soil" campaign. Under this bucolic propaganda, however, an exclusionary society was established that cast as pariahs wide categories of persons on political grounds, mostly from the leftist parties of the Third Republic, and on racial grounds, as in the case of foreigners and, more specifically, of Jews.[1]

The Vichy regime was confronted from its inception to the armistice constraints. In a train carriage near the Rethondes train station, the same one in which the Franco-German armistice was signed in 1918, the Nazi dignitaries had dealt France a humiliating blow in a clear revanchist spirit. France was stripped of most of its army, which shrank to a mere one hundred thousand men; its economic resources were channeled to the German war effort on top of footing the bill for the occupation troops; more than one million prisoners of war were sent to labor camps in Germany; and, finally, the French metropolitan territory was sliced in half by a demarcation line separating the northern half, ruled under German administration, and the southern half, the *zone libre* (free zone), under Vichy nominal control.[2]

Aware of sitting at the table of negotiations only by the grace of the Fuehrer, and perhaps ashamed by the disappointing results of the Battle of the Alps, the Italians came to the Italian-French armistice talks, which took place on 23–24 June 1940 in Rome. The Armistice of Villa Incisa, on the other hand, copied only the less severe clauses of the Franco-German armistice, such as the demobilization of the French army, the docking of the disarmed warships in French ports, and the obligation to store in depots all war materiel. However, it lacked the most punitive articles of the Rethondes armistice, such as the enormous indemnities imposed to cover the cost of the occupation troops.[3]

At Villa Incisa the French delegation was actually allowed to voice its opinion on several topics addressed by the first draft of the armistice. Manifold issues were smoothed over, in many cases to the advantage of France.[4] It was agreed that the Italian army would occupy only the territory that had been seized in the Battle of the Alps. The armistice pushed back the Franco-Italian border, known as the Green Line, but at most a mere ten kilometers inside the old border. This small strip of land was mainly dotted with pastures and a few rural villages, with only one medium-size town, Menton, in the Alpes-Maritimes. To ensure a buffer zone in the eventuality of future conflicts, Article 3 of the armistice compelled the French army to demilitarize the area up to a distance of fifty kilometers as the crow flies from the occupied territories, a border to be known as the Purple Line. Finally, at the behest of the Italian Army General Staff, Italian troops were permitted to cross the Green Line in order to facilitate the transportation of supplies to remote Italian outposts. This logistics line (the Red Line) would spark several conflicts between Italian officers and French local authorities. In all, thirteen communes were occupied: nine in the region of Savoy (Séez, Montvalezan, Sainte-Foy, Bessans, Bramans, Lanslevillard, Lanslebourg, Termignon, and Sollières),[5] two in the Hautes-Alpes (Montgenèvre and Ristolas), and two in the Alpes-Maritimes (Menton and Fontan). Additionally, small parts of land were seized in other communes, especially in the Alpes-Maritimes and in the Basses-Alpes. In the end the Italian occupation zone spanned 82,217 hectares and in theory encompassed a population of more than 28,000 (see map 1).[6] However, most of the population, especially in the case of Menton, had already fled before the beginning of the conflict. The Battle of the Alps had given the Italians little land, most of which was devoid of inhabitants, at a staggering cost in human lives.

One of the biggest consequences of the Armistice of Villa Incisa was the creation of the Commissione di Armistizio con la Francia (Italian Armistice Commission with France, or CIAF), which would play a major role in the Italian occupation of France. As underlined by Article 23, the CIAF was given the task of "overseeing and controlling . . . the enforcement of the present Armistice Convention." Officially sanctioned by a duce's ordinance, the new commission fell under the direct command of the Italian General Staff, the *Comando Supremo*.[7] Its organizational structure, housed in its headquarters in Turin, was pyramidal, with its president Gen. Pietro Pintor, commander of the First Italian Army in the Battle of the Alps until December 1940; followed by Gen. Camillo Grossi until June 1941; and, finally, from 16 June 1941 to 9 September 1943, Gen. Arturo Vacca Maggiolini. Below it were four under-commissions: three for each army service (army, navy, and the air force) and one called General Affairs, responsible for the protection of Italian citizens in non-occupied France.[8] The presidency's role was to issue general directives, rule on general matters, interpret the armistice clauses, and manage relations with the German Armistice Commission (CTA) and Vichy. The president charged the under-commissions with more specific questions pertaining to their field, and the under-commissions themselves delegated their tasks to different bureaus both in metropolitan France and in its colonial territories. With the Wiesbaden Accords (29 June), the two Axis powers had delineated their respective spheres of influence in the free zone, the French territory governed by the Vichy regime. The Italian zone was delimited on the western border by the Rhône and on the northern side by the Savoy region. Thus, the CIAF under-commissions established delegations in a zone that roughly corresponded to the one the Italian army would occupy in November 1942.[9]

The navy under-commission enjoyed permanent delegations in three major ports—Toulon, Ajaccio, and Bizerte—where it could keep an eye on the French navy. Similarly, an army office was established in Gap (Hautes-Alpes) to oversee the demilitarization of the Alpine border. French military installations had to be rendered inoperable by the dismantling of the artillery guns, and French engineers were ordered to remove all minefields and roadblocks. Moreover, several other army offices were created in relevant cities, such as Chambery, Annecy, Valence, Marseille, and Nice, to check French army depots and to supervise the demobilization of French troops.[10] In fact, Italian authorities were especially worried about a possible resurgence of a French threat, an idea that would soon become an obsessive leitmotif until the end of the Italian occupation in September 1943. The Comando Supremo was so suspicious of an eventual resurrection of the French army that it insisted that the Regio Esercito check police rosters, especially to "ensure that soldiers do not disguise themselves as civil servants."[11] Italians' worries about there being a revanchist spirit within the French army were confirmed by the nomination at the head of the French delegation of Turin of Adm. André Duplat, the former commander of the French Mediterranean fleet, which had successfully carried out bombing attacks on the port of Genoa a few days after the beginning of the hostilities. Duplat was a staunch believer in a strategy of antagonizing the Italians as much as possible and of procrastinating on Italian demands, either arguing that the dire condition of the French economy made certain demands impossible or quibbling about details and the interpretation of the armistice clauses.[12] After all, the French delegation estimated that in the "land of Machiavelli" the best tactic to get the best results from the negotiations was to tackle the issues indirectly.[13]

The Armistice of Villa Incisa was meant to deal with only the most urgent matters, primarily military questions, such as the disarmament of the French army. It is clear, then, that in the beginning the CIAF served only a military function, as confirmed by its first roster, in large part military personnel.[14] The vast majority of the twenty-six articles of the armistice convention dealt with military issues, such as the demilitarization of the French army and of its fortresses on the Alpine border, which needed urgent clarifications. In fact, only Article 21, which stated that Italian military and civilian prisoners in French prisons should be handed over to the Italian army, had any political relevance. This shortsightedness likely originated from the staunch Italian conviction that the war would end quickly. Confident that the forthcoming Battle of Britain would be the last campaign of the war, the Duce was looking forward to a peace treaty that would sanction the expansion of Italy in Europe, a wish he and Ciano repeatedly reasserted in the manifold meetings with Hitler and his foreign minister, Joachim von Ribbentrop, in the second half of 1940.[15] Thus, they were willing to wait until the aftermath of the conflict for the settlement of political questions such as their territorial claims on the County of Nice.

The definitive postponement of the invasion of Britain, as the German bombing campaign in the fall of 1940 managed only to steel the resolve of the British, upset Mussolini's master plan. Nonetheless, the Duce's ambition to incorporate Corsica and the County of Nice into the Italian state had not been tempered by the poor military results in the Alps. The Italians insisted unremittingly on their territorial claims, as they feared Germany and Vichy might form an alliance to the detriment of the Fascist regime.[16]

In truth the Italian worries were not exaggerated. The dogged resistance by the French naval forces against Anglo-Gaullist forces in Mers-el-Kébir (14 July 1940) and Dakar (23 September 1940) persuaded Nazi officials that French colonial troops would remain loyal to Marshal Pétain and could thus represent an important element in the control of trade routes to the colonies.[17] Therefore, in the Brenner Pass meeting in October, while giving assurance to the Duce that his territorial claims would not be unheeded, Hitler reaffirmed the importance of co-opting France into an anti-British alliance.[18]

Thus, the alarming scenario of being sidelined by the country's senior partner to the benefit of France was slowly materializing in the last months of 1940. On 24 October 1940 the famous handshake between Hitler and Marshal Pétain in Montoire formalized France's entrance "into the path of collaboration." Vichy was actively seeking to launch a new relationship with the Nazi regime. Not surprisingly, the negotiations between Germany and France emboldened Vichy officials to resist Italian wishes. The French authorities, both civilian and military, countered by using any kind of excuse to delay the implementation of the armistice. For instance, French military weaponry, ammunition, and materiel, which in theory had to be stocked in depots under Italian surveillance (Articles 10 and 11 of the Armistice of Villa Incisa), were concealed in dozens of stashes in isolated places, only to be found later by the Italian army after the November 1942 invasion.[19]

In light of the evolving political situation, the Italians counterattacked in several ways. First, Italian newspapers, encouraged by the Fascist establishment, started a massive campaign advocating the annexation of territories. Fascist publicists pompously predicted that "after the death of the French front, Nice, the Savoy region, Corsica, Tunisia, the French Coast of Somaliland, and other territories [could already be considered as] being returned to Italy or in the process of [being returned]."[20] Ezio Maria Gray, the vice president of the Chamber of Deputies, went even further by boldly titling his rather biased historical account, published in 1941, *Le terre nostre ritornano . . . Malta–Corsica–Nizza* (Our lands return . . . Malta–Corsica–Nice).[21]

More important, the CIAF gradually expanded its prerogatives by tackling issues that did not strictly pertain to the military field. As a matter of fact, until November 1942 the CIAF rapidly became the sole Italian interlocutor available to French authorities to discuss economic, military, financial, and especially political matters.[22] In the political domain its strategy was twofold: on one hand, it wanted to win over the local Italian population; on the other hand, the CIAF endeavored to challenge the French state on its own turf in order to compromise Vichy's sovereignty. Both strategies were geared toward the common goal of preparing the ground for a future Italian annexation; the incorporation of the Provence and the French colonies into the Italian empire quickly became the raison d'être of the CIAF. To this end, the excuse CIAF officials used to impinge on French internal affairs was Article 21 of the armistice. In it the Italian state had demanded the immediate liberation and subsequent handing over to Italian military authorities of all "the prisoners of war and the Italian civilians interned, arrested or condemned for political or military reasons or for any deed in favor of the Italian government."[23] The French delegation tried to minimize the reach of the article by stressing its one-time effect: only Italians who had been interned in concentration camps before the armistice fell within the range of Article 21. In addition, they argued, Italians freed by the French authorities should be repatriated immediately. Conversely, the CIAF retorted that the French state could not deny any Italian the right to stay on French soil if he was willing to return to his home. Furthermore, the Italian state claimed the right to intervene at any moment "during the whole armistice period to prevent all limitations to the personal freedom of the Italian citizens for reasons connected to the state of war or for acts or feelings in favor of their country."[24] In other words, while the French stressed the one-time effect of Article 21, the CIAF was adamant that the same article gave them the right to defend Italian citizens' interests as long as the armistice was valid.[25] Arguably much more was at stake than simply the fate of the few Italians on French soil. The French delegation understood that the Italians were using the only political article of the armistice to wrest part of French sovereignty for itself by challenging the French arrests. Clearly, CIAF officials were seeking to delegitimize Vichy as much as they were endeavoring to protect their compatriots.

That being said, the ratification of the armistice did not immediately improve the situation of the Italians held in internment camps. Some prisoners chose not to wait for the Italian authorities to act; they petitioned at once to the prefect of their department of residence for their liberation.[26] French camp commanders acted on their own volition, shrewdly guessing that in light of the stalemate in Franco-Italian talks regarding the interpretation of Article 21, many prisoners would resort to anything to recover their freedom. Commanders gave "their" Italians the opportunity to return to their homes in France and resume their lives, on the condition that they signed a declaration of loyalty to France. By doing so, the prisoner explicitly claimed political asylum and thus was de facto seen to be relinquishing his or her Italian nationality.[27] Camp commanders used openly menacing arguments in order to break the most stubborn Italians. Men were told they would not be able to see their families again unless they signed the declaration.[28]

In the meantime the CIAF hurried its campaign to have Article 21 enforced. Beginning in early July, two Italian military commissions, headed by Col. Edmondo De Renzi and Lt. Enrico Giglioli, visited the internment camps and provided a preliminary report of the appalling conditions, prompting the Italian state to demand the immediate release of all Italian prisoners.[29] After mid-July, French authorities began to comply, starting with the prisoners who had large families or who had been wrongly accused of Fascist militancy, but eventually moving to liberate even the most ardent Fascists.[30] By 28 October 1940 all Italians had been liberated from French prison camps except four hundred fuoriusciti in the Vernet camp, most of them former members of the International Brigades who had fought in the Spanish Civil War.

The liberation from internment camps was only the first step in what would be the long journey for these men as they rebuilt their lives. Many prisoners had lost their jobs and upon their return found themselves ostracized by their neighbors and the French administration. The Italian authorities faced the conundrum of how to help these former prisoners and, more generally, the Italian citizens in France, as well as how to protect them from possible French retaliation. To this effect the Italian state started to build up a network in the free zone, under the supervision of the CIAF General Affairs under-commission, to spread its influence. Starting in July 1940, consulate functionaries, attached to the Italian military bureaus in the free zone under Italian control, focused their work on alleged discriminatory acts, internments, or expulsions meted out to Italian citizens. Fearful that the activities of these functionaries would undermine their authority, Vichy officials asked in October 1940 if the protection of Italians could be entrusted to Red Cross offices, as such was already the case in the part of the free zone supervised by the Germans. Not only did the Italians refuse, but they also expanded their network by creating additional bureaus in Avignon, Cannes, and Bastia in December 1940.

The CIAF in the Côte d'Azur (1940–1942)

The Italians were not satisfied with this situation, as the legislative position of these civil officials was based on a rather subjective interpretation of Article 21.[31] They therefore embarked on further negotiations with French representatives in January 1941. The agreement reached on 4 February in

Turin upgraded these civil officials to Delegati per l'Assistenza ed il Rimpatrio (Delegates for the Assistance and Repatriation), who were formally charged with assisting the Italian communities in France and carrying out the repatriation of emigrants who were willing to return to Italy. To facilitate their task, the delegates were granted several privileges: the right to meet the local prefect and every Italian citizen; free circulation within their zone of competence; complete freedom to contact the Italian foreign ministry, the CIAF in Turin, and Italian border authorities by wire and mail; and the right to freely choose their staff.[32] In return, Vichy hoped that the Fascist militants would leave France and that the repatriation campaign would considerably thin out the Italian population, thus ultimately reducing the activity of and need for CIAF officials.

At first thought it is puzzling that the delegates were not given formal diplomatic titles, even though some of them had been consuls in France before the war and now had the same prerogatives, except for notary acts, that consuls had always enjoyed according to international law. The Fascist state, however, feared that the official opening of Italian consulates could be interpreted as an implicit acceptance of the non-Italian status of the contested territories, such as the County of Nice.[33] What is more, this compromise was in part the result of the strained relations between the Italian foreign ministry and the CIAF. In truth, the Italian diplomatic corps resented the intrusion of an organization headed by army officers, staffed with former Foreign Affairs employees, into what seemed traditionally the purview of diplomats. Their fears were not groundless; in January 1942, Franco-Italian diplomatic relations were renewed with the nomination of Ambassador Gino Buti as "political plenipotentiary" in Paris and Count Vittorio Zoppi as consul general to Vichy, but both men were granted only limited power by the Duce, who specifically asked them to refrain from taking any political initiative.[34] Thus, the CIAF kept their diplomatic privileges intact.

While the military delegations carefully supervised the demilitarization of the Alpine zone, the rounding up of French military materiel in guarded depots, and making sure that the Armée d'Armistice was not expanding outside the limits indicated by the German and Italian armistices, the civil delegations were assisting those emigrants who were willing to return to Italy by issuing certificates valid for repatriation.[35] The repatriation campaign had mixed results. At the beginning it enjoyed relative success, with repatriations peaking at five thousand per month until early 1941. Then their numbers stabilized at three thousand until the invasion of November 1942, when they plummeted to fewer than one thousand each month.[36] The gradual petering out of the campaign was attributable to several factors, among them a renewed belief in the imminent annexation of the County of Nice in light of the Italian army invasion. On the other hand, the explosion in numbers at the beginning of the armistice period reflected the traumas suffered in the internment camps and the surge of discriminatory behavior following the Battle of the Alps. All in all, from October 1940 to March 1943, more than seventy thousand Italians repatriated to Italy.

More important, CIAF delegates stepped up to help the Italian emigrants in France. Before the official inception of the delegations in February 1941, Italians, even those harboring Fascist loyalties, brought their complaints to the French police.[37] With the establishment of the delegation, the CIAF offices such as those in Nice had quickly become a bureau of grievances for the Italian community. The CIAF delegation proved invaluable to Italians who had lost their jobs for economic or political reasons and, more generally, for those who had been discriminated against, allegedly or not. Italians were asking for assistance in matters as diverse as pensions, admissions to seniors' homes, speeding tickets, apartment sales, and disputes over untilled land.[38] The Nice CIAF delegation also received numerous grievances lodged by Italian citizens who were at loggerheads with their French neighbors for even more trivial reasons. Anything from a disputed right-of-way, noise at night, a dog urinating on a fence, or unpaid rent sparked stormy exchanges. Italians were supposedly tagged with racial slurs such as "Spaghettis," "Macaronis," and "Sales Piémontais" and were often invited to go back to Italy to eat "Mussolini's bread" or "polenta."

Quarrels were made worse by misunderstandings arising from linguistic challenges, because the majority of Italians in France, including those who arrived in the interwar years, were poorly educated. First-generation emigrants did not go to French schools and were unable to understand or communicate in French. In fact, the difficult challenge of trying to explain to a French bureaucrat the particulars of an individual's situation in Italian and the Italians' mistrust of the French state were probably the main reasons for the decision of many to file their complaints with the CIAF delegation. Italian officials encouraged this type of behavior both for propagandistic reasons and as a means of connecting with the local Italian community. In some cases shrewd petitioners played the xenophobia card, understanding that their case would be more interesting to the CIAF if an anti-Italian element was involved. Thus, they tended to exaggerate any slurs that directly attacked Italy and the Italians. Petty quarrels between neighbors that in time of peace would have been resolved by justices of the peace easily took on dramatic proportions in a time of occupation. After all, if someone's dog barked each time his Italian neighbor mentioned Mussolini's name or whistled Fascist anthems, surely its master was feeding him communist ideas.[39]

Not all the issues stemmed from petty quarrels or language barriers. In some working environments the Italians were truly discriminated against. Vichy had unilaterally declared null and void every prewar Franco-Italian treaty and accord on the grounds that the state of war had severed all legislative ties between the two countries. In particular, the abrogation of the 30 September 1919 treaty, which had granted Italian workers the same social rights as their French counterparts, had severe repercussions for the Italian community. At a time of faltering economy, foreign workers, especially Italians, were the first targeted for layoffs. Employers sometimes used detention in internment camps as a reason to fire Italian employees. That certainly seemed the case with the dismissal of some Italian emigrants working in the port of Marseille on 11 June, the day the war was declared.[40] If the latter cases were the result of private initiative, French authorities seldom objected to it. Italian entrepreneurs were sometimes cut out of calls for tender, as Vichy legislation gave municipalities the authority to refuse to outsource public works to companies managed by foreign entrepreneurs.[41] In the Alpes-Maritimes department, Italian entrepreneurs fared little better.

Of course, xenophobic measures in France had not been unique to the Vichy regime. As analyzed by Julie Fette, foreign and recently naturalized lawyers and doctors had already been banned in the 1930s to practice in France, on the grounds that their poor training and uncertain mastery of French would lower the quality of those professions.[42] However, the *maréchal's* regime significantly accelerated this xenophobic trend. Fed by the resentment provoked by the humiliating defeat in June 1940, an array of laws curtailing the civic rights of foreigners on French soil was rapidly implemented. The distrust of foreigners was enshrined in the 17 July 1940 law that restricted access to civil service to only those French citizens whose fathers were of French nationality.[43] This watershed legislation, coupled with another law passed five days later stating that any naturalization after 1927 could be subject to revision, especially targeted the Jews as part of the anti-Semitic campaign of the Vichy regime. However, in the Côte d'Azur it had dire consequences for many Italian emigrants. Not only were recently minted French citizens thereafter denied any possibility of employment in the civil service, but also those who were already working in public administration were fired on the spot. In the Alpes-Maritimes every Italian working at a municipal level was laid off.[44] Doctors and lawyers, unless French and born to a French father, were forbidden to practice.[45] Italian delegations vehemently protested against these discriminatory regulations with mixed results. Italian physicians, including those born in France from an Italian father, were no longer stricken from the professional registers.[46] However, they still had to apply to be reintegrated in the medical corps, and their requests were at times denied by Vichy prefects.[47]

If the Italian delegations took great pains to help these professionals, it was because these doctors and lawyers were sometimes Italian notables who actively supported or at least sympathized with the Fascist cause.[48] In fact, in return for the Italian state's protection against discrimination, the Italian CIAF expected these professionals to bridge the transition with the rest of the Italian community. Lawyers, along with the delegates, helped destitute Italian families resolve legal problems, such as evictions, breaches of contract, or even criminal charges, by taking care of legal expenses and providing free assistance. Local Italian doctors and pharmacists helped with the distribution of drugs sent by the Italian army.[49] Furthermore, the CIAF created a network of outpatient clinics, attached to every delegation office, which could even perform minor surgery and blood tests.[50]

The Battle for Food

With living conditions worsening daily in Vichy France, food assistance was probably the major asset of the CIAF delegations in terms of winning the hearts and minds of the Italian and, to a lesser extent, of the non-Italian population in the Italian-controlled free zone. Indeed, the everyday life of the French population was profoundly affected by the war. After the French defeat, the Nazi state plundered without scruple, seizing raw materials and food supplies, justifying such actions by referring to Article 18 of the Franco-German armistice, which stated that the "expenses of the German occupation army will be borne by the French government." The food issue was aggravated by the fact that the German occupation zone encompassed regions that produced more than three-quarters of the nation's production of wheat, butter, and sugar.[51] In addition, more than four hundred thousand agricultural workers, many either casualties of the Battle of France or prisoners of war in German stalags, were missing at the crucial time of harvesting. Accordingly, the free zone's population experienced an increasing deficit in food supplies from the onset of Vichy's regime. On 27 September 1940, at the express behest of the Germans, Vichy refined the use of ration cards. A variety of basic products such as bread, milk, rice, sugar, meat, and coffee became available only upon the submission of appropriate ration coupons to the vendor.

Southeastern France was more severely hit by rationing than most of the other French regions, beginning as early as the Phoney War in 1939. During the interwar years, farming productivity in this region was well below the French average because of the rugged landscape, extended urbanization, and underdevelopment of the agricultural sector. The Alpes-Maritimes relied heavily on nearby departments not only for food but also for raw materials and fuel.[52] One of these food-producing departments, the Basses-Alpes,[53] was at the beginning of the war less affected by food rationing than its more developed counterparts along the French Riviera.[54] This state of grace, however, rapidly deteriorated; farmers complained in the summer of 1942 that the government's fixed prices for products such as wheat, pork meat, and potatoes were so low that they were making hardly any profits. Farmers then illegally started selling their goods at exorbitant prices to city dwellers coming from the coastal departments, who made extensive trips in search of food that was unavailable in city markets. For that reason, in flagrant contrast to Vichy's propaganda praising the rural France Éternelle (Eternal France),[55] farmers were openly labeled in many regions as unscrupulous hoarders of food, profiting from the desperate needs of the French population.[56]

Compounding the declining agricultural output of rural areas, the ravages of war disrupted the food supply network by cutting the main axes of communications between the various departments and with the colonies.[57] No wonder, then, that the official rationing system started to crumble in larger cities such as Nice and Cannes as early as April 1941. Police reports noted alarmingly that "some staples are becoming increasingly scarce: skimmed milk, eggs, fruits," while meat had become so rare that "the majority of consumers do not even use all their [monthly meat] coupons."[58] Furthermore, in the French Riviera, Italians in Nice traditionally had specialized in small grocery stores, lacking both the capital and the skill to start bigger companies. This monopoly of the distribution of food worried Vichy officials, as the regime food policies thus largely depended on the goodwill of individuals who might possibly be working to undermine the regulatory system.[59] Italian grocers were accused of making illicit profits by selling goods under the counter at exorbitant prices or only to Italians. Using the excuse of gas rationing in France, the local prefecture selectively gave permission to a few noteworthy companies deemed "of primordial importance for the supplying of the department," few of which were Italian-owned, to circulate with any kind of gas-propelled vehicles, two-wheelers included. Italian grocery owners voiced their anger to the CIAF delegation, but there was little Italian officials could do in the face of Vichy regulations.[60]

Not only did the Alpes-Maritimes department under-produce basic staples such as wheat and milk, but it also sheltered a significant minority of wealthy families, who had no intention of compromising their standard of living. As public confidence in the Vichy rationing system eroded, an extensive and lucrative black market developed in occupied France. In the words of one historian, "Almost everything was for sale during and immediately after the occupation."[61] Admittedly, the "Système D" is probably the phrase that embodies the essence of the experience of occupied France, for no matter the department or the social class, one who had lived in France during the occupation was bound to deal either directly or indirectly with the black market.[62] Trips by French civilians into the countryside in search of food, at first tolerated by Vichy to complement one's meager weekly rations, increasingly became a way to evade the draconian rules of Vichy *ravitaillement* (resupply) as consumers linked directly with producers. Ironically, the peasants, who in the ideology of the National Revolution represented the backbone of the France Éternelle, never failed to fuel the black market in spite of Vichy officials' threats.[63]

If nothing else, however, in the long term clandestine transactions worsened the food issue as black market prices skyrocketed, keeping all but the most basic food outside the reach of the French population. In this bleak context, Axis occupying powers and Vichy waged a propaganda war over welfare services in an effort to endear the French. Vichy made wide use of the Secours National, a war relief organization born at the beginning of the First World War and then revived by the Daladier government in October 1939. As the German tide washed over France in the summer of 1940, the Secours National, along with the French Red Cross, was given the important role of assisting the millions of French who had been displaced by war.[64] As the occupation continued, the Secours National morphed from being an emergency agency to a full-fledged welfare behemoth, which in the 1943 calendar year distributed nearly eight million food rations and more than one-and-a-half million articles of clothing.[65] In providing relief to the poor and needy, Secours National officials never failed to beat the drum of the Révolution Nationale, as in the unrelenting distribution of millions of Pétain's portraits.[66] Understandably, Italian authorities moved to the counterattack; in the Italian-occupied city of Menton, the head of the Italian administration forbade the posting of placards by the Secours National, allowing fund-raising only if done discreetly without "fanfare or public demonstrations."[67] However, in unoccupied Nice, CIAF officials could do little more than file a perfunctory report on the Secours National, whose campaign and fund-raising were publicly endorsed by both the mayor, Jean Médecin, and the bishop of Nice, Monseigneur Paul Rémond.[68]

Concurrent to thwarting Vichy relief agencies, CIAF officials thus turned to a program of food distribution to poor Italian emigrants. Two thousand tins of condensed milk in the Alpes-Maritimes alone were distributed over one year in 1940–1941. This charitable act was crucial not only because it came at a time when fresh milk was becoming a rarity but also because Italian women were denied the priority card created on 18 June 1941 to allocate extra shares of milk to women with at least two small children.[69] The Italians organized a network of soup kitchens to increase the daily food intake of the most destitute. For obvious propagandistic reasons, the Italian part of the population was helped first, but the Italians also tried to reach out to the French populace. However, it seems that the result did not live up to the expectations, as the Italian soup kitchen had fallen from serving 20,000 meals in the interwar period to 750 in 1941.[70]

There was little humanitarian sentiment underpinning the relief campaign promoted by the Fascist state in France. That the CIAF delegates' actions were inspired mostly by political reasons is also evident from their open contempt for the Italian communities in France. In a scathing report, the vice-consul of Nice, Count Borromeo, admitted that the popularity of the soup kitchens did not constitute proof of the Fascists' appeal among the Italian community in France. The vast majority of the Italian workers were modest people with relatively low incomes and even less education. Their first and foremost worry was to provide food for their children and to find employment in the stagnant job market. Thus, Borromeo bitterly concluded that "the very aspirations to see Nice being returned to Italy, most of the time, are in the mind of a plain laborer or of the conscientious carpenter only the most genuine expression of his hope of seeing an improvement in his living conditions."[71] Count Quinto Mazzolini also dismissed the Italian community as individuals with "poor intellectual level" (*basso livello intellettuale*), further adding that the colony "did not shine either in their past history, their way of life or civil obedience" (*precedenti, costumi e disciplina*).[72] In fact, the many destitute living in the Italian community in a territory claimed by the Fascist state were nothing less than a "shame" (*disdoro*) that hurt Italian prestige at an international level. Derogatory remarks regarding Italian permanent residents in France were not confined to southern France. An inspector of the Fasci all'Estero sent to Paris was appalled by the poverty he found among the Italian community in Paris. He deeply deplored the relief campaign promoted by Italian agencies in France, because it benefited only those who were "more skilled at whimpering" (*più abili a piagnucolare*).[73] Italian officials thus acknowledged that the relief campaign would benefit merely the more indigent part of the Italian population on French soil. On the other hand, most of the Italian notables, with a few exceptions, were loath to side with the Fascist state, as they were either sincerely grateful to their host country for their prosperity or were wary about losing all the benefits they had accumulated over the years. These harsh judgments about Italian communities in France likely stemmed from the Italian diplomatic personnel's prejudice against the destitute. Hailing from the upper bourgeoisie, if not from the nobility, CIAF officials thought that material poverty inferred not only intellectual paucity but also moral slackness. No wonder, then, that they had hardly connected with the majority of the Italians in France.

In addition to being fought in occupied France, the "Battle for Food" was waged all across Europe and even worldwide; occupying armies and occupied populations clashed bitterly, sometimes to the last morsel.[74] Even though France did not reach the harrowing depths of mass starvation found in other Axis-occupied countries such as Greece and Russia, the French population did suffer from hunger. Arguably, CIAF officials exploited the deficiencies of the Vichy food distribution system to drive a wedge between the populace and the regime. They strove to undermine the newly created French state from within by exploiting the frail legitimacy of a regime born of a crushing defeat that had cut its territory in half. The actions of the CIAF official who was mediating to reinstate Italian workers who had been laid off or to get an Italian mother access to the *carte alimentaire* (ration card) reserved for French women with toddlers were not merely affecting the local economy but were also impinging on French internal affairs. Through his efforts he directly challenged the authority of Vichy prefects and the French jurisdiction. More than any alleged humanitarian effort to relieve the Italian populace, undermining the Vichy regime to prepare for a future annexation of France was the main reason, if not the only reason, behind CIAF activities in the French Riviera.

CHAPTER 3

ITALIAN IRREDENTISM AND FRENCH PATRIOTISM IN THE CÔTE D'AZUR

To further undermine the French state in preparation for a possible annexation of the French Riviera at the end of the war, and in spite of the aristocratic disdain they harbored for the local Italian immigrants, CIAF officials attempted to fully mobilize local Fascist militants, many of them already imbued with the irredentist rhetoric of one day seeing the Italian flag over the County of Nice. However, the first clashes happened on neutral ground. The Principauté de Monaco (Principality of Monaco), a sovereign country since 1861, was really a hyphen between Italy and France in the interwar years. It stood midway between Nice and the Italian border, and its population was as much Italian as it was French. That Italian community, however, was heavily divided between a hard-core group of fuoriusciti based in Beausoleil, a commune in the Alpes-Maritimes, and a growing pro-Fascist cell in Monaco, supported by the Italian consulate. Several incidents erupted between 1934 and 1936 following the opening of the Casa degli Italiani in Monaco, but these violent episodes did not seem to deter people's affiliation to the Fascists, as allegedly up to 20 percent of the Italian adult population held a Partito Nazionale Fascista (National Fascist Party, or PNF) membership card between 1920 and 1943.[1] On 10 June 1940, after the Italian declaration of war, the Monaco police immediately arrested one hundred pro-Fascist Italians, who were later to be herded into French internment camps. After their liberation the Italian prisoners, embittered by the trauma of their detention, returned to Monaco, where they fueled the principality's tension with their account of the poor conditions while detained. On the opposite end of the political spectrum, the Italian leftist emigrants increasingly felt cornered between reactionary Vichy France and Fascist Italy.

On 11 August 1940, under the aegis of the Italian consulate in Monaco, a mass to commemorate the liberation of the internees of Saint-Cyprien and Vernet, officiated by Don Luigi De Biasi, himself a former Saint-Cyprien prisoner, was held in the Principality of Monaco. While the Italian church of the Moneghetti neighborhood was packed with former internees and Fascist militants, a mob of fuoriusciti and French anti-Fascists gathered outside and started to scream insults against Italy and the Italian regime. As the confrontation escalated to reciprocal open threats, the Monaco police showed up, but according to the consul's report, the only reason the situation did not degenerate into chaos and violence was the self-control of the CIAF personnel.[2] In fact, local Italian authorities in both Monaco and Nice openly accused the French and Monaco police of conniving with the fuoriusciti. They demanded and obtained the resignation of the Monaco head of police, Le Luc, and the incarceration of the most active fuoriusciti.[3] In response to accusations that the mass had been a trap to stir up the leftist expatriates, authorities pointed out that the officiating priest had previously obtained permission from the bishop of Monaco; the event had not been advertised in any newspaper; and it had been planned for seven o'clock in the morning. Moreover, allegedly no Fascist or Italian flags were hung up, and the sermon did not mention the political situation.[4] Notwithstanding an effort to keep a low profile, it seems doubtful that local Italian authorities did not anticipate that at a time of tension between pro-Fascist Italians and Italian political emigrants, the latter supported by French leftists, an event featuring previous internees and Italian officials in military uniform would not be perceived as open provocation.

CIAF delegates, however, found out that the mobilization of local irredentists was a double-edged sword. By December 1940 the head of the CIAF delegation in Nice, Consul Silvio Camerani, was suspiciously monitoring the whereabouts of several "shady characters" and "agents provocateurs" who had made contact with the CIAF delegation. He admonished his subordinates not to mingle with these individuals, as he feared these outspoken irredentists were being kept under strict observation by the French police.[5] Camerani's worries were well-founded. The French Ministry of Interior was keeping an eye on Italian Fascists such as Ezio Garibaldi, the grandson of the Italian national hero Giuseppe Garibaldi.[6] Ezio Garibaldi had fought in the First World War with the Légion Garibaldienne on the Argonne front, as had most of his siblings. However, the Garibaldi family had divided after Mussolini's rise to power: Sante Garibaldi remained loyal to his leftist origins while Ezio joined the PNF, becoming a deputy in the parliament from 1924 to 1934. After the armistice, Ezio renewed his ties with the irredentist cause. In December 1940 he founded the Gruppi d'Azione Nizzarda (Nice Action Groups, also known as GAN) in Rome. In the usual hyperbolic irredentist jargon, the GAN's constitution proclaimed that its overarching goal was "to contribute, by any means, to returning the land of Nice to the fatherland which was iniquitously torn from it in 1860 through blackmail and intrigue [*sic*]."[7] The GAN was open to four categories of people: inhabitants of the County of Nice who were willing to contribute to the "incorporation of the territories not yet freed, to the Fascist Motherland";[8] Garibaldi's legionnaires; PNF members; and veterans of the Battle of the Alps.

The fact that Garibaldi wanted to make inroads into the Regio Esercito was a telltale sign of the intended purpose of the GAN: to act as shock troops for a coup on the model of the Fiume putsch of 1919,[9] or, in the worst case, as fertile ground for a future military occupation.[10] Indeed, three hundred irredentists gathered in Menton on 21 December 1940.[11] The meeting, headed by Ezio Garibaldi, fueled wild rumors in the Côte d'Azur that Italian irredentists were preparing a Marcia Su Nizza (March on Nice), nicknamed after the October 1922 March on Rome, which had brought Mussolini to power. At the end of April 1941, reunions were organized by local GAN with the help of the PNF in support of the cause of Nizza Italiana in major Italian cities, especially in the regions bordering France. On 28 April, Ezio Garibaldi chose to celebrate the Giornata D'Azione Nizzarda (literally translated as "the Day of Nicean Action") in Savona, an important city at one hundred kilometers from the French border.[12] The tone was set by the historical flag of the County of Nice being mounted behind the stage, surrounded by the banners of the local towns and Fascist organizations. The first speaker, the national GAN inspector, Gustavo Traglia, started his speech by eulogizing the soldiers who had died in the assault of the bunker of Saint-Louis Bridge in Menton, some of them hailing from the Liguria region. He then listed all the alleged French wrongs that had been made against Italy and the Italians, ranging from French colonial greediness in North Africa to the massacre of Aigues-Mortes.[13] Traglia then advocated the return of the County of Nice, including the Principality of Monaco, to its legitimate homeland: Italy. Ezio Garibaldi briefly spoke, announcing that the Fascist state had officially sanctioned the GAN that very day by incorporating it in the PNF. Finally Garibaldi concluded the meeting with the flamboyant rallying cry "*O Nizza o morte!*" (Nice or death). Aside from the GAN, Garibaldi launched a newspaper, *Il Nizzardo*, to promote the irredentist campaign. Published weekly from 15 March 1942 to 27 June 1943, *Il Nizzardo* took its name from an 1860 Italian newspaper that had campaigned against the French annexation of the County of Nice. Its first issue set the tone. In his front-page column Garibaldi proclaimed the paper's own rallying cry, "*Nizza fino alla morte*" (Nice until death), and gloated over the impending conquest of the French irredentist lands.

Il Nizzardo was merely echoing the wishes of irredentist militants in the County of Nice who were already excitedly anticipating the coming of Nizza Italiana, when "the oppressors will become the oppressed."[14] Their Monaco fellows were no less enthusiastic. Irredentists were already speaking of "sunbathing in the shade of our flag." One veteran of the First World War could not wait to meet the Italian army and planned to "put a wine keg in front of his house to drink with soldiers, especially his fellows, the Alpini."[15] However, it is debatable whether the desire to see Nice incorporated into the Italian state only reflected deep irredentist feelings among the Italian population. Some Italians living in Nice complained about the strict food rationing in the Alpes-Maritimes and hoped that the coming of the Italians would improve their living conditions.[16] Others viewed the incorporation of Nice simply as a way to see their Italian relatives without the hassle of border controls at a time when Vichy, and sometimes the Italian authorities, openly discouraged traveling between the two countries.[17]

The brazen attitude of the GAN, however, was shunned by Italian officials in France, who complained that the irredentist campaign was harming Italian interests in France. Boastful proclamations of an imminent Italian conquest of the Côte d'Azur by hordes of Blackshirts (the Italian Fascist movement's paramilitary wing) had the effect of radicalizing the French population, thus thinning the already meager chances of winning over the local populace to the CIAF welfare campaign.[18] As a consequence of this contempt for local irredentists, Count Quinto Mazzolini, the CIAF delegate in Nice, forbade any Gruppi D'Azione Nizzarda demonstrations without his consent. In addition, he explicitly prohibited the disclosure to *Il Nizzardo* of any information stemming from his reports about the French authorities in the Alpes-Maritimes. Mazzolini even went as far as to veto the nomination of the son of Lieutenant Colonel Bandini, one of the most virulent *Il Nizzardo* editorialists, to the CIAF military delegation in Nice.[19] Mazzolini's distrust of the GAN, however, went beyond a simple difference of opinion over strategy. He questioned the sincerity of some GAN leaders, accusing them of riding the wave of irredentism for reasons of self-interest. He was upset that some of these leaders were criminals, charged in Italy with a variety of crimes such as desertion, theft, and criminal bankruptcy fraud.[20]

One episode can serve to underline Mazzolini's contempt for the irredentists in Nice. On 16 May 1942 a major Italian newspaper, *La Gazzetta del Popolo,* reported a brutal physical and verbal attack on Italians by Frenchmen in Nice. But it soon backfired, badly embarrassing the Nice CIAF delegation. Mazzolini discovered that the two victims, notorious irredentists, were completely drunk when they started quarreling with a horse carriage driver and his clients. The xenophobic motivation was also ruled out because the French had not known the nationality of the two Italians. Significantly, Mazzolini angrily stated that the two individuals were "among the worst I had ever seen among the ten thousand who had come to my office in one year," and that the *Gazzetta del Popolo* recounted the episode "in a way totally contrary to the facts, so that the version should be regarded as completely false."[21]

Yet the irredentists and the CIAF found common ground against their common enemy, the French local authorities, who fought to counter the irredentist propaganda. The Fascist state equated the Alpes-Maritimes to the 1860 County of Nice, which in the past had belonged to the kingdom of Piedmont, and thus stressed its Italian heritage. Vichy, which had already lost half of the French territory to the Germans and with its empire in dire straits, was very reluctant to part with any part of its metropolitan territory. Therefore, the prefecture of the Alpes-Maritimes and the CIAF delegations in Nice and Cannes, along with *Il Nizzardo,* fought a war of propaganda, resounding speeches, and never-ending negotiations over regulations and reports on one another's activities.

The CIAF delegate in Nice, Silvio Camerani, started criticizing the local French authorities as soon as he was back in France, devoting special attention to the bishop of Nice, Monseigneur Rémond, and to the prefect of the Alpes-Maritimes, Marcel Ribière. Both were accused of launching, with the help of the two Nice newspapers, *Le Petit Niçois* and *L'Éclaireur de Nice et du Sud-est,* a campaign with the two-pronged aim of belittling the prestige of the Fascist state and reasserting the French character of the County of Nice.[22] Furthermore, Camerani accused Monseigneur Rémond of fueling the patriotism of the French clergy while ostracizing clergymen who sympathized with the irredentist cause.[23] Camerani's successor, Count Mazzolini, was even more vitriolic in his criticisms of Monseigneur Rémond, unceremoniously labeled as the man who "perfectly summed up the fanaticism of the French officer and of the Gallic clergy always obsessed . . . with nationalist ideas instead of divine ones."[24] In addition, *Il Nizzardo* blamed Monseigneur Rémond for his uncooperative stance, and his speeches were always carefully monitored for any anti-Italian ideas.[25] *Il Nizzardo* became the most outspoken vehicle of an Italian campaign aimed at defaming the French authorities in the Alpes-Maritimes. Ribière was held responsible for the supposedly thriving Gaullist movement and for the general hostility directed against the Italian CIAF delegation. Even Jean Médecin, the senator-mayor of Nice, was targeted for backing a proposal to rebuild the Vieux Nice,[26] which, in the mind of the irredentists, was an effort to destroy the most tangible proof of Nice's Italian heritage.[27]

The irredentists' contempt was well placed, as both Vichy representatives in the Alpes-Maritimes were known for their staunch patriotism and their firm opposition to any Italian annexationist aims. It was widely known that Monseigneur Rémond, a former military chaplain on the Rhine front, was fiercely anti-Italian, especially after the backstabbing of June 1940.[28] Monseigneur Rémond's hostility toward Italian annexationist claims was supported by Marcel Ribière. First cousin of the conservative politician and former prime minister Pierre-Etienne Flandin, Ribière was a hard-line Pétain-ist, who believed that his mission was twofold: to spread the word of the National Revolution as far as possible and to preserve the territorial integrity of southeastern France. The first goal was achieved by implementing, to the letter, all directives issued by Vichy. More than 550 municipal officials in Nice alone were fired after the 17 July law; 35 municipal councils, most of which were leftist municipalities such as Grasse and Saint-Laurent-du-Var, were disbanded; people affiliated with Freemasonry were forced to resign following Vichy's 13 August 1940 law against secret societies; and notori-ous communist militants were hunted down and incarcerated in internment camps.[29]

Coincidental to the political cleansing of the department, a widespread campaign to glorify Marshal Pétain was carried out. Indeed, owing to the fact that the marshal owned a country house in Villeneuve-Loubet, the may-ors of nearby villages obtained official permission in March 1943 to rename the region La Vallée du Maréchal.[30] Pictures and portraits of the "Hero of Verdun" were hung in every municipality in place of the traditional bust of Marianne.[31] In the Alpes-Maritimes, Pétain was especially revered because of the high concentration of veterans in the region. Indeed, the Légion Française des Combattants (LFC), created in July 1940, was made up of war veterans from the First World War and a select few from the Second World War and was intended to be the chief vehicle for implementing the National Revolu-tion. The LFC became the eyes and the ears of Vichy, and its adherents were encouraged to report any activity that was directed against the new moral and political tenets to the police authorities.[32] With its 28,000 members, in a population of 516,000, the LFC in the Alpes-Maritimes, headed by one of the most decorated veteran of the French army, Joseph Darnand, received a lot of attention in CIAF fortnightly reports.[33] Besides, local Ital-ian authorities were alarmingly dismayed by the degree of cohesiveness and coordination between the LFC and the Vichy youth organizations. The birth of a more militant part of the LFC, the Service d'Ordre Légionnaire (SOL), in December 1941 also worried CIAF officials, as the radicalization of the legion might have presaged the rebirth of a revitalized French army.[34]

To be sure, Pétain's worship in the Alpes-Maritimes was harnessed to a broader campaign to stress the French character of the County of Nice and to preserve France's territorial integrity. In November 1940 a Nice newspaper, *L'Éclaireur du Sud-Est* published the controversial pamphlet "Nice est Bien Française" (Nice Is Really French) written by the most famous Nice historian, Louis Cappatti.[35] Local newspapers were also used by French authorities to advertise the start of public works to be carried out in the department. Country roads were paved and widened, and Vichy chose to centralize the cinematographic activity of the free zone in Nice's Victorine Studios, shooting interior scenes there. The goal of this vast campaign was twofold: first of all, public works created jobs at a time when the French economy had ground to a halt due to the war. But more important, by investing money, Vichy wanted to send a clear message to the local population and the Italian state alike that the French government was not forsaking the Alpes-Maritimes department.[36]

Most conservative regimes make wide use of heroes who are considered to embody the nation, virtue, and spirit of sacrifice, and in this regard Vichy was not an exception. Vichy's panegyrists chose to exploit a traditional heroine who had been canonized in 1920, Joan of Arc. Her cult was not a novelty in France; since the nineteenth century, the French Romantic movement had lionized the "Maiden of Orléans." The apogee of her cult, however, was reached after the armistice in the form of a blunt message: Joan of Arc was a French heroine who fought foreign invaders. The Vichy propaganda shrewdly tied the marshal's cult to devotion to Joan of Arc. For instance, *L'Éclaireur du Sud-Est* sponsored an essay contest in 1941 for school pupils themed "De Jeanne d'Arc à Pétain, la France continue."[37]

Nothing, however, stirred French nationalism in the region as much as Italian irredentist claims. After the Giornata D'Azione Nizzarda in April 1941, French officials counterattacked. Across the free zone a massive celebration was held on 11 May, Joan of Arc's saint day, to rally the populace to the new regime. In Nice the celebrations were organized in grand style: flags, rosettes, tricolored ribbons, and portraits of Pétain were distributed for free. Twenty-five thousand school pupils paraded in front of Joan of Arc's statue, placed by the organizers on the stairs of the Church of Notre-Dame. More than twenty thousand members of the Légion Française des Combattants marched on the Promenade des Anglais and gathered for a mass, officiated by Monseigneur Rémond, near the Monument des Morts (Monument for the Fallen Soldiers).[38] Nice's historical center was also decked with flags in demonstration of the national fervor of its population.

Until the Italian military invasion in November 1942, Nice remained one of the cornerstones of the Révolution Nationale. To bolster the *francité* (frenchness) of the Côte d'Azur, Admiral François Darlan, the minister of foreign affairs, of defense, and of the interior, and the de facto deputy of Marshal Pétain, visited Nice on 9 October 1941.[39] Darlan's visit was just the first of the many official trips between February and October 1942 made by leading Vichy officials, including state secretaries Paul Marion (Information) and René Belin (Work), and leading French fascists such as Philippe Henriot, Charles Maurras, and leader of the Parti Populaire Français (PPF), Jacques Doriot. All of these orators harangued the Nice populace, to the point that Nice earned the nickname of "*fille aînée de la Révolution nationale*" (eldest daughter of the National Revolution).[40]

Marshal Pétain never visited Nice. Vichy's officials acknowledged such a visit would probably trigger a backlash from the Italian government, as it would be interpreted as a provocation with possible repercussions from the Italian state. His influence, however, was pervasive. On both Joan of Arc saint's day and during Darlan's visit, Pétain was at his country house in Villeneuve-Loubet for the whole day, which was hardly a coincidence. On both occasions he was visited successively by important local notables such as Prefect Ribière, Monseigneur Rémond, and Joseph Darnand, among others. His symbolic presence in the department was so important that wild rumors spread that Pétain had attended Darlan's speech incognito and that he himself would visit Nice one month later.[41]

Vichy mass rallies in the French Riviera not only showed the support the regime could still boast in the region but in the minds of French nationalists were also useful occasions to unmask closeted irredentists. Indeed, those who refused or neglected to hang flags or ribbons during patriotic events were allegedly threatened by the populace.[42] In one case an Italian woman was labeled a troublemaker when she hung up a black skirt instead of a French flag.[43] French authorities, however, while harnessing nationalist fervor, were wary not to fuel the fire of anti-Italian sentiments. If nothing else, an eruption of ethnic violence between the two communities could have been used as an excuse for the Italian army to step in. Ribière issued an appeal inviting the population to retain its composure and reminded everyone that "any incident could harm France's interests."[44] According to CIAF officials, local Vichy officials so refrained from alluding to Italian irredentist claims in their speeches that they "could have been given in any other French city."[45] In fact, it was the leaders of the LFC, backed up by the prefect and the head of the legion, François Valentin, who silenced the few voices in the crowd yelling anti-Italian slogans on Joan of Arc's saint day.[46]

French anger continued to zero in on members of CIAF delegates, seen as the embodiment of the state that had turned on France. The French population was increasingly upset at the sight of individuals strolling around their towns in the military uniform of an enemy country they considered to have not truly defeated France. Indeed, jokes targeting the Regio Esercito abounded in the free zone, especially after its poor performances in Greece and North Africa in 1941. For instance, a cabaret artist, Pierre Dac, in a sketch performed at the Nice Nouveau-Casino, explained that his car did not need any gas to back up, because the reverse gear used "macaroni" as fuel.[47] In another instance, in Haute-Savoie, one group of Compagnons de France, a Vichy youth organization, cried on stage, "Les Macaronis vont se faire casser la gueule" (The Macaronis would have their faces smashed in), a clear reference to the Battle of the Alps, provoking hilarity and cheers among the audience.[48] Sometimes the French population resorted to more indirect means to express their contempt. Songs parodying famous Italian or French songs sprang out of the blue starting at the end of 1940. One version of "La Marseillaise," rechristened "Allez, Enfants de l'Italie," become widespread in Monaco and Nice in March 1941. The song belittled Italian military prestige from the very first verse ("Allez enfants de l'Italie / Le Jour de fuite est arrivé"), then ridiculed their poor campaign in the Balkans ("Il nous faut quitter l'Albanie / si nous ne voulons pas y crever") (Let's go, children of Italy / the day of fleeing has arrived! . . . We have to withdraw from Albania / if we don't want to die there) and finally derided the most important Italian war decoration, calling it the "Order of the Hare."[49] This parody of the French anthem was by no means the only one circulating in the Alpes-Maritimes. In February 1941, at the village of Breil-sur-Roya near the Green Line, a twenty-year-old was caught humming the Fascist anthem "Giovinezza" (Youthfulness) in the Breil patois, a local dialect similar to Italian. Interestingly, the song already hinted at the beginning of the rationing in Italy ("Avant que l'on chante Jeunesse / 40frs par jours on gagnait / Maintenant que l'on chante Jeunesse / On meurt de faim et de faiblesse") (Before singing Youthfulness / we earned 40 francs per day / Now that we are singing Youthfulness / we die of starvation and weakness).[50]

Most of the anti-Italian songs were based on popular songs for children or came from the milieu of the youth, thus underscoring its juvenile nature.[51] In early June 1941 several Italians in Nice received tracts in their mailboxes addressed to them specifically and containing anti-irredentist slogans such as "Nice est Française" (Nice is French) and "Mort aux Piémontais" (Death to Piedmontese). The perpetrators of the tracts were later identified as two young individuals, ages seventeen and eighteen, with no link whatsoever to any political organization.[52] However, one should not patronizingly dismiss rebellious acts of teenagers in occupied France as adolescent narcissism. Many young men and women over time organized in various organizations, which in the autumn of 1943 were reunited in the Forces Unies de la Jeunesse Patriotique (literally, "The United Forces of the Patriotic Youth") to help "adult" Resistance groups.[53]

All of these episodes underlined the seed of contempt for the Italians that was growing within the French population. In a brilliant attempt to underline the momentary Italian retreat against the Greek army, anonymous adult hands tagged a wall in front of the new Italian territory at the Pont de l'Union checkpoint in Menton with the words "*Grecs, ici c'est la France*" (Greeks, this is France).[54] In some instances, French adults became quite creative in expressing their feelings: oil drums shipped from Antibes to Italy as part of the renewal of economic ties were tagged with derogatory slogans such as "*Abas [sic] Mussolini mangeur de macarons*" (Down with Mussolini, the macaroni-eater) and "*La Grèce c'est plus forte que l'huil [sic] de ricino*" (Greece is more powerful than castor oil).[55] To preserve their anonymity, the perpetrators tagged only the side facing the ground when the drums were in vertical position; thus the insults were discovered only when the drums were unloaded on the other side of the border.[56]

The Italian delegates certainly felt the brooding hostility around them, even though they interpreted it as a reflection of the French people's reputedly chauvinistic haughtiness and disdain for all non-French. Italian officials were loath to admit that the Battle of the Alps had resulted in a strongly negative reaction among the French population, especially in the border regions. It was not uncommon for local Italian officials to receive anonymous letters with death threats, but sometimes the contempt was expressed in face-to-face confrontations. On 9 May 1941 two young men, upon seeing members of the Nice delegation of Sea Traffic Control, provocatively yelled, "*Vive la France, à bas Mussolini!*" Chased by the two Italian officials and two French gendarmes, the young men were able to sneak into a soap and washing powder factory and escape capture. The successful flight of the culprits would have settled the matter if some factory workers had not started to sing "La Marseillaise." One of the delegates lost his temper and yelled back, threatening the workers with possible imprisonment. The placating attitude of the other Italian delegate and the policemen notwithstanding, the excited Italian official became outraged as yet another worker cried aloud, "*Vive la France, à bas Mussolini!*"[57] Disputes between Italian representatives in France and the local population were not limited to the Alpes-Maritimes. Digne-les-Bains, the capital of the Basses-Alpes department, was the scene of two minor incidents in April 1941. In one instance two members of the small CIAF delegation in Digne were allegedly barred from entering the village cathedral for the celebration of Palm Sunday by a few young men and girls who mocked them. It seems, however, that the incident was the result of a misunderstanding: the young French themselves had been denied entry because the cathedral was packed beyond its capacity.[58] In another instance the head of the local Italian delegation, Lt. Ercole Viscardi, furiously kicked a drunkard in the street who was hurling half-slurred insults about Italy. Not satisfied, Viscardi threatened to punch a French captain who had objected to what he thought was excessive action by the CIAF official.[59] The Italian delegation in Corsica, too, was not immune to the populace's resentment. On 25 August a CIAF official, while strolling in Ajaccio, was hit on the nape of his neck with a rifle cartridge case thrown by an unknown passerby. Later that day a wall of the city's main street was tagged with the ominous graffiti, "*A quand la Saint-Barthélémy de la Commission?*" (When will there be a Saint-Bartholomew for the [Italian] Commission?).[60] In fact, clashes between CIAF officials and the French population happened in most of the departments under Italian control to such an extent that all prefects felt compelled to call for calm. For instance, the prefect of the Alpes-Maritimes in March 1941 issued such an appeal, asking the population to "maintain vis-à-vis members of the Control Commission the most reserved and correct attitude."[61]

Mutual suspicion between Italians and French sometimes erupted into violent confrontations between French and Italian nationals. On the night of 30 October 1940, Pierre Weck, eighteen years old and French, was strolling home from the movies with a few friends and his sister in Monaco. On the way, he ran into two Italians who were allegedly yelling "*Viva Mussolini, Vive le Duce!*" Weck asked them to stop their singing and in reply got punched. He then fell while fleeing, was repeatedly kicked in the head, and a few days later succumbed to his wounds at the hospital.[62] This tragedy caused an uproar in the French community. Wild rumors spread that the Italian surgeon who treated Weck had indicated in his report that the youth had died from hitting his head on the pavement, thus exonerating the two assailants.[63] The Italian consul in Monaco, Antonio Sanfelice, confirmed the Italian surgeon's explanation. In his report of the incident, Sanfelice asserted that the French group had started the confrontation and that Pierre Weck was particularly virulent in his insults "because of the support of several friends or maybe to act as a braggart to impress some girls." As soon as the two Italians had threatened to beat him, Weck ran and slipped on the sidewalk, mortally injuring himself by hitting his head on the paving. The consul's report, moreover, accused the local LFC, which had provided legal support to the victim's family in the trial, of adding to the tension by stirring up a nationalist campaign in describing the death of Pierre Weck as "a hateful Fascist aggression."[64]

Pierre Weck's death happened in the first months after the Battle of the Alps and, coupled with the previous incarceration of allegedly Italian Fascists in June 1940, the unfortunate incident could have foreshadowed the beginning of xenophobic violence. Yet, notwithstanding the increasing uneasiness in the department stemming from the tightening of rationing and the growing fear of an Italian invasion, no major crime based on xenophobic motivation was recorded after the Weck incident before the Italian military invasion in November 1942. Even the CIAF delegate in Nice, Quinto Mazzolini, admitted that the CIAF delegation often exaggerated the threat for propaganda reasons when he wrote, "I often explain the facts [incidents between French and Italians] to the French authorities with the *necessary dramatization*, but to the Royal [Foreign] Ministry I have to concede that at the present time, the Italian community in the Alpes-Maritimes lives almost undisturbed."[65] Xenophobic riots between Italians and French simply never happened, and the relations between the two communities never completely deteriorated.

This relative calm stemmed from two factors: first of all, the absence of widespread violence could be attributed to the high degree of integration of the Italian immigrants into the French society. While undeniably some Italian separatists were provocatively fueling the fire of irredentism to set in motion an open confrontation between the two communities and the two states, the majority of the Italian community in the French Riviera stayed put, refusing Italian welfare services even at a time of great need and prudently preferring not to meddle into politics. Moreover, mixed marriages were common and with good reason: the two communities were largely Catholic and shared common cultural roots such as similar dialects and similar cuisine. This cultural proximity, which later could also explain the minor impact of the Italian military occupation when Italian soldiers and the local population came to a modus vivendi, was a factor even before the occupation. Second, both communities were in an *attentiste* (wait-and-see) mood, waiting for the armistice situation to clarify itself. Even the most ardent anti-Italian inhabitants were cautious in expressing their contempt, in case of an Italian invasion.[66] The same attitude was certainly present in the relationship between CIAF and Vichy officials as both sides waged an indirect war of propaganda and quarrels over Italian immigrants' rights. Yet CIAF officials indeed knew they were treading dangerous ground in the free zone and therefore paid lip service to Vichy sovereignty in order to minimize confrontation with the French state and the local population. Conversely, Vichy prefects, while resenting the Italians' interference in public matters, avoided making rash moves until the coming of an eventual peace treaty. Of course, in this war of nerves, each of the participants cast baleful sidelong glances to the enemy. Not surprisingly, the Deuxième Bureau, the French military intelligence service, carefully monitored both German and Italian armistice commissions.[67] CIAF officials, too, were not idling as they used money and food to build spying networks.[68]

However, CIAF delegations never fully trusted the Italian populace who were willing to help them, the irredentists. To be sure, the two parties still shared the same overarching goal of seeing the Italian flag fly in the County of Nice one day. They dissented, however, on how to achieve this objective. The irredentist movement openly voiced its opinion by any means and aimed to foment nationalist riots within the Alpes-Maritimes, hoping to eventually compel the Italian army to cross the border. This outspoken attitude achieved nothing except to breed hostility toward the Italian community and the CIAF. Still it remains undeniable that CIAF officials, even though they did not fully trust people from the local irredentist movement, were forced to rely on them, since they were the only faction in France sympathizing for the annexation cause. Indeed, CIAF delegates never lost sight of their ultimate mission, which was to prepare for the future annexation of the free zone. All the CIAF fortnightly reports carefully analyzed the French internal situation with the goal of identifying which forces might eventually oppose any invasion. In the words of Mazzolini, "We never failed to provide any possible support to the idea of our territorial claims."[69] Of course, at least until November 1942, this annexationist policy was always carried out in a semi-clandestine way for fear of alarming Vichy officials.

CHAPTER 4

A Prelude to Full Occupation

The Occupation of Menton (1940–1942)

The iconic coastal town of Menton is widely acclaimed even today for its Mediterranean charm. Indeed, nestled between the Alpine mountains to the north and east and its magnificent shoreline to the south, Menton, thanks to its subtropical climate and breathtaking view of the Mediterranean Sea, was a favorite spot for upscale tourists, mainly from northern France, England, and, since the interwar years, the United States. However, this bucolic setting was the theater between 1940 and 1942 of a forceful, albeit inchoate, colonization campaign of Fascist officials that would considerably alter the society of the Italian-French border region. To be sure, contrary to the free zone, where Vichy prefects still had the final say in internal matters in the area occupied after June 1940 by the Italian army, at least until November 1942, Italian administrators had complete control over the entire occupied zone. Therefore, local CIAF officials could openly express their desire of annexation without incurring the anger of French authorities. This strategy served two purposes: first, the Italians wanted Menton to become a model of Italianization for the consumption of both Italian and French public opinion, and most important, with the reconstruction of Menton and the occupied zone, the Italians, especially the CIAF, were willing to experiment with a policy of colonization, which, in the minds of the Italian leaders, would later carry over in all irredentist lands.

This policy was not well accepted by local Italian military commanders, for the new strip of conquered land held a crucial role in security matters, which they believed superseded its political value. The Italian army was endeavoring to create a new buffer zone between Italy and France in order to both prevent any future invasion of the French army and screen individuals who transited from France to Italy. Arguably, this security strategy did nothing to facilitate the task of Italian civilian officials who strove to restore the zone—especially its biggest town, Menton—to its former glory with a two-pronged campaign that was intended to encourage former inhabitants to return home and tourists to visit the area. Therefore, when the occupation zone expanded to include a wider territory of southeastern France in November 1942—and contrary to the German-occupied area, where Wehrmacht commanders were progressively sidelined in favor of Gestapo executives and SS commanders—the internecine rivalry between Italian army commanders and Italian CIAF officials over occupation policy in France was ultimately won by the former, who emphasized security measures over political interests. Initially, however, the power lay with the CIAF, who did not lose time underscoring the importance of the zone.

On 5 November 1940 a separate bureau, the Amministrazione dei Territori Occupati (Administration of Occupied Territories Bureau), was created in Turin, headed by an Italian prefect who supervised the civil commissars and the Italian civil administrators of the municipalities in the Italian occupation zone. It was crucial for the Fascist authorities to reestablish legal order in the occupied zone immediately, as the departure of the French civilian authorities a few days before the war had left a jurisdictional vacuum. Thus, on 30 July Mussolini issued the "Proclamation Concerning the Administration and the Judicial Organization of the Occupied Territories," which officially sanctioned the coming of the occupied territories under Italian jurisdiction.[1] Appointed by the Italian High Command, this zone's civil commissars were subordinated both to the Administration of Occupied Territories Bureau at the central CIAF headquarters in Turin and to local military commanders, especially with regard to questions of public order.[2] Nevertheless, each civil commissar, whose purview encompassed one municipality, still enjoyed a high degree of autonomy, and his role mirrored that of the French prefect in Vichy France. Any French decree issued by French local or national administrations had to be approved by the Italian authorities before becoming law in the occupied zone.[3] Thus, civil commissars quickly became the supreme civilian authority in the occupied zone.

The proclamation warned that civil commissars could release from their duties local French authorities who had abandoned their posts prior to the conflict and did not return within ten days. This provision was probably meant to force a limited number of French civil servants to return to the occupied territory. The presence of French mayors, in particular, was important to both the Italian and the French states, but for diametrically opposed reasons. The Italians were hoping to effect a smooth transition from French to Italian administrations, drawing on the knowledge and experience of the

French functionaries, as well as to lure French citizens into moving back to the occupied zone. Vichy itself was interested, for reasons of prestige, in order to ensure a continued presence of some representation of French state authority. To this end, Vichy instructed the former administrative personnel who had previously fled the German advance to resume their work in the occupied zone.[4] In the case of Menton, nudged by the prefect of the Alpes-Maritimes, the mayor of Menton, Jean Durandy, agreed to do so, crossing the new border (the Green Line) on 29 June.[5]

This did not mean that the Italians were willing to embrace the old administration as if nothing had happened. Durandy was joined after two months by only a handful of municipal civil servants, mostly clerks, handpicked by the Italian authorities. Strict rules were enforced by local Italian authorities in the entire occupied zone. Mayors and the bare minimum of municipal office workers needed were allowed to return to their alpine villages, but other functionaries were forbidden to follow suit.[6] No other French official—not a firefighter, a policeman, or member of the Renseignements Généraux,[7] not even a postman—was allowed to resume his prewar position. All of these officials were forced to relocate across the border—in the case of Menton, at Roquebrune-Cap Martin.

This moderate yet condescending attitude toward French officials reflected the Italian two-pronged policy. In the short term the occupation zone needed to be rebuilt, especially in the case of Menton, and its infrastructure restored. French administrators were tolerated insofar as they could help restore the economic and social network of the occupied zone. Yet the Italians always saw them as an intrusive presence that would be dismissed as soon as the situation stabilized. After the short, yet quite destructive, military offensive in the Battle of the Alps, the Italians were confronted with the poor state of the zone. Parts of Menton had been ruined by Italian shells and street combat. To add insult to injury, the city had had to endure widespread looting. Italian authorities pointed an accusatory finger at the retreating troops of the Armée des Alpes. While it is possible that French troops may have occasionally looted, it is clear that the Italians were the major culprits. Taking advantage of the forced exile of two-thirds of Menton's inhabitants and almost all farmers in the countryside,[8] some Italian soldiers, as vengeance for their fallen comrades, rampaged through the streets, combing whole neighborhoods in search of portable yet valuable goods such as silverware or lingerie. Summer villas of rich English citizens were targeted first for their luxury goods and because of the certainty that their owners would not return soon to lay claim to their property.[9] Italo Calvino, who would later become one of the major twentieth-century Italian novelists but was at that time a Fascist *Avanguardista* (Vanguardist), testified to the devastation in Menton he had witnessed when he toured the occupied zone with his fellow Vanguardists.[10] Everywhere, the desolate streets were littered with broken glass, and broken doors lay ajar. The walls of buildings were defiled with patriotic slogans such as *W il Re, W il Duce, W i morti,* and *W la Cosseria.*[11] The *razzia* (raiding) also spread to the small villages in the Italian occupied zone. In Breil, for instance, a schoolteacher complained in July 1941 that the furniture of her house had been illegally moved to the new Italian civil commissar's house.[12]

With the rebuilding of the infrastructure under way, the Italian authorities turned to their overarching objective of integrating Menton and the occupied zone into the Italian empire. Although trade barriers between the occupied zone and Italy were lifted, they were instituted between the zone and France.[13] The Italian lira was made the official currency while the French franc was officially demoted to a second-rank currency, its exchange rate set at an outrageous thirty lire for one hundred francs.[14] The proclamation was even more drastic in its revamping of the judicial system. The French were left with only a justice of the peace, who doubled as *juge d'instruction* (examining magistrate). This same magistrate, however, was carefully supervised by an Italian military prosecutor and had to abide by Italian penal and civil laws.[15] Any crime committed against the Italian military forces was to be prosecuted by a special Italian military tribunal.[16] Finally, depending on how far the case might progress, one could appeal only within the Italian legal system to the Turin Court of Appeals.

With the integration of the occupied zone into the jurisdictional, political, and economic framework of the Fascist state, the Italian authorities set in motion their long-term goal of Italianizing the whole occupation zone, Menton in particular. In the convoluted language of the Italian bureaucracy, the goal of every civil commissariat was "to endeavor as much as possible to contribute to giving a typically Italian imprint. To this end, it should enact a series of measures similar or parallel to those adopted in the national territory and implement a daily and concrete activity through the Italian commissars' offices, with the general aim to achieve a substantial inclusion of this area into the life of the Italian nation."[17] This campaign developed in two directions. First of all, local Italian authorities were to root the Italian language, customs, and traditions in the newly occupied territory. In the meantime, local administrations would be purged of the few remaining French civil servants, who would be replaced by Italian ones.

It is a truism that the national language is one of the pillars upon which a nation rests. In fact, since the end of the nineteenth century, mandatory schooling was one of the principal vehicles used by modern nation-states to instill a national consciousness in their populace. Pupils were taught to realize that they shared a common culture and history.[18] This was the plan of the commissariats; nevertheless, the Italianization of the occupied zone was uneven. In the Alpine occupied zone the Italians tolerated the reopening of French schools. The reason for the difference was simple: fewer efforts were made to provide school services in Italian in the northern Alpine departments (Savoy, Hautes, and Basses-Alpes), because they were not the primary objective of the irredentist plans.[19] On the other hand, the County of Nice, as well as Tunisia and Corsica, ranked high in the expansionist agenda of the Fascist state. Italian irredentist panegyrists insisted that the French Riviera "belonged unmistakably by the nature of its people, the language spoken, its customs and the religious, civic and warlike spirit [to Italy's western Riviera]."[20] Therefore, Italian officials took great pains to create new Italian schools in the area of the County of Nice that had been included in the occupied zone. Because of its demographic and symbolic importance, Menton was a special target of this policy. By October 1942 the Italian administration had set up no less than nine Italian schools, ranging from day care to secondary schools, with more than one thousand pupils enrolled.[21]

Coincidental with the development of Italian schools, the Italian authorities refused to allow the French schools to reopen. This odd situation spurred the French community in Menton to swiftly take steps to protect their cultural heritage. French teachers and other educated citizens organized clandestine lessons in private houses and even cellars.[22] Starting at the beginning of October 1942, the French community went as far as to set up fee-paying French lectures, taught by two clergymen and a university student. Realizing that the civil commissar would never give them permission to teach even in private settings, the French ecclesiastical authorities disguised the lessons as Catholic catechism.[23] Italian authorities reacted quickly to what they deemed a threat to Italian sovereignty in the occupied zone. The unofficial schools in San Michele and Sacro Cuore's churches were closed in early November, and the French priests were strictly admonished not to stray again from Italian regulations.[24] Things were no different in the rural parts of the department. In the municipality of Fontan, the school offered classes only in Italian, with an Italian teacher who came daily from across the border. Pupils who wished to study in French had to take private lessons, paid for by their families.[25] The same situation popped up in the hamlet of Isola, where the intransigent commissar Guido Botto refused to allow the return of the French teacher until May 1942.[26]

Tied to the issue of the education system was the question of clergy. Both the Italians and the French realized the significance of controlling Catholic worship in a region where church influence was still strong. In the County of Nice and the bordering Liguria and Piedmont regions, rural villages were built around churches and the social fabric was woven through local parishes. Clashes between the local French Catholic Church and the Italian one were not new. In the late 1800s the Italian Church had sent priests or missionaries to France to address the needs of the growing Italian community, which was otherwise unable to understand the sermons or confess, even though the French Catholic clergy were not always happy with what they viewed as an intrusion into their congregation.[27]

Again, policies varied markedly between departments within the occupation zone. It seems that the farther the department was from Menton, the more lenient the Italian authorities were about enforcing occupation policy. Bishops enjoyed free access to those parts of their dioceses located in the Maurienne and Tarentaise valleys in Savoy, even without safe-conducts.[28] On the contrary, in the Alpes-Maritimes the Italians and the French, not surprisingly, locked horns. The bishop of Nice, Monseigneur Paul Rémond, who in light of his patriotism was quickly identified by Italian officials as a nefarious influence, used his position to undermine the authority of the Italian Catholic Church. Appealing to the highest Vatican authorities, he successfully lobbied against the bishop of Ventimiglia's coming to Menton, fearing that such a visit could be construed as a step toward the incorporation of Menton into Ventimiglia's Italian diocese. Italian authorities lashed back by denying Monseigneur Rémond a safe-conduct to visit Menton, forcing him to delegate his prerogatives to the eldest clergyman in Menton, Canon Ortmans.[29]

The conflict even trickled down to the parish level. From the moment of the creation of the occupation zone, Italian authorities had tried to persuade local parish priests to deliver sermons only in Italian but were forced to accept masses in French, due to the limited availability of local priests who spoke Italian and their reticence to alienate their old parishioners. Even those who spoke Italian were not necessarily cooperative. In Fontan, a small hamlet in the Alpes-Maritimes divided in half by the new border (the Green Line), the priest, Don Antonio Pellegrino, categorically refused to preach in Italian. The civil commissar did not dare expel him from Fontan, as Don Pellegrino had been officially supported in his decision by the Vatican, which in this instance ruled that Fontan, as much as Menton, was still to be considered part of the diocese of Nice. However, Don Pellegrino was prohibited from crossing the border to officiate in the free zone and was

severely admonished by the civil commissar when he preached a mass on
Joan of Arc's name day.[30] In the hamlet of Le Bourghet, Italian authorities
had even less success. A curate from the nearby commune of Saint-Étienne
de Tinée had to cross the Green Line nearly every day to act as both parish
priest and schoolteacher. This problematic situation stemmed from the local civil commissar's decision to appoint an Italian who had no knowledge
of French language and was thus unable to communicate with his French
pupils.[31]

The forced Italianization was not limited to education and religion, but
touched other aspects of daily life as well. In Menton road signs were
changed to conform to Italian signage, and new milestones were erected
to mark the kilometers to Rome.[32] Street names were renamed after the
myths and heroes of Italian Fascist propaganda. Thus, "Promenade du Midi"
changed to "Passeggiata Mare Nostrum,"[33] "Promenade Georges V" became
"Passeggiata Italo Balbo,"[34] and several streets were dedicated to fallen
Italian soldiers of the Battle of the Alps.[35] The topographic upheaval in
Menton included Italianizing the names of stores and buildings: "Palazzo
del Comune" replaced "Hotel de Ville," and grocery stores were renamed
alimentari.

The forced colonization of the occupied zone was further implemented
by Italianizing local administrations. Between 1941 and 1942 the number
of Italian civil servants swelled dramatically as new bureaus were created at
the civil commissariat to help in the reconstruction of Menton. At the same
time, Italian authorities dismissed the most important French civil servants,
such as Menton mayor Jean Durandy. Durandy had been given express permission by the Italians to return to Menton, and the occupation authorities
had wanted to use him as a decoy to lure the French population to return to
Menton. Therefore, at the beginning, the relations between Durandy and the
Italian authorities were courteous. In fact, the mayor had been so accommodating that the Alpes-Maritimes prefect Ribière dryly complained that
"the mayor, Mr. Durandy, does not act as a resolute French."[36] Indeed, as a
sign of favor, the three chief Italian dignitaries in Menton, among them the
civil commissar Giuseppe Frediani, attended the mayor's wedding reception
on 16 October 1941. As a token of goodwill, Durandy and his new wife
also accepted the Italian authorities' invitation to spend their honeymoon
trip in Italy.

However, this forced cohabitation petered out shortly thereafter. Municipal functionaries, as the sole representatives of the French state, were bound
to become the target of the Italian irredentist campaign. As time went by,
Durandy and his staff had lost their usefulness in the eyes of the Italian

authorities now that the transition period was over. This new hostile stance was embodied in Frediani, who made the point in June 1942 that the French town council in Menton enjoyed only a fictitious decision-making power. Frediani had been slowly but steadily draining the town council of its rights, passing them over to Italian officials.[37] By 1942 it became clear that he was the real puppet master behind the council. The Italians first targeted the head of the mayor's personal staff, Marcel Barneaud, who was given a one-week ultimatum to leave the city in April 1942 for alleged anti-Italian espionage and for immoral behavior. The future *Combat* resistant was openly accused of traveling to France to deliver political and military reports on Menton.[38] To tarnish his reputation even further, the Italian authorities hinted at a possible affair, a slander that his wife vehemently denied.[39]

That the sand in the French mayor's hourglass began to flow was evident by the launching of a campaign to discredit Durandy himself. The full frontal attack came in the 6 September 1942 edition of *Il Nizzardo* with an article titled, "The Hopes of the Mayor of Menton." Allegedly, Durandy had been heard in a café in Nice uttering scornful remarks about the Axis powers and predicting that 1943 would be a turning point in the war. The journalist wryly concluded the article by advising the mayor to be more careful in the future.[40] The mayor did not get a chance to heed the advice, however. Even though Durandy immediately wrote a letter to the civil commissar firmly denying the article's allegations,[41] the Italian authorities had already decided to exile the mayor and to take advantage of the upheaval to dismiss the entire town council.[42] To replace the French mayor, the prefect for the Administration of Occupied Territories, G. B. Marziali, picked an Italian engineer born in Menton and known for his Fascist sentiments, Giovanni Marenco. Not surprisingly, *Il Nizzardo* hailed the appointment of Marenco as the "end of the misunderstanding," created by having "a French mayor and a French town council [ruling over] the very Italian [*italianissima*] Menton."[43]

If the Menton civil commissar was adamant about crushing the last remnants of French sovereignty, he tolerated the Mentonese autonomist movement, probably stemming from the desire to sever the bonds tying Menton to its French heritage while underscoring its cultural affinity with the Italian peninsula.[44] Moreover, the civil commissar in Menton keenly understood that by fostering the local autonomist movement—the Comité des Traditions Mentonnaises, which consolidated in February 1942—Italian authorities could make inroads into the French part of the Mentonese population. For this reason, the *comité* enjoyed relative political and economic freedom.[45] Its president, the controversial Marcel Firpo, became the head of the Ufficio

Assistenza per il Rimpatrio dei Mentonaschi (Office for the Repatriation of the Mentonese Population).[46] The newly created organization, which took over the rooms in the city hall previously occupied by the French police superintendent, was given the tasks of enticing Mentonese refugees to return and providing assistance to them upon their return to the city. An article in the *Giornale di Genova* described in flattering prose what awaited the Mentonese emigrant entering the office: "In the waiting room, a notice in pure Mentonese stated: 'Here you are at home.' This will give the emigrants who get back the certainty that they could express freely their wishes. . . . Greeted by the Head of the Office Marcel Firpo, a pure blood Mentonese, with his proverbial kindness, the emigrants will find an almost brotherly assistance. . . . The news of the establishment of the assistance office has had very positive feedback."[47]

The Italian state was not the only one interested in repatriating the ten thousand displaced Mentonese still living in southwestern France, mostly in the Pyrénées-Orientales department. Vichy too encouraged them to return by extending grants to Menton refugees who returned home.[48] By sending back French citizens, Vichy endeavored to reassert Menton's French character. Moreover, their hosting department, the Pyrénées-Orientales, which had already sheltered four hundred thousand Spaniards fleeing the Spanish Civil War during the 1930s, was after a month already on its knees as feeding and lodging thousands of refugees became the serious social and economic burden.[49] Notwithstanding the Secours National campaign to entice inhabitants of hosting departments to welcome refugees with "open arms" (*a bras ouverts*), its inhabitants increasingly grumbled about the newcomers, especially in a period of increasing rationing and food shortages. Arguably, this brooding conflict heightened the homesickness (*dépaysement*) of the Mentonese.[50]

However, Menton's refugees were reluctant to accept Vichy's offer for several reasons. First of all, most of the people had lost their belongings in the looting at the cessation of hostilities, and in some cases they had lost even their houses or shops. French refugees were compensated by neither the Italian state, as the Italian decree of 26 October 1940 regarding damage related to war events limited the indemnification to Italian citizens, nor the French state, as French loss adjusters were forbidden to come to Menton to evaluate the extent of material damage.[51] This important issue was further worsened by a currency exchange rate that was clearly disadvantageous for the French, a fact that even Giuseppe Frediani could not deny.[52] Moreover, French citizens would be cut off from any French administration, with the exception of the municipal authorities, and even they had only infrequent contact with the department's administration in Nice. Finally, as a condition of returning to their homes, French refugees from Menton were required to obtain a safe-conduct from Italian authorities.[53] The bleak prospect of being subjected to Italian laws without the possibility of appealing to French authorities dissuaded more than one possible candidate. This sense of isolation was further heightened both by the new postal policy in the occupation zone (letters sent to France were not only charged international postage rates but were also carefully scrutinized by the Italian censors) and by the impossibility of phoning France, a privilege enjoyed by only the Italian authorities.[54] While food supplies were better in the Italian occupied zone than in Vichy's territory, chiefly because the population of Menton received food from the Italian army and, outside Menton, also from the French ravitaillement services, the French understood that this dependency left them at the mercy of the Italian occupiers.[55]

If this situation was not enough to discourage prospective returnees, the 6 April 1941 decree was a cold shower for many. Prewar Fascist legislation unilaterally deemed each individual of Italian descent to be an Italian citizen, even if he or she had previously relinquished their nationality in order to become French. The 6 April decree, however, took this law even further, severing these individuals' ties with France. The Fascist state deemed their French nationality to have lapsed and thereafter considered them to be full Italian citizens. This new status had a dangerous implication. French citizens of Italian blood could well "receive the postcard" from the Genoa or Turin military district and be drafted into the Regio Esercito.[56] Local fears worsened when in 1941 the Italian authorities ominously conducted a census of every male between seventeen and twenty-four years of age in the occupied zone.

In response to these moves by the Italian occupation authorities, Vichy attempted to coerce those young Frenchmen who were living in the Italian zone but working in the free zone to enlist in the French forces, threatening them with imprisonment if they failed to do so. In retaliation, the Italians canceled the men's safe-conduct passes, even though this measure effectively choked off the economic recovery of the Italian occupation zone by drastically increasing the number of jobless men.[57] Moreover, in light of the ongoing war effort, even those who were deemed unfit for military duty, including minors age fourteen or older and women, could eventually be called to perform the *servizio obbligatorio del lavoro* (mandatory work service). Given that approximately one-fourth of the population in the region was Italian or had been naturalized in the 1930s, the potential impact of the

6 April decree was significant. The French delegation in Turin vigorously protested to no avail. Conversely, the Italians were adamant that no residents in the occupied zone could be enrolled in the French Armée d'Armistice, probably fearing that any French military service would provide the seeds of rebellion.[58] Italian authorities were so anxious about a possible fifth column emerging in the occupied territory that even youth organizations such as the Chantiers de la Jeunesse were banned.[59]

In light of the ongoing tension between the two countries and the dire prospect of living a precarious life in a foreign city, the Mentonese refugees ignored the repatriation campaign. In April 1941 fewer than sixty-eight hundred people were living in Menton, compared to twenty-one thousand in 1939. This number increased to only seventy-two hundred by the end of the occupation in 1943. Consequently, in late 1942 three out of four inhabitants in Menton were Italian, whereas in 1939 they had represented only one-fourth of the total population.[60]

Unable to persuade Menton refugees to return, the Menton civil commissars sought to recruit Italians to Menton.[61] Starting in 1941 a major propaganda campaign that depicted Menton as the embodiment of the dawn of a new Italian empire unfurled in Italian newspapers and magazines. The Duce himself had visited the town only one week after the end of combat, on 1 July, in order to underline the importance of Menton in the Fascist expansionist discourse.[62] Significantly, the railroad line between Ventimiglia and Menton was not only reopened but also electrified as a way to reinforce Menton's link to the Italian territory. The local tourist office, the Costa Azzurra di Mentone, commissioned several leaflets that praised the geographic beauty of Menton along with sites such as the Saint-Louis Bridge, where Italian and French troops had clashed in June 1940. Moreover, a notorious postcard of the Fifteenth Army Corps portrayed an Italian soldier using the butt of his rifle to topple a border milestone engraved with the words "France 1861," a clear allusion to the 1861 incorporation of the County of Nice into France.[63] The Fascist state was so determined to use Menton as the symbol of Italy's resurgence that the city enjoyed an unusual abundance of food, at least until July 1941, at a time when both France and Italy had already fallen into daily rationing.[64] The campaign had the two-pronged goal of enticing workers, mostly from the Liguria region, to settle in Menton and of helping restore the key sector of tourism. This colonization policy, denounced by both Vichy and French civilians, met with some success, as one out of five inhabitants of Menton in 1941 had not been living in the city before the war.[65]

The Woes of Menton

Nevertheless, the French Riviera town of Menton was hardly the idyllic place it had been before the war. It was still half deserted, its image blemished by soaring unemployment and the impossibility of communicating with the French free zone, the result of a break in the telephone network. Even basic utilities needed for everyday life, such as gas, water, and electricity, were in short supply.[66]

The Italianization campaign, the plummeting of the standard of living, and the extenuating negotiations for the distribution of basic utilities served to exacerbate the already strained relations between the French and Italian communities. Tensions in Menton between the isolated French minority and the Italians were building daily, tearing the delicate social fabric of the town. To the outrage of the French community, on the night of 10 April 1942, unidentified vandals toppled the bust of the *République* (referring to Marianne, the national symbol of revolutionary France) in the central square of Menton, which symbolized the 1860 annexation of Menton by France. Brazen Fascist activities such as a weekly Saturday parade of Avanguardisti and Balilla youths in their black shirts and the celebrations on 23 June of the anniversary of the "capture" of Menton were considered provocations by the French population. Fights erupted in the bistros between Italian soldiers and French youths, the latter eventually ending up in jail for a few days. Shops owned by outspoken Fascist militants were targeted by French youths and their windows shattered with stones.[67] Anti-Italian graffiti and anonymous pamphlets belittling the Italian invasion and inviting the Italian soldiers to desert were common.[68] French citizens who collaborated with the occupying authorities, such as Marcel Firpo, the head of the Office for the Repatriation of the Mentonese Population, had their houses defaced with insults such as "Sellout" (*Vendu*) and "Traitor" (*Traitre*).[69]

The Italianization campaign ran into serious limitations outside of Menton as well. For a local holiday in Fontan, the civil commissar brought a musical band from Italy to play in the central square, only to the general indifference of the local population.[70] The French populace's attitude was hardly surprising. The replacement of the word "*Mairie*" with the Italian equivalent "*Municipio*" on the façade of Fontan's town hall during the first days of the occupation clearly demonstrated that, as in Menton, the Italian authorities had no qualms about pursuing their plans for the Italianization of the County of Nice.[71] For the same reason, in 1942 the French population in Fontan abandoned the local celebration of Epiphany, despite the fact that they would miss the distribution of children's toys, food, and money.

The French likely resented the unscrupulous use of the Twelfth Night for propaganda purposes and its Italianization in the form of *Befana*.[72]

To counter the hostility of the local French, the Italians finally had to resort to repressive instruments to curb anti-Italian acts. These ranged from the denial of safe-conducts to persons who were believed to have an anti-Italian or anti-Fascist agenda to meticulous body searches at border checkpoints; from apartment inspections to open intimidation.[73] Arrests and imprisonment were the ultimate punishment. From June 1941 to January 1943 more than twelve hundred people were arrested, most of them for illegally crossing the border, minor anti-Italian activities, or simply on suspicion of such. For example, the arrival of Axis dignitaries such as Hans-Gustav Felber, one of the German commanders in charge of southern France, in December 1942 triggered a wave of preventive arrests. A sojourn in jail was generally a first step toward expulsion from the occupied zone to the free zone, and thus the time in jail was often short.[74]

The ongoing repressive campaign in the occupied zone hinted at the problematic result of the Italian occupation in the border zone; the real test would be how the colonization system operated in actual practice. It is not an understatement to conclude that the Italian experiment in the occupied zone was a serious failure. The Italians had underestimated the patriotic sentiment of the local French population, who did not intend to relinquish their own nationality and heritage. The aborted revival of Menton was also the consequence of the Italians' dismal failure to win the hearts and souls of the local population. The French inhabitants who had fled the Italian invasion did not go back to live in the occupied zone, because they feared being cut off from the French state and being ostracized. Moreover, the city was still in shambles in 1942, both structurally and economically, a factor that hardly seduced any prospective Italian colonist. Indeed, the new administration was unable to solve the financial cost of the occupation. The Italian state had injected 800,000 lire into the local economy, but this was just a fragment of the 195 million lire estimated by the civil commissariat as necessary to completely refund the local population for war damages.[75] The massive expenditure required to pay for the expanded numbers of personnel and for the public works projects needed to rebuild the city irritated more than one ministry in Rome, at a time when every lira was needed to bolster the war effort in the Balkans and in North Africa. Furthermore, the public cost of the occupation could not be alleviated by taxation, owing to the fact that in an effort to encourage the repopulation of the territory, between 1940 and 1943 no income or property taxes were levied in the occupied zone. In addition, an inspection stemming from the CIAF headquarters in Turin uncovered several cases of corruption and abuse. In a very revealing and scathing letter, G. B. Marziali, the prefect of the Administration of Occupied Territories, reported a sudden suspicious rise in unnecessary expenditures and budget irregularities, a result of leisure trips being reported as business travel, inflated bills for propaganda leaflets, unscrupulous use of vehicles and long-distance calls, and outrageous expenses for the luxurious renovation of the commissariat's building.[76] In the same letter, Marziali chastised Frediani for hiring employees without permission from Turin. Consequently, he considerably restricted Frediani's freedom of action and strongly advised him to pursue a policy of austerity.

As damaging for the Italian occupation as the malpractice of its officials were the internecine rivalries within the Fascist state. Conflicts between different seats of power mirrored the vested and conflicting interests of the Italian national ministries. Several ministries, such as the Ministries of Interior, Foreign Affairs, and Popular Culture (MINCULPOP) vied for control in order to further their own particular interests. In his June report Frediani had requested an extension of his power so that he could deal with the frictions between the different departments in the commissariat.[77] In the same report, Frediani affirmed that as a militant of the PNF he was shunned by the Italian military *presidio* (garrison) in Menton. This conflict was much more than mere political antipathy, as it was indicative of two fundamentally different and ultimately irreconcilable policies. On the one hand, Frediani had based his policy on the development of local tourism, the only activity that could have bolstered Menton's prestige and economy in Italy and abroad. Under his supervision, the city saw a partial normalization of its life: schools opened, the food distribution network became more organized, and the reopening of the local casino and some hotels attracted a few tourists. A massive propaganda campaign carried out by local and Italian national newspapers touted Menton as the ideal spot for a relaxing sojourn. Under the supervision of Frediani, the Comité des Traditions Mentonnaises celebrated the rebirth of the new town by authorizing a Menton exhibition stand at the 1941 Milano Fair, one of the most important in Europe. The Menton exhibit was graced with a chorus in traditional costume who delighted the public, among them King Vittorio Emanuele III, with its repertoire of songs in Mentonese dialect.[78] Despite the choir's tour in the neighboring regions, which won flattering reviews, even the comité's campaign was partly hamstrung by strict controls at the Italian border.

In strident contrast with Frediani's policy, military authorities prioritized the security of the region over its economic recovery and always underscored that until the peace treaty was signed, the occupied zone was considered a *zona d'operazione* (operation zone). Supported in their decision by the local head of the state police, Inspector Rosario Barranco,[79] they tightened their grip on the borders, believing that every visitor could be "a possible spy or a currency trafficker."[80] Italians wishing to enter the occupied zone had to apply for a permit issued by the Italian police. This burdensome procedure, which could take as long as thirty days, discouraged one-day visits from nearby regions and severely hampered any chance for Menton's tourist industry to return to its past levels of success.[81] In April 1942 the military Italian authorities relaxed the border crossing by allowing members of the Partito Nazionale Fascista into Menton on the strength of their membership cards.[82] However, it was not enough for Frediani, who opposed this rigid policy because it hindered the resuscitation of tourism, the only activity that could have bolstered Menton's economy and prestige. In the end, Frediani was ultimately forced to yield, only because the 30 July 1940 decree stated that the civil commissar was subordinate to local military commanders, especially on security matters. The Italian invasion in November 1942 would seal all the borders of the occupied zone, once and for all dooming tourism in Menton.[83]

Therefore, the Italian occupation was seriously weakened by its conflicting goals: it was a military occupation designed to secure the border and prevent the French army from rising from its ashes, but it was also concurrently used by the Fascist civilian administration as a means to promote Italy's image both in the peninsula and worldwide. The two agendas were not compatible, and the tension would only worsen after November 1942. In truth the dualism between the Italian army and the civilian authorities was not the only issue explaining the failed development of Menton. The forced Italianization campaign was as responsible as the military contingency. The prefect of Imperia, Marcello Tallarigo, wrote a terse letter to the interior ministry underlining the dreadful approach undertaken by CIAF commissars in Menton, who were guilty of using the same blatant colonization policy carried out in Albania, Africa, and the Balkans. Instead, Tallarigo explained, it would have been "advisable to implement from the beginning a homeopathic diffusion of the Fascist ideology, given the fact that the organism we were confronted with had never been very receptive to a prescription with the double tag of Italian and Fascist."[84]

Franco-Italian Entente in the Alps

Indeed, when the Italian authorities implemented a more nuanced approach to the local population, unloading the occupation of its political undertone, the results were much more satisfactory and cohabitation between occupied and occupiers became easier. For example, Montgenèvre, a small village in the Hautes-Alpes department, underwent a successful reconstruction, orchestrated by the local civil commissar, Marquis Saporiti, after having been partially destroyed by the deluge of bombs in the 1940 June offensive. According to Fascist propaganda, the village was rapidly rebuilt and even outshone its former self, quickly becoming a thriving Alpine resort.[85]

The case of the Presidio of Maison-Méane in the Basses-Alpes department was itself emblematic of the emerging entente between Italian soldiers and the French populace. The Armistice of Villa Incisa had given the Italians a small strip of pasture lands on the eastern border of the Basses-Alpes. The utility of the occupied French land was minimal even for strategic purposes, as the Regio Esercito had failed to secure locations, apart from Menton, that would be effective as bridgeheads in the face of any prospective invasion, especially in wintertime. The Italian garrison in Maison-Méane initially consisted of one company of the Alpine Divisione Cuneense.[86] Starting in late 1940, the elite Alpine divisions were progressively transferred to the Greek and Eastern fronts, passing the baton to units of the Guardia alla Frontiera (GaF), an Alpine corps created in 1937 with the task of manning the defensive network of forts on the Italian side of the Alps.[87] Beginning in 1941, even a few GaF units were relocated to the east to cover the abysmal human cost of the Greek and Russian campaigns.[88] As a result, the garrison of Maison-Méane never exceeded five hundred soldiers, half of them only temporarily quartered there, waiting to be sent to other theaters of war.[89]

Notwithstanding the continuous renewal of Italian units in the Alpine outposts, a peculiar modus vivendi between the Italian occupation army and the French population in the rural regions emerged progressively. Maison-Méane was rather isolated from the rest of the region, and continuous avalanches and heavy snowfalls made the movement of supplies extremely difficult.[90] However, while the extreme climatic conditions heightened the sense of isolation felt by the Italian soldiers, they also brought the soldiers closer to the local population. In addition, many of the Alpine troops came from similar regions just across the border, such as the Valle d'Aosta or the Piedmont, and therefore had more cultural affinity with the local populace than with the rest of Italy.[91]

From the onset of the occupation, the Regio Esercito supplied the occupied hamlets with free food, although starting in January 1941 the quantity of these supplies gradually diminished due to the tightening rationing of food in the Italian peninsula.[92] Granted that this policy had a clear propagandistic purpose, as was the case in Menton, it set the mood for cordial, and in some instances even friendly, relations between civilians and soldiers, as in the village of Larche. There, in October 1940, the prefect of the Basses-Alpes alarmingly noted that because of the food coming from Italy and the good manners of the Italians, "a wave of popularity seems to be taking shape in Larche toward our former opponents" to the point that "some people envisage with serenity the prospective annexation of their village."[93]

The popularity of the Regio Esercito was also enhanced by bringing an effective health service system to the region. Italian military doctors were dispatched to remote areas to practice "freely and with dedication."[94] It is true that people in the occupied zone did not really have a choice in medical care, as French doctors from the free zone were strictly forbidden by the occupation authorities to practice in the occupied zone. However, in some cases even the French population living in the free zone near the Green Line did not hesitate to turn to the Regio Esercito's doctors, because the French physicians had more limited access to drugs than their Italian counterparts. Furthermore, the inhabitants of the isolated hamlets found it easier to reach Italian doctors just across the border than French physicians living in larger French towns, especially in emergencies, such as on 27 July 1942, when a child in Larche, Basses-Alpes, was seriously injured by falling on a wooden stake.[95] This was not an isolated case. As a matter of fact, the whole population of the border village relied on the Italian military doctor, a routine local French authorities tried to discourage, apparently without much success.[96]

Some young French women were especially interested in mixing with the Italian soldiers. It was not uncommon for French girls to seek out the Regio Esercito's officers, much to the dismay of French authorities. In Vichy's eyes these casual relations were intolerable because they compromised the girls' morals. In Vichy's patriarchal society, women were cast solely as diligent housewives and mothers; therefore they were not supposed to indulge in vain pleasures or casual relationships.[97] What is more, as a way to demarcate itself from the decadent Third Republic, Pétain's regime had strictly outlawed public dancing as of July 1940. Dancing and partying were held to be indecorous when so many Frenchmen had been killed or were languishing in prisoner-of-war camps. After all, Pétain had argued that France's defeat had been the result of the moral breakdown of French society. The *esprit de jouissance* that had replaced the *esprit de sacrifice* was reified not only in public dancing but also in other facets of everyday life, such as cinema, music, literature, prostitution, and gambling.[98] Thus Vichy officials frowned upon any fraternization with Italian troops.

In one case three young girls paid a visit to the Italian guardhouse at the border near Larche in December 1941. The sub-prefect of Barcelonnette reproachfully wrote in his report, "Some accordion tunes were heard, which probably indicates that they spent the whole afternoon dancing with Italian soldiers."[99] In another case, on 31 May 1942, three girls, two of them the daughters of the mayor of Larche, met with Italian officers to play football. The French official in his report insisted self-righteously that "[the girls] went so far as to undress in front of the soldiers to play in shorts." Moreover, it appeared that the eldest daughter of the mayor, Hélène V., had actually flirted with the Italian captain in command of the outpost of Maison-Méane. Aside from its moral undertone, the report is particularly significant for its articulation of the grave consequences that, from the standpoint of French officials, such fraternization threatened. Hélène worked in the Larche commune and thus had access to French mail. The French official was worried that top-secret documents from Vichy could end up in Italian hands through unprincipled exploitation of the girl's naiveté.[100]

Italian soldiers and French civilians had a symbiotic relationship in these Alpine regions in that the Italians enjoyed the company of French civilians who alleviated the tedious boredom of guard duty in isolated border passes, while the local population certainly derived benefits in the form of goods and services. The result is that the locals tended to forget that they were dealing with enemies. In the scathing words of a French gendarme, "Self-interest is more powerful than the [patriotic] feeling" (*L'intérêt a plus souvent force que le sentiment*).[101]

In fact, the population obtained fresh supplies from either the French ravitaillement services or the Italian army, sometimes from both.[102] Moreover, French authorities were flabbergasted to discover that, starting in 1940, shop owners in the occupied zone had no qualms about selling unregulated quantities of rationed goods such as dairy products and meat at prices significantly higher than the state-imposed limit, or even bartering them for manufactured goods such as shoes or clothes.[103] As seen before, the black market was by no means confined to the occupied zone, but it is evident that the geographic location of the occupied zone and the limited nature of French sovereignty over it favored its evolution as a hub in a strong clandestine network in goods. For instance, selling cattle from the French free zone in the occupied zone became widespread, with cows selling at 50 percent more than their legal French price due to the official and fixed currency exchange rate, which so favored the Italian lira.[104]

If we compare the situation in the Alpine frontier with that of another border region, the Basque borderlands dividing Spain from southwestern France, it becomes rather evident that several circumstances, besides pure pragmatic reasons and cultural proximity, were favoring a cordial cohabitation.[105] For a start, the Germans arrived in southwestern France in the winter of 1942, when the French Resistance movement was shaping up; the Italians, on the other hand, moved in at an earlier time when Resistance activities in France were minimal. Furthermore, the geopolitical situation of the two regions was quite different. Spain was still a neutral country, notwithstanding Hitler's incessant demands to lure the Spanish nationalists into joining the Axis. Thus, the Spanish territory across the Pyrenees would be widely used by Basque *passeurs* to smuggle people escaping the Vichy regime,[106] such as cornered Jews, Allied pilots, and, from February 1943, young Frenchmen escaping the Service du Travail Obligatoire (STO).[107] None of this drama happened along the Alpine border, as few people wanted to cross the Alps into Italy, at least until Italy stayed in the Axis camp. Finally, politically speaking, the Basque borderlands were quite a tinderbox, with a fairly consistent part of the population being anarchist or socialist militants, many of whom were Spanish republicans in exile. This leftist substratum proved a fertile terrain to plant the seed of an active Resistance network. The Basque borderlands soon became a place where resisters and Germans played cat and mouse in a dangerous paroxysm that led to some ruthless reprisals on the local population. The Alpine sector, on the contrary, harbored few political activists, especially in the very sparsely populated mountainous areas, as most of its inhabitants were farmers and herders with little political inclination. Therefore, the thinly deployed Italian garrison in the area had little to worry about and could focus on establishing fruitful relations with the locals.

Thus, the success of the relationship in the Alpine region demonstrated that Italian soldiers and French civilians could establish significant relations if the occupation was unloaded of its political undertone. In regions that ranked high in the irredentist propaganda, such as the County of Nice and Menton, little entente was possible, because every single act, even the most helpful, was seen by the other side as propaganda to endear the local population to either the French nationalist or the Italian irredentist cause. This indeed could explain the dreadful outcome of the occupation of Menton, which in the mind of the Fascist intelligentsia should have been the jewel in the crown of the Italian empire but instead became a thorn in its side. In fact, the Italians made the same mistake as the Vichy regime by wanting to rebuild the foundation of the house while the roof was on fire. The Fascist regime, prisoner of its own irredentist propaganda, could not wait until the peace treaty to transform the new zone into an Italian colony. By rebuilding while the war was still raging, the Italians took a great risk, which at the end of the day did not pay its dividends. Italian officials grimly acknowledged that the halfhearted revival of Menton was hurting the prestige of the Italian state abroad as much as the Italian military's appalling performance in the Battle of the Alps.[108] It was clearly a missed opportunity for the Fascist state, which could have more effectively exploited the experiment of colonizing a small territory before proceeding to a more populated one such as the County of Nice. The failure of the Italianization campaign in Menton probably shaped the occupation policy of November 1942. The Italian army's top-ranked leaders did take note of the impossibility of furthering Italy's political goals at a time when the demands of the war suggested that security and strategic issues were more important. Thus, when the full-fledged occupation started in November 1942, the army would set aside the political goals and focus solely on military matters.

PART III

THE ITALIAN OCCUPATION

OF SOUTHEASTERN FRANCE:

NOVEMBER 1942–SEPTEMBER 1943

CHAPTER 5

THE NOVEMBER 1942 INVASION

In November 1942 more than 150,000 Italian soldiers deployed in the French free zone following the Allied invasion of North Africa. The Italians occupied nine departments of southeastern France, a vast zone that was delimited by the Rhône on its western border and the Savoy to the north. Many "unredeemed lands," such as the County of Nice, Savoy, and Corsica, were occupied effortlessly by the Italian army in just a few weeks. No wonder the irredentist movement hailed this occupation as the achievement of the *Mare Nostrum,* Italy's full control of the Mediterranean Sea. However, what was in theory a political victory shortly became a strategic nightmare. The Italian army was overstretched in different theaters of war all over Europe and North Africa. The deployment in France had also depleted the already thin defenses of the peninsula's coastline. Poorly organized, suffering from low morale, and lacking resources in terms of both manpower and materiel, Italian soldiers wearily spread out along the French Mediterranean shore. In fact, Fourth Army cadres were as worried about a possible uprising by the French population as about a possible Allied invasion. The Italian military, therefore, was not interested in any short-term policy of colonization or Italianization that would exacerbate the hostility of the French populace. The Menton experiment was never repeated, to the utter disappointment of both CIAF officials and local irredentists.

Rumors of a prospective Italian invasion of the free zone had started as soon as the ink of the Armistice of Villa Incisa dried. The famous painter Henri Matisse, who had fled the German advance in June 1940 by moving to his villa in the Cimiez neighborhood in Nice, was already complaining in September 1940 that there was "such widespread fear that Nice may be occupied at any moment."[1] In fact, whenever Italian state officials felt that the French were cheating or dragging their feet in the negotiations, plans to invade southern France were once again reviewed. However, the situation radicalized considerably in 1942. Rumors of an invasion increased exponentially in the Côte d'Azur. At first the offensive was supposed to take place on 21 April, the birth date of the city of Rome;[2] the next possibility was 30 April, when Senator Ermanno Amicucci, the author of the propagandist book *Nizza Italiana,* gave a particularly virulent irredentist speech.[3] May was even more frenzied, with three possible dates (10, 24, and 28) being bandied about. It was unclear who spread these panic-inducing rumors and for what reasons. The CIAF accused real estate speculators who wanted to convince the populace to hastily sell their assets, which would inevitably depreciate with any invasion.[4] In the eighth issue of *Il Nizzardo* (3 May 1942), an anonymous journalist titled his column "Le Jour viendra" (The Day Will Come). A French title in an otherwise Italian publication had a double inference. On one hand, according to the columnist, French agents provocateurs were creating a red herring in the form of speculation about a possible Italian invasion. These subtle maneuvers supposedly kept the French populace focused on the external threat. On the other hand, the ominous title was a reminder to the French authorities that they were playing with fire. Using agents provocateurs could backfire, as an Italian invasion of the County of Nice was going to eventually happen and the irredentists would use the army to take revenge on local authorities.[5]

The escalation in irredentist propaganda matched pace with the worsening of Franco-Italian relations. Pierre Laval's return in April 1942 worried the Fascist hierarchy, who feared that his reappointment meant a closer rapprochement between Vichy and Berlin. In spite of reassurances from German officials, this suspicion was confirmed in the meeting between the CIAF and CTA (Franco-German Armistice Commission) in Friedrichshaven held 10–17 June 1942. The head of CTA, Gen. Oskar Vogl, mollified the CIAF by stressing the superiority of the Axis powers with regard to Vichy but also insisted that Germany and Italy should be generous with Vichy. As the war began to turn against Germany, the Germans were prepared to offer France compensation in order to get full access to its industrial resources and to get the support of its colonial army. The CIAF president, Arturo Vacca Maggiolini, furiously replied that Italy could not accept the minimization of its territorial claims, since the latter were the main reason for Italy's entry into the war in the first place.[6] Mussolini and the leadership had not budged from their position of the summer of 1940. They demanded that Italy should be fully rewarded for its war effort and that the Axis should reject any major collaboration with France on the grounds that Vichy would probably ask for compensation in return for its help.[7]

Therefore, the army was instructed to lay out in May 1942 a strategic plan for a prospective invasion, the Esigenza Ovest (Plan West, or simply known as Esigenza O). The occupation was to focus strictly on the territory claimed by Italy: the County of Nice and the Savoy region.[8] However, in July 1942 the Italian senior military was asked to change the invasion plan to encompass the whole Mediterranean coastline up to Toulouse in southwestern France. This drastic shift in strategy stemmed from the evolution of the war. The Western Allied powers were seeking to open another front in order to take the pressure off the Soviet Union. The Italian Army General Staff wanted to ensure that France's Mediterranean shores would be adequately defended as rumors of a possible Allied landing in southern France grew in intensity.[9] If the Allies were successful, a bridgehead in southern France would give the Anglo-Americans a base to carry out military operations against Italy and Germany. Therefore, the very nature of the future Italian invasion of France was shaped by strategic requirements as the Axis powers aimed to secure "Fortress Europe" against an enemy landing on a crucial strategic point.

To be sure, the British-American invasion of Algeria and Morocco on 8 November 1942, code-named Operation Torch, triggered the occupation of southern France by German and Italian soldiers. The Axis feared that the northern Mediterranean area was next in line for an Allied invasion. Moreover, the Germans no longer trusted the Vichy regime. Notwithstanding Pétain's immediate call to resist, Hitler was furious about the ambiguous attitude of some high-ranking officers, in particular the obfuscation of Admiral Darlan, who just happened to be in Algiers to visit his ailing son. Prime Minister Laval, who went to Munich the next day, 9 November, with the daunting task of convincing Nazi officials of Vichy's loyalty, was severely chastised by the Fuehrer.[10] The "North African Imbroglio" had finally managed to unite Germans and Italians on the issue of France after two years of dissension. Both Galeazzo Ciano and Hitler agreed that a joint invasion of France was absolutely necessary to prevent a possible Allied landing on that country's Mediterranean shore.[11]

At 9:55 P.M. on 10 November, the chief of the Italian Army General Staff, Gen. Vittorio Ambrosio, wired the formal order to the Fourth Army to begin the latest version of the Esigenza Ovest, at 7 A.M. the next morning. The Fourth Army was divided into three *Corpi d'Armata* (Army Corps, or CA), each one with its own task: the I CA (GaF mobile units, 20th Alpini Sciatori [Alpine Skiers], the Rovigo [Italian division] in reserve), which was deployed along the upper part of the border, would occupy the Alpine departments from the Savoy to the Hautes-Alpes, mainly through the Modane

and Bourg-Saint-Maurice valleys; the XXII CA (GaF, Taro, Emanuele Filiberto Testa di Ferro [EFTF], and Pusteria) was assigned to the center and
was given the targets of Basses-Alpes and upper Alpes-Maritimes; the XV
CA (Lupi di Toscana, Legnano, and Piave divisions) would deal with the
coastline. The XXII and XV CA units were given the task to push up the
river Var and then farther west to the line of Cannes–Grasse–Entrevaux.[12]

As had been the case in June 1940, most of the units quartered on the
French border were unprepared for action. The I CA was in its winter barracks down in the Turin valley far from the border; the key division of the
XXII CA was moving east to defend the Liguria coastline; the XV CA had
no divisions within thirty kilometers from the border.[13] Moreover, many
divisions were still severely undermanned. Although orders were issued re-
calling every officer, noncommissioned officer, or soldier on leave, it did not
solve the problem.[14] The efficiency of the Fourth Army was further marred
by the chronic paucity of materiel that continually plagued the Italian army
in the Second World War. In October 1942, alarming reports from Fourth
Army commanders underscored the dearth of essential materiel such as
shoes and food.[15]

Furthermore, the Italian Alpine forces had been repeatedly weakened in
1942 by the decision of the Italian Army General Staff to use full divisions of
the Fourth Army as reserves to relieve other units fighting in hotter theaters
of war such as Russia, Greece, and North Africa.[16] In September the Italian
Army General Staff was so worried about a possible attack on North Africa
that two divisions quartered near the French border, the RECo. Cavalleggeri
di Lodi and the Centauro, were sent to Libya. Just hours before the North
African Allied landing, the Piave was ordered to move to Naples in order
to bolster the defenses of the Campania coast.[17] The commander of the
Fourth Army, Gen. Mario Vercellino, complained that the impact of those
directives was to reduce his units to the point of compromising the occupation of southern France. He insisted on keeping the Piave, as it was one of
the only motorized units of the Fourth Army, and he considered it essential
to his operation. In a last-minute decision, the SMRE, aware of the poor
mobility of the Fourth Army, agreed to leave the mechanized companies
of the Piave Division on the French border, notwithstanding the fact that
its commander, Gen. Ugo Tabellini, was already in Rome to supervise the
transfer of the other half of the division.[18]

At 1 A.M. on 11 November the SMRE (Stato Maggiore dell'Esercito, or
Italian General Staff Army) postponed "crossing the Rubicon" by twenty-
four hours, to the night of 11–12 November.[19] Then, fifteen minutes later,
the SMRE reversed its orders and General Vercellino was invited to cross

the border "on 11 November at noon with as many forces as he could muster."[20] Senior Fascist officials and the Italian military command were torn between the strategic risk of overstretching the already strained logistics of the Regio Esercito and the political need to move deeper into France and occupying as much land as possible in order to facilitate its possible annexation at the end of the war. Indeed, in all likelihood the decisive factor was the knowledge that two German armies—the First from the Atlantic Coast and the Seventh from central France—were going to invade the free zone at 7 A.M. on 11 November in what became known as Operation Anton. If the Italian army wanted to take the coastline and southern France for itself, given its relative lack of mobility it had to act immediately.

The County of Nice, the most heavily populated Italian region in southern France, was easily occupied by Regio Esercito's troops because of its short distance from the Italian border.[21] However, the SMG (Stato Maggiore Italiano, or Italian General Staff) was worried about the two other coastal cities with important Italian communities, Marseille and Toulon. Italian officials agreed that both cities ideally should be occupied by Italian troops as a means to control the whole Mediterranean coastline and as a mark of prestige. A too swift German advance might indeed ruin the party.

Thus, the Italian chief of the general staff, Gen. Ugo Cavallero, immediately phoned Vercellino.[22] The new order was to occupy as much territory as possible. Cavallero exhorted the commanders to push forward "day and night," adding optimistically that troops should be transported by train. Occupying the territory became mandatory to the point that "resupplying should not be prioritized."[23] Cavallero's directive remained nothing more than wishful thinking. The SMG soon discovered that their strategy was far too ambitious. The SMRE's master plan for the occupation of the Mediterranean coastline up to Toulouse would have necessitated at least twelve fully motorized divisions.[24] Moreover, hopes of taking Marseille were soon dashed. When the Tenth Armored Division of the Felber Armeegruppe stormed the capital of the Bouches-du-Rhône department on the afternoon of 12 November, the Piave units were still some fifteen kilometers from Toulon.

The difference in mobility between the two partners stemmed in part from the Germans' savvy exploitation of the railway. The Franco-German armistice of June 1940 had established a board of German engineers who had been assigned the task of managing the French railway network in the occupied zone. Furthermore, a Franco-German commission in Lyons had supervised the integration of the French railway network into that of the Germans. It is not surprising, then, that the Germans succeeded in moving three entire divisions by train on 11 November.[25] The Italians, on the other hand, were slower to mobilize. Units of the XXII CA, which were already located far from the Alpine border, were further delayed by the shortage of railway carriages and locomotives in Piedmont. To make matters worse for the invaders, the Italian army was short of truck drivers and trucks. Old trucks broke down in the middle of mountain trails, leaving entire companies stranded and forced to continue their journey on foot. In some cases the disorganization of the convoys was such that entire units got lost and had a hard time finding their way back (the local population apparently enjoyed giving false directions to the befuddled drivers).[26] Not surprisingly, it took up to ten days for several units to reach their headquarters in Cannes and Grasse, a mere seventy-five kilometers from Menton.[27]

The lack of cooperation on the part of the French CIAF delegation was instrumental in crippling the deployment of the occupation army in the free zone. Several I CA and XXII CA units were delayed when the French delegation in Turin denied the Italian convoy permission to use the French network, notwithstanding the local civilian authorities' fear of the consequences of having to billet these troops in their communes.[28] This farcical situation thus forced the Lupi di Toscana Division to cover 150 kilometers by foot in three days in order to reach its destination in the Grasse region. Intense negotiations just defused the situation on 15 November. Italians were finally authorized to run two daily trains from Modane and Menton to both supply and move their garrisons.[29]

The transportation issue had severe repercussions on Franco-Italian relations. Vichy's refusal to allow the movement of Italian troops on its railway network became the Italians' justification for invading the Savoy region. Italian officials argued that quartering troops in Savoy would not have been necessary if the French had allowed the Regio Esercito's trains on French tracks. Outraged French officials retorted that the occupation of Savoy had minimal strategic value in any operation against an Allied landing, because the Savoy region was not part of the Mediterranean coastline.[30] French fears were heightened when Italian newspapers celebrated the occupation of southern France as the culmination of the irredentist campaign. All of these factors reinforced the French belief that the Italian army was using short-term and questionable strategic "needs" to achieve the Italians' ultimate goal in the occupation of France: the future annexation of the contested territories.[31]

The French, however, had misconstrued the Italian motives. The Italian army's sole interest, at least in the short run, was strategic and not political. In both its telegram formally ordering mobilization and the subsequent phone call to the Fourth Army command, the SMRE insisted that the Italian army should "retain a reserved attitude [*contegno assolutamente riservato*] without any reference to irredentism or any political claims," and should not open fire unless attacked first.[32] Even Italian officials such as the civil commissars were instructed to be accommodating toward Vichy's representatives.[33] Along this line, SMRE directives instructed the commanders to inform the French population that "[the invasion] will be carried out exclusively to oppose Anglo-American operations in the demilitarized zone."[34] To this effect, Italian military airplanes dropped thousands of leaflets in the County of Nice and in the Alpine valleys. Written in both Italian and French, their message asked the population for their cooperation and stressed the temporary nature of the occupation, in an effort to quell fears of a possible annexation.[35] To reinforce this effort, Mussolini, following the advice of the CIAF president, Vacca Maggiolini, denied Ezio Garibaldi and all other irredentist leaders' permission to enter the French territory with the Italian troops.[36]

It would be wrong to see this self-restraint as a change of heart regarding Italian territorial ambitions. The Duce and his topmost advisors still believed that the irredentist territorial claims were absolutely legitimate. However, they reluctantly recognized that the timing was not right to effect a political annexation such as the one carried out in Menton in June 1940. The contingency created by the Allied landing in North Africa forced the Italians to temporarily shelve their expansionist plans. The defense of the Mediterranean coastline had to be the top strategic priority. The Axis powers could not afford any internal French military action while the Allies were gathering their troops just across the Mediterranean. The SMRE's long-standing fear of a resurgent Armée d'Armistice fed this decision. They had continued to be suspicious of the French government's loyalty, considering its attitude toward the Axis powers as dubious (*dubbio*) at best.[37] As well, the Italians were especially worried that a guerilla insurrection, possibly fed by Gaullists and former members of the army, could erupt in the event of an Allied landing on the French Riviera.[38]

In retrospect, the worries of the Italian army were exaggerated. Neither the Vichy army nor the Resistance had the potential to organize a full-scale rebellion against an army that even in its paucity in equipment and men was still operational and equipped with heavy weapons and armored cars. Military intelligence had its faults, but so did that of the CIAF. It was not uncommon for CIAF officers in French territory to write up erroneous or exaggerated evaluations based on scanty evidence or shaped by their own worries about a French uprising.[39] Indeed, the situation was very different from what had occurred in June 1940. Now the demilitarized zone, along with the vast demobilization of the French army, ensured that the Italians had control of the system of Alpine bunkers and army depots. Thus, there was little opportunity for a rapid French mobilization. In a few isolated cases, soldiers sang "La Marseillaise" or hid their weapons. In most cases, French officials surrendered their arms.[40]

This widespread passive behavior was not a coincidence, but stemmed from directives from above. A fierce debate raged among Vichy's upper echelons over the policy the French state should adopt in light of the new military contingency. Hardliners such as Gen. Jean-Édouard Verneau, the future leader of the Organisation de Résistance de l'Armée (Resistance Organization of the Army), and Gen. Jean de Lattre de Tassigny felt that the French should exploit popular resentment and rise up against the Nazis. In response, some officers of the Armée d'Armistice near Montpellier tried to organize an insurgent movement, but their fanciful project was immediately crushed by their division commander. In fact, the majority of the Armistice Army still remained faithful to Pétain. Thus the directive issued by the war minister, Gen. Eugène Bridoux, two hours after the beginning of the German invasion was heeded by almost all officers. All units were confined to barracks and were instructed to offer no resistance. On the contrary, when called upon they were instructed to provide full cooperation.[41] French local authorities were to be courteous, if not helpful. In Bourg-Saint-Maurice and Grenoble, Italian units were politely received by the local mayors.[42]

Nonetheless, the Italians took no chances. In every single village along the Franco-Italian border, border guards and gendarmes were forced at gunpoint to hand over their individual firearms and in some cases were even arrested and confined to jail.[43] In Castillon, a small village thirteen kilometers north of Menton, the Italian soldiers cut the telephone wires upon arriving, thus isolating the village from the outside. The local mayor, along with the few gendarmes and border guards there, were confined to the school and released only at dawn. At the border post of the Pont de l'Union in Menton, Italian units spearheading the invasion broke the border fence; tore down the French flag, replacing it with the Italian one; disarmed border guards; and arrested a few passersby.[44]

The nervousness of the Italian troops was in part a result of the logistical difficulties arising from a hastily prepared invasion. Aside from the already mentioned bottleneck at the border, accommodations for thousands of soldiers were not easily found. In their push toward the occupation of the Basses-Alpes, Italian soldiers of the Taro Division were forced to bivouac in the middle of the downtown plaza in Castellane.[45] Officers often resorted to quartering their troops in the biggest buildings available: churches, gendarmeries, schools, and sometimes hotels or private houses.[46] The last alternative was the most problematic. The high number of vacation houses along the coastline rapidly became the alternative of choice for local commanders in search of accommodations for their units. However, as in June 1940, the lack of control, the landlords' absence, and the relative poverty of the rank and file resulted in an explosion of looting. In Roquebrune-Cap-Martin several houses were sacked for goods as diverse as silverware, linens, clothes, kitchen utensils, and liquor. Hungry soldiers emptied the cellars and the orchards of any edible staple.[47] In some cases the soldiers resorted to outright theft, breaking into garages in search of food and stealing vegetables in gardens.[48]

Indeed, feeding thousands of soldiers, most of them young men with healthy appetites, quickly became a critical concern. Troops entering France were often left to live off the land. The Italian troops had to requisition bread and cheese in Castellar the day after crossing the border.[49] In one case a squad of forty soldiers who, upon arriving in Nice, found themselves ignored by the Italian army food service turned to the local Casa d'Italia for food, to the amusement of the local French populace.[50] In light of the alarming reports pouring into his office, the prefect of the Alpes-Maritimes, Marcel Ribière, issued a telegram on 12 November stressing that even Italian troops were bound by French legislation. Thus, "no staple [should] be delivered to the operations troops unless authorized by the Ravitaillement Général. . . . Only French ration tickets are valid."[51] Ribière insisted that local authorities should do everything in their power to enforce Vichy's regulations as a way to affirm that the French government was still in control of the free zone. In a message sent a few days later to the sub-prefect of Grasse and to the department's mayors, Ribière was insistent: "You are not occupied. The Italian troops are not occupation troops, but operation troops [*troupes d'opérations*]. . . . The sovereignty of French authorities is integrally preserved."[52]

The expropriations were not so much a result of an Italian desire to wrest sovereignty from Vichy, but a reflection of the disorganization of the Regio Esercito. Most French reports emphasized the diverse lines of conduct between Italian units. For example, the attitude of the Italian soldiers in Breil was absolutely correct, unlike the expropriations by their fellows in the nearby villages.[53] In fact, the police commissar in Breil observantly noted, "The majority of the Italian detachment commanders acted, while occupying the villages of this sector, in such different ways that one got the impression that they followed more their personal feelings or resentments than the instructions their leaders had given them."[54] Many French reports stressed the demoralized attitude of the average Italian soldier. The logistical disorganization made obvious to even the most casual observer the inchoate nature of the Italian invasion, reflected in the numerous remarks about the Italian soldiers' individual carriage. A bystander in Nice noted that many of the soldiers "were marching hanging their heads, looking demoralized in their down-at-heel shoes."[55] The local population judgment of the invading army was without appeal: the Italian soldiers were "in somber mood, tired and defeatists" (mornes, las et défeatistes). These soldiers, "thin as cuckoos" (maigres comme des coucous), were so poorly equipped as to look like "an operetta army in filthy rags" (troupes d'opérettes en vêtements crasseux), to the point that "their misery had ended up moving the populace's sympathy" (fini par émouvoir la pitié générale).[56]

The morale of the Regio Esercito was reinvigorated by the warm greetings they received from the Italian population in France. In Digne, Italian civilians gave the troops hot beverages to fight the Alpine cold.[57] In Roquebrune, Italian irredentists, who mistook the advancing columns as the onset of the March on Nice, offered wine, fruits, and flowers from the wayside.[58] Yet the Italian soldiers were more embarrassed than happy to be greeted in Nice by black-shirted men showing off the Roman salute. One soldier, upon seeing a man making the Fascist salute, allegedly scolded him to put his hand down and invited him to take his place as a soldier instead.[59] The Italian soldiers were not the only people annoyed by these irredentist demonstrations. French civil servants stressed that "the behavior of these [Italian] foreigners who had been well received and who often had grown rich in our country" was severely criticized by the French populace.[60] On the night of 13–14 November in Cap d'Ail, the houses of those who had celebrated the coming of the Italian troops in the streets a few days before were painted with xenophobic slurs.[61] In Antibes, too, houses of known Italian irredentists were smeared with pitch and in a few instances even became the target of hails of stones.[62] The same report, however, stressed that no incidents had occurred between the French civilian population and the Italian soldiers. In fact, Italian and French reports alike agreed on the relative uneventfulness of the first days of the Italian occupation of the free zone. The Italian soldiers, having received strict orders to avoid any attitude that could be interpreted as political, such as fraternization with the irredentist movement, and perhaps ashamed of invading a land they had not conquered but had entered almost on the sly, did little to provoke a reaction from the local populace. On the other hand, the French population and army, directed by the local authorities and the military commanders to avoid any opposition to the Italian military operation, may have eyed the invaders with hostility but refrained from actively opposing the Italian advance.

However, to insist that the Italian invasion and occupation went smoothly would be misleading, for it would diminish the impact the Italian occupation had on the Côte d'Azur. The Principality of Monaco is an interesting test case to demonstrate how far the Italian commanders were willing to impinge on local politics. Perched dramatically on a large rock, and dominated by the imposing build of the Grimaldi Castle, Monaco enjoyed in 1940 the traits that are still dominant today: an autocratic monarchy, whose popularity rested on the appeal of a gorgeous landscape and a fiscal haven for unscrupulous individuals. To be sure, the Grimaldi dynasty, one of the oldest ruling families in the world, made a risky but, in the long run, profitable bet by building a casino in 1866 in the neighboring Monte Carlo area. With its ups and downs, the principality thrived in the next eighty years as snobbish dandies, crooks, and starlets huddled around roulettes and game tables.[63] In the words of English playwright William Somerset Maugham, the Riviera and Monaco were a "sunny place for shady people."[64]

At the beginning of the war, Prince Louis II wisely chose to watch the war from the sidelines of neutrality. That is not to say that Monaco was a passive spectator of the occupation of France. In fact, Italian reports worriedly noticed that German middlemen, among them Carl Schaeffer, the German controller of the Bank of France, were making inroads in the Monaco financial world, especially to seek control on the SBM (Société des Bains de Mers et des Étrangers), which as the owner of the casino and the most important hotels was arguably the most powerful company in Monaco.[65]

A certain connivance with the Germans notwithstanding, in November 1942 Monaco was still officially a neutral state. The Esigenza O, the Italian master plan for the invasion, was clear on that point. The units of the XV CA that had to push along the coastline were not to cross into Monaco's territory unless attacked by Monaco units or if defending French troops sought refuge in the principality.[66] Regardless of this order, a few units crossed the frontier into Monaco, as the Moyenne Corniche, one of the roads linking Menton to Nice, bordered the neutral state. This act of trespass, although limited in nature, was enough to stir up the nationalistic zeal of the Italian irredentist community. More than four hundred people, twenty of whom donned black shirts for the occasion, gathered in front of the prince's palace and in the Place des Armes chanting "*Monaco Italienne*" and "*Vive Mussolini*" and singing Fascist anthems.[67] But the demonstration was short-lived, and during the next few days, the situation reverted to pre-invasion normalcy, except for a small contingent of Italian soldiers left guarding the railway line.

The tension, however, escalated at the state level on 14 November. The Italian consul in Monaco, Stanislao Lepri, formally asked for the collaboration of the principality in the Italian invasion, later to be sanctioned by a deployment of a Regio Esercito detachment within the city. In the face of the Italians' insistence, Emile Roblot, Prince Louis's minister of state, flatly refused, solemnly declaring that the invasion of the principality would fundamentally violate the internationally neutral position of the sovereign state of Monaco.[68] The real target of the Italians was not Monaco's monarch or his government, but the American consul in Monaco, Walter Oberaugh. To understand why the Italian foreign ministry was so interested in the U.S. consul, it is necessary to return to October 1942. As admitted by Oberaugh in his autobiography, the U.S. consulate in Nice had clandestine contacts with the French Resistance in the south of France.[69] On 5 November, Oberaugh, at that time consul in Nice, was urged by the U.S. embassy in Vichy to open a consulate in the principality as soon as possible. This diplomatic move was no coincidence. Officials in Washington realized that the onset of Operation Torch would mean the end of diplomatic relations with the Vichy regime. The Italians resented this intrusion of diplomatic personnel of the most important Allied state into a territory that was considered within the Italian sphere of influence, rightly fearing that the consulate would act as a hub of Allied propaganda and espionage.[70]

This diplomatic wrangling did not prevent the Italians from advancing their program. On 16 November starting at noon, Italian units closed every access to Monaco, whether by sea or by land. They then invited all the American citizens to stay home. In the face of this imminent threat to the neutrality of his realm, Prince Louis wrote to both Pope Pius XII and even to the Fuehrer himself complaining of this breach of Monaco sovereignty.[71] The pro-French population was also mobilized. On the morning of 16 November the mass at the Monaco Cathédral Notre-Dame-Immaculée for the commemoration of the dead princes of Monaco turned into a demonstration of support for the Grimaldi dynasty.[72] The crisis rapidly escalated. On 17 November, Italian soldiers, guided by the vice president of Monaco's *Fascio*, as well as an employee at the Italian consulate, Guido Bruni, stormed the U.S. consulate and locked up the consul and his personnel on the second floor.[73] The prince, along with Minister Roblot, reiterated their protests and threatened to break diplomatic relations if the American consul was not allowed to leave the consulate.[74]

The atmosphere grew increasingly tense as the most prominent irredentists used the situation to settle scores with some of their political and personal adversaries. On 17 November a former prisoner of Saint-Cyprien, Georges A., shielded by two Italian soldiers, was caught illegally checking papers in the streets of Monaco. Taken in for questioning by the Monaco police, he was later committed to prison for "usurping the responsibilities of the state" (*usurpation de fonctions*). A few hours later, thirty armed men led by Domenico S., an employee of the Italian consulate, broke down the door of the prison and freed the irredentist.[75] In some cases the irredentists targeted people with whom they had quarreled in the past, leading to their arrests by the Italian army. Already on the morning of 12 November, Italian officials, with the help of soldiers of the Regio Esercito, had arrested approximately ten individuals—mostly in Nice, both Italian fuoriusciti and French citizens.[76] It appears that even local Italian irredentists actively participated in the blitz to capture Italian anti-Fascists, such as in the case of the arrest of the former communist mayor of Ormea (Cuneo), Carlo Bava.[77] These sudden seizures in the former free zone raised a commotion among the populace and prompted the prefect of the Alpes-Maritimes to send a formal letter of protest to the Italian local authorities on 19 November.[78] The commander of the XV Army Corps, Gen. Emilio Bancale, replied the next day that the wave of arrests would cease immediately.[79] These orders originated from the head of the Italian forces in France, Gen. Mario Vercellino, who, in a short telegram on 20 November to the SMRE, ordered the immediate cessation of any activity of the "political police" and "counterespionage."[80]

Shortly thereafter the Italians moved toward a harsher policy. The order to terminate the arrest of civilians in the former free zone was explicitly called off by the Duce on 24 November and relayed by the Fourth Army command on 25 November.[81] According to this directive, Italian military commanders had to ask the French authorities and police forces to take into custody "dangerous individuals . . . whenever possible and convenient [for the Italians]." In practice, Italian commanders, who deeply mistrusted Vichy officials, often took the situation into their own hands. Between the end of November and the beginning of December, Italian authorities resumed the rounding-up of fuoriusciti in Nice, among them Paul A., a former army officer who had emigrated to France before the war for his political ideas, and Armand A., an Italian socialist who admitted campaigning for the enlistment of Italians in the French army and for taking part in the screening of alleged Fascist Italians after the declaration of war on 10 June 1940.[82]

The first few days following the 11 November invasion exposed some of the features found later in the Italian occupation: its chaotic and improvised nature, where commanders were left to fend for themselves and had to creatively improvise; its moderation and suspicion toward the French population as Italian units cautiously tiptoed into France; its ambiguous attitude toward the irredentists, both shunned for their awkward, at times goofy, nationalism and sought after for their logistical help and for providing useful intelligence; and its ambivalent relationship with Vichy authorities, nominally still in charge of the former free zone, but in reality barely tolerated by the Italian military commanders. Thus, the first period of the occupation established the triangular relationship between Italian military, French population, and Italian immigrants that would shape the Italian occupation of the French Riviera.

CHAPTER 6

THE ITALIANS SETTLE IN

The First Months of the Occupation

The ambivalent attitude seen in the first weeks of deployment was also at the heart of the Italian occupation policy. The Italians had to strike a delicate balance between a more lenient and flexible approach intended to ingratiate the civilian population and a harsh policy of rules set in stone. On one hand, the Italians wanted to avoid antagonizing the French population, as they had no forces to spare to deal with a prospective pro-Allied insurrection, and they wanted to accommodate French prefects, because they needed the local authorities for routine administration. On the other hand, the Italians did not want to appear too lenient, for fear of losing prestige in the eyes of the Italian community in France. Moreover, establishing their authority in the occupied zone through application of a rigorous policy was also a sign to the French government and the French civilian population that the Italians would not tolerate any interference in the implementation of their occupation.

These shifts in approach can also be seen with a careful look at another document issued on 20 November 1942.[1] In a message to all Fourth Army commanders, Gen. Mario Vercellino warned that the relative calm and the absence of reaction in the occupied territories should not lull the Italian army into thinking that the population would remain forever passive. On the contrary, he admonished, the current situation should be acknowledged as the calm before the storm of an Allied invasion by sea, probably supported by a Resistance uprising. It was a frightening scenario to contemplate, especially in light of the inherent deficiencies of the Italian army. The Fourth Army lacked air support, and its deployment would be marred by logistical issues such as the poor road and railroad networks in southern France, most of which were not under Italian surveillance, and the total dependence of the Regio Esercito on the already existing French communications network. For those reasons, Vercellino emphasized the new strategic tenets of the Italian occupation: the importance of deploying reserve troops, useful not only to dam any possible leak in the coastline defenses but also as a way to quell any possible French rebellion; the implementation of an Italian military radio network and a liaison network utilizing motorcycle or bicycle couriers; and the creation of army depots to guarantee supplies of materiel in case of crisis.

The two last parts of the document, titled "*Provvedimenti di carattere politico*" (Political measures) and "*Provvedimenti di carattere informativo e di tutela del segreto militare*" (Measures of informative nature and for the protection of military secrets), shed further light on the policy that would be implemented by the Italian occupation army in the next months. Vercellino was skeptical about the possibility of finding a modus vivendi with local authorities because of bad blood and divergent state interests. However, relations with the civilian populace were an entirely different matter. Winning the hearts and souls of the populace would be a difficult task; nevertheless, the Italian army was directed to strive to earn the respect of at least part of the local population, thus "cracking the solidarity of resentment" (*incrinare la compattezza del risentimento e la solidarieta' nel rancore*). Thus, Vercellino deemed it important to implement policy "without faltering or weakness but at the same time without harshness or brutality." Italian troops and their commanders should always demonstrate propriety and composure (*correttezza di forma and compostezza di vita*) toward both the French authorities and the civilian population. However, the Fourth Army command directive also stressed in its last part that the Italian soldiers should limit any kind of contact with the civilian population to a bare minimum. This warning was the result of Italian intelligence reports that Allied agents were trying to fraternize with the rank and file in order to gain valuable information and to sow seeds of discord by encouraging the soldiers to desert and by spreading defeatist and scaremongering rumors. To thwart this anti-Italian propaganda, Italian commanders were asked to keep a watchful eye on their underlings. Conversely, the careful use of informants was crucial to garner intelligence on anti-Italian organizations, be it Resistance- or Vichy-based. To this effect, local commanders were told to seek help from the CIAF delegates, who, as Italian officials with established social networks, were well suited to act as local counselors.

The paranoid attitude of the Italian forces was not entirely groundless, as demonstrated by the unfolding of events at the naval base in Toulon. The main French naval base of the Mediterranean had sheltered the core of the French navy since the debacle of June 1940. Following Article 12 of the Armistice of Villa Incisa, the warships had been disarmed and left without fuel to thwart any possible effort to join the Gaullist forces in Africa. The vigorous opposition of the French navy against its erstwhile ally, the British fleet, at Mers-El-Kébir (3 July 1940) and Dakar (23–25 September 1940), changed the view of the Axis powers, who interpreted this as solid evidence that the French navy was loyal to the Vichy regime. Thus, the Germans, and, more reluctantly, the Italians, agreed to ease the armistice clauses regarding the navy.[2] The relaxation soon ceased with the Allied landing in North Africa and the subsequent occupation of southern France. The Germans were worried about the allegiance of the French troops after the confusion caused by Admiral Darlan's betrayal. On 11 November the Fuehrer himself wrote an incendiary letter to Marshal Pétain, bluntly questioning the loyalty of the French troops in the event of an Allied landing. The fear of a possible French reversal of strategy was heightened on 12 November by an order issued by Adm. Jean de Laborde, the head of the French navy, to the Toulon navy to warm up the battleships' engines. In any event, the Germans and the Italians would have been unable to reach the Toulon zone at the beginning of the invasion, and therefore they were obliged to leave the French navy command in place. Thus, Adm. André Marquis, the *préfet maritime* of Toulon, was left in control of the Place de Toulon (Stronghold of Toulon), which stretched east along the peninsula of Hyères to the cities of Saint Raphaël and Saint Tropez.

It was clear, however, that the Axis local commanders were increasingly uncomfortable with the French equivalent of two full divisions in the stronghold, some of which were battalions of the Armée d'Armistice.[3] A telegram from the Italian Army General Staff dated 24 November reported that "the behavior of the French forces is becoming more dubious and even less clear," so much so that he believed Italian units should be ready to advance in case French units in Toulon joined the coming landing invasion.[4] In reality the Regio Esercito was hardly prepared to take Toulon. The reduced enlistment of its divisions, coupled with severe deficiencies in the armored forces, had already impeded the Italian forces' attempt to take Marseille, notwithstanding the large Italian community living there.[5] The Germans, well aware of the poor condition of the Italian army, were loath to rely on the Italian units for the forthcoming Operation Lila. Therefore, they did not even bother to notify the XXII CA command, which was fifty kilometers north of Toulon in the town of Brignoles, until the German divisions of the Felber Armeegruppe were already besieging the *préfécture maritime* of

Toulon, Fort La Malgue. Presented with a fait accompli, the Italians had no choice but to be relegated to the sidelines by occupying the village of Hyères, twenty kilometers east of Toulon, and a few airfields.[6]

Operation Lila turned out to be a serious tactical blunder. German troops failed to reach the arsenal before the battleships and the submarines were either scuttled or, in some rare instances, scurried away to join the Gaullist forces in North Africa. In all, more than eighty vessels, including fifteen destroyers, three battleships, and twelve submarines, were purposefully sunk by French navy personnel. The Axis engineers salvaged only a few ships and divided up the scuttled ships for scrap metal.[7]

The occupation of Toulon was in fact the key element in what was a much larger operation by the Germans and the Italians to disarm the Armée d'Armistice. The Fourth Army command issued a directive at 11 A.M. on 27 November, ordering Italian troops from the three Italian army corps in France to disarm all French military units and to confine them to their barracks, separating the officers from their soldiers. Meanwhile, Italian squads were ordered to ensure that no military goods were smuggled from French armistice depots and to secure all air bases to prevent any defection by the French air force.[8] These tasks were carried out at once. French troops were disarmed in department administrative centers such as Digne, Gap, Annecy, Grenoble, and Nice, while air bases and important armistice depots were brought under Italian control in Orange, Le Pontet, Valence, and Grenoble. The whole operation went without a glitch, apart from occasional halfhearted protests by French officers. Interestingly, the only problems experienced by Italian units were created by their German counterparts. Strategic airbases in the Rhône valley, along with their armistice depots, while officially in the Italian occupation zone, were seized by Wehrmacht troops. An Italian unit was dispatched to Chambery only to find the administrative center of the Savoie department already occupied by German soldiers.[9] These areas were handed over to Italy only three weeks later, starting on 15 December.[10] That same day, the Italian navy command in France, headed by Adm. Vittorio Tur, took over the administration of the port of Toulon.[11]

At the heart of the problem in the relations between Germans and Italians was the difference in their views on the occupation of southern France. The Wehrmacht was worried exclusively about a possible Allied landing on the Mediterranean coast. The occupation of Marseille and Toulon was done solely for strategic considerations, because the two cities were the most important ports in southern France and because the Italian army was incapable of securing cities of such an important size. The Italian army too had strategic and military motivations for the push and sought to grab as many French army depots and supplies as they could before the Germans could put their hands on them. However, they had other underlying motivations as well. First, their inferiority complex vis-à-vis their senior partner and the French army, especially after the debacle of the Battle of the Alps, surely played into the Italian decision to occupy as much territory as possible. The Italians' purpose was to demonstrate that they could contribute to the defense of France. Furthermore, the Italian army was certainly not oblivious to the political motivations behind the invasion. The Fascist state wanted to show to the Italian population in France that it could defend the interests of its citizens who were spread along the French coast. Therefore, it is understandable that the failure to take the two major cities with important Italian communities, Marseille and Toulon, deeply stung Fascist and military officials.

Regardless of motivation, the Italian Army General Staff had no choice but to leave Marseille and Toulon to the Wehrmacht. If nothing else, the deployment in France had dangerously strained the military resources of the Italian army as it depleted the reserves that would have been used to defend the Italian coastline. The Italian front along the Italian shores was already overstretched. The seventy-six hundred kilometers of coastline suddenly became an enormous burden for the Regio Esercito, given the fact that many of its divisions were still mired in North Africa, the Balkans, and France. Confronted with the strategic dilemma, the Italian Army General Staff opted to prioritize the defense of the peninsula. A directive on 7 December to Fourth Army commanders stated that the task of their units was primarily "the occupation and defense of French territories . . . and the defense of the national soil." The directive minimized the French occupation, stating that while the Italian army should watch over the French coastline and the Swiss border, only a minimal Italian presence was needed in the most important cities and in the French armistice depots.[12] The SMRE then started to recall units quartered abroad in order to bolster the Italian coastline defense.

The Conflict between CIAF and Regio Esercito

In light of the recent events, Italians and Germans met in the forest of Görlitz on 18 December 1942 to update their policy vis-à-vis the Vichy state. Hitler, while still distrustful of the French, favored a moderate stance, feeling that the Axis powers still needed the Vichy administration to ensure the maintenance of public order in the French territories. This "useful sovereignty fiction" was instrumental to avoid the cluttering French soil with additional

Axis troops and civil servants at a time when the Italian and German armies were already lacking able men.[13] However, the Germans were not shy about reminding the French who was at the helm of occupied Europe. On 27 December, Gen. Alexander von Neubronn, the Wehrmacht representative in Vichy, gave the French government an official note that sanctioned what had already happened one month earlier: the handing over to the Wehrmacht of all the armament, materiel, and buildings of the former French army. Moreover, the document added that "the French government should support by any means the orders of the Supreme Commander West."[14] In other words, Vichy remained in charge of the normal administration but was now a mere vassal of its Teutonic neighbor, a condition made real by the loss of its two biggest strategic assets: the colonial empire and the navy.[15]

The German declaration was based on Article 3 of the Franco-German armistice, which stated, "In the occupied French regions, the German Reich exercises the right of the occupant power" (*puissance occupante*). This important article did not have any equivalent in the Armistice of Villa Incisa. Thus, the Italian pretensions rested on shakier legal ground. The Italians, however, were undeterred. The Commissione Consultiva per il Diritto di Guerra presso il Consiglio dei Ministri (War Law Advisory Committee of the Council of Ministers) came up with a solution to solve the potential impasse. The commission, basing its judgment on Italian and international war jurisprudence, noted that the armistice had not ended the state of war between Italy and France. As a matter of fact, the Italian board of jurists argued that by occupying French territory without the consent of its sovereign state, the Italian army had started de facto a wartime occupation (*occupazione bellica*). Therefore, the commission concluded, "The occupation of an enemy territory entails the effective replacement of the authority of the state which has the jurisdiction over the occupied territory, with the authority of the occupying state."

This new status held important legal repercussions. First of all, "the occupant armed forces bring with them their own legal laws and their own jurisdiction." In other words, Italian soldiers could not be prosecuted by French justice courts, no matter the severity of the crime. More important, any person committing a crime against the Italian armed forces, their personnel, or their employees would be judged by an Italian military court in Turin. Second, the document continued, "the occupant authorities assume the civil administration of the occupied territory, *which could be carried out also by using the local authorities*" (emphasis mine). In fact, the Italians, paralleling Hitler's notion of the "useful sovereignty fiction," gladly relinquished daily administration to Vichy civil servants for both political and pragmatic reasons. However, the text insisted, this was an "autolimitation" (underlined in original), as the Italian state reserved the right to take over the civil administration at any moment for reasons of security and prestige.[16]

On 16 January a note was sent from Rome to the Laval government via Gen. Avarna di Gualtieri, the Italian Army General Staff representative in Vichy, that reiterated the major details of the conclusion of the War Law Advisory Committee. The note from Rome explicitly underscored the importance of CIAF officials as guardians of the Italian immigrants in France. French police authorities were required to communicate any arrest of Italian citizens to local CIAF representatives. No penal proceedings could be initiated and no deportation orders could be executed against Italians without the prior consent of local Italian authorities. Finally, CIAF requests for administrative concessions, such as special permits for ration cards or exemption from the *Relève,* were expected to be granted.[17] Thus, at first sight it seemed that after November 1942 the role of the CIAF had greatly expanded. Starting on 1 January 1943, Delegates for the Assistance and Repatriation who had operated in the former free zone since February 1941 were officially upgraded to the role of Italian consuls. This unilateral decision was made possible by the new events, for the November 1942 military occupation had ended any potential ambiguity regarding the sovereignty of the free zone: the opening of consulates that could have been previously seen as the implicit Italian acceptance of the authority of Vichy France in the contested territories was now touted by the foreign ministry as the prelude of the Italian annexation of southeastern France.[18]

Nonetheless, relations between Italian civil and military authorities in France were often tense. The commander of the Fourth Army, Gen. Mario Vercellino, and his underlings did not hesitate in expressing their contempt for the CIAF officials in France. The CIAF representatives resented the intrusion of the military into what they deemed their private hunting ground, both in terms of territory (the former free zone) and activities (the care of the Italian emigrants' interests). Moreover, they feared that the proverbial uncouthness of military men would shred the web of networks they had woven locally over two years, both within the local Italian communities and with the French administration. Army commanders, on the other hand, objected to any interference by Italian civilians in the operation of their military occupation. Thus, on major decisions CIAF delegates were often sidelined by local commanders of the Regio Esercito. For instance, upon his arrival in Nice on 14 November, the commander of the Legnano Division orchestrated a ceremony to pay homage to Garibaldi without informing, let alone inviting to the event, the CIAF delegate in Nice, Consul Alberto Calisse.[19]

This episode should not be dismissed as an example of personal antipathy, but as a sign of a profound structural issue plaguing the Italian occupation of France. Italian military and civil authorities clashed, sometimes bitterly, over their roles in occupied France. The army's role was theoretically limited to military and security matters. However, they quickly extended their influence over affairs that were the CIAF's prerogative, maintaining that every political issue could impinge on both the prestige and the security of the army. For instance, Regio Esercito commanders took an interest in the fate of Italian citizens in French jails, treading on CIAF toes when they did so, because the liberation of Italian prisoners had always been considered part of the armistice (Article 21). At the end of November, allegedly in retaliation to a wave of arrests carried out by the Italian occupation army, the French authorities in the Alpes-Maritimes incarcerated a score of Italian immigrants for "public order reasons." The head of the Legnano Division, Gen. Giovanni Marciani, immediately demanded a list of the arrested Italians from the prefect and their immediate release from the Vernet prison camp, and this without previously consulting Consul Calisse.[20] On 11 December the EFTF and the Legnano divisions switched their occupation zones, but the new commander in Nice followed in the footsteps of his predecessors. He informed the prefect that the Italians in the Vernet camp had to be sent back to the division command, explicitly ordering that the Nice consul "not meddle in this affair."[21] In light of the alarming reports from the Italian consul, the Ministry of Foreign Affairs immediately wrote to its liaison attached to the Fourth Army, Count Vittorio Emanuele Bonarelli di Castelbompiano, to ask General Vercellino to intercede with his local commanders.[22]

But Bonarelli's reply bore bad tidings. After two meetings with the head of the CIAF, Vacca Maggiolini, the commander of the Italian occupation army in France, insisted that the CIAF delegations should fall under the army umbrella, for any of their actions could impinge on occupation policy and thus had to be preventively authorized by local military authorities.[23] Vercellino's claims were strongly supported by what was happening on the German side. The German Armistice Commission (CTA) was already merging with the German Army Command in the West (Oberbefehlshaber West, or ObW) headed by Gen. Gerd von Rundstedt, and the ObW had progressively taken over the CTA tasks. The remnants of the CTA in Wiesbaden had been relegated to a minor jurisdictional role.[24]

Undaunted by the German example, Vacca Maggiolini at once counterattacked by writing a memorandum to Vercellino in which he argued in earnest that, notwithstanding repeated French violations, the Armistice of Villa Incisa was still in effect. As a matter of fact, for Vacca Maggiolini, "the Franco-Italian Armistice is the only document which exists and the armistice commission is the only agency which embodies in an official and indisputable way the position of superiority of the victorious Italy over vanquished France."[25] The CIAF president decided to bring the issue to the attention of the head of the Italian General Staff, Gen. Ugo Cavallero, but Cavallero's response proved evasive.[26] Vacca Maggiolini, fearing that the restructuring of the CTA foreshadowed a similar fate for the CIAF, tried to strike a compromise. In a memorandum sent to Cavallero on 6 January 1943, Vacca Maggiolini agreed that the CIAF military under-commissions (army, navy, air force, and armaments) should be integrated into the Fourth Army administration. However, he insisted the CIAF should keep its role as enforcer of those matters assigned to it by the armistice, such as the management of the French army depots and the liberation of Italian prisoners.[27]

On the issues of Italian prisoners, however, the army commanders refused to stop interfering. On 6 January 1943 Vercellino sent a message to all Fourth Army commanders, emphasizing in bold letters that any arrest of Italian citizens on French soil weakened the prestige of the Italian occupation army. The Regio Esercito was thus honor-bound to free their compatriots in prison, especially those whose only crime was to have fraternized with the invading army. If French authorities refused to comply with the army orders, local commanders were invited to free the prisoners, *manu militari* if necessary. While Vercellino underlined the importance of coordinating the effort with the local Italian state representatives, he added that the latter were especially useful as lightning rods to channel the protests of the French authorities. In other words, their role was to be a passive one: to relieve the army of the burden of endless quarrels with Vichy.[28] That not much had changed, despite Vacca Maggiolini's protests, was demonstrated by a report a few days later. The Nice consul, Calisse, complained to the CIAF president that the head of the Delegazione Esercito Controllo Scacchiere Alpino (Army Delegation for the Control of the Alpine Front, or DECSA) in Nice, a former CIAF bureau that had been attached to the Fourth Army administration on 9 December 1942, was tampering in the consul's business—namely, the protection of Italian citizens.[29] From then on, until the end of the occupation, the CIAF would be progressively deprived of its role as guardian of the Italian community in France, to the advantage of local military commanders.

Shoring Up the Mediterranean Coastline

By the beginning of 1943 the military situation was stabilizing in the Italian occupation zone. The total number of Italian soldiers in France had reached 185,000 at the beginning of the occupation but fell abruptly in December 1942 to 115,000 and then stabilized at 170,000 between January 1943 and July 1943 with the addition of two coastal divisions.[30] The deployment of the Fourth Army clearly underscored that the defense of the Mediterranean coast was the strategic priority of the occupation of the former free zone; 70 percent of its roster was amassed within fifty kilometers of the coastline.[31]

Beginning in January 1943 the Italian army in France endeavored to bolster the coastal defenses. To this effect, the territory was divided into two zones: the combat zone, stretching from the coastline inland roughly thirty kilometers, and the rear zone, encompassing the rest of Italian-occupied France.[32] The combat zone was by far the most important of the two, as most of the Italian units were huddled along the coastline. Italian military leaders deemed it the most probable location for any Allied invasion. The zone thus needed to be cleared both of its inhabitants and of Vichy organizations.

To this end, the Italians had no qualms about expropriating buildings to quarter their troops. Sometimes domestic security needs matched strategic considerations. For instance, Fort Carré, an imposing sixteenth-century structure overlooking the port of Antibes, was requisitioned because the fortification was strategically well placed atop a hill and because it housed the Chantiers de la Jeunesse, a Vichy youth organization that the Italians feared was becoming the vanguard of a future army of resistance.[33] More serious and problematic for the Italian commanders was the removal of the local population from this zone, as the coastline was the most heavily populated zone in southern France. Army commanders began by encouraging the population, with the help of the prefects, to relocate at least four or five kilometers inland, while in the meantime forbidding anyone to move to the combat zone, even if just temporarily, either for weekends or for the summer. As a matter of fact, to enter the new buffer zone, civilians needed a laissez-passer from the local prefectures approved by the Italian army.[34]

The coastal defense impinged on the everyday lives of not only those who lived near the coastline but also those who worked at sea. Once settled in France the Italian army had forbidden fishing at night for security reasons, to the dismay of local fishermen.[35] In late January 1943 even fishing during the day was forbidden, a decision that caused a flurry of protests among the local population, for the seafood industry was an important resource at a time of heavy rationing. In the face of the protests, a week later the Italian military authorities authorized fishing in the Mediterranean but with tight restrictions: the crews and the boats were inspected by Italian soldiers both upon departure and upon their return to harbor. Those few boats allowed to sail at night had to take Italian border guards with them.[36]

It is evident, then, that the Italians were willing to strike deals with the local population only insofar as the security of their coastal defense system would not be compromised. The agreements reached with the French fishing community did little, however, to lessen the impact of the Italian occupation, for the buttressing of the coast significantly altered the vista of the Côte d'Azur. Against any prospective Allied beachhead, the Italian army dotted the combat zone with *capisaldi* (strongholds)—fortified positions surrounded by minefields and barbed wire, packed with machine guns, mortars, and antitank weapons with a wide range of fire.[37] No French civilian was allowed to enter their premises, and the Italian military authorities started to evacuate the population living near the capisaldi out of fear of possible spies and in dread of civilians getting in the way should the Allies strike.

Yet the impact of the Italian combat zone, however disruptive for the local population, should be reconsidered if compared to its German counterpart, which operated under stricter regulations. In April 1941, fearing a possible Allied landing on the Atlantic shoreline, the German military supreme authority in France, Gen. Otto von Stülpnagel, ordered the creation of a buffer coastal area, dubbed *zone côtière interdite* (Forbidden Coastal Zone), stretching from Hendaye in southwestern France to Dunkerque at the border with Belgium.[38] The buffer zone, stretching twenty to forty kilometers inland, soon became off-limits for all non-Germans, except the few, mostly locals, who could obtain a pass from the local German *Kommandaturs* and those who worked for the organization Todt, the German construction firm that later in 1942 had the responsibility to shore up the Atlantic fortifications in western France, the Atlantic Wall.[39]

If the Atlantic Wall significantly reinforced the western coastline, the strategic picture for the Axis forces defending the Mediterranean shore was at its bleakest. After their victory in Tunisia in May 1943, the Allies held complete mastery of the sea and the air in the Mediterranean theater. This advantage gave them the choice of the battleground. The Axis had to dilute their defenses along thousands of kilometers of coastline, because the Allies' target for an attack could not be predicted. The Italian army commanders were indeed skeptical about the effectiveness of this defensive network on the French Mediterranean coast. After a tour of the Italian coastline defenses in December 1942, General Vercellino scathingly noted that "the fieldworks carried out until now are more a testimony to the goodwill of the executors than the solidity of the fortifications." He described the fortifications as "fit at best to stand the sporadic incursions of a few airplanes or shots from light naval units, [but] they are bound to shatter under massive air bombardments, which could not be hindered by the modesty of our anti-aircraft defenses." Urging front units to reinforce the bunkers with concrete walls, Vercellino advised reserve units to be prepared to move quickly to relieve any pressure on capisaldi. His logic was that a wise use of reserves placed so as to swiftly intervene at as many points as possible would go some way toward blunting the important strategic edge that the Allied forces enjoyed by having the freedom to choose the site of the landing.[40]

Vercellino's orders for a more equitable redistribution of forces soon became wishful thinking. Italian commanders disconsolately noted the chronic shortage of men, in that they could raise the number of troops in their division only by drawing from other units in the Fourth Army. Therefore, the fragile blanket of the Italian occupation army was always pulled in different directions, laying bare one or more services at any one time. Crews in the fortifications and guarding arms depots had to be kept to a bare minimum as more manpower was required for the mobile units patrolling the coastline.[41] To make matters worse, no soldier could be moved from coastline outposts, because local commanders had been given orders to defend the coastline "with feet in the water" (*piedi nell'acqua*). In other words, the Italian army was expected by the Italian Supreme Command to make a stand on the beaches of the Mediterranean with insufficient personnel. Ultimately, local Italian commanders were compelled to use soldiers from reserve units for important chores such as guarding armistice depots, patrolling city streets, and anti-paratrooper activities. Thus, the cannibalized reserve units would be unable to back up frontline divisions in the event of an Allied assault.[42] The transfer of manpower from one army service to the other was merely robbing Peter to pay Paul.

The dearth of human resources in the Fourth Army also had a negative impact on the quality of its units. The Italians were worried about airborne troops parachuting behind the rear lines, linking up with French insurgents, and sabotaging key infrastructure and roads. For this reason the Fourth Army created the *nucleo antiparacadutisti* (NAP, or anti-paratrooper units), each consisting of forty soldiers commanded by an officer. However, these second-line units were also second-rate units; their armament was extremely light and their roster was filled with the dregs of the Fourth Army such as truck drivers, other non-fighting personnel, and middle-age reservists. Those in the latter category were especially unfit for units whose task of intercepting airborne troops required men who were capable of quick action and constant patrol.[43] Moreover, NAP soldiers displayed an abysmal deficiency in military techniques while drilling; in one instance it took one and a half hours for an NAP unit to arrive at the scene of a prospective parachute landing, in part because the NAP leader fell back asleep after the alarm was sounded.[44]

The Unruly Occupation Army

Another problem the Fourth Army had to deal with is that the average soldiers' training and morale left much to be desired. Even one month after their deployment to France, soldiers had a hard time orienting themselves in the new territory and easily got lost. Officers lacked even a basic knowledge of the procedures for calling for support from the artillery or reserves.[45] One of the criticisms leveled against regular soldiers and officers alike was their excessive search for comfort. For instance, the locations of regiments' or battalions' headquarters were sometimes too far from their batteries or units, as commanders preferred to stay in cozier inland positions than in weather-beaten locations near the coastline.[46] In some instances officers and soldiers agreed to place their lodgings as far as possible from each other in order not "to hamper each other's freedom." In other words, at least some officers were turning a blind eye to the irregular behavior of their subordinates just as they themselves did not abide by the rules.[47] Vercellino was appalled, for example, to discover that many soldiers were idling about on New Year's Eve 1942 and on the first of January, justifying their laziness with the excuse that the period was a holiday in Italy in normal times.[48] More important, soldiers were the first to break the curfews established by the local commanders. Unarmed privates were caught strolling in town on days when all leave had been suspended for security reasons after bombing attacks,[49] and officers often failed to return to their barracks after evening curfew, preferring to stay with civilians in movie theaters or bars.[50]

The sloppiness in discipline worsened the gaping holes in the Italian security network. Soldiers were ordered by their commanders to stop civilians from taking pictures near Italian military camps and beach fortifications. However, it appears that soldiers were not only allowing passersby to take pictures in the vicinity of the Italian military sites, but they even encouraged civilians to include them in the pictures![51] Italian sentries failed to stay focused on their tasks. Soldiers were found guilty of "abandonment of post or violation of orders," mostly to indulge in vices such as drunkenness and sex. Some soldiers could not resist, it seemed, the appeal of bars and women even while on guard duty.[52] Sometimes their absence hid darker motivations; one sentry exploited his position as guard at a railway station to steal from the railcars.[53] In another instance, the same sentry abandoned his post to sexually harass a small child.[54]

This negligence was reflected in the shoddy carriage of the soldier of the Fourth Army. Local commanders were extremely condemnatory of their underlings' appearance: soldiers left the collar of their military shirts open, arguing that they were too tight to be buttoned up; their uniforms were messy and threadbare; tunics and trousers were dusty and sometimes even stained; belts hung loose. Even worse, soldiers strolled around with their hands in their pockets. Noncommissioned and junior officers were indifferent to the soldiers' infractions most of the time, and with good reason, as they were sometimes the first to offend, especially with regard to their interactions with women. Vercellino's report especially condemned officers who chastised Italian privates for indulging in frivolous relations while being themselves incautious in their affairs.[55]

To be sure, the Fourth Army's general and commanders were not bothered by the moral questions raised by the troops having relationships with local women if they were limited to simple sexual gratification. A reflection of their male chauvinism, they felt soldiers were entitled to "physiological satisfaction of sexual needs" (*soddisfazione fisiologica delle necessità sessuali*).[56] In fact, a military chaplain ruefully commented that "a very impressive immorality is pervasive; kindly souls, in the face of the appeal of sex forget their dearest family ties [*affetti più cari*], their most intimate bonds [*vincolo più intimo*], [and even] their more important duties."[57] Thus, the army commanders tolerated the use of brothels, which were carefully divided between those reserved for officers and those for the rest of the army.[58]

Obviously, prostitution was practiced not only in brothels but also in hotels and even private houses.[59] However, Italian military authorities openly discouraged relationships outside brothels for two reasons. First of all, they feared the spread of venereal disease among the ranks of the Regio Esercito; to avoid this, prostitutes in brothels were required to undergo periodic examinations by Italian army doctors.[60] Second, the senior officers of the Italian army were afraid that love affairs would cement into stable relationships. This was frowned upon not only because it was morally inappropriate for Italian officers to be seen in public with women of an enemy nationality but also for security reasons. Between the sheets Italian soldiers and officers could easily blurt out confidential information. Pillow talk was dangerous. Therefore, Italian generals did not hesitate to use heavy-handed tactics to cut off any temptation. For instance, one navy officer in Cannes fell in love with a Brazilian dancer and moved into her apartment, making no effort to keep their relationship secret. This brazen act was too much for the local Italian commander.[61] The navy officer was transferred to another city and his lover placed under house arrest in a small inland village.[62] In fact, the Italian military police suspected the Brazilian dancer of being part of a Resistance network whose members were being carefully monitored by the Italian counterespionage operation. Italian fears were not entirely groundless. In at least one instance, a soldier who befriended an Italian woman came to believe that she was part of a Resistance network. He set out one evening to spy on her and was beaten, apparently by members of the Resistance, as a warning.[63]

The loquaciousness of the average soldier, however, was not confined to the bedrooms of squalid bordellos or to the comfortable beds of sultry women. Officers and soldiers of the Regio Esercito were just as careless in public spaces like streets, plazas, and public transportation.[64] While being interrogated by the Italian police, one enemy spy confessed that he had obtained key information on the Italian war situation merely by overhearing the conversation of two Italian officers in a train compartment.[65] It is evident that members of the Italian occupation army took few precautions to safeguard military intelligence. As a matter of fact, officers used the French telephone network extensively to communicate between units. Not only were their conversations taped, but in some cases Italian officers used the phone in French police offices, where French gendarmes could easily eavesdrop on their conversations. Vichy officials apparently were not the only ones who had access to Italian communications; the Resistance had allegedly installed wiretaps on Italian military telephone lines.[66] Furthermore, the Italian war ministry deplored the "careless loquaciousness [*loquacità imponderata*] of soldiers, who discuss and talk with relatives and friends about directives issued by Italian military authorities, causing serious damage to the security of military intelligence."[67] Some soldiers in France had few qualms about spreading alarming news through the post. In a probable effort to make the account of the invasion more dramatic than it really was, one Alpine soldier quartered in Savoy wrote at the beginning of December 1942 to his family, "It has been one week that we have been fighting the French; they are giving us a good thrashing [*botte da orbi*], . . . [the unit quartered] in Val Cenischia has already suffered sixty or more casualties."[68]

The failure of ensuring the protection of military intelligence was only part of the problem, for the Regio Esercito also did a generally dismal job in securing the main roadways in southern France. Owing to the large extension of its occupied territory coupled with an insufficient number of soldiers, the Italian army established checkpoints only on the arterial roads. These checkpoints were manned by a squad of six soldiers, led by a noncommissioned officer, one interpreter of the Regio Esercito, one Italian carabiniere (Italian military police), and one French gendarme, whose presence was important if only to ensure that no violation was committed by the Italian soldiers.[69] The Italian directive explicitly stated that the gendarme "should not check either the travelers or the cargo in the car, but only attend and facilitate the check." However, to the dismay of local commanders, some Italian NCOs, out of laziness, permitted the French gendarmes to overstep their bounds and actively check inside cars as well as examine identification papers.[70] Once again, criticism on the part of the Italian army's higher echelons highlighted the excessive nonchalance of the Italian soldier in France when checking cars. "Leniency and effeminacy," which translated into "smiles, bows, and ceremonies," were deemed unacceptable.[71]

Sometimes this "effeminacy" hid a disconcerting naiveté. One carabiniere failed to inspect inside a truck painted with a Red Cross emblem, taking its authenticity at face value.[72] This gullibility assumed grotesque proportions in January 1943 when an unscheduled German plane landed at an airport guarded by the Italians. The German pilots justified their emergency landing by blaming their poor navigational skills, for they had lost their way in French airspace. They replenished the plane's tanks and took off after a few hours. A terrible doubt crept into the soldiers' minds when they remembered that the pilots had drawn a sketch of the camp. Later the Italians were dismayed to find out that no such plane or crew existed in the German records.[73]

This last episode underscored the paramount danger of enemy intelligence gathering that faced every occupation army. Italian commanders incessantly reminded their subordinates that Allied spies could easily mask their real identity behind Italian or German uniforms. Thus sentinels were expected to check the identification papers of every unfamiliar officer, no matter the grade. However, the army warned, even papers could be falsified, and therefore, guards had the right to question the officers and, if doubt subsisted, to report them to their command.[74] Nevertheless, it appears that not only did soldiers fail to check papers, but they also had the disconcerting habit of disclosing military information to unfamiliar officers without even checking their identity.[75] Yet there was more here than merely carelessness and lack of motivation among the NCOs and the rank and file. Italian soldiers regarded their officers with a reverential awe that sometimes bordered on outright submissiveness. When sentinels or junior officers asked for papers, they were sometimes chastised by Italian officers who haughtily refused to comply.

This issue became so recurrent that General Vercellino publicly disciplined a senior officer for having denied his travel papers to a junior officer, and who, in retaliation for the check, had reported the junior officer.[76]

This snobbish attitude had been a recurrent feature of the Italian army since its inception. A serious gulf existed between the Regio Esercito officers and their underlings, due to the privileges enjoyed by the officer corps at a time when the rank and file was coping with a sudden decrease in their standard of living. In a circular issued on 25 January 1943 and widely distributed to all the officers of the Italian occupation army, Vercellino sternly rebuked his officers when he noticed the "little interest officers bore in the continuous and overwhelming needs of their soldiers" and the "double standards" (*due pesi e due misure*) between officers and soldiers in terms of the conditions of service. Vercellino singled out the most flagrant double standards:

> When wine distribution is erratic or inadequate, it irritates the soldier to see the van of the officers' mess full of bottles and flasks pass through. When the tobacco distribution is inadequate and the canteen has none, it irritates the soldier to see the officer light cigarettes, one after another. When strategic reasons, or simply railway traffic, call for a limitation on leaves, it irritates the soldier to see the officer sent on leave because "the use of a few seats in first class carriages does not hamper the service." When you remove from the senior soldier, who is far from his family, the possibility of seeing his relatives, oftentimes it irritates [the soldier] to see young officers show off the conquest of venal women.[77]

The flagrant disparity between officers and soldiers in the Regio Esercito was certainly not limited to the Fourth Army. In August 1941 the war ministry issued a directive to inquire about the possibility of adopting a common ration and distribution system not only for units operating on the front line but for all the units in the field. A fairer food distribution system, it was thought, would help strengthen the bond between the officer corps and the soldiers.[78] The result was disappointing. All officers agreed that on the front line the officers' mess was a luxury that could not be guaranteed. Indeed, in the North African and Greek campaigns, officers of frontline units tended to eat the same rations as their soldiers for logistical reasons, since it would have been too problematic to distribute separate menus. However, the majority of the officer corps fiercely rejected the proposal, generally for specious reasons. First of all, they argued that the soldiers themselves reacted oddly to seeing officers eating at their mess. The presence of their own officers made them uncomfortable. Soldiers were so amazed by the novelty that some thought it was a part of a collective punishment inflicted on the officer corps for the campaign's poor results. Furthermore, the generals feared that eating together might lead to "excessive familiarity and loss of prestige" and would put at risk the officers' esprit de corps. Second, the hierarchical rationing system was instrumental "in putting the officer in the physical and psychological condition necessary for the accomplishment of his difficult task" and was therefore needed "for the purpose of the officers' morale." As Gen. Riccardo Balocco, commander of the Fifth Army Corps pointed out: "[The privileged ration system] would prevent dietary dysfunctions stemming from the fact that cadres, most of them reserve officers, are accustomed, due to their [sedentary] life of study and office, to a light and brain tonic (tonica-nervina) diet, easily digestible and with little fat, while the soldier-farmer or blue collar loves rich and fatty staples (large quantities of bread, bacon, stew)."[79] In other words, the Italian army was still nurturing an officer caste mentality, stemming from the Bourbon army, which was completely counterproductive in the 1940s.[80] In marked contrast to the Regio Esercito, the Wehrmacht stressed the necessity of creating a strong bond between officer and soldier called *Kameradschaft,* a bond that went beyond the simple acceptance of military hierarchical authority.[81] The Italians were amazed to see that German units trained with their commanders, who led the regular soldiers in the attack. More important, the Italians were shocked to see that "up to the division command, officers eat the same meal as the rank and file."[82]

Perhaps the comparison with the Wehrmacht could provide at least a partial explanation as to why discontent was spreading through the Italian ranks. An artilleryman of the 48th Regiment of the Taro Division openly vented his anger about how the mess rations of the regiment were not on par with those of the regiment's command. Only the strong intervention on the part of the commander of the soldier's battery prevented the situation from degenerating into open rebellion.[83] Tensions between officers and troops could escalate into open insubordination. Soldiers went so far as to threaten higher-ranking officers with death, most often while under the influence of alcohol.[84] In a few isolated cases, soldiers had no qualms about coming to blows. A gunner of the 58th Artillery Regiment of the Legnano Division killed a staff sergeant in cold blood for allegedly insulting him by calling him a "son of a bitch."[85]

It is interesting to note that the gunner was sentenced to only thirty years in prison, a relatively mild sentence for the murder of a noncommissioned officer. The explanation reflected the cardinal importance of the value of the family in Italy, especially with regard to the figure of the mother. The military court had recognized extenuating circumstances on the grounds that insulting the gunner's mother was a severe provocation, especially for a soldier from southern Italy. In a similar episode a lieutenant who had punched a soldier twice for calling the officer's mother a whore got his sentence reduced by two-thirds.[86] The latter case, however, hinted at the leniency of Italian military justice when prosecuting officers. In March 1943 a lieutenant repeatedly punched a private who had refused to lend him a deck of cards. What is informative about this episode is not only the arrogance of the officer, who had overstepped his authority by demanding a personal belonging from a subordinate, but also the fact that at first the unit command had tried to downplay the incident and blame the soldier. Only the overwhelming number of witnesses forced the upper echelons to act, and even then the officer was sentenced to only four months.[87]

Conversely, any insubordination by the rank and file was perceived as an attack on the Italian occupation army as a body and was severely dealt with. The simple act of insulting an officer could get a soldier into serious trouble; for instance, Romano V. of the Taro Division was sentenced to four years of prison for having slandered his officer by calling him "*cornuto*" (bastard) in front of his fellows.[88] Soldiers were aware of the untouchable aura surrounding the officer corps. In a telltale episode an Alpine soldier of the 20th Raggruppamento Alpini Sciatori, Giuseppe L., menacingly yelled to his unit commander, "Only mountains stand still; we will meet [after the war] in civilian clothes."[89]

From these examples, one could get the impression that the Regio Esercito was an institution rife with tension between officers and soldiers, weakened by a serious lack of discipline. However, the Italian army, and the Fourth Army in particular, had many officers who proved not only qualified but also concerned about the well-being of their subordinates. For instance, a 223rd Coastal Division captain lent some soldiers of his unit to local farmers to use as laborers. All the wages were reinvested in buying four sheep, as well as staples at the army canteen. The food was split equally among the soldiers and the officers to augment the daily rations, with a special allocation to those who had worked for the farmers.[90] In another example, a battalion commander complained about the transfer of two of his most able junior officers to another unit. The commander explained that the officers were "most loved by the rank and file" and that, upon their departure, many soldiers could not hold back their tears.[91]

Thus, there were many officers, and not just isolated cases, who were conscientiously fulfilling their responsibilities. They faced a daunting task in keeping the soldiers' attention riveted on the war at a time when the front line seemed thousands of kilometers away and the luscious landscape of the Côte d'Azur lulled them into complacency.[92] To bolster the men's fighting spirit, Italian commanders of elite divisions made much of the reputation of their units. Upon his arrival in November 1942 at the head of the Legnano Division, General Marciani issued a directive to be read to all Legnano soldiers that emphasized the major battles fought by the two major regiments, the 67th and the 68th.[93] Officers headed reading groups that analyzed newspapers and Italian agency news with the goal of reinforcing the Fascist propaganda.

Italian commanders did acknowledge that they needed to do much more than simply insist on Italian military traditions or praise the Fascist regime to boost the Italian soldiers' morale. Stranded far away from the front but also from his family, the soldier risked falling into apathy. Therefore, the MINCULPOP sent to France not only Italian and German propaganda documentary reels but also lighthearted movies to be played using motion-picture cameras mounted on trucks (*autocinema*) or in French movie theaters rented by the Italian army.[94] Each army corps created its own musical band that traveled from unit to unit, performing concerts and comedy shows. Hobbies such as chess, checkers, and cards were openly encouraged, while intra-division football and bocce tournaments enjoyed wide success.[95] Furthermore, the Italian army supplied Fourth Army units with books and gramophones, and efforts were made to give elementary-level courses to illiterate soldiers.[96]

The army thus partially contained the loss of morale experienced by the Italian soldiers in France by enhancing their leisure options and bolstering a sense of community within units. Yet one should not be overly optimistic. No embellished newssheet could hide the appalling string of defeats that had occurred since the beginning of the war. The Battle of the Alps, the North African campaign, and the invasion of Greece were indelible stains on the Regio Esercito's World War Two record, and they were not counterbalanced by any significant victory. A war that had been incessantly touted as the war that would lead to the rebirth of the Italian nation had become a desperate defense of the fatherland. Beginning in late 1942 the tide of war had decidedly changed, and Italy was looking more like a cornered dog than a defiant lion. After Operation Torch, the Allies had taken control of the entire North African coastline except for Tunisia, which eventually fell in May 1943. After that they dominated the Mediterranean Sea and openly threatened Sicily.

For the soldiers the major consequence of this reversal in national fortune was that army leaves became increasingly difficult to obtain. At the beginning of 1943, leaves became available once again, a decision explicitly made by the military command to boost the morale of the Italian troops abroad, as many men had not seen their homes for at least a year. Unfortunately, the decision had one significantly damaging effect. Soldiers who had been led by the military censorship to believe that the home front had been spared by the war were shocked to see firsthand the great economic difficulties experienced by their families and the devastation of the Allied bombing attacks. The plummeting of the Italians' standards of living, which had been expunged from official Fascist reports and newspapers, instantly became common knowledge among the rank and file. Upon their return to France, soldiers rapidly spread the upsetting news to their comrades in arms, who in turn became worried about their relatives.[97]

In spring 1943, following rumors of an imminent Allied invasion of Sardinia and Sicily, the Italian army declared the two fortified islands operations zones and sealed their borders. Thus, the Italian Supreme Command decided once again to cancel all leaves for Sicilian and Sardinian soldiers, for it feared they would desert en masse if given the opportunity to get back home. Not surprisingly, this decision fueled anger and resentment among the soldiers. Some went so far as to forge documents that reported dying relatives in order to get permission to visit their families. Others simply deserted.

Desertions were certainly facilitated by the proximity of the Italian peninsula and the porosity of the Franco-Italian border. Moreover, most soldiers who deserted did so while in Italy, using their leaves as an opportunity to vanish into the countryside, sometimes shielded by relatives and friends. Yet desertions never became an endemic problem. Records of the Fourth Army show that there was only a steady trickle, even in 1943, averaging sixty desertions every two months, roughly one desertion per day over the whole period. What is more, the statistics included the cases of soldiers who had returned late from their leaves. These men were generally punished for a short period and then reintegrated in their units. Nonetheless, the possible impact of these acts of insubordination on the overall morale of the rank and file cannot be dismissed. The evolution of the attitude of the Italian military leaders is enlightening in this regard. At the beginning of the conflict the Italian General Staff did not fully grasp the long-term implications of the multiple desertions, and their policy was therefore very lenient. The Duce's proclamation of 20 June 1940 indicated that sentences of ten years or less for any criminal offense would be postponed until the end of the war. This lax policy was reinforced by another decree, issued on 9 July 1940, which widened the use of suspended sentences, even for desertion, provided the soldier did not defect to the enemy.[98] This was in marked contrast to the policy of ruthless disciplinary action for any form of insubordination in the

First World War. Giorgio Rochat, a leading Italian military historian, suggests that because Mussolini and his generals believed in June 1940 that the war would end in a few months, they thought that suspending the sentences would keep the soldiers of the Regio Esercito focused on the war. As time went by, however, they became worried about the mounting resentment of the soldiers of a war that had been poorly led and the growing list of failed campaigns. Thus, the protraction of the global conflict forced the Italian army to enforce stricter rules. Sentences were suspended only if they did not exceed three years, and thus, desertions, which were punished with between five and fifteen years, were automatically excluded from any suspension.[99]

At the same time, the morale of the German army was also worsening. But the German commanders had a considerable advantage compared to their Italian counterparts. The Wehrmacht could boast striking successes against Poland, in Scandinavia, and against France. Joseph Goebbels's Ministry of Propaganda made sure to capitalize on these triumphs throughout the war. Furthermore, the German commanders never failed to underline the differences between the German and Italian campaigns. This contempt was expressed even at the rank-and-file level. In fact, news was leaking that the Axis front in Russia was crumbling and that relations with the Wehrmacht had become stormy, if not downright hostile. In the laconic words of a Fourth Army bulletin, "The support of the Germans for our troops was not what would have been reasonable to expect."[100] This lack of cooperation also shaped the French theater of war. The Delegazione Trasporti Militari (Military Transport Delegation), which was in charge of the transportation and distribution of Italian military goods in France, felt the sting of ostracism at the hand of the Germans, in addition to the uncooperative attitude of French railway workers. In particular, members of the Organisation Todt requisitioned French locomotives that had been leased to the Italian army, allowing the Italians to use them for only a limited time at the end of each day.

In light of this situation, it is not surprising that relations between German and Italian soldiers were at best ones of "mutual respect, but without familiarity."[101] Italian soldiers openly complained that German pay was much higher than theirs,[102] and this disparity, on top of the already strained relations between the regular troops and their officers, was aggravated by the fact that, inexplicably, the soldiers of the Fourth Army were not receiving the special allowance generally given by the Italian army to troops of units quartered outside national territory. Thus, they could save very little money to send to their own families or to pay for extra food and staples at the unit canteen.[103] Food, its quality and quantity, became a recurrent complaint in every single report of Fourth Army commanders for the whole occupation period. In a scathing report General Vercellino neatly summed up the *cahiers de doléances* submitted by his local commanders: bread "shows up poorly baked or preserved, . . . the quantity of the individual bread ration is not always honored, . . . the wine is sometimes undrinkable, and the tobacco distribution is lagging."[104] The general's ire was aimed at the Fourth Army Intendenza (Service Corps) for failing to provide even the most basic staples. The reply from the head of the Fourth Army Service Corps was immediate. Gen. Raffaello Operti excused his underlings, stating that the poor quality of the bread and wine was a result of the inherent deficiencies of the Italian military transportation network. For lack of gas and trucks, most of the staples had to be shipped via train. Thus, the distribution bottlenecked at the French-Italian border, as the only railway line linking northwestern Italy to the Côte d'Azur, the Genoa-Mentone-Nice-Marseille, became overcrowded and was often the target of the Allied bombing campaign.[105]

Operti's report also hinted that the supply issue was due to not just disruption by Allied bombers but also because of the fragile Italian economy: "Italy is a poor country and did not become richer on 11 November." Indeed, the disarray of the Fourth Army mirrored the breakdown of the Italian economy. The Italian populace was hit hard by the war. The conflict had already reduced salaries to subsistence level, and starvation threatened great numbers of people, especially city dwellers. In March 1943 widespread strikes broke out in major centers in northern Italy, the heart of the Italian industrial region. As a consequence, Italian military authorities were unable to reliably supply their troops. Wine was unavailable for weeks, as were other diverse goods such as radios, razor blades, and soap.[106] Soldiers' socks and boots were already worn down by years of war, because the Italian army had lacked the material to repair or replace the threadbare uniforms.

In essence the strategic worsening of the Italian campaign, the deterioration of the Axis entente at both state and grassroots levels, in addition to the material conditions of the average Italian soldier cast an ominous shadow across the overall morale of the Fourth Army. Cracks in the Italian army's morale were so widespread that even French authorities could not help noticing them. A member of the Renseignements Généraux who watched the screening of an Italian Luce newsreel in the courtyard of the nearby Italian barracks from his apartment's balcony noted that the appearance of the Duce on screen did not spark even a single cheer or any applause.[107] In March 1943 a local commander alarmingly reported that "many Italian soldiers, while talking with French civilians in shops, quickly confessed to tiredness or even of demoralization," because they had been serving continuously since the beginning of the hostilities.[108] Perhaps, then, the unruliness of the regular soldiers in France indicated a growing malaise spreading contagiously within the rank of the Fourth Army. By refusing to dress appropriately, incautiously flirting with women, and disobeying orders in general, soldiers were increasingly casting themselves as civilians and behaving as such as a way to express their desire to go back home. And arguably the melancholy was reinforced by the absence of a front line and by the similarities in landscape and people of the French Riviera with the Italian peninsula. Thus, as a graffiti etched on the walls of the Regio Esercito barracks in Digne dismally summed up: "*Duce, Vogliamo pasta suta pano* [*sic*], *vino e congedo*" (Duce, we want pasta, bread, wine, and discharge).[109]

CHAPTER 7

LIFE UNDER THE OCCUPATION

Soldiers and Food

At the inception of the Italian occupation of November 1942, the Côte d'Azur was already experiencing serious food shortages. The agricultural production of southeastern France was severely underdeveloped, as all the prewar investment had focused on building tourism infrastructure. Thus, the agricultural output could not cover the regional needs. Everything from flour to vegetables, from hay to meat, had to be imported from the interior. In addition, the local distribution network had been severely disrupted by the war. Unquestionably, by the end of 1942 Vichy's ravitaillement services were certainly not able to keep up with the rations allocated.

To be sure, the settling in of an army of hundreds of thousands of soldiers, which would have impacted the food distribution of any region, had the immediate effect of twisting the knife in the already moribund rationing system of southeastern France. Hungry men in their prime, unable to find a decent meal because of the dysfunctional nature of the Italian army supply system, quickly turned to the black market, exchanging goods that were unavailable on French soil such as gasoline, women's stockings, and shoe soles for staples such as meat, eggs, and fresh cheese that could complement their mediocre diet. Mirroring the situation in the German-occupied zone, the coming of an occupying force brought a powerful actor in France that had the leverage to semiofficially fuel a black market of hard-to-find delicacies. In some cases, though, desperate Italians even resorted to outright theft and break-ins. These acts seriously strained relationships with the local population.

In 1942 the Vichy ravitaillement system was already creaking. At the top of the food chain, farmers were increasingly confronted with serious impediments to production, ranging from shortages of fertilizer and seeds to a lack of oil and gas for their agricultural equipment. It certainly did not help that 1942 and 1943 suffered extensive droughts in both the spring and summer seasons. Moreover, the rural communities complained about the strict price controls imposed on dairy products at a time when the war was driving up the prices of raw materials dramatically. Unsurprisingly, the peasants were not motivated to sell their goods to the Vichy ravitaillement services, which bought at prices fixed at a level that did not even cover the farmers' basic expenses. Thus, farmers sold their goods on the black market or bartered them.[1] By 1943 the situation in the major cities had become nothing short of drastic. Vegetables such as tomatoes and onions disappeared from market stalls, and only the cheapest ones, such as Jerusalem artichokes (*topinambours*) and cabbage, remained available. Even these were becoming a rarity; cauliflower was cut into small parts to meet everyone's ration tickets. Dairy products such as milk and butter also became difficult to obtain; fresh fruit was nowhere to be found, nor was olive oil; and tickets for *matières grasses* (fat) were worth nothing more than the paper on which they were printed. Weekly rations of meat in Nice fell to ninety grams, bones included.[2]

When people did manage to get something to eat, it was not uncommon to discover that the quality of the goods was abysmal: sausages and cold cuts turned black within hours of being sold, and local authorities reported several cases of food poisoning.[3] The appalling state of the food supply stemmed not just from the disrupted food distribution network but was also due to the outright dishonesty of some shopkeepers and producers. Dishonest shopkeepers fobbed off watered-down milk (*lait mouillé*) as natural cow's milk and sour wine (*vin piqué*) as red wine. Vichy inspectors became so concerned about the black market that every good sold was required to have its price tag attached. This measure did not stop some merchants from using counterfeit tags on their products; artificially colored water was passed off as orange or lemon juice, and articles of clothing were tagged as silk when they contained none. In some extreme cases the staples were outright toxic; bread was made with ashes or even sawdust to increase its weight.[4]

Because of these problems, the "have-nots," most of them city dwellers, vented their frustration at a number of targets. Farmers were the first scapegoats. Antagonism between urban and rural inhabitants was not new to France, but it reached new heights in these times of dire restrictions. In the words of an exasperated retired grocery owner, "The producers, in light of the growing presence of clients and the advantage of selling their wares directly at their farms, without costs, at unlimited prices, disregard any taxes or state regulations, and desert city markets, hence the absence of staples in the city."[5] The population's anger was echoed by Marcel Delpeyrou, the prefect of the Basses-Alpes, one of the rural departments expected to feed the Côte d'Azur. In his monthly reports Delpeyrou never failed to mention the severe disruption of the food distribution network, which was due in part to the illegal market fostered by cattle breeders and grain producers, both groups openly hostile to Vichy's price policy.[6] At the beginning of 1943, spontaneous demonstrations in front of municipal halls in Antibes and Nice by desperate housewives demanding food were an alarm bell that the rationing system was teetering on the edge of an open chasm. Protests widened to schools. Pupils erupted in anger, for the French state was incapable of supplying school cafeterias, so much so that some schools had to close their boarding programs.[7]

The inability of local French authorities to address the inequities of the food distribution considerably undermined their prestige in the eyes of the local population, but that was nothing compared to the rumors that were spreading in Nice regarding the privileges enjoyed by the local notables. According to another Italian report, local Vichy authorities were widely corrupt and in league with the traffickers.[8] One story recounted that a delivery boy bringing goods to the prefecture accidentally dropped a "large basket filled to the brim with white bread." This rumor was followed shortly by another in which a delivery boy was mistakenly arrested by the French gendarmerie while transporting twenty liters of olive oil to the bishop's palace in Nice. It is likely, and the Italian military report did not deny it, that these were slanders deliberately spread by irredentists and maybe even by Italian authorities, for they were directed against two of the staunchest opponents of the Italian military occupation: the Alpes-Maritimes prefect, Marcel Ribière, and the bishop of Nice, Monseigneur Rémond. They had been accused of hoarding two key rationed staples, bread and olive oil, that had become rarities in southern France and were found only on the black market. However, the widespread acceptance of these rumors by the populace was a telltale sign that the Vichy regime's popularity was quickly declining.[9]

To justify their failure in administering the food ration system effectively, local Vichy authorities blamed the Italian occupation. Their reports never failed to emphasize how the Italian army was drawing heavily on the local market to supply its soldiers. In truth, Italian Army Corps commanders had been instructed to stock up on fresh staples such as fruits and vegetables using local wholesalers to avoid the difficulty of transporting supplies from

Italy. In early December 1942 a gendarmerie report noted that fresh vegetables had vanished from market stalls as soon as the Italian army had occupied the free zone.[10] In the Alpine regions the Italians bought lumber for heating and forage for their horses and mules, especially in the first critical months after the invasion.[11] The population was especially enraged that the Italian army food services were permitted to buy significant quantities of staples, even at market stalls, without having to stand in line.[12] There is no question that the addition of 160,000 soldiers to the region broke a food distribution network that was already on the verge of collapsing.[13] In the face of an extreme shortage of food combined with high Italian demand, prices for dairy products and fresh vegetables skyrocketed. One kilo of butter, which normally sold for 120 francs, cost 750 francs in October 1942; one liter of olive oil rose from 160 francs in October 1941 to 1,500 francs by March 1943. Italian army reports made it clear that wholesalers could not keep up with their contracts as local production fell precipitously.[14]

Inevitably, the increasing food deficit of the region fueled an already thriving black market in the Côte d'Azur. Disregarding the strict prohibition on any kind of transaction between Italian soldiers and French civilians, a mutually beneficial barter system came into being as soon as the Italian units settled in the former free zone. On 22 November, a few days after the invasion, a restaurant owner in Nice was found with a bag containing seven kilograms of beef to be delivered to Italian soldiers.[15] Mutually profitable exchanges were concluded with French civilians accepting virtually any kind of good or equipment to which Italian soldiers had access. Horse feed made by grinding carob pulp (*energon*) was traded for potatoes, shoes for money, and fuel for food. Fuel, in fact, became a primary currency for all kinds of illegal transactions; it was often exchanged for wine (a meaningful barter, as wine was considered as important as food in an army made up of farmers and workers).[16] The fuel trade was particularly successful in rural departments like the Basses-Alpes, where local farmers desperately needed it. Between December 1942 and January 1943, four Italian soldiers stole sixty liters of gas from their units' depots and bartered it for ten kilograms of potatoes, ten kilograms of beans, and one rabbit.[17] On 15 January two truck drivers of another unit quartered in the Basses-Alpes siphoned off a few liters of gas from their vehicle and exchanged it for potatoes and olive oil.[18]

The most striking features of both cases was not just that they happened almost as soon as the Fourth Army units had settled down in their locations but also that they continued over time. For the above reasons the Fourth Army military tribunal handed down sentences intended to send a message, ranging from eight months to three years. In spite of this the dubious bartering practice became widespread, for even unit officers were seen striking deals with civilians. In Méailles, a small village in the Basses-Alpes, an officer, along with a few soldiers of the Regio Esercito, was sent to legally buy three hundred kilograms of potatoes. He approached a local producer, offering to barter fuel or pasta for two or three calves. The lieutenant explicitly stated that this latter trade was not part of a regular requisition or purchase, but was to be considered a black market deal.[19]

In most instances the troops bartered Italian goods found in army de-pots in France, which were relatively easy to pilfer. Sometimes, though, the scheming was much more elaborate. Some soldiers smuggled goods across the border—a much riskier business but not uncommon. For instance, six soldiers sent to Italy by their commander to buy rice and other staples not available on the local market also brought back extra bags of rice and forty-liter demijohns of olive oil. Bewildered military authorities discovered that these soldiers, under the cover of regular food distribution, had created a black market network supplying restaurants in the Côte d'Azur with hard-to-find consumer goods.[20] In fact, smuggling olive oil, which sold at eight hundred francs per liter on the black market, was a lucrative business. Several other smuggling rings were dismantled by the Italian authorities. Among them was one headed by an Italian lieutenant, a former restaurant owner in Italy.[21]

Smuggling of goods into and out of France was not just done by Ital-ian soldiers; Italian civilians also participated, smuggling gold jewelry and French perfumes.[22] Even Italian civil servants actively participated in the black market. A clerk of the CIAF delegation in Nice was caught with jewels and wads of Italian banknotes in his coat pockets.[23] Sometimes the diligence of Italian border guards led to unexpected results. One soldier returning from leave was prosecuted for attempting to bring three kilograms of to-bacco and several pairs of stockings and socks across the border. However, upon careful examination the Italian military tribunal realized that because of his perfect bilingualism, the soldier was a member of the Service "I," the counterintelligence bureau present in every Fourth Army unit. The confis-cated goods were meant to reward French informants, and the soldier had been authorized by his field officer to buy them in Italy. This case, which in itself was emblematic of the lack of communication between different services in the Italian occupation army, was closed with an embarrassing acquittal by the Fourth Army tribunal.[24]

Italian soldiers' black market activities were not the aspect that most damaged the reputation of the Italian army in the eyes of the local populace. Thefts and burglaries by soldiers of the Regio Esercito were more frequent and their effects more visible than contraband across the border. In fact, they became so endemic on the Côte d'Azur as to become a recurrent worry for anyone with valuable goods or staples. French prefects' desks threatened to collapse under the stacks of local authorities' reports.

The easiest prey for the pillagers were the railway cars used to transport food for both the Italian army food service and the Ravitaillement Général. In most cases a few individuals, under the cover of shadows, sneaked into a railway station to grab whatever food and other goods they could carry.[25] Both Vichy and Italian military authorities incessantly deplored the loss of goods. The prefect of the Basses-Alpes, for instance, complained to his Bouches-du-Rhône equivalent that during the night of 12 December a group of Italian soldiers had broken the lock of a wagon parked inside the Digne station and stolen five hundred kilograms of potatoes.[26] On the other hand, a report of the Delegazione Trasporti Militari (Military Transport Delegation) of the Fourth Army underlined the constant "thefts from Italian railways car transporting food, a plague which shows no sign of abating."[27]

To curb the wave of robberies, the Italian army established squads of carabinieri and soldiers to patrol the railway stations. However, in a few cases the same persons who were supposed to be guarding the carriages were found pilfering goods. Two sentries of the Carnoules (Var) railway station were caught stealing a chunk of red meat from a refrigerator carriage.[28] In another incredible episode, two French policemen noticed, while walking beside the depot in Cannes Bocca, that an Italian soldier was stealing goods from a wagon. The French gendarmes dashed to arrest him but stopped abruptly as two Italian sentries interceded, giving the pillager time to flee the scene. In the ensuing presumably heated conversation, the Italian sentries feigned ignorance, asserting that neither had seen anyone approaching the wagon.[29]

While all of these robberies undoubtedly added to the strain on the food supply, the general population was not all that aware of them. Nevertheless, the plundering of orchards and kitchen gardens directly affected the lives of French civilians. Unfenced fields became easy targets for bands of Italian marauders, who pillaged anything edible, from cabbage to potatoes, from onions to lettuce.[30] The French population was well aware of the many thefts committed by Italian soldiers. The mayor of Mandelieu, a village near Cannes in the Alpes-Maritimes, bitterly complained to Vichy police authorities that fields were often plundered at night. He insisted that while it was difficult in the dark to distinguish more than black shadows moving along these fields, their proximity to Italian encampments and the trails of heavy military boot prints left no doubt about the culprits' identity.[31]

It happened occasionally that local commanders sent patrols in search of pillagers. In January 1943, at Saint-Laurent-du-Var, a soldier found stealing vegetables was shot in the leg while fleeing an Italian patrol.[32] Records of the Fourth Army indicate that, on average, fifty to eighty soldiers were arrested each month for theft, about 30 percent of the total arrests.[33] These numbers were in line with the average for the Italian army in the Second World War more generally.[34] However, it is safe to assume that the thieves who were actually caught and charged were only the tip of the iceberg, as Italian soldiers and officers often turned a blind eye to minor offenses. With the dearth of men, and facing a possible Allied invasion and partisan insurrection, the theft of goods from French fields was ranked low on the scale of threats. Additionally, some officers and NCOs felt it would not be advisable to systematically punish troops for every minor infraction. They feared that a hard-line policy would sour relations between soldiers and officers and considerably deplete the already insufficient number of soldiers on French soil. Thus, the sentences passed by military tribunals appear to have been relatively lenient in the treatment of thefts unless the stolen goods were the property of the Italian army. Finally, we should not underestimate the pressure put on honest soldiers by their unscrupulous peers. One corporal who had denounced some privates who were responsible for the theft of honey and chickens received death threats from the culprits.[35]

Given this permissive attitude, some soldiers became bolder and bolder and began targeting livestock, not hesitating to break doors and locks of shacks and pigpens, even though this "violence on goods" was considered an aggravating circumstance by the military courts.[36] The logical next step in the ladder of offenses was to break into private homes. Hungry soldiers smashed windows, grabbing whatever food they could find.[37] Sometimes they resorted to creative tricks to force the owner to hand over his goods. Two privates, passing themselves off as Italian army police, tried to intimidate a farmer, arguing that the small bonfire he had lit in front of his house was a beacon for enemy planes. Threatening him with a hefty fine, the carabinieri impersonators agreed to ignore his error in exchange for three rabbits.[38] In another classic swindle, an Italian soldier, under the pretext of waiting for the military courier to arrive at the village, invited himself into a home for a glass of wine with the owner while an accomplice tried to break into the rabbit hutch out back.[39]

Break-ins into private houses were few, however, as the risk of being caught was high. Owners did not hesitate to do anything they could to find the culprits, as the stolen goods often represented the entirety of their often meager stores and the difference between survival and serious hardship. Instead, many

Italian soldiers resorted to a more direct way to get food: shoplifting. Staples as diverse as cheese, condensed milk, *mortadella* (Italian cold cuts), and sugar were stolen from shop shelves.[40] The populace was particularly incensed by the fact that the soldiers were even shoplifting non-consumable and non-essential goods as diverse as cameras, postcards, souvenirs, and jewels.[41]

Friction in Everyday Life

The Italian army affected the population's everyday life not only by indulging in black market activities and theft but also by misusing public goods in galling ways. Just a few days after their deployment in southern France, some soldiers were found washing their clothes in a tank that stored the water supply for several apartment buildings, oblivious to the clear health issue that they were contaminating the residents' drinking water.[42] Lacking fuel to keep warm during the cool and humid nights of southern France, Italian soldiers had no scruples about cutting down trees, whether on private property or public land.[43] If the disorganization of the Italian invasion was as much to blame as the lack of discipline among the Italian rank and file, other incidents reflected a marked lack of respect for French laws. French civilians accused the Italian soldiers of shooting domestic pets.[44] The Italians also had the nasty habit of hunting game without any recognition of French hunting regulations.[45] French reports noted with alarm that these hunters also endangered the local population, for stray shots came perilously close to hitting farmers cultivating their fields and even people strolling in village streets. In fact, military court records report at least one case of a French civilian shot in the leg by an Italian soldier who was hunting hares.[46] Italians had even less compunction about fishing, commonly using explosives to increase the size of their catch.[47]

Even though fuel was scarce and traffic on the roads was light, Italian soldiers considered themselves racing pilots and were responsible for several accidents involving cars and trucks. On 30 January 1943 a speeding Italian truck driver lost control of his vehicle on a bend in the road and mortally injured a French pedestrian.[48] In August 1943 an Italian motorcyclist, while driving at top speed in the village of Sisteron, hit a French civilian. Not content with having injured the civilian, the Italian officer not only abused the French gendarme who was writing down the motorcycle's license plate but also insulted passersby.[49] In another unfortunate incident a French truck whose driver failed to pull over to let an Italian car pass became the target of several shots to its tires. In the face of protests from the French prefect, the Italian commander in Digne icily commented that this "natural reaction" of the Italian soldiers was simply the consequence of the careless driving of "French drivers who did not comply with traffic regulations, especially when they are near Italian military vehicles."[50] Reckless driving also directly impacted the Italian army. An Italian army driver swerved into the opposite lane to avoid crashing into a horse-drawn carriage. In doing so, the truck collided with a car of Italian carabinieri coming from the opposite direction, killing one officer and severely injuring an NCO.[51]

Additionally, soldiers of the Regio Esercito had assumed responsibility for maintaining law and order from the French security forces. However, as traffic policemen their tactics were at times unorthodox. Cyclists who failed to stop in the face of soldiers' challenges risked slaps or even a severe beating.[52] These incidents sometimes escalated into fights, as in the case on 9 December 1942 in Nice when French citizens came to an unlucky cyclist's defense and ended up in a brawl with Italian irredentists, who vigorously backed up the soldiers.[53] Even essential services such as ambulances and public transportation were not spared. On 19 January 1943 the driver of an ambulance carrying two sick people had the misfortune of crossing an Italian military procession in the streets of Nice. Given the urgency of his task and having received the green light from an NCO, the driver moved forward, thus cutting the procession in half. An officer, deeming the move of the French civilian an impudent affront to the Italian army, immediately rushed to punch the driver in the face. Only the intervention of a French agent prevented the situation from escalating.[54] Vichy officials were also targeted, as they were considered both a challenge to the authority of the Italian army in France and a possible threat in the case of an anti-Italian insurrection. French gendarmes who patrolled at night to enforce the curfew were in a few instances chastised by Italian military patrols, especially when the former hailed the soldiers or directed their flashlight beam into the soldiers' faces.

The occupation army was in constant fear of possible attacks from the French population. This fear lay behind the curfew measure established by the Italian garrison commander in the small village of Gattières after a sentry opened fire on an individual who upon approaching the camp and being ordered to stop, instead precipitously fled the premises.[55] The obsessive dread of a possible insurgence sparked yet another incident. A tax collector was arrested in mid-January in Nice and his gun was confiscated. The arrest stemmed from a misunderstanding: the French civil servant had been seen showing his gun to one of his fellows in a café. A witness who thought the two tax collectors were possible resisters reported the incident to an Italian patrol, who proceeded to arrest the alleged insurgent.[56]

Nervous Italian soldiers were also prone to overreact when they believed they had been mocked or insulted by Frenchmen. On 14 December 1942 an Italian squad stormed the gendarmerie of the small village of Vence in response to an alleged rude gesture made by a French gendarme at an Italian column the day before. Even though the situation was quickly defused when it became clear that the whole incident was the result of a misunderstanding, the population of Vence was shocked by the excessive use of force.[57] French police officers were often suspected of scoffing at Italian troops. An Italian officer accused two gendarmes of making fun of *bersaglieri* (marksmen) troops, whose distinctive wide-brimmed hats were decorated with black capercaillie feathers.[58] The Italians seemed exceptionally sensitive, perceiving insults even where none was intended. A gendarme who failed to greet a passing Italian officer was considered to have insulted him, even though at the time the gendarme was focused on hunting down poachers.[59]

This arrogance and prickliness disturbed and angered the French, who sometimes reacted with sarcasm and irreverence. A customer in a bar who, upon hearing an Italian soldier slandering the French army for not being able to resist the Wehrmacht in June 1940, replied that it did not matter, because the Americans would soon come to free the French, was immediately arrested and brought to Italian army local headquarters.[60] A common site for these kinds of confrontations was the bistro, as a result of immoderate alcohol consumption by Italian soldiers. In January 1943 four soldiers in Thoard, Basses-Alpes, who had been refused wine fired several shots into the sky to intimidate the owner.[61] In June 1943 a brawl in a bar in the village of Manosque, Basses-Alpes, between French customers and Italian soldiers rapidly escalated into a wider street fight.[62] However, Italian commanders and local French authorities managed to contain the incidents, avoiding with their moderation more serious ethnic confrontations within the population.

To fully gauge the effect of the Italian occupation on everyday life, one should put it in the context of the occupation of France. Indeed, as far as illegal activities were concerned, French civilians and German soldiers alike were as much to blame as the Italians. Since the beginning of the occupation, the Wehrmacht had few qualms when it came to imposing draconian requisitions and concurrently buying enormous quantities of food on the black market, with the long-term effect of destabilizing the Vichy distribution network and of skyrocketing food prices.[63] Since January 1941, its intelligence branch, the Abwehr, under the supervision of Hermann "Otto" Brandl, had developed an organization of four hundred people who acted as mediators with French entrepreneurs wishing to evade Vichy's stringent rules and lured by profitable deals with the occupying power.[64]

In the meantime, as the failing Vichy distribution system could not keep up with the demand of a hungry population, many people increasingly resorted to either illicit trade or theft to satisfy their needs, often at the expense of the weaker or more honest part of the population. French POWs' parcels were often targeted by unscrupulous individuals.[65] Thefts of foodstuffs and ration cards had become a daily event in the Côte d'Azur as early as 1941, way before the Italian occupation of the French Riviera. Thieves raided ravitaillement offices for ration tickets, even blowing safes to get them. This situation became so widespread that Vichy increased the penalty for those who distributed or used counterfeit or illegal ration tickets, in some extreme cases sentencing felons to life in prison.[66] Moreover, thefts were not limited only to food or the ration system but encompassed a wide variety of goods. For instance, an average of four bicycles were stolen each day in the city of Nice.[67]

As a matter of fact, the Italian presence was sometimes convenient. Some civilians were quick to blame the soldiers of the Regio Esercito in order to cover their own crimes. In January 1943 the CEO of a French distribution company complained to the prefect of the Alpes-Maritimes about the numerous robberies targeting the wagons that transported food from Marseille to the department of the Alpes-Maritimes. SNCF (Société Nationale des Chemins de fer Français), the French national railway company, openly accused the Italian soldiers of the thefts. However, the manager of the distribution company suggested that some of the robberies may have been committed by "unscrupulous SNCF employees [who] used these thefts as an excuse to carry out their own." In support of his theory, the CEO accused SNCF of having allegedly ordered its employees to blame the occupation army as a way to avoid having to refund the plaintiff companies.[68] The CEO's suspicion is corroborated by the sheer data on thefts in railcars, as in 1942 alone more than 134,000 thefts occurred, which resulted in 18,334 individuals arrested and 2,983 SNCF employees dismissed.[69] Italians, thus, were used as scapegoats by French officials to cover the deficiencies of the Vichy rationing system. While there is no doubt that the arrival of hundreds of thousands of soldiers strained the precarious food balance in the French Riviera, by 1943 the Vichy rationing system was in dire straits with daily caloric intake for individuals falling from 1,365 in 1941 to 1,080 in 1943.

If nothing else, the sheer number of trials for black market deals attested to the gargantuan proportion of black market activities. For instance, dairy products and meats, which had become rarities in Vichy-regulated markets by 1943, became so widespread on the black market that some people estimated that illicit transactions of meat equaled the lawful ones.[70] The Italians therefore only delved in and amplified a subterranean economy that was already thriving. It is important to recognize that the occupied population, too, significantly shaped the occupation period and that trading activities were two-way relationships. Both the soldiers of the Regio Esercito and the inhabitants of the Côte d'Azur were eager to partake in black market activities, aware that it was the best means to stave off the incessant hunger. In doing so, Mussolini's soldiers had perfectly integrated in the "sunny place with shady people."

CHAPTER 8

Military Repression,
Civilian Resistance

The Italian Repression

Military occupations are traumatic experiences for the occupied population. Most aspects of everyday life must be negotiated with the occupier, the latter ultimately having the last say. Watching one's daily space narrow—and in some cases, such as with the combat zone, disappear—arguably had a negative impact on one's sense of security.[1] Familiar landmarks were gone while routine habits were hindered by total strangers with weapons, sometimes barking incomprehensible words. On the other hand, soldiers of the occupying army also no doubt felt alienated in an unfamiliar environment inhabited by a population who eyed them at best suspiciously and at worst with cold hatred. Mindful of the inherent pitfalls of an occupation in a region loaded with political undertone, the Italian military officers successfully implemented a realist strategy to avoid escalating the confrontation with the local population.

Yet at the same time, the army still needed to guarantee the security of its troops, so they requested the aid of other security agencies to help them root out any possible resistance threat.[2] At the head of the civilian security forces in the Italian occupation zone was Rosario Barranco, the controversial head of the Italian political police in the Alpes-Maritimes.[3] Barranco's early career was that of a brilliant civil servant who served the Fascist regime, but without really compromising himself or dabbling in politics. His excellent record, exemplified by seventeen service citations received in the interwar years, along with his knowledge of the French language eventually brought him to Nice in March 1939 as police attaché to the Italian consulate. After the armistice Barranco came back to Nice on 24 July 1940 to work as part of the local CIAF. He was assisted in his task by a staff of functionaries, among them Luigi Civilotti, the former *Fascio* secretary in Cannes, and Osvaldo Angrisani, who was killed by resisters on the night of the 14–15 April 1943.[4] While the political police office in Nice was certainly instrumental, working in collaboration with the Vichy police, in the arrests of several fuoriusciti living in the Côte d'Azur, such as the future head of the Italian Communist Party, Luigi Longo (known in France by the pseudonym Luigi Gallo), it appears that Barranco acted more out of a sense of duty than a staunch belief in Fascism.[5]

In addition to Barranco's office, other security agencies moved into the former free zone in the wake of the Italian occupation starting in November 1942. The SIM (Servizio Informazioni Militare, the Italian military intelligence service) sent two agents to Nice—Carabinieri Major Giuseppe Valenti (alias Salerno) and Carabinieri Captain Tisani (alias Pescara, Mario di Resta, or Aresta)—both from the XV CA carabinieri unit.[6] Moreover, the army had its own counterintelligence agency, the Ufficio Informazioni (Ufficio "I"), operating at a divisional level since the inception of the occupation.[7] The first task of the Ufficio "I" was to monitor Fourth Army troops for any sign of defeatism.[8] Every Ufficio Informazioni received a grant from the division to build up a network of informers, divided into two categories: permanent agents (*agenti fissi*) and occasional agents (*agenti occasionali*), all handpicked from among pro-Italian activists in the local population.[9] Their informers' task was to provide information on anti-Italian organizations, either Resistance- or Vichy-based, and to update the army on the public opinion's views of the occupation army. Often, intelligence officers did not have to search far, as unscrupulous local individuals showed up at the Italian garrisons eager to be recruited, either moved by Fascist ideals or for more base reasons such as petty quarrels and greed. Informers were rewarded with not only money but also cigarettes and food such as rice and meat.[10]

A typical example of an informers' ring tied to a local Ufficio "I" was located in Antibes starting in December 1942. Three Italians, a couple owning a bar and a former Italian army veteran living in France, and two French, a civilian and a former French captain, spontaneously showed up at the local Italian garrison, volunteering to become informants.[11] The Ufficio "I" immediately asked the Nice CIAF delegation for any background information on the prospective agents. A few weeks later the delegation informed the Ufficio "I" that the Italian army veteran was extremely unreliable. Information he had provided the CIAF before November 1942 turned out to have been distorted by his personal biases. As well, the French captain had apparently lied about his participation on the eastern front in the ranks of

the Wehrmacht.[12] In spite of the dubious reliability of some of their informers, the Italian army still made use of their information as they swept over
Antibes on 4 January 1943 and arrested twenty persons.

As the three Italian security agencies (Italian political police, SIM, and
Ufficio "I") built their separate spy networks among the local population,
this intricate web of espionage at times caused confusion within the Italian
intelligence network. First, the three organizations were not always eager
to share their data. To be sure, it was not rare for informants already on
the payroll of one agency to be contacted by recruiters of other agencies
who ignored the fact that the former individual was already working for
the Italian cause.[13] The issue of overlapping tasks and conflicting networks
was in part clarified by the December 1942 tour in the occupation zone of
the head of SIM, Gen. Cesare Amè, and his talks with General Vercellino.
It was agreed that police operations would be headed by both the political
police and SIM, as confirmed by instructions given to various units before
a January roundup of alleged anti-Italians.[14] Fourth Army units were asked
to provide logistical support by way of escorts for the arrested persons and
trucks, while CIAF personnel were given the thankless task of warding off
the expected complaints from French authorities.[15] However, relationships
between the different agencies still remained strained, even after the clarifications. In particular, Barranco and Vercellino could not stand each other.[16]
And it appears that the army frequently had the last say in decisions.

Regardless of these differences, all the Italian organizations operating in
the newly occupied territory ultimately coalesced in the face of the ongoing
menace of an internal French insurrection. To prevent this dreaded scenario,
Italian authorities quickly enacted a strategy of massive arrests. However,
the implementation of this policy waxed and waned over time, and the Italian army was always quick to tone down its implementation after a scare.
We have already seen that from the beginning of the occupation of the free
zone the Italian army was willing to arrest individuals, most arrests resulting
from denunciations made by Italian informers. After protests made by French
authorities, this strategy was called off on 20 November 1942 by Vercellino,
only to be reinstated by the Duce five days later. Following the late November
crisis that ended with the seizure of Toulon and the subsequent disarming of
the Armée d'Armistice, the Italian Army General Staff, fearing an uprising by
the French population, gave permission to take hostages (*prendere ostaggi*)
from among either the local notables or anti-Italian activists. However, the
order remained vague, as they did not specify what to do with the hostages,
leaving the decision to the discretion of the local army command.[17] This
order was soon scaled down on 12 January by another directive stating that

in case of attacks, "[the local Italian units] should not detain hostages, but only arrest the individuals responsible for the offences."[18]

That is not to say that the Italian army halted its repressive campaign. The 12 January document itself insisted that even "those who are suspected of complicity" could be arrested. Moreover, some units still kept lists of local dissidents who were to be taken hostage in case of attacks, even though their use was limited by the fact that the detention of hostages was to be carried out only "in case of urgent needs" (underlined in original).[19] On 28 January a Fourth Army command directive insisted on enforcing the "absolute protection by any means available of the physical and spiritual integrity of the Italian Armed Forces." Thus, Vercellino stated, if the perpetrators of the attacks on Italian troops could not be found, local commanders would have to resort to collective sanctions (sanzioni collettive), ranging from mild reprisals such as curfews and the temporary detention of suspects and witnesses to severe ones such as the deportation or internment of local French authorities. Yet it is worth noting again the self-limitation of the Italian army. The more severe sanctions could be ordered only by the higher echelons of the Fourth Army, such as division commanders or the Fourth Army commander. Moreover, Vercellino himself warned, "Collective sanctions are a delicate weapon [arma delicata], abuse of which is very dangerous." Thus, he appealed to the sensibility and the tact of local commanders to select a sanction that was commensurate with the gravity of the offense and the local mood of the population. More pragmatically, the commanders were to gauge the "effectiveness that the sanctions will have [to better local conditions]."[20] This rather down-to-earth approach of the Italian army's upper echelons underscored the uncertainty of the Italian policy in the first months of the occupation, balancing a hard-line stance that was intended to quash any sign of rebellious behavior against a softer policy favoring a modus vivendi with the population.

Collective sanctions were, in fact, seldom implemented in the Italian occupation period. However, starting in December 1942, arrests rapidly escalated, changing from a pattern of individual arrests, to raids leading to multiple arrests, and finally, as of May 1943, to massive roundups. Periodically, Italian troops, guided by local informers and headed by SIM and Italian police functionaries, stormed apartments and houses arresting individuals accused of allegedly being part of anti-Axis organizations or of having anti-Italian sentiments. The roundups followed several criteria, such as the nationality of the arrested. On 26 December 1942 a wave of arrests hit the Polish community in Nice. Apparently the arrests were triggered by an incident involving a young Pole who had fired a shot at an Italian soldier, although another rumor suggested that a Pole had been using a radio transmitter to communicate with Allied secret services. Whatever the true reasons, more than twenty Poles, mostly journalists, officers of the former Polish army, or civil servants of the defunct Polish state, were arrested.[21] On 17 January 1943 the Italians went so far as to arrest the Polish consul in Monaco.[22] Other citizens from Allied states were also targeted, such as British and Americans, as the Italians feared that every Allied foreigner was potentially a spy. Most of the British citizens were apprehended in three distinct sweeps: on 28 December 1942 in Monaco, in Nice on 9 January, and in Cannes on 26 January.[23] The majority of arrested people were either Italians (roughly one hundred people in total) or French nationals (roughly seven hundred). Both communities suffered from waves and individual arrests throughout the Italian occupation. Nevertheless, the French bore the brunt of the repression disproportionately. The French numbered four times as many as the Italians in the general population, yet the number of French arrested was seven times that of Italians arrested.

Some arrests were brutally carried out. Suspects were normally picked up in the evening or in the middle of the night. They were seldom given time to dress, with the Italians reassuring them and their family that they were not being arrested and would come back in, at most, half an hour. The suspects were then driven to Villa Lynwood, the former vacation house of an English citizen, which sat on the hills of Nice with a breathtaking view of the Mediterranean Sea. Here, members of the SIM and the political police interrogated their prisoners, resorting in some cases to physical and psychological torture.[24] One common technique described by resisters in their memoirs was the *giro* (circle), a torture consisting of walking the detainee in chains for hours, or even allegedly for days, in a corridor until the unfortunate detainee dropped from exhaustion or agreed to confess his misdeeds.[25] In another example of physical and psychological abuse, one prisoner, accused by an Italian irredentist of having denounced him to the French authorities in June 1940, later complained of having been beaten by members of the Italian political police and by his neighbor. The Italians allegedly forced the prisoner to drink castor oil and, in the face of his refusal, beat him, causing him to faint. The suspect, however, was lucky. He was released shortly thereafter, but not without having been first severely rebuked and warned to leave the Italian irredentist alone.[26] Those who were deemed dangerous to Italian security were shipped to the various internment camps administered by the Regio Esercito.

The Italians used a variety of camps to hold their prisoners, depending on the reason for their arrests. Those who were suspected only of being part of

Resistance groups or having anti-Italian feelings but had not committed any actual offense against the Italian army were transferred to the internment camp in the village of Sospel, a village north of Menton, situated near the border between the 1940 June occupied zone and the former free zone.[27] At the end of May 1943 these prisoners were transferred to a new camp in Embrun (Basses-Alpes), a former French penal colony.[28] In response to the sheer number of arrests following the spring 1943 escalation of violence in the departments occupied by the Italians, the Italian army created an internment camp in Modane (Savoy), this one reserved for communist and Gaullist militants.[29] Living conditions in all the camps were harsh. A detainee complained to his daughter that the prisoners were given only two hundred grams of bread a day, with just a meager bowl of soup for lunch and dinner.[30] That being said, families could visit their relatives in the camp, a privilege not many detainees in Axis prisons enjoyed. What is more, British and American citizens were treated fairly well.[31] The sincerity of the Italian commanders' attitude is unclear; perhaps some of them were already "playing it safe" with Allied citizens, understanding that the tide of war had turned and that it behooved them to ingratiate themselves with the possible victors. That said, it is important to note that the special commission consisting of the head of Fourth Army carabinieri, members of the Ufficio "I," of SIM, and of the political police, which met periodically to review the prisoners' dossiers, freed people of all nationalities for humanitarian reasons.[32] For instance, fourteen French prisoners were freed from the Modane camp in July 1943 for health problems, which had made further detention dangerous for them.[33]

Sospel, Embrun, and Modane, however, were reserved for suspects who had not been arrested on specific charges. Those who had committed actual offenses against the Regio Esercito were referred to the military court of the Fourth Army, which operated in the small border village of Breil-sur-Roya. Given its exceptional nature, its sentences were never publicized, and even its existence was unknown to all but the French intelligence service and the detained persons.[34] Those awaiting trial were generally detained either in Breil, Menton, or occasionally in Turin. As in the other detention centers, conditions for the prisoners were harsh but seldom unbearable. Acts of kindness were not uncommon; one prisoner stated to the French police upon his release that the Italians had even transferred him to a hospital to cure a temporary illness.[35] Some prisoners underlined the sympathetic attitude of the Italian jailers, who sometimes alleviated the imprisonment by giving them extra food and cigarettes.[36] Sentences were rather mild, and acquittals and suspended sentences were not rare, especially for minor offenses such as alleged insults to Italian troops.[37] In fact, the Italian tribunal clearly understood that some of the accusations had been made in bad faith by individuals slandering their neighbors. Gen. Alessandro Trabucchi, the head of the Fourth Army staff, warned the Italian commanders of the danger represented by members of the Nice Action Groups (see chapter 3) who used the Italian soldiers to settle petty quarrels with neighbors.[38] If anything, the people prosecuted were surprised that trials were held with equity and with a real defense provided by military attorneys, and most considered the verdicts to be fair.[39]

However, these arrests were frowned upon by local French authorities, because they clearly undermined the sovereignty of the French state. Local Italian army commanders preferred to focus on strategic and security matters, leaving regular administration to local authorities. However, sometimes confrontation was unavoidable. The prefect of the Alpes-Maritimes, Marcel Ribière, repeatedly protested the campaign of wanton arrests carried out by the Italians.[40] In addition, the Italians did not hesitate to arrest French civil servants. Ange B., a French citizen who, as a Monaco police auxiliary, participated in the arrests of Italian irredentists in June 1940, was himself arrested on 28 December 1942.[41] On 24 January 1943 it was the turn of Jacques Galli, the *chef de division à la préfecture,* one of the closest collaborators of the Alpes-Maritimes prefect, who was taken into custody by Italian police officers under the prefect's formal protest.[42] As was the case with the Menton mayor, Durandy, the Italians hoped to catch "the big fish" by first getting the "small fry." As mentioned before, Prefect Ribière had been at loggerheads with local Italian authorities since 1940 because of his hard-line anti-Italian attitude. The occupation of November 1942 only worsened the conflict, and increased Italian infringements on Vichy's authority considerably hardened Ribière's stance. The Italian army's protection of the Jews in the department, in flagrant opposition to Vichy's Jewish policy in the German zone of herding French and foreign Jews into concentration camps, contributed to the institutional conflict in the Alpes-Maritimes.[43] Moreover, the Italians criticized the préfecture for its ineptitude in thwarting the wave of sabotages and attacks on the Italians. Thus, it was inevitable that, pressured by the Italians, a frustrated Ribière submitted his resignation in late April 1943.[44]

A few other Alpes-Maritimes notables also came under attack. The mayor of Nice, Jean Médecin, had already been blacklisted by the CIAF in November 1941 for speeches filled with nationalistic undertones.[45] In a scathing report, Quinto Mazzolini, the Nice CIAF delegate until May 1942, summed up the story of the Nice administration in the first half of the twentieth century, focusing on the Médecin family, who had allegedly misappropriated municipal funds originally designated for repairing the city's infrastructure.[46] As in the case of Ribière, tensions increased with the military occupation of November 1942. Italian authorities were certainly not impressed by a May 1943 report from Jean Médecin that denounced the brutal and massive intrusion of the Italian police into the daily life of Nice's inhabitants. The confidential report, written after a massive roundup on 6 May 1943 and intended to be seen only by Vichy authorities, was leaked to the Italians.[47] Médecin had done nothing to hide his contempt for the Italian's repressive policy, and he expressed his solidarity with the arrested persons by greeting them, one by one, at the railway station before their departure for the Embrun internment camp.[48] It is plausible that the occupation authorities then pressured the mayor to quit. The Nizzardo stepped up its campaign against the Nice municipal administration.[49] On 27 July 1943 Jean Médecin stepped down and Nice remained without a mayor until its liberation in August 1944.[50]

The Italians were not always successful in ousting hostile notables. For instance, Monseigneur Rémond, the nationalist bishop of Nice, kept his position until the end of the war, to the dismay of local irredentists, who saw the unwillingness of Italian authorities to arrest him as a worrying sign of "weakness."[51] In fact, rumors abounded that the cellar of his residence was stacked with weapons.[52] Perhaps the Italian Fourth Army command did not dare detain the bishop for fear of incurring the Vatican's ire and because of the likely backlash it would spark in an army whose rank and file were mostly of Catholic faith. Thus, the Italians bothered only minor clerical figures, such as a Nice abbot who had allegedly railed against the Italian occupation during a marriage celebration.[53]

The Resistance in the Côte d'Azur

Italian army commanders, however, were more concerned by underground organized opposition. The Resistance in the Côte d'Azur started in 1940 after the French defeat, but as everywhere else in France, its first steps were hesitant. The Resistance in the Alpes-Maritimes in the first months of the Vichy regime remained largely, in the words of the Alpes-Maritimes specialist Jean-Louis Panicacci, "the deeds of a few individuals, . . . their action often confined to debates, epistolary exchanges, listening to Radio-London."[54] The shock of the defeat along with the widespread popularity of Marshal Philippe Pétain were probably key factors in explaining the slow start of the French Resistance.[55] In the whole free zone, a few movements such as

Franc-Tireur, Libération-Sud, Combat, and Témoignage Chrétien au Sud eventually sprang to life, but their action centered mostly on Marseille and Lyons.[56] The situation did not improve in 1941, notwithstanding the fact that Jean Moulin had gone underground at the beginning of that year following his sojourn in Nice. Acts of resistance did not go beyond the occasional leaflets directed against Vichy and expressing fear of an Italian occupation, or school pupils' slurs directed against Pétain, which were probably more a result of youth rebelliousness than a true Resistance consciousness.[57] Even pangs of hunger did not stir up the population to oppose the Vichy regime. Quite the opposite, people were adamant that without Pétain the rationing would have been far worse.[58]

If the French Resistance was reserved in its activities until the second half of 1942, the same could be said for Italian leftist expatriates. Southern France was known in the interwar years as a strong militant base for the fuoriusciti. In the Alpes-Maritimes alone, the Unione Popolare Italiana (UPI), a movement created in 1937 from the merging of all Italian anti-Fascist organizations, could boast more than five thousand militants.[59] However, the UPI was fatally weakened by internal conflict between the two major political factions: the communists and the socialists. That rift widened dramatically after the Nazi-Soviet Pact in August 1939. Socialists, who strongly opposed the pact, left the UPI along with some communists. This secession could not have happened at a worst moment; first the Third Republic and then the regime of Vichy cracked down on the Italian leftist network in southern France. As mentioned earlier, a few hundred fuoriusciti were put in internment camps or under house arrest, and Vichy shrewdly traded Italian leftist leaders, such as Luigi Longo, for French citizens who had been jailed in Italy at the beginning of the hostilities.

Starting in January 1942, Jean Moulin, Gen. Charles de Gaulle's envoy in metropolitan France, endeavored to unite three of the most important Resistance groups (Combat, Libération-Sud, and Franc-Tireur). Their military branches, which later merged into the Armée Secrète organization, were probably responsible for a wave of attacks meant to destabilize the Vichy regime. Several months before the Italian occupation, starting in the second half of 1942 and continuing in 1943, offices of collaborationist groups such as Jacques Doriot's Parti Populaire Français (PPF) and the Parti Franciste,[60] and of Vichy organizations such as the Légion Française des Combattants (LFC), the Service d'Ordre Légionnaire (SOL), and the Légion des Volontaires Français contre le Bolchevisme (LVF) were bombed or set alight.[61] Businesses that were working for the Axis powers were also attacked: a movie theater in Nice that showed German propaganda movies was set on fire in October 1942;[62] a newsstand owner was threatened with having his business burned if he kept on selling collaborationist and pro-German newspapers and magazines;[63] and in May 1943 a bomb exploded in the Préfecture of the Alpes-Maritimes, although it caused only minimal damage.[64]

Yet it was the Italian military occupation of the Côte d'Azur in November 1942 that finally galvanized the local fuoriusciti to become active. The Armée Secrète strategy was concurrent to the campaign against the Italian occupation orchestrated by the communist fuoriusciti, who were led by Emilio Sereni.[65] Anti-Italian resistance fell into three categories: efforts to undermine the Italian soldiers' morale; the sabotage of infrastructure essential to the Italian army, especially the railway network and the telephone lines; and as the occupation continued, direct attacks on Italian soldiers. The fuoriusciti wanted to weaken the Italian army from within by infiltrating its ranks with spies and agents provocateurs. To this end, they tried to approach lone soldiers either in cafés or in bistros to persuade them to desert, playing on their desire to return home. Italian officers complained that soldiers were even invited by fuoriusciti to their homes for a glass of wine or to wash their clothes, where the conversation would turn to the news from other fronts.[66] The Italian military authorities took this menace very seriously. Gen. Roberto Olmi of the Legnano Division insisted that soldiers should be encouraged with the reward of extra leaves and money for reporting suspicious attitudes among civilians. Conversely, failure to do so could lead not only to a soldier's indictment but also to collective sanctions against the soldier's unit.[67] Yet Italian officers soon discovered that this policy was being abused when some soldiers denounced French citizens as having defamed the Fascist regime or the Italian army only because of the prospect of special leaves.[68] In some cases the incentives paid off: one soldier feigned interest in the offer, only to lure the recruiter to a meeting that ended in arrest and a hefty twenty-year sentence.[69] Therefore, the fuoriusciti also pursued other, more indirect and less risky ways to spread their propaganda. They published a newspaper called *La Parola del Soldato* (The Word of the Soldier), which was distributed by either dropping it furtively in front of Italian barracks during the night or simply leaving it on the sidewalk. The paper invited the Italian soldier to desert and join the ranks of the Resistance against the German army. By emphasizing the poor conditions of the average Italian rank and file, the paper endeavored to drive a wedge not only between the soldiers and their officers but also between the Italians and the Germans. According to the newspaper, the Germans were sleeping in "cozy bunks" at first-class hotels that were heated by coal stoves while the Italians had to cope with beds made of "four wood boards on two rickety trestles" in shacks barely warmed by inadequate wood stoves.[70]

Of course, the views in the *Parola* were biased and tended to exaggerate the divide between the two armies. Yet, as mentioned before with regard to wages and living conditions, it is likely that this particular indictment held a kernel of truth. Besides, the newspaper's editors seemed to be well informed on the whereabouts of the Fourth Army, as an article mentioned that leaves to Sicily, Sardinia, and to southern Italy more generally had been canceled. It is difficult to gauge the extent of the anti-Axis presence in the ranks of the Italian army. However, it is probably enlightening that in August 1943, Italian commanders complained that the Italian communists were infiltrating the ranks of the Fourth Army.[71] Their worries were well-founded: in a trial of the Italian communist organization in the Alpes-Maritimes in late August 1943, four of the thirty-four accused were soldiers of the Fourth Army.[72] That a profound malaise permeated the army was clear when General Vercellino himself irately complained that soldiers were openly singing "rebellious songs" (*inni sovversivi*) in front of their officers.[73] The fuoriusciti cleverly exploited the period of confusion following the ousting of the Duce in July 1943, but defeatist ideas apparently had seeped into the Italian army long before the fall of the Fascist regime.

In addition to fostering the seeds of defeatism within Italian ranks, the local Resistance endeavored to discourage the local population from helping the occupation army. Thus, they also widened their attacks to include the shops and houses of notorious Italian irredentists. People who openly displayed their support for the Italian troops or who brazenly demonstrated a pro-Fascist attitude received death threats or had their shops bombed. On 8 February 1943, in Antibes, several makeshift bombs were found in the shops or houses of Italian Fascist militants who had been previously singled out as informers for the Italian army in a tract distributed in mailboxes throughout the city.[74] Infiltrating army ranks and intimidating the irredentist minority in the Alpes-Maritimes were only the first steps of a strategy to weaken the Italian war effort. The local Resistance also resorted to more direct means to oppose the Italian military occupation. No attacks were carried out by the Resistance until the end of 1942, as they were gauging the size of the Italian army and its occupation policy.[75]

In January 1943 the internal Resistance in the former free zone consolidated into the Mouvements Unis de la Résistance (MUR).[76] Under the guidance of its commissar for military affairs, Henri Frenay, the military wing stepped up its efforts to fight the occupation. First, its members targeted railway and telephone lines. Railway lines were crucial for moving troops and goods, and the local Resistance was aware that the line between Genoa and Marseille, which ran parallel to the coastline, was key to feeding the Italian units deployed along the Mediterranean shore. Therefore, beginning in January 1943 they unleashed a series of attacks on the railway line; boulders were hurled onto the tracks and explosive devices were planted, targeting tunnels and bridges especially.[77] To stop the wave of sabotage, the Italian units, which were already short on men, requested the assistance of local authorities. French police officers, border guards, and even members of the newborn Milice Française were commandeered to patrol the railway lines.[78] However, this measure did not stop the wrecking of the railway lines, which continued unabated throughout the occupation, as did the regular sabotage of telephone lines.[79]

At the same time, local Resistance fighters decided to step up their struggle by taking direct aim at Italian soldiers. It is unclear if the first attacks attributed to the Resistance were truly the deeds of resisters or the result of the deep sense of insecurity pervading the Italian army in France. For instance, on 4 January 1943 in Cagnes-sur-Mer, the exhaust roar of Italian military motorcycles was apparently mistaken as rifle shots.[80] A few days later, an Italian sentry posted near railway tracks was shot in the leg, the bullet allegedly fired from a passing train. However, further investigation uncovered a somewhat confusing picture in which the evidence did not corroborate the soldier's account. In fact, the police and the population suspected the soldier had voluntarily mutilated himself in order to be sent home.[81]

If nothing else, these incidents demonstrated the edginess of the Italian soldiers. Yet, until February, direct strikes on Italian troops were rare and not very effective. A bomb hurled near Italian barracks in Nice detonated without causing much damage.[82] In fact, the same report mentioned that explosive devices that had been used by the Resistance so far were of poor quality and failed to explode most of the time. In his February report, Vercellino downplayed the Resistance's action as "a few attacks . . . which caused no severe consequences."[83]

By March 1943 local resisters had grown bolder. A CIAF office (Border Control and Surveillance Delegation) in Cros-de-Cagnes had its telephone lines cut and was the target of a bomb.[84] Four bombs were thrown into the courtyard of the Caserne Dugommier, former barracks of the French army in Nice, now occupied by Italian units. Even though only one of the four bombs detonated and it caused only minimal damage, the French report noted that the devices had a more "destructive power" than those previously used by the Resistance.[85] This impression was confirmed on 10 April 1943 when a powerful detonation shook the night in Cannes. The door of a garage loaned to members of the local CIAF office was blown in by a bomb hung on its doorknob, causing some damage to the vehicles inside.[86]

Summer 1943: The Apex of Violence

The situation escalated at the end of April 1943. The Axis front on North Africa was collapsing as Allied troops advanced into Tunisia, the last African territory still in the hands of the Axis powers. With repeated acts of sabotage, the local Resistance was hoping to contribute to the prospective Allied invasion of the French Mediterranean shores by weakening the already shaky Italian distribution system. The Italian Army General Staff was becoming increasingly worried that the internal situation was radicalizing at a time when there were serious risks "in the short term [brevissima scadenza] of enemy operation against our coastline."[87] At a local level the Italian Army General Staff's stern warning trickled down to the units quartered in France. Army corps commanders warned that the Anglo-American offensive strike in Tunisia might trigger "turmoil and hostile acts" (fermenti e atti ostili) in France.[88] In other words, the Italians' greatest fear—of being caught between the hammer of an Anglo-American landing and the anvil of a French insurrection—was taking shape.

Units deployed on the coastline were reminded by a dispatch from the Italian General Staff that they should continue to strictly enforce the 10 January regulation that had divided Italian-occupied France into two zones. It also ordered that a strict curfew from 11 P.M. to 4 A.M. be enforced in the combat zone starting on 27 April.[89] The Fourth Army command communicated the new regulation to the prefectures of the coastline departments, the Alpes-Maritimes and the Var, which in turn relayed the information to all the major newspapers, and posters to that effect were placarded in every city and town.

The twenty-seventh of April 1943 would be remembered in the story of the Italian occupation for more than just the beginning of the curfew. That evening three officers of the local Italian garrison were gunned down while waiting for the trolley in the center of Nice. One of the officers, Lt. Giorgio Tobino, died a few hours later from a severe hemorrhage, the first Italian soldier to die in the French Riviera during the occupation.[90] No suspect was found. The local Italian military commander immediately blamed the French police for "guilty negligence, if not of outright complicity." The commander warned that if the culprits were not found by 5 May, the Italian army would ask for the dismissal of both the prefect of the Alpes-Maritimes, Ribière, and the head of the Nice police, Paul Duraffour.[91] In the meantime a longer curfew than originally planned was imposed in Nice, from 9 P.M. to 5 A.M., and all the theaters, cinemas, and public halls were closed until further notice. Finally, the city of Nice was required to pay a hefty fine of three million francs by 29 April at noon.[92] Italian military authorities were determined to punish the population as a whole. Concurrently, wild rumors were spreading that the Italians would be handing over the occupation to the German army, or, even worse, to local irredentists who would use it to pursue personal vendettas.[93]

No immediate punishment was implemented by the Italians, however. On the contrary, the funeral of the Italian officer was uneventful in its somber ceremony and no major incident erupted in the following days.[94] Local military authorities were probably keeping the irredentists at bay. At first, then, the Italian army reacted surprisingly passively to the death of its first soldier of the occupation. In addition, the military took measures to reduce the troops' exposure. Italian commanders advised their officers to avoid settling in isolated apartments or villas where their security could not be assured.[95] Soldiers going to the movies were required to return to their barracks before nightfall.[96] Furthermore, officers who had to leave their barracks after curfew were instructed that they should always be armed and accompanied by other soldiers.[97]

The Italians were not idle. On 1 May the Fourth Army command had issued a note to the entire coastline army corps detailing an upcoming roundup in Nice of "communist" elements. The operation was to be headed by the highest officer of the Fourth Army military police, the carabinieri. The local Italian garrison would be supported by the EFTF (Emanuele Filiberto Testa di Ferro), a reserve division quartered farther inland, along with a few hundred carabinieri from other units and even two regiments of the elite unit Legnano. Everything was prepared in minute detail: all the major routes leading to Nice were closed starting from 10 P.M. on 6 May; the arrests of suspects began shortly thereafter. The suspects were herded into the Nice racetrack, where military doctors checked the health of prisoners to make sure it would be compatible with detention. Those who passed the physical were sent to the Modane internment camp. The operation took a full day, with the Italian army's supply services ordered to prepare more than one thousand meals for all the prisoners and their guards.[98]

In spite of being the largest roundup to date and the expectation that it would catch hundreds, the result was underwhelming. As in most counter-insurgency theaters, massive dragnets seldom end up with significant results. For instance, in February 1942 the Italian occupation army in Slovenia built a fenced perimeter of barbed wire that surrounded the Slovenian capital city,

Ljubljana, an enormous feat that, in the minds of Italian commanders, would separate Slovenian Resistance leaders in the city from partisan units in the countryside.[99] This massive effort was followed in the summer of 1942 by a wide counterinsurgency sweep in the province that produced few results but alienated the local population.[100] The Italian operation in Nice was far from being successful, but at least, unlike the Slovenian operation, which cost the lives of thousand civilians and soldiers, it did not involve severe reprisals. Its results, however, were disappointing for the Italians: Vercellino's short telegram to the Italian Army General Staff on 8 May 1943 flatly stated that only 225 individuals had been arrested.[101] Communist fuoriusciti in the Alpes-Maritimes who had been responsible for several bombing attacks, including the one at the Caserne Dugommier, were arrested only a few months later, between June and July 1943.[102] In fact, according to a French police report, most of those arrested were not even communists, let alone fuoriusciti. Various notables, officials working in the Nice municipality, lawyers, engineers, and a few retired policemen and army officers, were among the victims of the raid.[103] Some of those who were arrested had no links whatsoever with the Resistance but were guilty only of having quarreled with their neighbors.[104] Indeed, the raid was flawed from the start, because the Italians' intelligence was based on unreliable sources such as local irredentists. The local commander may have been encouraged to use irredentist informants by an order from General Vercellino that directed the head of the Nice stronghold, the commander of the I CA division, to use the Nice Action Groups (GAN) to spread Italian propaganda.[105] Something went wrong, as, according to a French informant who had leaked confidential information garnered at a GAN reunion a few days after the raid, the Italian authorities were furious with local informants who used the army to win petty rivalries with neighbors. In the future, they declared, informants would be held responsible for their denunciations and would be punished for perjury if the denunciation proved to be groundless.[106]

In view of the unreliable intelligence, a few prisoners were freed within days.[107] The uneasiness in the Fourth Army high echelons over the faulty operation could explain the surprisingly lenient occupation policy of the Italian army in the following days. On 8 May the Italian army relaxed its grip by reducing the curfew to 11 P.M.–4 A.M., and theaters were again opened until 9 P.M. This decision would have been logical if the Italians had the feeling that the situation was calming down after the sweep of the communist organizations. However, one day before the curfew was reduced, on 7 May, the Italian army was attacked again. At noon two men on bicycles threw two bombs inside the Hotel Francia, which had been requisitioned by the occupation army.[108] The two bombs were intended to inflict maximum damage, being aimed at the officer's mess at a time when it normally would have been filled to its capacity. As fate would have it, lunch had been postponed that day and no one was injured.[109] Thus, surprisingly, the Fourth Army command had decided even after the bombing attack to lighten the occupation policy, probably in an attempt to avoid any escalation of violence.

However, the gamble did not pay off in the short term. The attack on the officers' mess was the first of a wave of strikes against the Italian army in May 1943. On 11 May an Italian motorcycle patrol was ambushed in Trinité-Victor, a hilly suburb north of Nice. Four men suffered minor injuries.[110] The day after, a bomb was thrown into an Italian military gas depot.[111] On 14 May a bomb exploded on the windowsill of a school in Marseille that housed Italian units in transit. Seven soldiers were injured and one of them died a few days later.[112] On 16 May another bomb exploded in Cannes near the barracks of a Fascist Milice unit, injuring one.[113] After every incident Italian local authorities enforced strict curfews and carried out roundups of citizens, choosing their targets from informers' lists and from among passersby, with little success in finding the real culprits. Many of those arrested were released very quickly.[114]

June 1943 was relatively uneventful if compared to the previous months. Few incidents of sabotage were recorded, and there were no direct attacks on Italian soldiers, apart from an officer in Nice who was found unconscious in an alley, having been beaten. However, the Italian army did not publicize the incident, allegedly because the attack stemmed from a dispute over a woman.[115] With much more serious consequences was the retaliation against an irredentist couple on 5 June 1943. Two individuals entered a cobbler's shop in Nice and shot the owner, Giuseppe Moraglia, and his wife, Serafina. The two murderers, later arrested by French police officers while fleeing the crime scene, were two Italian fuoriusciti, former members of the Italian Communist Party who had decided to punish the Moraglia couple, as they had been responsible for the arrest of anti-Fascists in Nice.[116] In a controversial decision the Italian commander of the Nice garrison, Gen. Giuseppe Andreoli, disarmed GAN members after the assassination and increased curfew hours, but only for GAN members. It is obvious that the Italian military commander feared that the GAN's desire for revenge would escalate the spiral of violence in the Alpes-Maritimes, and full-fledged civil war was the last thing the Italian commanders wanted when they needed to concentrate their meager resources on repelling a forthcoming invasion.[117]

July was a different scenario. Bombs detonated in front of French col-laborationists and Italian irredentists' stores, or on the threshold of Vichy organizations such as the Légion Française des Combattants.[118] Sabotage of railway tracks was frequent even near Italian outposts.[119] In fact, the Italians were so exasperated by the recurrent destruction of their lines of communication that at least in one instance they held hostages, threatening to detain them indefinitely if the perpetrators were not found.[120] However, the severity of this sabotage was nothing compared to the bombing attack on the Davico restaurant in Nice. At lunchtime on 20 July a man entered the restaurant, which was packed with Italian soldiers, and threw a bomb. The explosion left five people on the ground, three of them in critical condi-tion. One of the wounded, an Italian private, later died at the hospital. The other two who were severely injured were Nino Lamboglia, a university professor who had openly espoused irredentist ideas, and his secretary, each of whom suffered one leg amputated by the blast.[121] The true target of the attack had been the head of SIM in Nice, Major Valenti, who was having lunch with his collaborators.[122] The attack was publicly rebuked by French local authorities. The prefect released a statement that described the bombing attack as "loathsome and cowardly."[123] The Contrôle Postal revealed that even the local French population opposed the resisters, not out of sympathy for the Italian occupation army, but more out of fear of Italian reprisals. If nothing else, it certainly shows that French civilians were as weary of the war as Italian soldiers.[124]

Confronted with increasing Resistance activity in the region, Italian mili-tary authorities never really hardened their repression, which was also at-tested to by the low numbers of casualties directly tied to the occupation. Of the roughly one thousand individuals detained in Italian prisons in the ten months of the occupation, only two persons, a fifty-six-year-old American citizen and the president of the Nice Chamber of Commerce, Francesco Becchi, died as a result of their detention.[125] The two prisoners were not the only casualties tied to the Italian occupation period. In particular, two cases made the headlines. On the night of 9–10 January 1943, Giacomo D. C. of the Cadore Battalion escaped from his unit's prison, where he was being detained for having incited some comrades to desert, and fled in the night, taking with him a rifle and some hand grenades. His escape ended in tragedy a week later on the Savoy border. Driven by hunger, the soldier broke into a farm and killed its owner, a French border guard who had grown suspicious.[126] In another unfortunate instance, a gendarme in Digne was murdered by three Italian soldiers who had been caught poaching. The incident sparked widespread indignation in the small department of the Basses-Alpes. Local Italian authorities promptly reacted to defuse the crisis, a fact acknowledged in French reports. They immediately investigated and located the culprits, who were prosecuted in a military trial held in Digne and sentenced to twenty-two years each. The population was not entirely satisfied with the verdict, as they had demanded the death penalty. Yet the local command made the trial public and the judgment was passed quickly as a token of goodwill. Moreover, the Italian army donated an important sum of money to the gendarme's widow as compensation for the loss of her husband.[127] If in the instances of the two prisoners a fair share of responsibility for their deaths lay with the Italian army for its detention of individuals in frail health, in the latter two murder cases the responsibility of the Italian army was not so obvious. The murders were carried out by Italian soldiers who were disobeying orders and thus did not commit their crimes as soldiers of the Fourth Army. These crimes cannot be ascribed to Italian occupation policy. In fact, local Italian commanders incessantly warned sentinels to use their weapons only as a last resort, even against railway saboteurs.[128] Of course, the official reasons to avoid firing needlessly were very pragmatic, because the commanders considered a resister much more useful taken alive, so as to be interrogated. Nevertheless, it is plausible to think that army commanders also wanted to avoid having nervous sentinels shoot innocent passersby.[129]

To conclude, commanders of the Fourth Army managed to rein in their subordinates, eschewing any form of instinctive reaction. Indeed, the situation on the French Riviera was a far cry from the infernal cycle of reprisals and counter-reprisals that inflamed the Balkans, as Yugoslavian partisans incessantly ambushed Italian patrols and outposts, while Italian garrisons razed entire villages, shooting suspects and deporting its population. Vercellino's directives in the French Riviera never echoed the scathing words of an exasperated Gen. Mario Roatta, commander of the Italian occupation army in former Yugoslavia, who instructed his subordinated commanders to retaliate partisan attacks "not 'tooth for a tooth,' but by a 'head for a tooth.'"[130] Thus Italian commanders and Vichy authorities successfully brokered a pace that, albeit uneasy, did save the French Riviera from descending into the bottomless pit of guerrilla warfare.

Army Commanders against CIAF Officials

This low-profile approach irritated local irredentists and CIAF personnel, who believed the Italians should exploit this opportunity to start an Italianization if not an outright annexation. The CIAF, along with the foreign ministry, had a more political approach to the occupation and thus held different objectives than the military. Their long-term goal, reaffirmed incessantly in their reports, was the political, cultural, and economic integration of the Provence region into the Italian nation. As early as 1941 the Italian finance minister, Thaon de Revel, had commissioned a study to investigate how the Italians could penetrate the local economy by investing in crucial sectors such as tourism and the gaming industry (casinos).[131] Cultural integration was the task assigned to Nino Lamboglia, a university professor and curator of a local museum in Bordighera, an Italian village near Menton. Lamboglia, the author of several books underlining the Italian character of the County of Nice, had been watched carefully by the French police even before the occupation as he toured various Nice museums, taking pictures of documents and historic relics that could prove the Italian nature of the region.[132] For these activities Lamboglia was expelled from France in April 1941. In the wake of the Italian invasion, he returned to the Alpes-Maritimes and continued to inventory relics in Provence museums.[133]

Lamboglia's mission was only one facet of a wider plan for cultural penetration espoused by the Italian minister of culture, Giuseppe Bottai. A January 1943 memorandum from Bottai is especially revealing. The minister approved a project proposed by Senator Mattia Moresco, the director of the Istituto di Studi Liguri, for the creation of a program of Provençal studies.[134] The program would involve experts in different fields such as archeology and art history, linguistics and history, who would travel to France for research. The fact that the Istituto di Studi Liguri was known as a major cultural hub for irredentist scholars was a good hint at the overarching goal of the program. In fact, the memorandum explicitly underscored "the advisability that the military occupation of Nice and the Provence should be followed by an immediate cultural campaign which could be carried out by transferring some of the activities of the Institute to Nice, especially a few courses and conferences." This campaign, the memorandum continued, would stress Provence "as a Ligure, Roman, and Mediterranean land whose history and tradition . . . could be easily integrated into the Italian culture." It should be noted that the Italians were merely following the example of the Germans, who, in the wake of the German occupation, had allegedly brought to France "some scholars whose role was to underscore all the traits and documentation of the Germanic influx in France throughout the centuries." The culture minister concluded his memorandum by underlining the importance of this cultural campaign, which could greatly benefit the activities of the Italian foreign ministry and reinforce Italy's future territorial claim. Thus, it is evident that civilian Italian authorities were already laying the groundwork for the political annexation of occupied France. In February 1943, under the aegis of the Ministry of Culture, Lamboglia published a book with the evocative title of *Nizza nella Storia* (Nice in History), a monograph that explained the historical ties between Nice and Italy. Moreover, conferences were organized at the University of Nice to prove scientifically the cultural bonds between Provence and Italy.[135]

It was inevitable that these goals would clash with the moderate policies of the Italian army, which had no immediate interest in annexing the newly occupied territory. The growing battle between the two agencies led to the emasculation of the CIAF in March 1943, which thus became subordinated to the Fourth Army. Effective on 1 April the three CIAF military bureaus (army, navy, and air force) were integrated into the Fourth Army's administration. More important, the General Affairs Bureau in Turin was reduced to a liaison office linked to the Ministry of Foreign Affairs and now headed by Bonarelli di Castelbompiano, the ministry's liaison officer at the Fourth Army headquarters and, in this way, subordinated to the military as well.[136]

The official rationale behind these changes was to smooth the negotiation process between local Italian military and French authorities. Indeed, previously any communication between the local army commander and the French civil servants had to be channeled through both Italian and French chains of command via CIAF, the French liaison bureau attached in Turin, and finally to Vichy. Now the Italian local commanders could talk directly to local notables and needed to report only the results to Vercellino. However, the real reason behind this reorganization was the desire of the Italian army command to remove the CIAF from any matter that could impinge on the occupation. Local commanders seized control over a number of key responsibilities that had been assigned to the CIAF, such as the oversight of French army depots. The army also created *nuclei di collegamento e controllo* (control and liaison units), which were attached to the French prefectures without informing the CIAF presidency. These were expected to replace the CIAF delegations.[137]

One of the consequences of this reorganization was a severe disruption of the Italian informant network. Some officials who worked in France for CIAF under-commissions were dismissed from their jobs, which led to a serious break in the stream of information.[138] Thereafter, even the release of the CIAF fortnightly bulletin on the political and economic situation in the Italian occupation zone, which had been compiled by the various bureaus in France, became unreliable.[139] The head of the CIAF, Arturo Vacca Maggiolini, lamented the fact that the Fourth Army command refused to send a fortnight report, choosing instead to send a skimpy monthly report that left the CIAF in the dark as to what was happening in France. The CIAF had been reduced to a dry husk by the reorganization.[140] The true hub of power in the occupied zone had shifted to the headquarters of the Fourth Army in Menton.

The brewing conflict between the CIAF, backed up by the foreign ministry, and the Fourth Army, backed up by the Italian General Staff, had ended in a clear victory for the military. Fourth Army commands had complete control over policy in occupied France, while the CIAF's power now rapidly dwindled. The CIAF was increasingly attacked over both issues in terms of its legitimacy and its efficiency. In a memorandum issued on 16 July 1943, War Undersecretary Antonio Sorice wrote to the head of the Italian Army General Staff, Gen. Vittorio Ambrosio, openly accusing CIAF officials of holding their offices out of nepotism or favoritism (*raccomandati*). Sorice also claimed that CIAF personnel living in Turin were squandering the CIAF's budget on a life of luxury, inexcusable in a city that had suffered repeatedly from heavy Allied bombardments.[141] Sorice's indictment of CIAF officials echoed a deeper resentment on the part of the army quartered in France. The rank and file in the Fourth Army resented the special allowance given to CIAF members in France, especially after March 1943, when they had far fewer duties and responsibilities.[142] CIAF personnel in France were also suspected of using their offices to pursue their own private interests, by using their travel privileges to establish black market networks.[143]

Apart from the loss of prestige, it was evident that by the summer of 1943 the CIAF was outliving its purpose. Vacca Maggiolini threatened to resign several times and was stopped only by General Ambrosio's persuasiveness.[144] However, the general's soothing words could not hide the stark truth: CIAF had been reduced to a secondary role, far from any decision-making process, and was often bypassed by Fourth Army commanders. As an example, an Italian army convoy arrived at the Vernet internment camp in June 1943 to transfer most of its Italian prisoners farther east without even informing the Italian consul in Toulouse, who had been working incessantly for two years to speed up the liberation process of the internees. The bewildered consul found out about the operation only by chance the day after, when the commander in charge of the operation asked the consulate to send a telegram to warn the Fourth Army services of the incoming convoy. The consul was furious, as he felt that this had discredited the consulate in the eyes of local French and German authorities.[145]

No surprise, then, that CIAF officials struck back, criticizing the Italian army's policy. The CIAF delegate in Nice, Spechel, attacked the Fourth Army command after the attack at the Davico restaurant. With the support of the Italian foreign ministry, Spechel severely criticized the 9 P.M.–5 A.M. curfew imposed after the attack, questioning the usefulness of a nightly curfew and acidly noting that the bombing attack had happened in broad daylight in a public place "supposedly guarded by the Italian police and soldiers." The curfew would not only restrict civilians from having access to entertainment events in the evening but would also force "the population to shut themselves away in insalubrious and overcrowded neighborhoods." In fact, the consul argued that strict regulations such as these that impinged indiscriminately on everyone's life would drive a wedge between the Italian army and the local population, thus advancing the Resistance's goal of breeding a climate of suspicion in the Alpes-Maritimes.[146] The army's reply was venomous. General Vercellino belittled the CIAF delegate's argument as an example of "the simplistic mentality of an official, who, shortly after coming to Nice, already sees himself as the perfect judge of the situation." He went on to defend the Fourth Army's policy, affirming that the limited number of incidents was a clear demonstration that the Italian security policy was harsh enough to be a threat to possible resisters but lenient enough not to stir a massive uprising.[147]

Spechel's interest appears less the result of a genuine concern for the well-being of the local Italian and French community than the desire to avoid alienating the population, in anticipation of the future annexation of the County of Nice. His criticism, however, was unusual, as officials in the foreign ministry tended to complain more about the laxity of the Italian military policy in France than of its harshness as in the case of Spechel. At the end of May 1943, Foreign Minister Giuseppe Bastianini sent a reproachful report to General Ambrosio, deploring the complacent attitude of the army commanders, whose moderate and tolerant policy could be interpreted by the local Resistance as a sign of weakness. This situation was especially damaging to the Italian interests in regions targeted for future annexation, he thought. In fact, the foreign ministry was explicit that the policy should ideally "protect and indirectly favor the local separatist and irredentist movements while preventing any opposition to the Italian political penetration from French authorities and police."[148] The foreign minister's doubts stemmed from two venomous reports by the CIAF delegate in Corsica, Ugo Turcato, on Italian military policy in Corsica. The foreign ministry plenipotentiary made a jab at the local Italian commands by dismissing them as prone to "excessive tolerance and weakness" (*eccessiva tolleranza e debolezza*). He insisted that it would be necessary to shore up the Italian police, Blackshirts, and military forces on Corsica while cracking down on enemy radio propaganda. This hard-line approach would require an "energetic and resolute command." Moreover, the CIAF delegate had bitterly complained about being sidelined along with the irredentist movement in November 1942 while, conversely, Italian military commanders enjoyed a frank relationship with the Corsica prefect Paul Balley. The report concluded that a drastic change in occupation policy was necessary in light of the future annexation of the island.[149]

Turcato's harsh stance against Vichy authorities had not always been consistent. In June 1942, in another report to the foreign ministry, the Italian consul openly criticized the irredentist movement in Corsica and their "bungled actions" (*pasticci*). This time the Italian diplomat recommended a moderate tone to the propaganda that would "avoid directly bashing France, its institutions, especially its army," as many Corsicans considered themselves Frenchmen as much as Corsicans.[150] This surprising change of mind, which is akin to the evolution of the attitude toward the irredentist movement of the Nice CIAF delegation, can be explained by the evolving political-military situation in southeastern France. Before November 1942, CIAF delegates were wary of openly displaying annexationist ideas, as the very existence of the CIAF delegations was still contested by Vichy. After the Italian invasion, Italian CIAF delegates along with irredentist movements became bolder in their demands. However, the CIAF officials' attacks on the occupation policy of the Fourth Army were certainly part of a battle within the Fascist state between the army and the Italian foreign ministry. CIAF delegates, like Turcato, who dreamed of being nominated civil commissars with the same prerogatives as those in the Italian-occupied zone were outraged at being cast aside by local commanders and lashed back, complaining to their superiors about the alleged ineffectiveness of Italian units quartered in France.[151]

The above examples were reflective of the Italian commanders' conflict with CIAF officials over occupation policies. The criticism of the Fourth Army by the politicized staff of the Italian Armistice Commission arguably depended on the outrage of having been sidelined by the military authorities since November 1942. This jealousy, though, was heightened by the presumed leniency of the Italian military toward French nationalism and their coolness toward Italian irredentists. The biggest fear of the Fourth Army command was to further destabilize a situation that was already partially compromised by the inherent weakness of the Italian army's deployment in

150 THE ITALIAN OCCUPATION OF SOUTHEASTERN FRANCE

southeastern France. For an army that was already overstretched and suffering poor morale, the defense of the Mediterranean coastline would have been a daunting task in itself, let alone if they also had to deal with internal rebellion. Thus, the Italian commanders had to implement security measures that would disrupt the daily lives of the local population as little as possible. Moreover, any political rhetoric had to be set aside, as annexationist propaganda would probably be the best way to rally the whole population behind the banner of French revanchism.

Presidio Militare di Mentone

Il Comandante del Presidio Militare di Mentone rende noto che nella zona d'occupazione, compresa tra il vecchio confine e la linea d'armistizio, é fatto

divieto

1.) - di entrare in zona d'armistizio senza il prescritto salvacondotto o lasciapassare;

2.) - di transitare per i valichi non autorizzati;

3.) - di soffermarsi in prossimità di accantonamenti, postazioni od opere militari;

4.) - di portare binoccoli, macchine fotografiche e cinematografiche, eseguire disegni o rilievi e raccogliere dati di carattere militare;

5.) - di usare comunque teleobiettivi od obiettivi panoramici.

Nei casi di comprovata necessità *(motivi di lavoro, ecc.)*, saranno rilasciati, a richiesta, speciali permessi in deroga ai divieti di di cui ai n. 4 e 5.

I trasgressori alle disposizioni del presente bando saranno puniti a norma di Legge.

I CC. RR., la Milizia Confinaria e l'Autorità di P. S. sono incaricati della esecuzione del presente bando.

Dato a Mentone, il 7 Gennaio 1941 - XIX

Il Comandante del Presidio
Colonnello Mario Bellini

Tip. Mentone via Prato 6.

Poster issued by the Italian Military Commander in Menton, forbidding, among other things, entering the armistice zone without safe-conduct, to loiter around, take pictures, or sketch on paper military outposts or barracks, 7 January 1941. (Archives Municipales de Menton, 5Fi00194)

COMMISSARIATO CIVILE
DI MENTONE

IL COMMISSARIO CIVILE

Vista la necessità di effettuare il censimento degli appartamenti, negozi ecc.
di proprietà di cittadini inglesi, russi ed americani;

Visto l'art. 3 del Bando del DUCE 30 Luglio 1940 XVIII°;

ORDINA:

Art. 1

Tutti i proprietari di stabili situati in Mentone dovranno presentare - **entro il 25 Luglio 1941 - XIX.** - denuncia scritta al Commissario Civile degli appartamenti, negozi, alberghi, magazzini, autorimesse, ecc., concessi in affitto a cittadini di nazionalità inglese, russa, americana.

Art. 2

Le denuncie dovranno essere presentate su appositi stampati da ritirarsi a cura degli interessati presso il Commissariato Civile e dovranno contenere tutte le indicazioni richieste dal modulo stesso.

Art. 3

In assenza dei proprietari degli stabili sono tenuti a presentare le predette denuncie gli amministratori delegati, le agenzie incaricate, i custodi o i portinai.

I trasgressori alla presente ordinanza saranno denunciati a termini della legge di guerra.

Mentone, li 10 Luglio 1941 - XIX·

IL COMMISSARIO CIVILE
Virgilio Magris

Tip. Mentonesse - Via Prato, N . 10

Poster issued by the Menton civil commissar urging landlords to report apartments, shops, hotels, warehouses, etc. rented to English, Russian, or American citizens, 10 July 1941. (Archives Municipales de Menton, 5Fi00197)

Anniversary of the March on Rome, in Menton, 28 October 1941. (Archives Municipales de Menton, 5Fi00208)

Menton postcard, probably issued to promote internal tourism. (Archives Municipales de Menton, 3Fi00577)

A view of old historic Menton from the sea. (Archives Municipales de Menton, 3Fi00581)

French civilians with an Italian military doctor, date unknown, perhaps somewhere in the Alps. (Archivio dell'Ufficio Storico dello Stato Maggiore dell'Esercito)

Gen. Mario Vercellino, head of the
Italian occupation army in France.
(Archivio dell'Ufficio Storico dello
Stato Maggiore dell'Esercito)

Italian light tanks Fiat L6/40 entering Nice, November 1942. (Archivio dell'Ufficio
Storico dello Stato Maggiore dell'Esercito)

Italian soldier peering at the Mediterranean Sea, with a 75mm artillery gun taken from the French. (Archivio dell' Ufficio Storico dello Stato Maggiore dell'Esercito)

Italian guard post with Italian carabiniere, French gendarme, and Italian Alpine troops in the background. (Archivio dell'Ufficio Storico dello Stato Maggiore dell'Esercito)

CHAPTER 9

Collaboration and Accommodation

No military occupation rests solely on repressive measures alone; it also seeks a modus vivendi with the local population, whether coerced or not. These "collaborations" happened at various levels in occupied Europe, and their degree and extent certainly depended on the occupiers' policy. It was more difficult for a Pole and a Russian to collaborate with the German occupier than for a Dutch or Dane, as the former ranked at the bottom of the Nazi racial ladder. In other words, they were deemed unfit to live in the Nazi New Order, let alone to participate in its expansion.[1] On the other hand, Western Europeans occupied by Axis forces enjoyed much more room for maneuver, and thus were able, if willing, to enter, in Pétain's words, the "path of collaboration." Indeed, since the publication of Robert Paxton's groundbreaking book *Vichy France: Old Guard and New Order, 1940–1944,* it became much of a truism that the Vichy government, including not only its prime minister, Pierre Laval, but also Pétain himself, fully embraced the Collaboration d'État (state-level collaboration), whereby Vichy actively sought a collaboration beyond the armistice treaty in order to be considered a reliable partner in the prospective Nazi New Order.[2]

However, ordinary French also interacted with various degrees with the occupier, be it German or Italian. Philippe Burrin has divided these relationships into roughly three categories, which he labeled "accommodations."[3] The first accommodation is "a structural one imposed by the need to have public services that continue to function and an economy that does not collapse." That could be the case of French civil servants, such as the mayors who were asked to remain in office and take care of routine administration, and of entrepreneurs who were threatened to have their factories closed and their workers sent to forced labor in Germany if they did not comply with German demands. Those Frenchmen, cast by Werner Rings as "neutral collaborators," perfunctorily complied with the occupation authorities, not only for their own sake but also in the interest of the local community.[4] Theirs was an attitude with little ideological or political undertones and dictated by mere survival in a bleak wartime period, which, nonetheless, considerably helped the Axis war effort.

However, the desire to anticipate the needs of the occupier in return for material or social benefits was tempting for some. Those entering into "opportunist accommodations" sought to build sturdier bonds with the occupier, as, for instance, by participating in his celebrations, learning his language, or partaking in any other relationship not essential to someone's survival. The last category was probably the rarest of the three, if not the most outspoken and visible. "Political accommodations" entailed a firm belief in Axis propaganda and ideas, to the point of fully embracing its ideology, however morally despicable. This category encompassed people with different responsibilities, from Prime Minister Laval, who infamously proclaimed that he "hoped for German victory because without it tomorrow Bolshevism will be everywhere," to various individuals who willingly joined the German war effort on the eastern front as soldiers in the Wehrmacht (Légion des Volontaires Français contre le Bolchevisme, or LVF) and in the Waffen SS (33rd Waffen Division Charlemagne, or Charlemagne Division).[5]

The analysis of accommodation in the French Riviera presents some methodological hurdles that should be clarified. Its complexity, first of all, stems from the very nature of the sources used. From 1944 to 1949, in the wake of the liberation of France, in what was later dubbed the *Épuration légale* (legal purge), several *Cours of Justice*, one in each department, themselves regrouped into twenty-seven major ones (in the case of the French Riviera, Aix-en-Provence), were established by the ordinance of 26 June 1944 to prosecute individuals who had allegedly collaborated with the occupying powers.[6] More than 350,000 people were brought to trial, even though only 100,000 were eventually convicted.[7] Nice and the French Riviera in general were also the theater of violent reprisals against alleged collaborationists and Italian irredentists; in fact, it is possible some irredentists had already been killed by the summer of 1944.[8] Arguably, some testimonies can be dismissed as unreliable, as the accused downplayed their Fascist sentiments in order to avoid harsher penalties, or, on the other hand, rivals could embellish details to cast neighbor's quarrels as political. As a matter of fact, several factors such as the sheer number of cases, the difficult task of sorting reliable evidence based mostly on denunciations, and the dubious impartiality of courts made up of judges compromised with the Vichy regime, impacted the regular trial procedure in several French regions.[9] These limitations aside, the dossiers of the Cours of Justice in Nice are worth examining to grasp the motivations behind Italian nationals' accommodation.[10]

Tied to the irredentist community, those seeking a relationship with the occupants on political grounds were frequent visitors to Italian CIAF delegations, or Case d'Italia. Irredentists who were habitués of the parties at the consulate were identified as informers in the roundups carried out by the Italian police.[11] They often doubled as guards or ushers at CIAF delegations or at the Italian consulate in Monaco.[12] Emblematic was the case of Luigi T., nicknamed "the Death Messenger" (*Messaggero della Morte*) for his enthusiastic distribution of postcards calling on young Italians in Monaco to enlist.[13] A few individuals were even more useful, such as the building contractor who agreed to repair the Casa d'Italia of Nice free of charge.[14] The close relations between the local irredentist movement and CIAF delegations should not imply that irredentists had no ties with members of the occupation army. One of the most rabid Fascists in Nice, Guillaume Paolini, was a regular guest at the CIAF delegation, but he also had strong ties with the Fourth Army commanders, because he rented his garage to Italian officers. That explains why after being arrested by the French police for denouncing two neighbors, Paolini was released by an Italian military squad led by an angry officer who threatened to retaliate accordingly if the French police ever bothered Paolini again.[15] Most of these irredentists were sentenced to twenty years, but almost all were tried in absentia, having fled France as soon as they understood their cause was lost.[16]

The irredentist movement's impact on the Italian occupation should not be overestimated. During the postwar trials, in their vindictive search for collaborators, French prosecutors indicted for *intelligence avec l'ennemi* any individual who had had any relation whatsoever with either the CIAF or the Italian occupation army. To be sure, prosecutors pried into the defendant's past to look for a subscription or an endorsement of either the GAN, the March on Nice, or the Italian Fascist Party (PNF). To help them in the matter, the French police had found a list of the GAN and PNF adherents, twelve hundred names in all, carelessly left behind by hurried Italian officials when fleeing the Italian consulate of Nice in the summer of 1944.[17] It would be tempting to view the members of the GAN and the PNF as part of the irredentist movement in toto. Nevertheless, considerable evidence proves this link simplistic. Almost all the accused admitted being part of some Fascist organization, but many argued that they had been forced, swindled, or bribed to sign the paper. It also appears that irredentist recruiters inflated their numbers. One individual whose name was found on the GAN member list was a French police informer who had been tricked into signing a donation for the poor children of Italian emigrants in Nice that turned out to be a member form for the GAN.[18] Sometimes an emigrant was forced to subscribe; one resident in Beausoleil joined the PNF in order to spare his father, a well-known communist in the region, any trouble with Italian authorities.[19] In other cases the threat was more explicit; one irredentist recruiter warned a hesitant Italian that he could be shot and his parents living in Italy arrested if he did not embrace the irredentist cause.[20]

Even if it is assumed that all the people whose names were on the list retrieved in the Italian consulate were irredentists, it is clear that the Fascist and irredentist organizations represented only a small minority of the 150,000 Italians living in the department of the Alpes-Maritimes. Of course, this minority was extremely vocal, especially after the invasion of November 1942, and this explains the fear on the part of the French population of an Italianization led by irredentist leaders, as well as the targeting of individual pro-Fascist individuals by resisters. These irredentists, many of whom had emigrated in the 1930s and had integrated very poorly into the French social fabric, had been celebrating since June 1940 in anticipation of Nizza Italiana. "Nice is ours!" was the rallying cry in many irredentist circles.

Conversely, some Italian emigrants chose to ally with local Italian authorities because of the very tangible benefits that could come with it. Examples abound: One doctor joined the PNF as early as the 1930s in order to get a passport so that he could look after his businesses in Italy.[21] An Italian father registered his sons in the GILE (Gioventù Italiana del Littorio Estero), the Fascist youth organization established in 1937 to replace the Balilla organization, so that they could participate in holiday camps in Monaco.[22] Starting in 1943 many joined to avoid being conscripted into the Service du Travail Obligatoire.[23]

Opportunist accommodations were nowhere as evident as they were in business relationships. The Italian army had arrived in France with its own supply services, and the general staff's initial plan was to be fully autonomous of French suppliers. However, it became quickly evident that the Italian army would have to rely on local production, especially in foodstuffs, all the more so because the Italian peninsula itself was experiencing severe shortages. Therefore, Fourth Army commanders quickly established commercial ties with local producers, wholesalers, and retailers. At a grassroots level, grocery stores were often visited by Italian soldiers in search of staples to supplement their inadequate rations. It was not uncommon for Italian grocery owners to sell their goods, out of either patriotism or simple greed, to the Italian rank and file, in spite of Vichy's rationing regulations that forbade them to sell to anyone who did not have ration coupons for the corresponding staple.

Of course, some shrewd Italian entrepreneurs quickly realized that the presence of the Italian army was a boon that could be exploited profitably. A few individuals specialized in collecting manure from the horses of the Italian army, a lucrative business at a time when fertilizers were widely unavailable.[24] Wide profit margins were also made by businessmen who anticipated the needs of the Italian army, either by selling typewriters to the CIAF office in Nice and movie projectors to Italian units,[25] or by distributing coal and wood to heat the Italian barracks.[26]

In the tense atmosphere of a military occupation, these profitable relationships could backfire at once, as friendly entrepreneurs were often on the receiving end of French wounded nationalism. The case of Joseph C. is indeed emblematic. This Italian, who had spent sixty years of his sixty-eight years in France, was an entrepreneur with an established business in typewriters and cinema projectors. Recipient of the Chevalier de la Legion d'Honneur, an honor recognizing his participation in the First World War as part of the famous Garibaldiens de l'Argonne, Joseph C. was arrested in June 1940 and sent to an internment camp. The French accused him of having strong ties with the local Casa d'Italia, even though it appears his trips were not politically motivated. He was a prominent fund-raiser for the indigent in the Italian community. During his detention Joseph C. witnessed a Nice gendarme, Inspector Bagarre,[27] brutally attack an Italian irredentist, Ezio Cardone. The victim later denounced Bagarre, and Joseph C. agreed to testify. Bagarre was ultimately sentenced to fifteen days in prison and was temporarily dismissed from his job. After the war, having been reinstated to his office, Bagarre arrested Joseph C. Notwithstanding the fact that three of his sons were resisters, and that several Jews testified in his favor, the Italian entrepreneur was sentenced to two years for having had a business relationship with the CIAF and the Italian army. One could speculate as to how much Bagarre's influence, as well as the general climate of hatred of the Italians in postwar France, shaped the judgment.[28] In another controversial case, an Italian entrepreneur who had business relations with the Italian army started receiving death threats in the form of small coffins sent in packages to his mailbox. The businessperson was so scared that he complained to Italian officers. Fearing for his life and expecting the resisters to come to get him, he mistook German and Italian police officers for members of the Resistance and shot them through the door, severely injuring one. The Italian was clearly on the brink of paranoia. Later, two Frenchmen who had allegedly sent the coffins were arrested by the Italians.[29]

Profits made in time of severe austerities were widely regarded in postwar trials as illicit hoarding made by Italian immigrants, dismissed at that point as merely "guests" of France at a time when the population was enduring serious economic deprivation. In the vitriolic opinion of a French inspector, each of these individuals was "the typical Italian, who, after having profited from the French hospitality to earn an adequate living, had sided, when the time came, with those backstabbing France, probably as a way to thank us."[30] These entrepreneurs, in the minds of many French, were doubly guilty of having amassed a considerable fortune during the war years while helping the army of an enemy state. The popular opinion in postwar France cast them as Fascists or irredentists who maneuvered behind the scenes to prepare the ground for a future annexation. Of course, some of these Italians combined a flair for business with a staunch belief in the future Italian supremacy in southeastern France, but there was more to it than that.

The case of an Italian building contractor in Nice, Albert O., who was prosecuted in the aftermath of war for having worked for an enemy country, serves as a good example. The defendant's company had not been in good shape before the war, nor had its condition improved when the war started. His business was doing badly, as its chief clients were the local municipalities, which had had their funds drastically cut, one of the consequences of the enormous reparations that Vichy France was paying to Nazi Germany. In addition, and perhaps more significantly, many Italian businesses suffered from the backlash of the backstabbing of June 1940. The local population deserted Italian-owned stores and companies, as they did not want to fund what they deemed an Italian fifth column in the region.[31]

Albert O. and others like him, who were shunned by the French population regardless of their political ideas, were delighted to see a potentially good client, the Italian army, come to France. Albert O. testified that he was forced to work for the Italian Corps of Engineers, as otherwise his company would have been requisitioned. In the end, the defendant's company built three blockhouses and a few roads for the Italian army. However, while it is plausible that the Italians might have forced him to collaborate, it did not explain why Italian military engineers were often seen dining at his house. He did not refute the accusation, explaining that "speaking fluently Italian and working for them [the engineer officers], I had no reason to be on bad terms."[32] Thus, business relations could also easily lead to more intimate relations between occupiers and at least one segment of the occupied population, especially at a time when the Italian community in the Côte d'Azur felt ostracized by the majority of the French population.

Local Italian commanders who needed companies or local people to help their units settle or ameliorate their daily life in France opted for Italian civilians when they could, people with whom they could relate more easily, if just because of language, culture, and way of eating. Thus, strong friendships emerged from first hesitant contacts, built on inviting the soldiers to dinner or to have a drink, chatting, singing, and socializing in bars and shops. As Italy in the first half of the century was still the "Italy of the Thousand Bell Towers" (*L'Italia dei Mille Campanili*), one often related far more easily with people coming from the same region or even from the same city.[33] It was not uncommon for people coming from regions that had seen a consistent emigration toward France, such as Liguria or Piedmont, to meet close relatives and renew family ties even after decades.[34] Moreover, at a time when crossing the Italian-French border was very problematic for civilians, soldiers returning to Italy on leave were asked to carry packages and letters to the emigrants' relatives and to inquire about their whereabouts.[35]

Perhaps, then, extending Burrin's "accommodation" model, one could also see the attitude of Italian soldiers on the French Riviera as bent on opportunist accommodations. At a time of uncertainty for Italy's destiny and of deep melancholy, the Italians were eager to strike bargains to protect their short-term interests. Examples abound of symbiotic relationships between Italian occupiers and Italian occupied. An Italian from Cannes, having moved to the Alpine village of Isola for health reasons, immediately befriended the medical officer of the local Italian garrison, who kindly visited him and his mother-in-law at home.[36] An Italian villager in Castillon developed a steady friendship with the local commander, as his daughter worked as a nurse for the local unit.[37] In another mutually beneficial relationship, one Italian woman washed soldiers' clothes in return for food to supplement the meager rations of her children.[38]

This accommodating stance in the Italian rank and file had a positive effect on the mood of the occupation. A Vichy police report regarding the Basses-Alpes in May 1943 revealed that, because of the goodwill of both the soldiers and the populace, the atmosphere was much more serene.[39] By June, "thefts [committed by Italian soldiers] had more or less ceased."[40] By this time Italian soldiers had proven a boon to the local economy. Italian troops "[were] for some categories of shop owners such as coffee shop owners, watchmakers and perfumers a source of profit."[41] Moreover, many were impressed by the kindness of the Italian soldiers. A woman who had been run over by a car driven by a member of the Italian military was promptly taken by the soldiers themselves to the local hospital.[42] Relations also improved in the coastal regions. For example, the sub-prefect of Grasse took the time to write a letter to the I CA Italian commander to praise the deeds of two Italian soldiers who had helped French civilians put out a fire in a pasta factory.[43] At a grassroots level some Frenchmen were praising the Italian soldiers for being "good fellows" (*brave gens*) who were not terribly disruptive to French daily life. The local population therefore "no longer regretted that it was the Italians who were occupying [southeastern France] and not the Germans."[44] In some instances, relations between the Italians and the local population even became friendly, as in the case of an officer in Nice who gave some milk to a French family in return for their hospitality and "acts of kindness" (*gentilesses*) to him and his men.[45] Even attempts to export or import consumer goods in France sometimes hid more noble motivations. Some soldiers sought to help families in France who were having difficulty because of the extreme shortages of food. An Italian corporal gave eight loaves of bread, stolen from his unit kitchen, to a struggling Italian family in Nice who subsequently, on many occasions, invited him over to dine and washed his clothes as a token of gratitude.[46] This was not an isolated act. Another attempted to bring in illegal olive oil, eggs, and women's stockings as a way to thank his relatives in Nice for their hospitality.[47]

More ambivalent and complex were the relationships between the Italian men and local women. It would be a simplistic interpretation to view the relationships between soldiers of the Regio Esercito and local women only through the lens of prostitution. In many cases, local girls genuinely fell in love with Italian officers and soldiers in a way that strongly mirrored the relations between German soldiers and the derogatively called Filles aux Boches (literally, Girls for Krauts).[48] Nonetheless, both prostitutes and soldiers' lovers shared the common trait of being generally despised by the population. Every woman who befriended a soldier of either occupation army was almost immediately branded a harlot. Rich women were especially targeted, as their villas were often used by the Italian army to billet their officers, thus incidentally encouraging promiscuous contact between the Italians and their female hosts. After the war a fourteen-year-old girl was denounced by her neighbor for having indulged in a debauched life (*vie de débauche*) with Italian and, later, German soldiers. The denouncer, a sixty-year-old schoolteacher, was horrified by the scandalous attitude of the girl, who "embraced tenderly an Italian [soldier], each day a different one."[49] In another case a former Italian nun who had become a nurse for a rich widow was accused of an allegedly scandalous attitude regarding the Italian officers billeted in her employer's villa. A witness had seen her "hug [*embrasser*] three or four times" a few Italian officers. The neighbor was so outraged by the presence of what he considered a prostitute in a bourgeois neighborhood that he once yelled at her, "You lackey of Mussolini [*espèce de sale Mussolini*] would be better gone to a brothel than housed in a convent." Another neighbor accused the former nun of "dancing and laughing with Italian officers," an intolerable moral crime in Vichy France.[50]

As time went by, some relationships evolved into something stronger than simple flirtation. These love stories rarely enjoyed a happy ending owing to the fact that most of the Italian military left France precipitously in September 1943 with the declaration of the Italian armistice with the Allies. That was the case of a divorced Italian woman in the Alpine village of Isola who befriended a sergeant and then became his lover in February 1943. Against army regulations that forbade soldiers to live with women, the sergeant openly dated her and was extremely fond of her three small children, a godsend for an unemployed single woman with children to feed at a time of heavy rationing. The two had even talked about getting married. Unfortunately, the idyll lasted only a few months, until June 1943, when the sergeant's unit was sent back to Italy.[51] Sometimes women took drastic measures to continue the relationship in spite of the war. A twenty-one-year-old girl, tired of waiting for news from her fiancé, who had left Nice in September 1943, decided to cross the border in Menton illegally, paying a hefty two thousand francs to a guide, and then worked her way to her fiancé's town, only to be caught by German occupation forces in Italy and sent back to France.[52]

Such affairs were hardly surprising, given the fact that France was missing one and a half million of its men, who were in German prison camps and factories, and that the occupiers were largely young men in their prime. It is important to remember that promiscuous relationships between occupying soldiers and local women happened not only in France but throughout occupied Europe as well.[53] Women who fraternized with the enemy were unanimously vilified as deranged, either morally or psychologically, and after the war endured public scorn.[54]

In conclusion, the scenario of a demoralized yet life-enjoying army coupled with the complicity of a population that was culturally close to the occupiers created the conditions of several accommodations under the Mediterranean sun. However, they were much more multifaceted than believed by postwar French public opinion, who sentenced for intelligence avec l'ennemi and tagged as "dangerous irredentists" those who associated with Italian civil servants or soldiers. Postwar Nice courts acquitted several individuals who had been wrongly accused of misdeeds against the French nation by neighbors seeking revenge or to personal vendettas. In some cases it was evident that jealousy of a successful business could lead envious competitors to defame individuals. For instance, several Italian florists were falsely denounced in order to free up flower stalls in the Boulevard Thiers market, one of the most popular in Nice.[55] A bistro keeper enjoyed the same fate, as French prosecutors ultimately decided that merely serving Italian soldiers as regular clients was not on its own sufficient to qualify as intelligence avec l'ennemi.[56] In some rare cases, the Tribunal de Grande Instance (the superior court that handled indictable crimes) dismissed the charges, even if the accused had been found to have been an admirer of Mussolini until 1940, provided he could prove that he had not supported the irredentist goal of the annexation of the County of Nice.[57]

French police inspectors, however, were adamant that Italian nationals deserved little pity. They frequently accused the defendants of having repaid the generous hospitality of their host with pitiless betrayal. They therefore did not shirk from imploring the court to "show an exceptional vigor" in meting out "harsh punishments," as the defendants "should not again make a good deal."[58] In another words, many Italian collaborators were "the typical versatile Italian, who always try hard to benefit from present times."[59]

Indeed, one could agree to a certain extent with the French inspector that many Italians were able to cope with the new occupation authorities, thus weaving opportunist accommodations. Of course, whether the Italian emigrant fully grasped the severity of his or her action, every act or relationship with the military occupier carried out severe political implications. The Italian father who agreed to allow his kids to be taken under the wing of the consulate or the business accepting commissions from the Italian army may have suspected that his actions could eventually backfire, but in time of dire straits, short-term needs trumped long-term worries of being cast as enemies of France. And the above cases certainly warrant caution, as it is difficult for historians to cordon off politically motivated individuals from opportunists.

Serious Fascist militants in the Alpes-Maritimes, those who faithfully hung on the Duce's words, were outspoken in expressing their ideas in November 1942, their attitude in part tied to years of ostracism from the indigenous population. These poorly integrated immigrants, many coming from the lumpen proletariat, who had a hard time integrating in the interwar years, later used the Italian army's presence to settle the score with their neighbors, as in the case of Italian housewives in Marseille who shoved their way past rationing queues crying out for all to hear: "Priority to the victors!"[60] Yet these rallying cries remained stuck in the irredentists' throat as they realized in November 1942 that annexing the occupied territories was far from a priority for Italian military leaders. Fourth Army high-ranking officers were primarily interested in securing the shoreline in southeastern France from a possible Allied invasion while keeping a watchful eye for any local rebellion. Thus, while occasionally using them as informers, Italian military commanders refused to hand them weapons and never recognized their political associations. It was a wise policy, which not only had the short-term effect of avoiding the degradation of law and order during the occupation but also had the long-term consequence of avoiding ethnic clashes when the war ended.

CHAPTER 10

THE ITALIAN JEWISH POLICY IN FRANCE

This aspect of the Italian occupation has been without a doubt the most carefully examined by modern historiography since the end of the Second World War. As early as 1946, Léon Poliakov, one of the founders of the Centre de Documentation Juive Contemporaine published a book, *La condition des Juifs en France sous l'occupation italienne,* which first delineated how effectively Italian authorities in France had managed to shield the Jews in their occupation zone.[1] Later monographs have reinforced this paradigm, although some works more recently had questioned the extent of the Italian rescue.[2] It is important to examine the Jewish question again, however, as it sheds some light on the overall Italian occupation policy in southeastern France. The real debate lies in understanding the reasons for this surprising and lenient attitude. Yet only by setting the question in its historical context can one fully understand the motivations of the Italians.

The Italian Jewish policy could not be studied without first focusing on that of Vichy, as the former was a direct response to the latter. Arguably, though, Vichy's virulent hatred for the Jews was not borne out of the blue. In fact, French anti-Semitism had deep roots, beginning in the late nineteenth century with a surge of radical nationalism and conservative Catholicism. The nationalists considered the Jews a foreign body, insisting on their potential harmful influence on French society. Extremists in the Catholic movement insisted on the deicide nature of the Jews and their inherently destructive behavior. Indeed, the downfall of a Catholic banking house, the Union Générale, was blamed on speculations by the Jewish finance. All the anti-Semitic factions coalesced in France in the infamous Dreyfus Affair at the end of the century. Alfred Dreyfus, a Jewish artillery captain in the French army, was accused in 1894 of having smuggled military intelligence to the Germans. Subsequent trials revealed that many of the related documents under scrutiny had been forged. However, the general consensus held that Dreyfus was guilty: 80 percent of the press in France condemned him. Even if Dreyfus was ultimately vindicated, the trial revealed the underlying anti-Semitism of the time. A product of this brooding sentiment, L'Action Française, a nationalist movement with staunch anti-Semitic undertones and led by Charles Maurras, was born shortly after the end of the trial.[3] The First World War coincided with an ebb of anti-Jewish hatred in France as Jewish-French soldiers fought as valiantly as their Gentile fellows on the various fronts of the war. The economic crisis of the 1930s saw a resurgence of a rabid hatred of the Jews, a part of the wave of xenophobia spreading over Europe. The arrival in the 1930s of foreign Jews from all over Europe exacerbated this sentiment to the point that even French Jews resented this intrusion, for fear that a rush of new alien Jews could harm their long and painful process of assimilation into the French society.[4]

Indeed, indigenous anti-Semitism was heightened after June 1940 by the need to find scapegoats for one of the most egregious humiliations in the history of France. It is not much of a truism that Vichy's anti-Semitic policy had begun even before the Germans demanded the implementation of discriminatory measures. As a matter of fact, because most of the Vichy officials came from the conservative right, if not the extreme right, the Vichy regime from its inception had begun its own program of anti-Semitic discrimination, itself part of a wider xenophobic trend. Out of the fifteen thousand individuals who were stripped of their French nationality following the 22 July 1940 denaturalization law, more than six thousand were Jews. Racist activists in the traditionalist right-wing groups such as L'Action Française and in pro-collaboration newspapers such as *Je suis partout* and *Au pilori* were given free rein to spew their anti-Semitic rhetoric. Jews were unremittingly flagged as a foreign body in the fabric of French society. The 3 October 1940 Statut des Juifs (Jewish Statute), which forbade Jews to hold high-ranking public offices or comparable positions in media or teaching, officially launched *l'antisémitisme d'État* (state anti-Semitism).[5]

Vichy did not content itself with just ostracizing Jews from civilian society; it also actively sought to expel them from the free zone. It has been widely demonstrated that Vichy was instrumental in the pursuit of the Jews. It is important to note here that the anti-Semitic policies of Vichy and the Nazis differed, at least at the beginning, in one important aspect: whereas the Germans wanted to deport any Jew found in France regardless of nationality, Vichy initially sought to protect its nationals, both because of reasons of prestige and because there were veterans of the First World War among the French Jews. In a cynical example of realpolitik, they bartered the lives of foreign Jews for the safety, albeit in the end only temporarily, of French Jews.

The wickedness of this accommodating policy became glaring in the summer of 1942. On 4 July the head of the German police in France, SS Carl Oberg, and the secretary-general in charge of the French police, René Bousquet, struck a deal to dispose of the foreign Jewish population on French soil.[6] In the infamous *Rafle du Vél d'Hiver* (Vel d'Hiver Roundup) on 16 July 1942, thousands of French policemen rounded up more than twelve thousand Jews, who were later sent to extermination camps in Eastern Europe.[7] Of course, not all Vichy officials were fiercely anti-Semitic. Prime Minister Pierre Laval, for instance, was not so much anti-Semitic as he was a pragmatist. He used the Jews, especially foreign ones, as a bargaining chip in his endless negotiations with the Germans. But many Vichy civil servants, such as the heads of the Vichy's Commissariat General aux Questions Juives (Office for Jewish Affairs, or CGQJ), Xavier Vallat, and his successor, Louis Darquier de Pellepoix, who never hid their fierce hatred of the Jews and, along with pro-Nazi collaborationists, were always eager to use them as scapegoats for the woes of France.[8]

This was nowhere as evident as in the Alpes-Maritimes. After the occupation of the northern half of France, Jews started flocking to the French Riviera in great numbers, as wittily remarked by the playwright Tristan Bernard: "*Nous ne sommes pas à Cannes, mais à Kahn*" (We are not in Cannes, we are in Kahn).[9] This concentration of Jews ignited anti-Semitic propaganda in the region, which blamed the "rich Jews" for driving up food prices. The *nez crochus* (or hooked noses, as in anti-Semitic propaganda Jews were often portrayed as villainous individuals with hooked noses, full lips, and frizzy hair) were often accused of running black market operations, either by buying or selling illicit goods.[10] The Jewish population in the French Riviera was starting to feel the breath of the French police on the back of their neck, which made the same Tristan Bernard quip: "*Tous les comptes sont bloqués. Tous les Bloch sont comptés*" (All accounts are blocked. All Bloch are counted).[11] Racial hatred directed against the Jews erupted in violence on 16 June 1942 when PPF thugs pillaged the synagogue of Rue Deloye in Nice. The moment seemed ripe to tighten the noose around the Jews. The Bousquet-Oberg agreement paved the way for the roundup of approximately five hundred Jews in Nice on 26 August, mainly expatriates from Eastern Europe, Germany, Austria, and Russia, who were arrested and sent to the Drancy camp.[12] Prefect Ribière, who, along with Nice Police Intendant Duraffour, supervised the roundup, congratulated the police for "the way the [roundup] operations [of Jews] were carried out."[13] However, the greater part of the Nice population disapproved of the operation, so much so that the objects of their earlier scorn were now looked upon with pity.[14]

As a matter of fact, the massive roundups of Jews in the summer of 1942 and the heart-wrenching scene of entire families being violently deported struck a chord in the French public opinion.[15] French Catholic prelates openly expressed their disapproval of Vichy's policy for the first time.[16] The bishop of Montauban (Tarn-et-Garonne) voiced his outrage in an open letter that was read in all the churches of his diocese during the 30 August mass. Without ambiguity, the letter declared that "the current anti-Semitic measures are disrespectful of human dignity; the violation of the most sacred rights of the individual and of the family."[17] A few days later one of the most prominent figures of French Catholicism, Cardinal Pierre-Marie Gerlier, echoed Montauban's indignation in an open letter that stated, "We are witnessing a cruel scattering of families where nothing is spared, neither the aged, nor the frail or the ill."[18]

This opposition did not stop the government from pursuing its Jewish policy. Prodded by the German administration in France, which was already deporting Jews from the occupied zone to the east with the help of the French police, Vichy strove to send Jews from the free zone to the occupied zone, starting with foreign Jews. Vichy police, helped by the Sections d'Enquête et Contrôle, the security force of the CGQJ, unwaveringly hunted down Jews. The situation radicalized with the occupation of southern France in November 1942. On 10 December 1942, orders issued from Berlin demanded the immediate arrest and deportation of all Jews in France. One day later Laval signed a decree that required Jews to report to the nearest gendarmerie to have the word "Jew" stamped on their identity and rations cards.[19] This discriminatory measure was issued along with two other measures: Jews between the ages of eighteen and fifty-five of neutral or enemy nations were to be immediately incorporated into the Groupements de Travailleurs Étrangers, while Jews in coastline departments were to be transferred inland in the departments of Drôme and Ardèche.[20]

These later decisions sparked a flurry of reactions from both civilian and military Italian authorities, who felt Vichy authorities were interfering with the Italian occupation. The Italian CIAF delegate in Nice, Alberto Calisse, immediately pointed out to the prefect that Italian Jewish citizens were not subject to Vichy decrees.[21] The head of the Fourth Army general staff, General Trabucchi, issued a directive to all commanders on 30 December expressly pointing out that no Jew in the Italian occupation zone should be interned by Vichy authorities.[22] The opposition to any French action against the Jews was further confirmed by Inspector Barranco, the head of the political police in Nice, on 6 January 1943.[23] Barranco delineated the future Jewish policy of the Italian authorities in France: Jews were to be sent into forced residence in small villages in the Alpes-Maritimes and in the Basses-Alpes, preferably to hotels that could host the thousands of Jews of the Alpes-Maritimes without splitting up the families. Small Regio Esercito units would supervise and guard these Jewish refugees. In the opinion of Barranco, this policy would "answer a standard of justice and humanity" (*criterio di giustizia ed umanità*).

Not surprisingly, rumors of the Italians' benign attitude in the Alpes-Maritimes were already spreading like wildfire throughout France.[24] Jews flocked by the hundreds, if not thousands, to Nice, where they were received by a Jewish welfare organization, the Comité d'Aide aux Réfugiés (Refugees' Aid Committee, later known as the Comité Dubouchage, due to its location on Rue Dubouchage). The committee was informally recognized by the Italian authorities, and its importance should not be underestimated.[25] Aside from material aid, the committee issued temporary "identity cards," an important tool regularizing the positions of people permanently living on the margin of society. The identity cards de facto shielded the Jewish refugees from wanton deportation by the French authorities, as the refugees were selected by the Italians to be sent to forced residences.[26]

The rescue operations were organized by Angelo Mordechai Donati, a well-to-do Italian Jewish banker who had acquired an important position in France during the interwar years as president of the Chambre de Commerce Italo-Française (Franco-Italian Chamber of Commerce). Donati had settled in Nice after the French military defeat in June 1940 and continued his banking activities there, helped by the fact that he was extremely influential in Italian political circles, especially in the Italian foreign ministry. If the first CIAF delegate in Nice, Silvio Camerani, in his visceral anti-Semitism despised Donati, his successors' attitude was the exact opposite.[27] Count Mazzolini was an old friend, and their relationship dated back to their frontline experiences in the First World War, and even his successor, Consul Calisse, favored Donati's activities.[28] It is still a debate in academic literature whether Donati really had enough influence to soften Italian policy.[29] One thing is certain: his whereabouts were carefully scrutinized by the French. A police report in April 1943 mentioned his involvement in the rescue operations of the Jews flocking in Nice.[30] Moreover, an anonymous anti-Semitic report from June 1943, probably written by a militant member of a collaborationist group in Nice, denounced the nefarious influence of the "Jewish Pope" (*Pape des Juifs*) as the Côte d'Azur quickly became the "Jewish Paradise" (*Paradis des*

Juifs). In fact, Donati was not only hated by French anti-Semitic militants but also feared; he was allegedly an intimate friend of the Duce himself, and from the twisted perspective of the French pro-Nazis, that explained why whoever opposed him eventually ended up in an Italian concentration camp.[31]

In fact, the author of the virulent pamphlet was flabbergasted by the protection enjoyed by the Jewish community in southeastern France, a policy in glaring opposition not only to that of the Germans' but also to Vichy's. For this reason, on 14 January 1943 Prime Minister Laval complained to the Italian ambassador in Vichy, Avarna di Gualtieri, that the Italians were protecting not only the Italian Jews but the foreign Jews as well. As rightly asserted by Jonathan Steinberg, this later point was problematic for Vichy; the rescue of foreign Jews from deportation and even from French labor camps at a time when French Jews were being rounded up and sent to Eastern Europe was badly damaging to Vichy's prestige.[32] Indeed, the Jewish issue needs to be placed in the wider context of relations between Vichy and the Axis nations. The French brought this problem to their talks with the Germans. In a January 1943 meeting with the commander of the SS police in France, SS-Brigadefuehrer Oberg, René Bousquet, the secretary-general for the police in the Vichy ministry, bitterly complained about Italian CIAF authorities who were hindering the search for Jews in southeastern France.[33] Vichy authorities recognized that this was an issue they could use to drive a wedge between the two Axis partners while at the same time showing the Germans that they were willing to fully collaborate with them in their racial policy. Upon hearing about the situation in the Italian occupation zone, German officials in France vented their frustration to Berlin. High-ranking Nazi officials approached their Italian counterparts in late January and early February to inquire about the reasons for the Italian leniency. The German protestations eventually paid off. On 16 February the Fourth Army command communicated to the Oberbefehlshaber West (German Army Command in the West) that "dangerous Jewish elements" would be forcibly concentrated in places far from the coastline.[34] The tone of this document was harsh enough to reassure the Germans of the unity between Italian and German policy on this delicate aspect of the occupation. However, the directive of the general staff delivered to Italian local commanders, which established the forced residence of Jews and citizens of enemy states, took a much more neutral if not actually sympathetic tone toward the Jews. Jews were given a reasonable amount of time (five days) to reach their destinations, and both individuals older than sixty and women living alone were exempted from the directive.[35]

This directive appeased the Germans but did little to reassure the French, who were still dispossessed of their prerogatives in settling the Jewish question. It was only a matter of time before Italian Jewish policy would clash with Vichy's anti-Semitic campaign. At the end of February, the prefects of the Savoy departments, under precise directives from their government, which was seeking to meet German quotas for deportees to the east, organized roundups of foreign Jews. Italian military and CIAF authorities in the Savoy region instantly opposed, in many cases successfully, the deportations to the occupied zone. This position was confirmed in a telegram from the Italian General Staff to the Fourth Army command on 1 March, reiterating that French prefects did not have authority over any Jews, regardless of the Jews' nationality. Therefore, local commanders were required to prevent any action of Vichy authorities, if necessary by resorting to the arrest of any prefect tampering with the Italian policy.[36]

The Germans were certainly not impressed with the Italian army's opposition to the deportations. On 9 March, Joachim von Ribbentrop wrote a memorandum to the German ambassador in Rome, Hans Georg von Mackensen, asking him to suggest to the Duce that the task of rounding up Jews should be given to the French police, to the SS, or to the Italian Fascist police, because Regio Esercito cadres had proven unreliable. The Germans openly favored the third solution, as they thought the Polizia Politica would be as ruthless as the Gestapo in hunting down the Jews.[37]

At last, in the spring of 1943, it seemed indeed that the Italians would abide by the Nazi Jewish policy of massive deportations to the east. The Fourth Army was told by the Italian Army General Staff to refrain from intervening in the Jewish issue, handing over to Vichy or German authorities any Jew who had come to the Italian occupation zone after 26 March 1943.[38] Mussolini personally handpicked Guido Lospinoso as the new general police inspector to resolve the Jewish issue. The fact that Lospinoso was a police official who had worked in the Italian consulate in Nice in the 1930s tracking the fuoriusciti's activities in the Côte d'Azur was not reassuring to many Jews, who were worried that his nomination bore grim tidings. In fact, the Italians had no intention whatsoever in changing their Jewish policy. Lospinoso procrastinated, delaying his arrival in Nice until the beginning of May and refusing to meet with any German official for several weeks, thus sparking anger among SS clerks in France, who accused the new Italian official of having fallen under Donati's influence.[39] Indeed, in his recollections of the Nice period, Lospinoso mentions the crucial role of the omnipresent Jewish banker as the link between local Italian authorities and the Jewish community.[40] In addition, in a postwar interview with an

Italian newspaper, Lospinoso boasted about his role in saving the Jews.[41] However, Italian Jewish policy in France seems to have been an admirable concerto orchestrated between different musicians, perhaps coordinated by Lospinoso as director, rather than the work of a soloist. Neither the Italian police nor CIAF officials were willing to hand over the Jews to their German counterparts, and they both gladly supported the work of the Comité Dubouchage, which provided financial support for the rescue operation. The Italian army provided the logistical support needed to move the thousands of Jews from the coastline to the inland villages and the personnel to guard the Jews once there.

The "forced residences" were a godsend for cornered refugees who had nowhere to go. Nestled at the Alpine border with Italy, the village of Saint-Martin-Vésubie, gifted with snowfalls in the winter and cool mountain air in the summer, had been a popular tourist resort before the war. Its cozy chalets now became a marvelous haven for the exhausted Jews. The Italians were willing to let the Jews live as they saw fit, provided they stayed within the village and registered with the local Italian garrison twice a day. The Jewish refugees thus were able to recreate an authentic Jewish colony in the alpine villages.[42] For instance, in Saint-Martin-Vésubie, a local committee elected by the whole community was implemented to act as the vehicle for communicating any eventual issues or requests to the Italian military authorities. In what was probably a unique situation in Axis-occupied Europe, Jewish schools and synagogues were created.[43] In the words of a German Jew, "I saw some scenes I had not seen in a long time: Jews calmly strolling through the streets or sitting at tables outside cafés, chatting in English, German, and some in Yiddish."[44] Vichy Contrôle Postal confirmed that the Jews were ecstatic in their new residences: Italian soldiers were "kindhearted" (coeur d'or) and treated the Jews "in a very humane way." Indeed, the Jews were "extremely happy to be under the Italian army's protection."[45] In fact, the army was not only permitting the refugees to live a normal life, barring the fact that they were forbidden to officially work (some took the occasional odd job), but they were also shielding the refugees from Vichy's eager grasp. For instance, on 6 April, French gendarmes tried to arrest two Jewish women who had escaped a Vichy forced labor camp. The women not only refused to leave the village but also went to complain to the local Italian commander. Shortly thereafter, the local carabiniere commander chastised the two gendarmes by pointing out that the Jewish population in the village fell under Italian jurisdiction, and therefore the French police were not allowed to have any contact with them. It is impossible not to hear some irony in the Italian commander's words: "Notwithstanding the freedom they enjoy, you have to consider them as individuals living in a concentration camp surrounded by barbed wire, militarily guarded and which you should not come near."[46]

The Italians stayed true to their commitment to defend the Jews until the end of the occupation. Jews in increasingly great numbers flocked to the Italian occupation zone as rumors spread that the Italian zone was a safe haven for the Jewish population.[47] In July a Nice police report stressed the powerlessness of the French to stop the escape of Jews from Vichy labor camps to Italian army officials, who then redirected them to forced residence villages.[48] After the ousting of Mussolini on 25 July 1943 and the subsequent rumors of an imminent disengagement of the Italian army from the French front, Jews protected by the Italians stormed the Italian consulate in Nice to plead with the Italian authorities to send them to Italy. Even a harsh life in Italian concentration camps, they desperately cried, was a more preferable fate than to fall again into German clutches.[49] The urgency of the situation in occupied France was acknowledged by the Italian foreign ministry, which authorized its officials in France to give safe-conduct to Italian Jews requesting repatriation, even without the previous screening of the Italian interior ministry that was usually required.[50] Moreover, until the last days of August, when it was evident that the Italians would be leaving France soon, Italian authorities were still protecting the Jews from being drafted to the Service du Travail Obligatoire (STO) or to forced labor camps. This resolute stance triggered formal protests from Prime Minister Laval, who feared that the prestige of the Vichy regime would be seriously compromised if the Jews were exempted from the STO at a time when entire classes of young Frenchmen were forcefully sent in Germany.[51]

The last days of the Italian occupation were even more frantic. In early September the Italian army, under Lospinoso's directive, moved Jewish refugees who had been housed in inland villages closer to the Italian border in anticipation of a precipitous flight across the border.[52] A few days before the 9 September Italian armistice with the Allies, many Jews were transferred to Nice.[53] Donati was even working on persuading the Italian navy to lend some of their ships so as to bring the Jews to Italy. The operation fizzled, however, due to the utter panic that followed the announcement of the armistice, and for thousands of foreign Jews, Nice would become a grim trap where the Germans could hunt them down easily.[54] If the Italian authorities failed to organize a comprehensive plan to move the Jews to Italy, some local commanders took the initiative to bring their protégés with them when they withdrew to Italy.[55] That was the case in the alpine village of Saint-Martin-Vésubie. The local commander, Lt. Federico Strobino, upon hearing of the armistice, immediately phoned the commander of the garrison of Cuneo, the city on the other side of the border, to inquire about a structure that could house hundreds of Jewish refugees. Upon receiving an affirmative response, with the help of local Jewish leaders, Strobino set in motion the evacuation of the Jews in the village. Long columns of Jews escorted by Italian soldiers fled the village to cross the border through the Col des Fenêtres. The biblical exodus was a difficult trek, as the trail peaked at more than two thousand meters and was more than fifteen kilometers long. This trip, which would require quite an effort even for experienced hikers, was an excruciating experience for individuals heavily loaded with luggage, some of whom were either too young or too old to walk at more than a slow pace. The worst part, however, was probably the terror of the doom that was quickly approaching from behind, a nightmare that cornered Jews knew well enough. Yet it was not only this grave danger of being captured by the Germans that ultimately motivated frightened Jews to run for their lives over a difficult mountain trail. In a generous gesture, Italian soldiers set up supply points in chalets along the trail to aid the Jews on the journey across the border. Hundreds of Jews made it to Italy, but unfortunately the Germans, anticipating the flight across the Alps, had already occupied the Italian side and arrested most of the Jewish refugees, along with their Italian guides.[56]

The grim outcome of the Jewish odyssey should not diminish the significance of Italian soldiers risking their lives to save Jewish civilians at a time of stressful political turmoil on the Italian peninsula. Yet if historians agree that the Italian Jewish policy in France was in flagrant opposition to those of Vichy and the Germans, the academic community is much more divided on the reasons behind this choice, especially since the Italian protection of Jews fueled the myth of the Italiani Brava Gente in the immediate postwar.[57] Léon Poliakov and Hannah Arendt argue that the traditional humanism of the Italian people explained their generosity toward the Jews.[58] This paradigm has been refined by modern authors. Jonathan Steinberg, for instance, contrasts the modern German nation, where anti-Semitism grassroots operations were rampant, to the modern Italian nation, where Jews accounted for only a tiny part of the population and were well integrated in the Italian social fabric. As a matter of fact, anti-Semitism, especially in its biological form, was foreign to the Italian tradition. While German officers were trapped in their tradition of blind obedience and martial efficacy, their Italian counterparts were more traditional in their beliefs, which emphasized both the Catholic piety and the enlightened values of the *civiltà italiana*.[59] Daniel Carpi, on the other hand, emphasizes the absence of anti-Semitism in Italian army cadres and civil officials, attributing it to the failure of the Fascist regime to change the minds of its citizens.[60] Steinberg and Carpi also stress that Italian humanism was not the only factor explaining the benevolent policy of the Italians in southeastern France; political calculations were also involved in the Italian decision to save the Jews. Italian army leaders considered it their right to carry out any policy they deemed fit in southeastern France while CIAF officials were also interested in delegitimizing the Vichy regime in order to prepare for the future incorporation of the irredentist lands into Italy. Therefore, their behavior was part of a strategy to assert Italy's sovereignty on the former free zone. The Italians also endeavored to demarcate their occupation from that of the Germans in order to stress the fact that they were capable of coming up with an independent policy, reinforcing their position that Italy should be treated on an equal footing with Vichy in the Axis negotiations.[61]

This pragmatist perspective on the Italian Jewish policy in southeastern France has been strongly argued by both Jean-Louis Panicacci and Davide Rodogno. Panicacci insists on the fact that Italian benevolence was also the product of their farsightedness. Financial holdings of the Italian royal family, Vatican prelates, and even of high-ranking Fascist officials were deposited in American banks. Thus, the Italians did everything to endear the United States, whose Congress allegedly had a powerful Jewish lobby, in order to avoid having their assets frozen.[62] Both Panicacci and Rodogno note that the Jews were merely pawns in the complex relations between the Fascist, Nazi, and Vichy regimes. In fact, the Jewish question was often used by local Italian authorities to challenge any interference from Vichy and the Germans in what Italians saw as their zone of influence. Rodogno, however, goes further, minimizing the Italian efforts and insisting that there was no overarching policy to save the Jewish refugees, but only localized cases of bribed soldiers, whose slackness allowed the escape of cornered Jews.[63]

While it is much of a truism that the lack of discipline in the Italian army and the Italian desire to affirm their sovereignty played a strong role in shaping the Italian policy, these two factors do not themselves explain the soft Italian policy with regard to the Jewish question in France. Indeed, if it was only a question of asserting one's authority in the newly occupied territory, the Italians could have herded the Jews into concentration camps and then eventually dispatched them to the Germans without going through Vichy's security agents. In this case they could have maintained their sovereignty in the newly occupied zone without annoying their senior partner. Rodogno rightly asserts that the Jews were never a high priority for Italian commanders; indeed it is odd that they did not get rid of the Jewish refugees in the first months of the occupation. If nothing else, this cold, pragmatic policy would have had the double advantage of not having to use human and logistical resources to guard them later while in the meantime discouraging any Jewish refugee living in the occupied zone to travel to the Italian one. Thus, it is difficult to dismiss the Italian approach as coldly pragmatic. In fact, the absence of anti-Semitism among both Italian army cadres and foreign ministry officials is glaring and has been noted by many historians.[64] Italian officials were aware of the atrocities perpetrated by the Germans in Eastern Europe and of the fate awaiting the Jewish population in Europe. The Italian ambassador in Berlin, Dino Alfieri, for instance, sent a poignant memorandum to the foreign ministry, denouncing in shocking details the harrowing conditions of German concentration camps.[65] Other officials had been probably firsthand witnesses of German atrocities, like the Italian CIAF delegate in Nice, Calisse, who served as Italian consul in Sarajevo during the war. Moreover, it is unthinkable that a Jewish man such as Donati, regardless of his real influence with Italian local and national authorities, could have otherwise enjoyed any leeway in the Nazi inner circles.

The Italian policy of shielding Jews was effective until September 1943 because it was one of the only aspects of the Italian occupation on which army and CIAF officials wholeheartedly agreed. There is no hint to any dissension from Italian documents regarding this generous stance, and all Italian officials collaborated in it without exception. Even the irredentist movement failed to show any anti-Semitic signs. Of course, that does not mean the Italian state was bereft of anti-Semitic people, but at least in France they were certainly kept at bay. The Jews were certainly favored by the fact that they did not represent a threat to the security of the Italian army or to the ambitions of Italian expansionists. In that regard the Italian Jewish policy could be seen as a pragmatic one, careful enough not to stir up conflicts or create problems that were not directly tied to security matters. However, the Italians did not passively ignore the Jews, but actively assisted them and bettered their lives. Only the unfortunate events following the armistice meant that fewer Jews could be saved.

CHAPTER 11

DRAWING THE CURTAIN
ON THE OCCUPATION

The end of the Italian occupation of southeastern France was much more dramatic than its beginning. The disorganization of the Italian army, along with the sudden announcement of the armistice, changed what should have been a gradual disengagement from southeastern France to a complete rout back into Italy. This dramatic collapse made manifest not only the weaknesses of the Italian army, in the frailty of its logistic network and the poor morale of its soldiers, but also its strengths, in the form of a moderate policy that was not seriously questioned even in the last frenetic moments of the occupation.

The demise of the Italian military occupation in France paradoxically started right after Italian soldiers' hobnailed boots were traipsing into the French Riviera. To be sure, over the winter of 1942–1943 the plummeting of the standard of living in the peninsula due to incessant Allied bombings, disheartening food rationing, and fragmented news on foreign theaters of war swelled the number of Fascist notables, among them the Duce's son-in-law Galeazzo Ciano and the head of the Italian General Staff, Gen. Vittorio Ambrosio, who had had enough of Mussolini's disgraceful war strategy. In the Fascist Grand Council meeting of 25 July 1943, most of the twenty-six delegates voted against the Duce's motion to continue the war at the side of the Axis. A few hours later the Duce was dismissed by the Italian king, Vittorio Emanuele III.[1] This decision was a clear repudiation of the imperialist and aggressive policy of the Fascist regime. It was evident to many soldiers of the Fourth Army that the new government would soon order a withdrawal from the former free zone. The news of the king's decision and the hope of rapid repatriation sparked scenes of euphoria in soldiers and officers alike. According to a report by the prefect of the Hautes-Alpes, later confirmed by postwar interviews with former soldiers of the Fourth Army,

Italian troops cheered the news of Mussolini's demise to the point that officers "were celebrating with champagne" (*sabler avec le champagne*).[2] Italian commanders were certainly happy that the Duce had been replaced by Marshal Pietro Badoglio, a former army general who was loyal to the monarchy, but their joy was also tempered by the fear of a collapse of the already poor discipline in the Fourth Army. For this reason, on 27 July, Vercellino urgently sent a telegram to all units complaining about "the jubilation with debauchery and sustained squalls" (*esultanza con gozzoviglie e schiamazzi prolungati*), especially on the part of some Fourth Army officers. Vercellino tried to bolster morale by reminding the men that the waning of the Fascist regime was not the prelude to the end of the war and that the Allies were still fighting for "unconditional surrender" by Italy.[3] In another directive on 1 August, the Fourth Army commander reiterated his point by urging officers to avoid using the word "peace" at all cost.[4]

However, the political situation in Italy was rapidly evolving. The Badoglio government was trying to demarcate itself from the former regime. Italian soldiers were invited to refrain from any political activity or manifestation, and it was particularly meaningful that the order came from the new MSVN (Milizia Volontaria per la Sicurezza Nazionale, or Voluntary Militia for National Security—i.e., Blackshirts) national commander, Gen. Quirino Armellini.[5] Moreover, all outward Fascist symbols were being expunged. On 29 July the Roman salute, along with Fascist symbols such as the Littorio (a bound bundle of wooden rods symbolizing power and prestige), as well as Fascist mottos, were officially abolished.[6] Of course, asking soldiers who had been indoctrinated for years of Fascist propaganda to now instantly abandon the doctrine would have been, at minimum, very upsetting. The younger generation of soldiers especially, who had been schooled in Fascist principles and rhetoric their entire lives, was completely at a loss now that its absolute ruler had been removed like a common politician.

In fact, despite the continuous calls to order by the Fourth Army command, evidence that the end of the war was approaching led to the disintegration of army morale and discipline. Endemic issues of the entire Italian occupation, such as soldiers and officers openly familiarizing with local girls, became widespread to the point that it happened even "in smaller villages and even in the countryside, at every hour during the day and night, even in spite of curfews."[7] Indeed, Vercellino insisted that the death of an Italian border guard gunned down on 2 August near the Swiss border was more the result of poor enforcement of security measures than the partisans' prowess.[8] More important, soldiers were found singing "subversive songs," probably communist hymns such as "*Bandiera Rossa*" (Red Flag).[9] Yet these songs were much more than just symptoms of a profound malaise within the Italian army. They were also evidence that the Resistance was actively recruiting, and with a certain degree of success. Indeed, the downfall of the Fascist regime had been a boon for the fuoriusciti recruiters. The Italian General Staff sent an alarming report to the Fourth Army command that the fuoriusciti were intensifying their efforts to infiltrate the Fourth Army with propaganda and to expatriate in Italy, taking advantage of the confusion at the porous Italian-French border.[10] Moreover, in some regions, such as the Savoy and Corsica, the Resistance radicalized by killing and wounding Italian civilians and soldiers in ambushes and bombing attacks.[11]

Italian army cadres blamed these acts of violence on the inability of the French police to thwart Resistance attacks, even accusing them of outright complicity with the resisters. For this reason the Fourth Army command imposed draconian rules on the population.[12] The *Bando Vercellino* (Vercellino Proclamation), published by French newspapers in the Italian-occupied zone on 17 August 1943, ordered the death penalty for a wide variety of crimes ranging from the sabotage of military and communication infrastructure, to armed insurrection, to harming Italian soldiers and organizing into "subversive" groups. Even simply articulating leftist ideas (defined as "forwarding the violent implementation of a dictatorship of one social class, or the extermination of one social class, or the subversion of economical, political and social structures") could lead to a sentence of two to eight years in prison.[13] In reality the punishments were seldom carried out, except in Corsica and Haute-Savoie, two regions that had been unruly since the beginning of the Italian occupation.[14] On the contrary, the Fourth Army command asked local newspapers all over the occupied zone to publish a subsequent proclamation that granted amnesty to all those who by the end of August chose to surrender their weapons.[15] In all probability this clemency was dictated by the will of the occupying army to avert an escalation of an internal rebellion in a time of crisis. Moreover, it is true that the Italians had dismantled the two most important Resistance organizations in the Alpes-Maritimes: the Italian communist Resistance and the French Armée Secrète in the summer of 1943.[16]

Starting in late July 1943 the Italians set in motion their gradual disengagement from southeastern France.[17] In theory all units, with the exception of a few coastal divisions, were supposed to return to Italy by midnight on 9 September. Officially the Italians were moving their troops from France in order to shore up Italy's defenses, fearing that the Allies would soon attempt to invade the peninsula after their successful landing in Sicily in mid-July (Operation Husky). In hindsight one could not help but think that the Italians were also moving their troops out of the various theaters of war in preparation for an incoming reversal of alliance. However, the Germans were no dupes. The Nazi leadership already had been very suspicious of its erstwhile ally long before the ousting of Mussolini, as the master plan to disarm and subdue Italian units in France, code-named "Operation Alaric," had been drawn up as early as May 1943.[18] Undeniably, the Italian General Staff's hurried decision to withdraw important units from Provence did little to quell German suspicion. CIAF officials noted, "German officials are still polite, but any sentiment of camaraderie has vanished from their side."[19] An Italian army report, based on CIAF information, underlined that in SS circles the disengagement from France "was seen as a betrayal, and further heightened the feeling of antipathy against Italy, which had lain dormant until now."[20] At a meeting in Casalecchio between Italian and German military leaders on 15 August 1943, Gen. Alfred Jodl, the chief of the operations staff of the German Armed Forces High Command, ironically asked the head of the Italian Army's General Staff, General Roatta, if the units withdrawn from France "would be deployed in southern Italy or near the Resia and Brenner Pass [across the Italian-German border]."[21]

The Germans shrewdly played on the Italian need for extra units to bolster the peninsula's coastal defense in order to send some Wehrmacht units to Italy.[22] Of course, the real motivation behind the deployment of German units in Italy was to intimidate Italian local commanders and, if needed, to intervene in case of an Italian betrayal. More than anything, at the beginning, the movement of a substantial number of troops into the Italian occupation zone en route to the Italian territory unnerved the Italian soldiers. In the summer of 1943 friction between Italian and German soldiers became widespread. Local Italian commanders bitterly complained that the German soldiers and officers were arrogant and completely disregarded all Italian decrees, whether pertaining to traffic, the purchase of goods, or even regulation of private property.[23] Wehrmacht personnel were especially inclined to break Italian curfews, giving false permits to French bistro owners that allowed them to keep their establishments open. Italian patrols were flabbergasted by the lack of discipline on the part of the noisy and boisterous Germans who kept reveling all night long. In a few cases the officers offered the weak excuse that they did not know about the curfews, but in most cases they simply ignored Italian directives.[24] More important, German units in transit settled near Italian quarters "behaving like masters of the house, carrying out artillery barrages, marches and drills with the intent to intimidate" (*a scopo intimidatorio*).[25] It was glaringly clear that the fall of the Fascist regime had definitely strained relations between the Axis partners at all levels. Germans and Italians warily watched each other, each expecting the other to make the fatal move that would shatter the coalition.

The forty-five days between the Duce's dismissal and the armistice were tense in the Côte d'Azur but did nothing to prepare for the massive drama that unfolded on 8 September 1943, the date of the most terrible military disaster in the history of Italy. On 3 September 1943 the Fourth Army command received a directive called "Memoria 44" from the Italian Army General Staff, which outlined the plan to be carried out in the event of a German attack. Italian units in France were to be deployed to protect the main axes of communication and the passes at the border to counter any German invasion of Italy from France. In addition, the Italians were directed to attempt to outflank and attack any German troops either while on the move or while resting after marching. However, it is important to note that the directive gave absolutely no hint of the Italian-Allied negotiations that were ongoing at that time.[26]

In retrospect this directive was no more than wishful thinking. Italian units were extremely demoralized, as most of the soldiers could not wait to see the end of the war and to be repatriated. Their sense of loss was heightened by their poor armament, and the comparison with the highly efficient motorized German units replete with tanks and armored cars was unforgiving. The nail in the coffin of the Italian hopes to stop the German army was dealt by the 8 September armistice. Much ink has been spilled about the armistice between the Italians and the Allied powers.[27] All authors agree on the fact that the higher echelons of the Italian army were not left completely in the dark regarding the negotiations with the Allies. However, they were also not given any timetable for the imminent reversal of alliance. Of course, the confusion had originated from the botched negotiations between the two sides, which led to the armistice being signed on 3 September but announced by the Allies only on 8 September 1943 at 6.30 P.M., and then, still only unilaterally. This in turn forced the Italian king, Vittorio Emanuele, and the head of the government, General Badoglio, to make the armistice public on Italian radio one hour later. As incredible as it seems, the armistice declaration caught the entire Italian army off guard, as previously no warnings had been sent to army commands.

This inexcusable mistake proved even graver for Italian units quartered outside the peninsula. Military leaders of the Fourth Army command were shocked to hear of the armistice. General Trabucchi, the head of the Fourth Army General Staff, immediately phoned the Italian Army General Staff, only to be told that even its head, General Roatta, had found about the armistice only through the Allied radio broadcast and that the Fourth Army command was now on its own.[28] The appalling lack of directive from Rome doomed the Fourth Army. Each commander or soldier reacted with frantic panic in an atmosphere of "every man for himself." Soldiers were still scattered haphazardly all over the Mediterranean coastline, from Toulon to La Spezia, as some divisions were still in the process of transferring part of their units to Italy. This situation led to some grotesque scenes, such as in the case of the head of the Pusteria Division, General Magliano, who was arrested, along with his general staff, while dining with the commander of the local German garrison.[29] In most cases the Germans had little difficulty in disarming and arresting their former allies. German commanders surrounded the headquarters of the local Italian unit with tanks, artillery guns, and heavy machine guns, ordering the Italians to surrender. Disoriented members of the Regio Esercito, who until a few days earlier had been ordered to fraternize with their Wehrmacht colleagues, surrendered en masse, feeling abandoned by Rome. Remarkably, in some cases the Italians fought back vigorously. In Albertville, a city in Savoy, members of the Val Toce and Val d'Orco regiments fought through the night, cornered inside their barracks, killing four German soldiers and surrendering only at dawn. The city of Grenoble, the capital of the Isère department, saw a full-fledged confrontation that allegedly resulted in hundreds of casualties on both sides. The small Italian garrison in the Nice railway station refused to surrender and entered into hand-to-hand combat with the Germans in a "last-ditch stand."[30]

When the Italians were well led by resolute officers and were not confronted with overwhelming odds, they managed to counterattack with surprising efficaciousness, given the circumstances. A few units slowed down the German advance by blowing up crucial bridges and tunnels leading to Italy.[31] In the end, though, these *barouds d'honneur* did little to minimize the epic military disaster. The fate of the Italian soldiers was already sealed when the king, along with General Badoglio and the government, failed to inform the army of the armistice and then fled from Rome to southeastern Italy. Vercellino, who had managed to retreat with part of the Fourth Army command to Cuneo, a city across the Italian border, was forced to sign a directive officially disbanding the Fourth Army on 12 September 1943.[32] Thus ended, rather disgracefully, the Italian occupation of France, three years of occupation of a foreign soil that had gained only minimal resources for the Italian war machine and less prestige for the Italian state in exchange for continuous political, strategic, and military trouble.

The end of the occupation eerily matched its beginnings in June 1940 and September 1942, both in its strategic improvisation and utter disorganization. The local population was extremely surprised to see the Italian troops pick up and leave so precipitously, in an incredible din that turned into a complete debacle. A French truck driver in Saorge was forcefully recruited at gunpoint by an Italian officer to drive his vehicle, instantly loaded with Italian soldiers, to the Italian border.[33] In Breil soldiers sold their remaining Italian military stocks of food to the local population.[34] In one instance, in compensation for the occupation, generous officers willingly left military materiel such as trucks and gas tanks for the use of the local population.[35] In most cases, though, Italian troops hurriedly fled to the border, carrying with them a minimal amount of food or their personal weapons while leaving behind their ammunition and food depots to be plundered by the local population.[36] Soldiers threw away their weapons and ammunition in the bushes, unfortunately resulting in a few incidents of children naively detonating Italian grenades left behind by hurried soldiers.[37]

It is difficult to estimate how many soldiers of the Fourth Army were captured by the Germans in the days following the armistice. Scholars seem to agree that at least sixty-two thousand soldiers of the Fourth Army, thirty-seven thousand of whom were formerly stationed in France, ended up in German prison camps.[38] In some cases Wehrmacht commanders anticipated the moves of Italian units trying to escape their stranglehold in southeastern France. For instance, German soldiers intercepted an Italian truck convoy in Barcelonnette that had departed from Digne and was heading for the border.[39] Other Italian soldiers were even less lucky. An Italian soldier who, in an act of desperation, had clung to the back of a departing truck was mortally wounded by incoming German troops in Mont Agel.[40] Another one was found drowned in the river Tinée one week after the armistice.[41] Not all the Italians were captured by the Germans, however. Some found refuge in the mountains or were hidden by the local population. The Germans, of course, tried to dissuade the population from assisting the fugitives by posting bilingual posters that grimly reminded everyone that helping any Italian straggler or taking Italian weapons was considered a crime punishable by death.[42] Yet part of the local population, even the French segment, was quite sympathetic to the Italian soldiers' pleas of being stranded in a hostile territory controlled by an army who regarded them as traitors. A report from the Var prefect made clear how "many people were moved by the [Italian soldiers'] condition, and in a surprising shift of opinion, the very persons who had railed against them before suddenly expressed sympathy for them."[43] Italian POWs in Toulon were helped by the local population, especially women, with food packages to ameliorate their meager rations in the German prison camps.[44] Especially in places where the Italians had fought back, such as Grenoble, the populace could not hide their admiration of their dogged resistance in the face of overwhelming odds.[45]

That is not to say that the French population was sad to see the Italian army leave. On the contrary, there were scenes of jubilation across southeastern France, especially in the part of the zone that had been occupied by the Italian army since June 1940. If nothing else, the departure of Italian troops meant that the irredentist territories would not be annexed by the Fascist state. In Fontan a French flag was hoisted on the roof of the Mairie (city hall), and French inhabitants decorated the streets with flags.[46] The prefect of the Alpes-Maritime, Jean Chaigneau, was greeted by an ecstatic throng during his visit to reinstate the French administration on 12 September 1943.[47] However, this joy did not last very long, because the German occupation began to establish itself. The German police carried out massive sweeps of Jews in Nice, and these manhunts threw the whole department into an "atmosphere of true terror" (*atmosphère de véritable terreur*). The situation in the Alpes-Maritimes considerably worsened during the winter of 1943–1944 because of the incessant waves of arrests by the Germans on one hand and deadly Resistance attacks on both collaborationist organizations and the Germans on the other.[48] The Germans and their French cronies did not hesitate to torture, execute, or deport anyone who opposed their policy, catching in their nets a number of innocent victims. Emboldened by the Allied advance and the population's growing hostility toward both the Vichy regime and the occupation troops, Resistance fighters ramped up their sabotage and the number of direct attacks against their enemies. The inhabitants of the French Riviera, however, would have to wait until August 1944 to have their land finally freed from the German yoke, as Allied forces landed on the shores between Toulon and Nice (Operation Dragoon).[49]

CONCLUSION

How can we explain and characterize the nature of the Italian occupation of France? Arguably, it is a difficult task for the historian to give definition to a military occupation in the Second World War, given the sheer variety of different perspectives and experiences it entailed. The easiest way to evaluate the Italian occupation is to compare the occupation of Menton with the German occupations in Alsace-Lorraine and the November 1942 occupation with the successive German one in the French Riviera (September 1943–August 1944), and then compare it with the Italian occupations in the Balkans.

The occupation of the strip of land including Menton in the summer of 1940 bore some similarities with the German occupation of Alsace-Lorraine. In both cases the occupying power de facto annexed the two areas, reified by the new borders, even though neither armistices explicitly stated it.[1] Moreover, French political authorities were forbidden to return to the border areas or downright expelled, to be replaced by German or Italian civil servants. On the cultural side, in an effort to demonstrate the German character of the incorporated lands, Nazi leaders endeavored to forcefully Germanize the population with sweeping changes such as the Germanization of street names, the press, and schools. This "denaturalization," as in the Italian area, was increasingly uneven the farther one went from the German border: in Alsace it was strictly enforced; in Moselle it seems the local populace was still reluctant to forego their French even in public spaces.[2]

Notwithstanding these similarities, the German policy differed both in its breadth and its enforcement from the Italian one. Reflecting both the stronger position vis-à-vis the Vichy regime and the stronger historical grip on the Alsace-Lorraine, which had been incorporated in the German Empire from 1870 to 1914, the new Nazi rulers had better luck in harnessing the local resources for their war effort. To this effect, 130,000 men from Alsace-Lorraine were drafted into the Wehrmacht and sent to fight mostly on the Eastern Front.[3] The Germans were also more efficient in systematically hunting down the local resisters, who were either executed or interned in the infamous Natzweiler-Struthof concentration camp. Significantly, contrary to the Menton area, where Italian military authorities ultimately sidelined the civilian Fascist authorities, the new incorporated territories were headed by two Nazi hardliners, Gauleiter Joseph Brückel (Moselle) and Robert Wagner (Alsace), who, following the Fuehrer's will, would single-mindedly pursue the goal of making the Alsace-Lorraine a Nazi bastion.[4] In this regard the German effort was definitely more ideological-driven than the Italian effort in Menton and more ruthless in crushing any form of French patriotism.

An examination of the occupations in the French Riviera from November 1942 to August 1944 is also enlightening to gauge the heavy-handed German policy compared to that of the Italians. A 1949 report of the Comité d'Histoire de la Deuxième Guerre Mondiale made a point of the fact that the Germans had executed (*fusillés*) fifty people in the commune of Nice and had deliberately pursued a scorched earth policy while the Italians had not.[5] If one examines the raw statistics for the overall occupation of France, the differences become even more glaring. The Germans killed three times more people in the Alpes-Maritimes department alone than the Italians did in their entire occupation zone.[6] Data encompassing the whole German and Italian occupations are even more glaring in their disparity. According to 1940–1943 study made by Vichy officials, 1,317 French nationals were arrested, 806 executed, and 2,176 deported in the occupied zone, while the Italian zone capped at 24 arrested, with no execution or deportation.[7] Most of the casualties suffered by the civilian population under the Italian occupation happened in Corsica, where the local Resistance movement stepped up its opposition to the occupation in early 1943, ambushing and targeting Italian soldiers and policemen with surprising success.[8]

Evidently the Germans occupied southeastern France at the end of 1943 at the moment when the conflict in France inexorably downgraded into a civil war without quarter between hardliner collaborationist movements like the Milice Française and a more structured and efficient Resistance movement, whose ranks had swelled with *réfractaires* (draft dodgers) from the STO. But even taking into account the brutalization of the Second World War in 1944, one cannot help but notice a qualitative difference between the Italian and German occupations that goes beyond the mere numbers of casualties. Unlike the Germans, who unremittingly crushed any form of opposition to their power, no matter how harmless, and deliberately targeted people who did not pose any threat to their occupation, such as the Jews, the Italians tried to balance carefully the need for tight security measures in a situation where they faced the real possibility of a joint effort between the local French Resistance and an Allied landing on the one hand, and the need for a temperate policy to placate the local population on the other.

Comparing the Italian occupation of France and that of the Balkans is even more enlightening. The question is whether the occupations of France and of the Balkans were two sides of the same coin, both reflecting the ambitions of the Italian Duce to create an Italian empire where the new Italian *stirpe* (noble lineage) would dominate. After all, the attitude of the occupiers was very different in the two regions. In the Balkans the Italians behaved as colonizers, prone to wanton violence, including razing entire villages, executing bystanders, and deporting even the most vulnerable, such as children and women. In short, they committed war crimes. In France none of this happened. The occupation was certainly not a promenade and had a serious impact on the population, but it never derailed into harsh repression or, worse, into a civil war.

What can explain such different outcomes? For one, the two occupations evolved differently because of their varied time frames in the war and to the peculiarity of internal politics in former Yugoslavia and France. When the Italians occupied the Balkans in April 1941, the strategic initiative was still on the Axis side. The United States had yet to join the fray while much of Continental Europe was dominated by Axis forces. The Nazis were at the helm of their glory, an idea that seemed to have been confirmed by the first few weeks of Operation Barbarossa. This assurance of an ineluctable victory trickled down to Germany's partners. Indeed, the bravado tone in reports from Italian commanders and civilian officials brazenly underlined the superiority of the Italian civilization vis-à-vis the Yugoslavian one. Indeed, Italian reports in the first months of the occupation optimistically gloated over the "sense of trust in our institutions" of local civilians who had graciously bowed to the power of Rome.[9] Even when the Italian soldiers were brusquely awakened from their martial stupor by partisans' ambushes, the head of the Italian army in Slovenia, Gen. Mario Robotti confidently exhorted his troops to "hit hard" (*picchiare sodo*) in response to partisan propaganda.[10]

To be sure, the political chaos of former Yugoslavia amid widespread atrocities inured local Italian units to violence, enticing them to implement a ruthless policy.[11] The Balkans, ripe with atavistic ethnic conflicts, erupted in astonishing violence and widespread atrocities under the extraordinary circumstances of occupation during the Second World War. Serb Četniks, Croatian Ustaša, communist partisans, and Germans all participated in the orgy of blood with a savagery rarely seen in the Second World War outside of the eastern front. Confronted with such deep ancestral hatreds and aggressive partisan actions, the Italians retaliated with indiscriminate reprisals against the local population.

One thing is clear: the Italians acted more harshly in the Balkans than in France because they felt little sympathy for the Slavic populations. The Italian rank and file did not identify at all with the local populace, who they described in their memoirs as "feral beasts" whose lust for blood was as evident as their absence of hygiene. Italian commanders never showed their contempt for the "Balkan mentality" of the Slavs, always reminding the Italian soldiers that they were fighting cowardly insurgents who did not have the guts to face them in pitched battles. Arguably, Italian units had not been trained for counterinsurgency operations and adapted to the new nature of war only gradually. Moreover, one should not underestimate the virulent anticommunist sentiment of Italian senior officers, many of whom had lived through the vilification of the armed forces by socialist militants during the years following the First World War. Not surprisingly, this generation of middle-class officers gladly embraced the Fascist credo, if nothing else, for its anticommunist stance.[12] As Italian commanders often equated the partisans in the Balkans as communists, this could explain their uncompromising approach to counterinsurgency in the region. In light of the racial and political bias and the faulty strategy in the Balkans, Italian commanders resorted to carrying out reprisals as brutal as they were ineffective, with few attempts to win over the local population.[13]

The Italians were confronted in France with a radically different situation. One on hand, Resistance groups were a far cry from the audacious partisans in former Yugoslavia, who organized themselves in marauding bands that were capable even of assaulting Italian strongholds. The Resistance in southeastern France was still in its early stages and never coalesced into a united internal front, perhaps a consequence of the Italian army's occupation policy that most of the time was carefully calibrated to the gravity of the situation and never erupted into indiscriminate violence. Thus, Resistance groups mostly antagonized the Italian army by indirect means, sapping the soldiers' already low morale by spreading defeatist propaganda, with some occasional attacks on buildings and soldiers.[14] While the impact of these episodes on the morale of the Italian fante should not be underestimated, Italian fears of a French revolt led by Gaullist and communist resisters were groundless and point more to the prudent strategy of the Italian army than an organized effort from the Resistance in the region.[15]

It is therefore safe to say that the worst enemy of Italian army command-ers in southeastern France was the low morale of their troops, stemming from the growing sense that the tide of war had irremediably turned against the Axis side by the fall of 1942. This sense of inescapable fatalism was reflected at two levels: at a grassroots level soldiers' discipline was very casual, if not downright sloppy. After an initial period of assessment, the rank and file relaxed in the *dolce far niente* (pleasant relaxation in carefree idleness; literally, "sweet doing nothing") of the French Riviera. Tasks were carried out perfunctorily, without much enthusiasm. As the war dragged on, idleness and the cozy climate of the Côte d'Azur, while certainly in the short term being a welcome respite from the unforgiving conditions of the other theaters of war such as Russia and the Balkans, in the long run only heightened the melancholy of soldiers who in some cases had not seen their homes for more than a year and who understood their families in Italy may be in danger now that the front was approaching the peninsula. The Italian *fante* had one overarching desire: to return to civilian life and be reunited with his family. Thus, Italian commanders had a hard time keeping the sol-diers focused on the prospective peril of an Allied landing and of a possible French upheaval.

Indeed, the sense of frantic urgency, reified by the hasty deployment of Fourth Army units in November 1942, remained omnipresent in the higher echelons of the Italian army. Adding to the strategic nightmare of shoring up hundreds of kilometers of Mediterranean coastline with understaffed and demoralized soldiers, Italian commanders dreaded the hostility of the French population, who still resented the backstabbing of June 1940. At first the reaction of the population to the invasion was indeed one of deep hostility, as everyone feared that the occupation would be a prelude to the annexation of the contested territories. However, after the dust had settled it became evident not only that the Italian army had no interest in advanc-ing an irredentist agenda, to the chagrin of local Fascist militants, but also that the Italian soldiers were willing to strike local compromises as long as they did not negatively impinge on the security and the prestige of the occupying forces.

The latter aspect hinted, perhaps, at the most important insight into the true nature of the relationship between the Italian occupying forces and those living under the occupation. French police reports emphasized that the absence of incidents in the region was due to the "great number of Ital-ian citizens or people with Italian heritage."[16] Italian soldiers stationed in southeastern France shared a common culture, and in some cases even a common bloodline, with a significant part of the local population, owing to the ongoing migratory flux of Italian families since the middle of nineteenth century. These cultural affinities—or as Nicholas Doumanis put it, "a correspondence of values"—enabled occupiers and occupied to forge more easily symbiotic relationships, which in some cases went as far as love affairs or sincere friendships.[17] The same scenario happened in Corsica, where "longstanding cultural, linguistic and social connections" forged a bond between Italian soldiers and local civilians that transcended even the politics of a war occupation.[18] Moreover, Italian commanders were more reluctant to enforce harsh measures or mete out severe punishments against people who were akin to those living in the Italian peninsula. To be sure, it was not uncommon for Italian soldiers to discover relatives and people hailing from the same Italian region, or even from the same village.

How much did cultural and ethnic proximity, then, affect occupation policy? Nazi intelligentsia ranked the types of German administration needed in the occupied countries in four categories, based on local popular attitude toward the occupiers and racial proximity. They ranged from the "informal" administration of Denmark, which needed only a light touch, to the supervisory in France, followed by the "ruling" occupation in the protectorate of Bohemia-Moravia, and ending with the "colonial" iron fist for populations whose civilization and culture were deemed inferior.[19] Evidently, these categories followed a racial taxonomy whereby the lower in the Nazi racial hierarchy the occupied population was, the tougher the occupation policy. Thus, Poles and Russians deserved little autonomy, as their supposedly inferior nature precluded any possible alliance. The same categorization could be used for the Italian military occupations in the Second World War. Whereas the Balkans ranked in the last category of "colonial" policy and deserved little trust and even less respect, France enjoyed a "supervisory" treatment because of the occupiers' consideration for its population, acknowledged as akin to the Italian one if not in ethnicity, at least in culture. Thereby, accommodations were definitely easier to cultivate in France, as they did not feel degrading for the occupying Italian army.

One could wonder how much cultural proximity mattered. After all, the moderate occupation policy was heavily dictated by overwhelming circumstances and also by the parochial power struggle between Italian commanders and civilian authorities, which was ultimately won by the former. Two documents, both written in August 1943, are exemplary of the two different approaches of occupation policy in France. The first, written by General Vercellino to justify his considerate approach to repression, reads as follows: "Penalty measures are extremely delicate weapons that should be used only by those who do not stop judging solely on appearances, but also know the roots of the problems. The limited number of incidents and of confrontations that happened in Occupied France (with the exception of the Haute-Savoie region, where the presence of draft-dodgers worsens the situation) shows that the guidelines followed by the Army command are commensurate with the [security] needs."[20] A few days later a memorandum written by a senior official in Rome, C. De Constantin, denied any beneficial effect of a soft policy, which made the Italians appear as dupes (*minchioni*) whose gullibility (*dabbenaggine*) was mocked by the local population. Instead, he advocated a policy of force (*regime di forza*) that would legitimize the prospective annexation of the County of Nice. In other words, Italians were to act as victors, because the French population was irremediably hostile to the Italian cause. The prefect and the mayor in Nice had to be ousted and replaced by an Italian civil commissar, and part of the population was evacuated by force to make room for Italian colonists.[21] In short, De Constantin was appealing for a Balkanized occupation policy, in a stark reminder of what happened in the occupied zone, where German military authorities, more traditional in their approach of military occupations, were progressively sidelined by Nazi civil servants and SS cronies who had few qualms about enforcing an iron grip on metropolitan France.[22]

It would be too simplistic to cast the army as a moderate faction within the Italian state and the CIAF as the extremist one. The two organizations shared the same overarching goal, but they had different short-term objectives, and both aimed to be in charge of the new province. While CIAF officials strove to assert Italy's political legitimacy on the region, army commanders were interested only in the short-term strategic issue of shoring up the Mediterranean coastline, but there is no indication they opposed the ultimate goal of annexing the area in the long run. They were not oblivious per se to Fascist imperialistic propaganda, as the army had fully supported Mussolini's dreams of conquest.

In hindsight, the Italian occupation of France was tempered and its impact relatively light. Few casualties were directly the result of the occupation, and neither massacres nor executions were meted out. While this book has underlined the relative moderation of the Italian policy in southeastern France, it should not be construed as an effort to revive the moldy myth of the Italiani Brava Gente. After all, the temperance of the Italian army was the result of a variety of factors, none of which were directly related to a supposed benign nature found in the Italian soldier. The relative moderation of the Italian policy should not lead us to forget that the Italian occupation of the French Riviera was a military occupation of an enemy country.

Military occupations by the Axis were always seen by the local populace as a traumatic intrusion in their everyday lives and an attack on the nation's sovereignty. The intrusion was incessant, as occupiers and occupied had to live side by side during a difficult period. The Italian occupation heavily impinged on everyday life with its curfews, evacuations, and expropriations. The population was greatly angered by the wave of thefts committed by Italian soldiers at a time of great need. Waves of arrests that targeted people not tied to the Resistance were also a reminder that no one was really safe in Axis-occupied Europe during the Second World War.

NOTES

INTRODUCTION

1. *Irredentisti* stems from *irredento,* literally "unredeemed," called such because its supporters advocated the annexation of territories outside the Italian state on historical or ethnical grounds. The movement became stronger after the First World War, as the Italians were frustrated by the 1919 Paris Peace Conference. Italy had been handed the Trentino Alto-Adige and Trieste but had failed to secure Istria and Dalmatia; therefore, Mussolini had only to add fuel to the already blazing resentment following the "Mutilated Victory" (*Vittoria Mutilata*). For more about irredentism and its use by Fascist and Nazi ideology, see Aristotle A. Kallis, *Fascist Ideology: Territory and Expansionism in Italy and Germany, 1922–1945* (London: Routledge, 2000), 115–21.

2. For more on the Légion Garibaldienne and its contribution to the Franco-Italian friendship after the war, see Hubert Heyriès, *Les Garibaldiens de 14, splendeurs et misères des Chemises Rouges en France de la Grande Guerre à la Seconde Guerre Mondiale* (Nice: Editions Serre, 2005).

3. For more of the idea of Latinity in the First World War, see Salvo Mastellone, "L'Idea di Latinità (1914–1922)," in *Italia e Francia dal 1919 al 1939,* ed. Jean-Baptiste Duroselle and Enrico Serra (Milano: Istituto per gli studi di politica internazionale, 1981).

4. The Battle of Caporetto (24 October–19 November 1917) saw the Austro-Hungarian army, reinforced by German units, break through the Italian lines and advance deep into Italian territory for more than one hundred kilometers. The Italians, who did lose a staggering three hundred thousand soldiers between killed, wounded, and captured, nevertheless managed to shore up their front line and stop the offensive strike on the Piave River. The Caporetto offensive was the swan song of the Austro-Hungarian army, as the Italians regrouped and during 1918 recovered all the territories previously lost.

5. The Italians would lose another six thousand men before the end of hostilities in November 1918. For more on the Second Army Corps, see Giorgio Rochat, "Les

Italiens dans la deuxième Marne," in *Les batailles de la Marne, de l'Ourcq à Verdun (1914 et 1918)*, ed. François Cochet (Paris: Soteca, 14–18 éditions, 2004), 223–36.

6. Archivio dell'Ufficio Storico dello Stato Maggiore dell'Esercito (hereafter, AUS-SME), B1, b. 111/S, b. 13b, Ordine del giorno n°2300 op., Comando II CA, Diario Storico II CA, Allegato 98, 23 luglio 1918.

7. Davide Rodogno, *Fascism's European Empire: Italian Occupation during the Second World War* (Cambridge: Cambridge University Press, 2006); James H. Burgwyn, *Mussolini Warlord, Failed Dreams of Empire, 1940–1943* (New York: Enigma, 2012).

8. Enrica Costa Bona, *Dalla guerra alla pace, Italia-Francia 1940–1947* (Milano: Franco Angeli, 1995), 21.

9. G. Bruce Strang, *On the Fiery March: Mussolini Prepares for War* (Westport, CT: Praeger, 2003), 73. For the Italian involvement in Spain, see Brian R. Sullivan, "Fascist Italy's Military Involvement in the Spanish Civil War," *Journal of Military History* 59, no. 4 (2007): 697–727.

10. In 1938 the Italian consul in Nice opposed the seizure of Alpine refuges on the grounds that the French Alpine Club could retaliate by boycotting tourism in the Italian Alps. Thus, the war ministry decided to temporarily halt the expropriations. See Archivio Storico Diplomatico del Ministero degli Affari Esteri (hereafter, ASMAE), Affari Politici, 1931–1945, Francia, b. 35, fasc. 3, "Rifugi alpini francesi in territorio italiano."

11. Gianni Oliva, *"Si Ammazza troppo poco," I crimini di guerra italiani, 1940–1943* (Milano: Mondadori, 2006), 6. For an excellent overview of the myth of the "Italiani Brava Gente," see Filippo Focardi, *Il cattivo tedesco e il bravo italiano: la rimozione delle colpe della seconda guerra mondiale* (Bari: Laterza, 2013).

12. For more on the Italian occupation in the Balkans, see Tone Ferenc, *There Is Not Enough Killing: Condemned to Death, Hostages, Shot in the Ljubljana Province, 1941–1943* (Ljubljana, Slovenia: Institute for Contemporary History, Society of the Writers of the History of the Liberation War, 1999); Eric Gobetti, *L'occupazione allegra. Gli Italiani in Jugoslavia (1941–1943)* (Roma: Carocci, 2007); H. James Burgwyn, *Empire on the Adriatic: Mussolini's Conquest of Yugoslavia, 1941–1943* (New York: Enigma, 2005); Eric Gobetti, *Alleati del nemico, l'occupazione italiana in Jugoslavia (1941–1943)* (Roma: Laterza, 2013).

13. Amedeo Osti Guerrazzi, *L'Esercito italiano in Slovenia, 1941–1943, Strategie di repressione antipartigiana* (Roma: Viella, 2011). For the English translation, see *The Italian Army in Slovenia: Strategies of Antipartisan Repression, 1941–1943* (Basingstoke: Palgrave Macmillan, 2013).

14. A summarized version of the circular is available in Oliva, *"Si ammazza troppo poco,"* 173–201. In truth, the Italians never implemented a system of extermination camps like the Germans did, because their goals were not to annihilate local populations as much as to subjugate them; however, living conditions in their concentration camps were no less atrocious than in the Nazi ones. The concentration camp on the Rab Island in Croatia in particular accounted for at least three thousand dead out of fifteen thousand inmates.

15. Data on the Italian population in France, particularly in southeastern France, can be found in Anne Marie Faidutti-Rudolph, *L'Immigration italienne dans le sud-est de la France* (Gap, France: Ophrys, 1964).

16. For more on the evolution of the Italian immigration in France, see Pierre Milza, *Voyage en Ritalie* (Paris: Payot, 2004).

17. As one of the several examples of the contemptuous views of Italian occupation soldiers in the Balkans, Gen. Taddeo Orlando, commander of the Granatieri di Sardegna Division, in a November 1941 report, sanctimoniously erupted against the "Balkan savagery, from the uncouth spitting to bestial ambushes and banditism." Cited by Amedeo Osti Guerrazzi, *Non non sappiamo odiare, L'esercito italiano tra fascismo e democrazia* (Torino: UTET, 2010), 257.

18. I am particularly indebted here to the methodological approaches delineated by Philippe Burrin in his essay "Writing the History of Military Occupation," in *France at War: Vichy and the Historians,* ed. Sarah Fishman, Laura Lee Downs, Ioannis Sinagoglou, Leonard V. Smith, and Robert Zarestky (Oxford: Berg, 2000), 78–81.

19. Ibid., 78.

20. Ibid., 80.

21. According to the Hague Convention, "The authority of the legitimate power having in fact passed into the hands of the occupant, the latter shall take all the measures in his power to restore, and ensure, as far as possible, public order and safety, while respecting, unless absolutely prevented, the laws in force in the country." Article 43, Treaty IV, Laws of War: Law and Customs of War on Land (Hague IV), October 18, 1907; full text available at the site of the Avalon Project of the Yale Law School, http://avalon.law.yale.edu/20th_century/hague04.asp, accessed 24 October 2014.

22. Burrin, "Writing the History," 81.

23. Philippe Burrin, *France under the Germans: Collaboration and Compromise* (New York: New Press, 1996), 461–62.

CHAPTER 1. COUNTDOWN TO WAR

1. Strang, *On the Fiery March,* 256–65.

2. MacGregor Knox, *Hitler's Italian Allies: Royal Armed Forces, Fascist Regime, and the War of 1940–1943* (Cambridge: Cambridge University Press, 2000), 23–25.

3. For instance, Ford was not able to compete with Italian automobile company Fiat, which, along with its partner, Ansaldo, retained the monopoly on the Italian production of tanks and airplanes. See Knox, *Hitler's Italian Allies,* 40–42.

4. Ibid., 69–70.

5. Giorgio Rochat, *Le Guerre Italiane, 1935–1943* (Torino: Einaudi, 2005), 150–52.

6. For instance, the Italian navy and the Italian air force bitterly quarreled in 1939 over naval aviation, particularly about the number of planes allotted to navy operations. See John Gooch, *Mussolini and His Generals: The Armed Forces and Fascist Foreign Policy, 1922–1940* (Cambridge: Cambridge University Press, 2007), 489–90.

7. Ibid., 494–95.

8. In his diary Ciano recalled hearing Mussolini planning the reforestation of the Apennines in order to drop the average temperature in the peninsula. In Mussolini's mind this climatic change would toughen the Italians. Cited by Bianca Valota Cavallotti, "L'immagine fascista dell'impero," in *L'Italia e la politica di potenza in Europa (1938–1940)*, ed. Ennio Di Nolfo, Romain H. Rainero, and Brunello Vigezzi, 121–44 (Milano: Marzorati, 1986).

9. An analysis of the controversial letter can be found in Ennio Di Nolfo, "Mussolini e la decisione italiana di entrare nella seconda guerra mondiale," in Di Nolfo, Rainero, and Vigezzi, *L'Italia e la politica di potenza in Europa*, 25–33.

10. Strang, *On the Fiery March,* 340–41; Costa Bona, *Dalla guerra alla pace,* 12–17.

11. For more about the Franco-German war, see Julian Jackson, *The Fall of France: The Nazi Invasion of 1940* (Oxford: Oxford University Press, 2004).

12. The Duce allegedly declared to Badoglio in his typically crude style: "I need a few thousand dead so as to be able to attend the peace conference as a belligerent." Quoted in Pietro Badoglio, *Italy in the Second World War: Memories and Documents* (Westport, CT: Greenwood Press, 1976), 15.

13. Costa Bona, *Dalla guerra alla pace,* 16–17.

14. Renzo De Felice, *Mussolini il duce* (Torino: Einaudi, 1981), 2: 841–42.

15. Auguste Brachet, *L'Italie qu'on voit et l'Italie qu'on ne voit pas* (Paris: Marion et Flammarion, 1883), 38, cited in Paul Isoard, "Le 11 Novembre 1942," *Cahiers de la Méditerranée* 62 (June 2001): 189.

16. Caroline Wiegandt-Sakoun, "Le Fascisme Italien en France," in *Les Italiens en France de 1914 à 1940,* ed. Pierre Milza, 432–69 (Rome: École française de Rome, 1986); Luca De Caprariis, "'Fascism for Export'? The Rise and Eclipse of the Fasci Italiani all'Estero," *Journal of Contemporary History* 35, no. 2 (2000): 151–83.

17. Case d' Italia were basically social hubs for Italian-state endorsed organizations. For more on the Case d'Italia, see Caroline Pane, "Le Case d'Italia in Francia. Organizzazione, attività e rappresentazione del fascismo all'estero," *Memoria e Ricerca* 41 (2012): 161–80.

18. The Opera Nazionale Dopolavoro (literally, the After Work National Club), or OND, was created in 1925 to organize leisure and recreational activities under the Fascist regime. For more about the OND, see Victoria de Grazia, *The Culture of Consent: Mass Organisation of Leisure in Fascist Italy* (Cambridge: Cambridge University Press, 1981).

19. The most deadly attack involved the bombing of a restaurant near Nice where Fascist veterans of World War I had gathered, leaving three people dead and fourteen wounded. For an account of the clashes between Fascist and anti-Fascist organizations in the Alpes-Maritimes in the 1920s, see Ralph Schor, "Les Italiens dans les Alpes-Maritimes, 1919–1939," in Milza, *Les Italiens en France,* 583–87.

20. OVRA stands for Organizzazione per la Vigilanza e la Repressione dell'Antifascismo (Organization for Vigilance and Repression of Anti-Fascism), even though its real meaning has been contested.

21. SIM stands for Servizio Informazioni Militare.

22. Pierre Milza, "L'immigration italienne en France d'une guerre à l'autre: inter-rogations, directions de recherche et bilans," in Milza, *Les Italiens en France,* 29–30.

23. For instance, the words of an Italian farmer in southwestern France nicely echoed the thoughts of many Italian immigrants: "Basically, for us adults, politics were not interesting at all: but we accepted this propaganda [the Fascist one] due to the benefits, gifts, books, copybooks, newspapers, rice, pasta, which came with it." Jean Anglade, *La vie quotidienne des immigrés en France de 1919 à nos jours* (Paris: Hachette, 1976), 61.

24. Some examples can be found in Emilio Franzina, "L'émigration et l'imaginaire: France du rêve, France de souvenir," in *L'intégration italienne en France, un siècle de présence italienne dans trois régions françaises (1880–1980),* ed. Antonio Bechelloni, Michel Dreyfus, and Pierre Milza, 123–54 (Paris: Editions Complexe, 1995).

25. Mary Dewhurst Lewis, *The Boundaries of the Republic: Migrant Rights and the Limits of Universalism in France, 1918–1940* (Stanford, CA: Stanford University Press, 2007), 217–20.

26. *Journal Officiel de la République française,* 19 November 1939. The *Journal Officiel de la République française* is a daily newspaper in which all new laws and decrees of French ministries are publicized.

27. Archives Départementales des Alpes-Maritimes (hereafter, ADAM) 171 W 1, Ministère del'Intérieur, Cabinet du Ministre, dépêche n°12, Le Ministre de l'Interieur à Messieurs les Préfets, Paris, 14 décembre 1939, 4.

28. For instance, roughly thirty Italians, almost all anarchists or communists, were arrested in the Alpes-Maritimes, twenty-six of whom were imprisoned in the Vernet internment camp. See ADAM 30 W 101.

29. ADAM 616 W 241, 14 May 1940 directive from the Ministère de l'Intérieur to Messieurs les Préfets; emphasis mine.

30. Jean-Louis Panicacci, *Les Alpes-Maritimes, 1939–1945, un département dans la tourmente* (Nice: Editions Serre, 1989), 60.

31. ADAM 616 W 241, Rapport du Capitaine Laurenties, Président de la Com-mission des Ressortissants Italiens à Grasse à Mr. Le Préfet des Alpes-Maritimes, 17 juin 1940.

32. A complete list of the Italian residents who filed declarations of loyalty can be found in Archives Départementales des Alpes-de-Haute-Provence (hereafter, ADAHP) 42 W 81.

33. They were right, as several cases in the Bouches-du-Rhône attest that French prefects were eager to prioritize naturalization dossiers of prospective soldiers; see Lewis, *Boundaries of the Republic,* 238.

34. Such behavior would be severely punished after the war by the various Co-mités d'Épuration. The ADAM 318 W series has numerous examples of this kind of conduct.

35. The precipitous departure of the Italian ambassador in Paris and the few Ital-ians holding diplomatic passports or exit visas is described by Ambassador Raffaele Guariglia in MINCULPOP, *Gli Italiani nei campi di concentramento in Francia;*

documenti e testimonianze (Rome: Società Editrice del Libro Italiano, 1940), 15–25. The Società Dante Alighieri was an organization to promote the Italian language and culture around the world; it still exists.

36. Most of this information is from MINCULPOP, *Gli Italiani nei campi di concentramento.* This book was commissioned a few months after the armistice by the Italian minister of popular culture (MINCULPOP) in an effort to discredit the French state. The book is presented as a succession of memoirs and letters, sometimes with pictures of the original ones, written during or after the detention. Apart from obvious rhetorical exaggerations and the occasional glorification of the Duce, the book is a gold mine of interesting details, corroborated by testimonies from more impartial sources such as Leo Valiani, the future partisan leader, and Arthur Koestler, a Jewish-Hungarian author. See also Milza, *Voyage en Ritalie,* 352; Anne Grynberg, *Les camps de la honte, les internés juifs des camps français (1939–1944)* (Paris: Éditions la Découverte, 1991). Life in the Vernet camp is extensively covered in Arthur Koestler, *The Scum of the Earth* (London: Hutchinson, 1968), 101–130. Leo Valiani, an Italian communist who fought in the Spanish Civil War and who would later become a British secret agent in Italy, openly endorsed Koestler's book in his article "Io e Koestler nel campo di concentramento," originally published in the October–December 1983 issue of *Nuova Antologia,* an Italian journal of literature, and which appeared in the appendix of the 1985 Italian edition of *Scum of the Earth* (Arthur Koestler, *Schiuma della terra* [Bologna: Il Mulino, 1985], 249–60). An account of life in the Saint-Cyprien camp as seen from the perspective of a Spanish republican can be found in Manuel Andújar, *Saint-Cyprien, plage . . . : camp de concentration* (Clermont-Ferrand, France: Presses Universitaires Blaise Pascal, 2003). One of the most detailed books on the Saint-Cyprien camp and village is the book by Pierre Cros, *Saint-Cyprien, 1939–1945, le village, le camp, la guerre* (Canet: Éditions Trabucaire, 2001). Surprisingly, the book fails to mention the thousands of Italian prisoners who were interned in the camp. Saint-Cyprien is a renowned seaside town today.

37. The Saint-Cyprien and Vernet camps had been created in July and October 1939 respectively. In 1939 and 1940 more than 150 internment camps existed. For a complete list of these locations, see Marcel Bervoets-Tragholz, *La liste de Saint-Cyprien* (Bruxelles: Alice Éditions, 2006), 174–77.

38. Anne Grynberg and Anne Charaudeau, "Les camps d'internement," in *Exils et Migration, Italiens et Espagnols en France, 1938–1946,* ed. Pierre Milza and Denis Peschanski (Paris: L'Harmattan, 1994), 150.

39. Koestler, *Scum of the Earth,* 107.

40. "The Wind! Adjusting the entire life [of the concentration camp] at the whim of its music, in the trances of an infernal spirit, a historical malediction, The Wind!" Andújar, *Saint-Cyprien, plage,* 60.

41. Ibid., 71–72.

42. For the Savoy, see Henri Azeau, *La Guerre Franco-Italienne, Juin 1940* (Paris: Presses de la Cité, 1967), 52–53; for the Alpes-Maritimes, see Panicacci, *Les Alpes-Maritimes,* 61–62.

43. Pascal Molinari and Jean-Louis Panicacci, *Menton dans la Tourmente, 1939–1945* (Menton: Société d'art et d'histoire du mentonnais, 1984), 19–21. A firsthand description of the difficult living conditions of the refugees in the Pyrénées-Orientales can be found in ADAM, Fonds privés, 1 J 236, Victor Lefebure, *Récit manuscrit de l'évacuation de Menton et de la vie à Menton pendant la seconde guerre mondiale,* unpublished, Cahiers n°1, "L'histoire des évacués de Menton en juin 1940," 22–103.

44. ADAM, Fonds privés, 1 J 236, Lefebure, *Récit manuscrit de l'évacuation,* 8–9. Ironically, it seems that these same soldiers extensively looted the homes, especially the most isolated ones. See Molinari and Panicacci, *Menton dans la Tourmente,* 21.

45. Julie Torrie, *"For Their Own Good": Civilian Evacuations in Germany and France, 1939–1945* (New York: Berghahn, 2010), 37–38.

46. The drama of the refugees has been vividly described by Hannah Diamond, *Fleeing Hitler, France 1940* (Oxford: Oxford University Press, 2007).

47. A more detailed account of the Battle of the Alps is available in Emanuele Sica, "The Italian Army and the Battle of the Alps," *Canadian Journal of History* 47, no. 2 (2012): 355–78.

48. Vincenzo Gallinari, *Le Operazioni del giugno 1940 sulle Alpi Occidentali* (Roma: Ufficio Storico SME, 1981), 51–63.

49. An orographic study of the Alps can be found in ibid., 9–17.

50. For more details on the Maginot Line of the Alps, see Daniel David, "Les fortifications alpines françaises," *Revue historique des armées* 250 (2008): 4–15; J. E. Kaufmann and H. W. Kaufmann, *The Maginot Line: None Shall Pass* (Westport, CT: Praeger, 1997), 76–83.

51. Gallinari, *Le Operazioni del giugno,* 75. The Italians also had troops who excelled in mountaineering: the Alpini and the Guardia alla Frontiera, an Alpine corps created in 1937 for the task of manning the defensive network of forts on the Italian side of the Alps. For more on the Guardia alla Frontiera, see Massimo Ascoli, *La Guardia alla Frontiera* (Roma: Stato Maggiore Esercito, Ufficio Storico, 2003). Yet the Italian army lacked enough scouting units. See Washington National Archives, Archival Research Catalog (hereafter, ARC), T-821, Roll 130, IT A1163, Rapporto segreto n°11 al Duce sull'efficienza dell'esercito, Rome, 25 maggio 1940, 3.

52. AUSSME, N 1–11, DS 5, Protocollo 143, Comando II Corpo D'Armata on Operazione "M," Diario Storico 4° Divisione Alpina Cuneense, Allegato 5, 20 giugno 1940. As a matter of fact, the Italians believed the morale of the Armée des Alpes was already plummeting as early as the beginning of June, before the start of hostilities. See ARC, T-821, Roll 357, IT 4632, Comando II Corpo D'Armata, Situazione francese sul fronte del II° Corpo D'Armata al giorno, 6 giugno 1940–XVIII, 6 June 1940, 4–5. The Italians were confident that the French soldiers originating from the Italian diaspora would be the first to desert.

53. AUSSME, N 1–11, DS 18, Protocollo 5000/II/P.S.S. Comandante Taurinense General Micheletti, "Occupazione della conca di Bourg S. Maurice e S. Foy," Diario Storico 1° Divisione Alpina Taurinense, Allegato 14, 19 giugno 1940. In fact, Micheletti was more worried about alleged partisan bands of fuoriusciti.

54. Alberto Turinetti di Priero, *La battaglia delle Alpi, 10–25 giugno 1940, La Divisione Superga e gli Alpini nell'Alta Valle di Susa* (S. Ambrogio, Italy: Susalibri, 1990), 62.

55. Gallinari, *Le Operazioni del giugno,* 129. Amazingly, overconfident Italian high officers made the same mistake in the campaign against Greece, as they wrongly assumed that the Greek army would offer only minimal resistance at best. See Rochat, *Le Guerre Italiane,* 262.

56. Dario Gariglio, *Popolo italiano, corri alle armi! 10–25 giugno 1940, l'attacco alla Francia* (Peveragno, Italy: Blue Edizioni, 2001), 63.

57. Bernard Cima, Raymond Cima, and Michel Truttman, *La glorieuse défense du Pont Saint-Louis: Juin 1940* (Menton: Cima, 1995), 19–21; Molinari and Panicacci, *Menton dans la Tourmente,* 34–36, Gariglio, *Popolo Italiano,* 140–41.

58. Gallinari, *Le Operazioni del giugno,* 216–19. For the full text of the 21 June Protocols, see Romain Rainero, *La Commission italienne d'armistice avec la France, les rapports entre la France de Vichy et l'Italie de Mussolini, 10 juin 1940–8 septembre 1943* (Vincennes: Service Historique de l'Armée, 1985), 352–60.

Chapter 2. The Italian Armistice Commission with France (CIAF)

1. For more on the National Revolution, see Julian Jackson, *France: The Dark Years, 1940–1944* (Oxford: Oxford University Press, 2003), 139–65. Vichy anti-Semitic policies are discussed in chapter 10 of the present text.

2. For a thorough analysis of the impact of the demarcation line, see Eric Alary, *La ligne de démarcation* (Paris: Perrin, 2003). In truth the northern half of the French metropolitan territory was itself divided into an occupied zone; a forbidden or reserved zone, which included the Pas-de-Calais and the Nord departments, ruled by the German High Command in Bruxelles; and the Alsace-Lorraine region, which was annexed outright on 15 July 1940.

3. A good comparison between the two armistices is available in Rainero, *La Commission italienne d'armistice,* 47–49.

4. For instance, in the final armistice document no mention was made of the irredentist claims raised only a few days before in the 18 June memorandum. For more on the negotiations of 24 June, see Rainero, *La Commission italienne d'armistice,* 366–72.

5. The Region of Savoy comprises two departments, Savoie and Haute-Savoie.

6. Rainero, *La Commission italienne d'armistice,* 77–78.

7. The full text of the ordinance can be found in Rainero, *La Commission italienne d'armistice,* 391–92.

8. Some scholars argued that Mussolini deliberately decided that Turin, not Rome, should house the newly created administration in order to be able to fully control it as Supreme Commander of the Italian army, without any interference from ministers in Rome. See, for instance, Costa Bona, *Dalle guerra alla pace,* 58.

9. Rainero, *La Commission italienne d'armistice*, 58.

10. See ibid., 64–66. The book also boasts excellent organization charts of the CIAF; see *planches* n°5 and n°7.

11. Memorandum of Gen. Mario Roatta, 25 June 1940. See Rainero, *La Commission italienne d'armistice*, 383–90. It should be noted that these tasks were also applied to the French territories in North Africa and in the Middle East.

12. See Rainero, *La Commission italienne d'armistice*, 61.

13. ADAHP 42 W 81, Compte-rendu de la Conférence interministérielle ayant pour l'objet l'étude des problèmes posés par l'occupation et la propagande italienne tenue le jeudi 10 décembre 1941 à l'Hôtel Thermal à Vichy, 8.

14. Its military nature is also clear by reading the memorandum the head of the Italian Army General Staff, Gen. Mario Roatta, sent to the head of the CIAF, Gen. Pietro Pintor, on 25 June 1940. Rainero, *La Commission italienne d'armistice*, 383–90.

15. Costa Bona, *Dalla guerra alla pace*, 66.

16. For an evolution of the triangular and ambivalent relationship of the Axis powers and the Vichy regime, see Karine Varley, "Entangled Enemies: Vichy, Italy, and Collaboration," in *France in an Era of Global War, 1914–1945*, ed. Ludivine Broch and Allison Carrol, 152–70 (Houndmills, Basingstoke, Hampshire: Palgrave Macmillan, 2014).

17. French navy ships, including four battleships, had been moored at the port of Mers-el-Kébir in French Algeria since the armistice. The French were handed an ultimatum that urged them to either join forces with the British or have their ships disarmed and herded into British ports. After receiving French commanders' firm refusal of such terms, British ships opened fire, damaging or sinking almost the entire squadron, leaving 1,297 French sailors dead and 350 wounded. Dakar, the capital city of Senegal, was an important French colonial port in western Africa. Anglo-Gaullist efforts to capture the port were repeatedly foiled in a two-day confrontation.

18. Massimo Borgogni, *Mussolini e la Francia di Vichy: dalla dichiarazione di guerra al fallimento del riavvicinamento italo-francese (giugno 1940-aprile 1942)* (Siena: Nuova immagine, 1991), 141.

19. As a matter of fact, three illegal depots still existed in Nice and Grenoble in early June 1943. See AUSSME, D7, b. 38, Rapporto Mensile n°42 sull'attività della CIAF, 16 maggio 1943–15 giugno 1943, 11–12.

20. Nicola Marchitto, "Il primo mese di vittoriose operazioni," *L'Illustrazione Coloniale*, July 1940, 25, cited in Rainero, *La Commission italienne d'armistice*, 41.

21. Ezio Maria Gray, *Le terre nostre ritornano . . . Malta–Corsica–Nizza* (Novara: Istituto Geografico De Agostini, 1941).

22. Rodogno, *Fascism's European Empire*, 210–12.

23. For the full text of the draft, see Rainero, *La Commission italienne d'armistice*, 364.

24. ASMAE, Affari Politici, 1931–1945, Francia, b. 69, n°3867 sull'attività della Sottocommissione Affari Generali, 17 aprile 1943, 12.

25. AUSSME, D7, b. 7, Document 3/B, Nota sull'Articolo XXI dell'Armistizio. With the passing of time, Article 21 was used less and less to liberate Italians incarcerated after the armistice. Italians preferred to trade their freedom for that of French prisoners detained in Italian prisons.

26. As an example, see the letter of Vittorio D. from the village of Forcalquier (Basses-Alpes) to the prefect, ADAHP, 42 W 81. The letter, written on 5 July, was received by the prefecture. Vittorio D., found to have been wrongly accused of Fascist militancy, was eventually released on 14 July.

27. A facsimile of the "Declaration of loyalty to France" can be found in MINCULPOP, *Gli Italiani nei campi di concentramento,* 78.

28. For firsthand accounts of the declaration of loyalty, see ibid., 111–14, 141–42, 148–49. However, no data exists on the number of Italians who agreed to sign.

29. A succinct summary of both reports is available in ibid., 304–311. French authorities, on the other hand, firmly challenged Italian complaints about the generally poor conditions of the internment camps—for instance, describing Vernet as a *camp modèle.* See ADAM 616 W 260, "Conférence pour l'étude des problèmes posés par l'occupation et la propagande italiennes tenue à Vichy le 16 décembre 1940," 29.

30. See, for instance, the list of Italians resident in the Basses-Alpes who were freed from the Saint-Cyprien camp, ADAHP, 42 W 81, Lettre du Lieutenant Colonel Borallo, Commandant du camp de St-Cyprien au Préfet des the Basses Alpes departement, 24 juillet 1940.

31. AUSSME, D7, b. 7, Document 3/B, Nota sull'Articolo XXI dell'Armistizio, 1–2.

32. The full text of the agreement is available in Rainero, *La Commission italienne d'armistice,* 434–39.

33. ASMAE, Affari Politici, 1931–1945, Francia, b. 54, Ministero Affari Esteri, Nota sull'evoluzione dei rapporti bilaterali tra Francia ed Italia, 21 dicembre 1942, 3. The Delegations for Assistance and the Repatriation were officially converted to consulates only in January 1943 after the occupation of the free zone in November 1942.

34. Costa Bona, *Dalla guerra alla pace,* 122.

35. ASMAE, Affari Politici, 1931–1945, Francia, b. 54, Lettera al Conte Leonardo Vitetti, Direttore generale degli Affari Politici, Ministero Affari Esteri, 28 febbraio1942.

36. ASMAE, Affari Politici, 1931–1945, Francia, b. 69, n°3867, "Attività della Sottocommissione Affari Generali, CIAF," 17 aprile 1943, 27–28.

37. See, for instance, the quarrel between two Italian citizens, Joseph U. and Louis P., in ADAM 616 W 223, Rapport n°14.766-IV Commissariat Spécial de Nice au préfect des Alpes-Maritimes, 12 décembre 1940.

38. Starting on 27 August 1940, non-French were forbidden to buy any real estate.

39. Files of Italian grievances can be found in ADAM 104 W 2; 104 W 3; 166 W 29; 166 W 30; 166 W 31; and 616 W 261.

40. In August 1940 the CIAF vigorously protested and the workers were reinstated. ASMAE, Affari Politici, 1931–1945, Francia, b. 69, n°3867, "Attività della Sottocommissione Affari Generali, CIAF," 17 aprile 1943, 15.

41. ASMAE, Serie Armistizio Pace b. 1, n°107/A di Eugenio Mazzarini, "Situazione politica nella zona delle Alte Alpi nella seconda metà del gennaio 1941," 30 gennaio 1941, 5.

42. Julie Fette, *Exclusions: Practicing Prejudice in French Law and Medicine, 1920–1945* (Ithaca, NY: Cornell University Press, 2012). In truth, bound by a corporatist mentality originating from the ancien régime, French lawyers and doctors feared the competition of foreign counterparts who were open to practice for lower fees. This self-defense stance meshed well with the wave of xenophobia that was pervasive in the economic recession of the 1930s.

43. Ibid., 134.

44. ADAM 616 W 241, Lettre du Préfet des Alpes-Maritimes au Ministre de l'Intérieur, 14 novembre 1941.

45. Waivers were available only to former soldiers or sons of soldiers who had fought in the wars of 1914–1918 and 1939–1940 or by special dispensation granted by the minister of justice based on exceptional merit.

46. Archives Nationales (hereafter, AN), F7 16050, Secrétaire-général à la Famille et à la Santé, note du directeur-général de la Sûreté nationale, 7 décembre 1940. Cf. AN 2AG 606, Ministère de l'Intérieur to prefects, "Circulaire sur l'application de la loi du 16 août 1940 concernant l'exercice de la médecine, n° 186," 1 novembre 1940, cited in Fette, *Exclusions,* 167.

47. ADAM 616 W 260, Lettre n°6248/dic du Colonel Bonnet, Officier de Liaison à la Délégation CIAF de Nice au Lieutenant Plaja, Délégué à l'Assistance et au Rapatriement de Cannes, 1 décembre 1942.

48. See, for instance, the case in Nice of the lawyer Roberto A., a Frenchman born of an Italian father and a French mother. ASMAE, Affari Politici, 1931–1945, Francia, b. 59, n°1432 General Quinto Mazzolini, Delegazione all'Assistenza e Rimpatrio di Nizza, alla CIAF, Sottocommissione Affari Giudiziali, 31 dicembre 1941.

49. ASMAE, Affari Politici, 1931–1945, Francia, b. 69, n°3867, "Attività Sottocommissione Affari Generali, CIAF," 17 aprile 1943, 23–24.

50. ASMAE, Affari Politici, 1931–1945, Francia, b. 69, no date (probably autumn 1942), "Relazione annuale sulla collettività residente nella giurisdizione della R. Delegazione di Nizza," 7–8.

51. Dominique Veillon, *Vivre et Survivre en France, 1939–1947* (Paris: Payot, 1995), 102.

52. Kenneth Mouré, "Réalités cruelles: State Controls and the Black Market for Food in Occupied France," in *Food and War in Twentieth-Century Europe,* ed. Ina Zweiniger-Bargielowska, Rachel Duffett, and Alain Drouard (Burlington, VT: Ashgate, 2011), 171.

53. The name of the department was changed in 1970 to Alpes-de-Haute-Provence.

54. ADAHP, 42 W 40, Rapport mensuel du préfet des Basses-Alpes au Ministère de l'Intérieur sur l'opinion publique, 31 juillet 1941.

55. Vichy ideologues held the conservative belief that the rural population was tied to immemorial values such as family, motherland, and the soil. They thus called the peasantry and the rural world in general France Éternelle.

56. ADAM 166 W 1, Rapport n°5894, "Situation économique," Commissariat Special de Nice, 24 juin 1941. Conflict between city dwellers and farmers was endemic in the Limousin, Creuse, and Haute-Vienne departments. See Shannon L. Fogg, *The Politics of Everyday Life in Vichy France: Foreigners, Undesirables, and Strangers* (Cambridge: Cambridge University Press, 2009), 25–46.

57. For instance, cutting off trade with North Africa stopped imports of a variety of food such as wine, eggs, sardines, wheat, and olives. Jean-Louis Panicacci, "Le temps des pénuries dans les Alpes-Maritimes (1939–1949)," *Les Cahiers de la Méditerranée* 48 (June 1994): 191–92.

58. ADAM 166 W 1, Rapport n°4857, Commissariat Spécial de Nice, 30 avril 1941.

59. Lynne Taylor rightly asserts that in the new reality of the Vichy rationing system, tradespeople in general became "petty bureaucrats," working directly to implement the state legislation. In this new role they held a large discretionary power. Lynne Taylor, *Between Resistance and Collaboration: Popular Protest in Northern France, 1940–1945* (London: Macmillan, 2000), 154.

60. See, for instance, the case of Adolfo C., in ADAM 104 W 3, Lettera n°445 de la Délégation CIAF de Nice, cas Adolfo C., Cannes, 29 janvier 1942, and the reply of the prefecture, Note de renseignements n°419, 5 mars 1942. Occasionally, French authorities admitted to administrative mistakes and promptly corrected the wrongs. See, for instance, the complaint of three wine merchants on the scarcity of wine distributed, in ADAM 104 W 2, Lettre du Délégué à l'Assistance et au Rapatriement de Cannes à l'Intendant Directeur Départmental du Ravitaillement Général, 17 octobre 1941.

61. Richard Vinen, *The Unfree French: Life under the Occupation* (New Haven, CT: Yale University Press, 2006), 223.

62. For a good overall view of the black market, see Veillon, *Vivre et Survivre en France*. The letter "D" stands for the French word "*débrouillard*," or resourceful.

63. Robert Gildea, *Marianne in Chains: Daily Life in the Heart of France during the German Occupation* (New York: Metropolitan Books, 2003), 107–115.

64. Torrie, *"For Their Own Good,"* 45–46. As noted by the author, in the first months following the occupation of France, the Nazi equivalent of the Secours National, the National Socialist People's Welfare Organization, or NSV, took the helm of the relief effort in France for clear propagandistic purpose. By August 1940 the NSV was largely gone from France, perhaps because of Vichy protestations.

65. Jean-Pierre Le Crom, *Au Secours Maréchal!* (Paris: Presses Universitaires de France, 2013), 78. Additionally, the Secours National enjoyed the monopoly of fund-raising, much to the chagrin of the French Red Cross, which had to rely almost entirely on the Secours National's funds. Ibid., 52–53.

66. Ibid., 177.

67. ADAM 166 W 26, lettera 7886 T.O., "Manifesti di propaganda per il Secours Nationale [*sic*]," Prefetto per l'Amministrazione dei Territori Occupati G. B. Marziali ai Commissari Civili, 26 dicembre 1941.

68. AUSSME, D7, b. 19, Notiziario quindicinale n°27, 25 gennaio 1942, 27.

69. Foreign mothers could receive a priority card only if all of their children were French. The CIAF delegations protested to no avail. See ASMAE, Serie Armistizio Pace b. 8, Telegramma n°1159/632, Ambasciata Italiana a Parigi, and the subsequent French reply, Lettre n°1781/DIC Colonel Salmon, Officier de Liaison auprès de la CIAF de Nice, 5 novembre 1941.

70. ADAM 616 W 223, Rapport "Propagande anti-française exercée par les Italiens dans les Alpes-Maritimes," unsigned, no date (probably around March 1941), 29–30. To counter this strategy, the top-secret French report suggested a wider development of the *soupes populaires* in order to include destitute Italians.

71. ASMAE, Affari Politici, 1931–1945, Francia, b. 69, "Relazione annuale sulla collettività residente nella giurisdizione della R. Delegazione di Nizza," 22 gennaio 1943.

72. ASMAE, Affari Politici, 1931–1945, Francia, b. 68, "Relazione Console Italiano Mazzolini sulla sua attività a Nizza," 20 marzo 1943, Parte II, "Sulla Situazione Generale." The translation is taken from Daniel Carpi, *Between Mussolini and Hitler: The Jews and the Italian Authorities in France and Tunisia* (Hanover, NH: University Press of New England, 1994), 7. It should be noted that the word *precedente* in Italian also means "criminal record."

73. ASMAE, Rappresentanza italiana in Francia (1861–1950), b. 319, fasc. 7, Rapporto n°2335 Ispettorato per i Fasci Italiani in Francia, Parigi, "Situazione della collettività italiana," 17 dicembre 1941.

74. For a holistic work on the topic, see Lizzie Collingham, *The Taste of War: World War II and the Battle for Food* (New York: Penguin, 2012).

CHAPTER 3. ITALIAN IRREDENTISM AND FRENCH PATRIOTISM IN THE CÔTE D'AZUR

1. Pierre Abramovici, *Un Rocher bien occupé, Monaco pendant la guerre, 1939–1945* (Paris: Éditions du Seuil, 2001), 38–48.

2. ASMAE, Serie Armistizio Pace b. 20, Rapporto n°1548/288 Console Italiano a Monaco Sanfelice, Monaco, 11 agosto 1940.

3. ASMAE, Serie Armistizio Pace b. 20, Rapporto n°1610/309 Console Italiano a Monaco Sanfelice, Monaco, 24 agosto 1940.

4. ASMAE, Serie Armistizio Pace b. 20, Rapporto n°1640/315 Console Italiano a Monaco Sanfelice, Monaco, 7 settembre 1940.

5. ASMAE, Affari Politici, 1931–1945, Francia, b. 48, Notiziario politico quindicinale n°1340 Delegato CIAF di Nizza Silvio Camerani, Nice, 10 dicembre 1940.

6. ADAM 616 W 223, Dossier "Propagande anti-française exercée par les italiens dans les Alpes-Maritimes."

7. ADAM 166 W 10, Propagande Irredentiste Italienne, Rapport n°4845 A/S des Groupes d'Action Niçoise du Chef du Service Régional des Renseignements Généraux au Préfet Régional, 20 octobre 1942.

8. Ibid.

9. Although the secret Treaty of London (26 April 1915) had assigned Fiume (now Rijeka, Croatia) to Yugoslavia, the Italians claimed it at the Paris Peace Conference on the principle of self-determination, because a consistent chunk of the population was of Italian ethnicity. On 12 September 1919, infuriated by the stall in the nego- tiations, the nationalist poet Gabriele D'Annunzio along with two thousand Italian irredentists successfully ousted Entente troops (troops of the Triple Entente during the First World War—namely, French and English in this case) from the Dalmatian city and proclaimed Fiume an independent city. The irredentist coup lasted until December 1920, when an Italian navy bombardment forced D'Annunzio and his underlings to surrender the city.

10. In truth the GAN failed to make inroads in the Regio Esercito, as Italian soldiers were officially forbidden by the Italian Army General Staff to adhere to the irredentist organization. See ACS, CIAF, Commissariato civile di Mentone ed Ufficio informazioni (1940–1943), b. 1, n°3428 T. C. dal Prefetto CIAF Vittorelli, "Iscrizione degli appartenenti alle Forze Armata ai Gruppi di Azione Nizzarda," 14 giugno 1941.

11. ACS, CIAF, Commissariato civile di Mentone ed Ufficio informazioni (1940– 1943), b. 1, Rapporto del Commissario Civile di Mentone, "Riunione Gruppi Azione Nizzarda," Mentone, 21 dicembre 1940.

12. Most of the details on the celebration in Savona were found in an unsigned report, possibly a newspaper article, in the trial dossier of two Italian irredentists, Jean-Antoine and Jean-Claude A. ADAM 318 W 52.

13. The annual salt harvest in August always attracted a large number of Ital- ian workers to the small medieval town in the Gard department, despite signs of growing hostility from French workers. The French authorities largely ignored the mounting friction. This tension suddenly burst into a full-scale riot on 16 August 1893 when French and Italian salt miners turned on one another. For two full days Italian workers were hunted down by gangs of Frenchmen, leaving nine dead and several dozens injured, according to official reports. See Milza, *Voyage en Ritalie,* 131–38.

14. Records of letters intercepted by the police are available in ADAM 616 W 190.

15. All the taped conversations are available in ADAM 616 W 188, Fichier Mo- naco.

16. ADAM 616 W 190, Rapport n°773, 16 février 1941, and Rapport n°1169, 12 mars 1941.

17. ADAM 616 W 190, Rapport n°1871, 8 mai 1941.

18. ACS, CIAF, Commissariato civile di Mentone ed Ufficio informazioni (1940– 1943), b. 1, Rapporto n°977, "Gruppi d'Azione Nizzardi, Attività ed inconvenienti," Commissario Civile di Mentone, 20 gennaio 1941.

19. ASMAE, Affari Politici, 1931–1945, Francia, b. 59, Telespresso n°597 R. Gen. Quinto Mazzolini, Nice, 19 marzo 1942; ASMAE, Serie Armistizio Pace 08, Tele-

gramma n°16836 P.R. Gen. Quinto Mazzolini, oggetto: Sottotenente Bandini, Nice, 29 maggio 1942.

20. ASMAE, Affari Politici, 1931–1945, Francia, b. 68, Relazione del Console Italiano Mazzolini sulla sua permanenza a Nizza, 20 marzo 1943. The lengthy report was divided into three parts: the Italian community (*La collettività italiana*); General situation (*Situazione generale*); and Gruppi D'Azione Nizzarda.

21. ASMAE, Serie Armistizio Pace, b. 8, Telegramma n°15655 Mazzolini, "Articolo della *Gazzetta del Popolo*," Nice, 19 maggio 1942, and Rapporto n°1343 R delegato CIAF Mazzolini sul caso Giov. Battista B., David B., Ranuzzi, Nice, 26 maggio 1942.

22. ASMAE, Affari Politici, 1931–1945, Francia, b. 48, Rapporto n°1370 Silvio Camerani al Ministero degli Affari Esteri, Nice, 11 dicembre 1940.

23. ASMAE, Affari Politici, 1931–1945, Francia, b. 48, Rapporto n°1420 Silvio Camerani CIAF Sottocommissione Affari Generali, Nice, 17 marzo 1941. See also the subsequent report on the principal clergymen in the Alpes-Maritimes.

24. ASMAE, Affari Politici, 1931–1945, Francia, b. 68, Memorandum delegato CIAF Mazzolini al Ministero Affari Esteri, Affari Generali, Rome, 20 marzo 1943, Parte II, "Sulla Situazione Generale."

25. Jean-Louis Panicacci, "Un Journal Irrédentiste sous l'Occupation: *Il Nizzardo*," *Cahiers de la Méditerranée* 33/34 (December 1986–June 1987), 144–45.

26. Vieux Nice (The Old Nice) was the oldest part of the city, allegedly where many Italians lived and with many monuments harking back to the Piedmontese era.

27. *Il Nizzardo*, Anno IX, n°20, 26 luglio 1942, 2.

28. For more on Monseigneur Rémond, see Ralph Schor, *Un évêque dans le siècle: Monseigneur Paul Rémond (1873–1963)* (Nice: Editions Serre, 1984).

29. Panicacci, *Les Alpes-Maritimes*, 98–102.

30. ADAM 616 W 49, Lettre Secrétariat du Maréchal de France au Préfet Régional, Vichy, 27 mars 1943.

31. Marianne is one of the most prominent symbols of the French Republic and is officially used on most government documents. Vichy despised Republicanism, thus Marianne was cast out in favor of Petain.

32. For more on the Légion Française des Combattants, see Jean-Paul Cointet, *La Légion française des combattants* (Paris: Albin Michel, 1995).

33. See ADAM 616 W 61, Région de Police de Nice, Alpes-Maritimes, Fichier départemental, 23, for the statistical records. For Italian reports on the LFC, see AUSSME, D7, b. 15, CIAF Notiziario quindicinale n°10, 15–30 aprile 1941, 7–9.

34. AUSSME, D7, b. 18, CIAF Notiziario quindicinale n°30, 15–31 febbraio 1942, 30–31. The SOL later evolved into the infamous Milice Française, a French paramilitary group created in January 1943, whose primary role consisted of helping German personnel hunt down French resisters and Jews. For more on both of these organizations, see Jacques Delperrié de Bayac, *Histoire de la Milice, 1918–1945* (Paris: Fayard, 1969), and the more recent work, Pierre Giolitto, *Histoire de la Milice* (Paris: Perrin, 1999).

35. The complete text is available at the Archives Municipales de la ville de Nice (hereafter, AMVN), 2 S 241.

36. The CIAF clearly understood the implication of this campaign. See, for instance, AUSSME, D7, b. 15, CIAF Notiziario quindicinale n°10, 15–30 aprile 1941, 13.

37. Panicacci, *Les Alpes-Maritimes,* 107.

38. *L'Éclaireur du Sud-Est,* 12 mai 1941.

39. ASMAE, Affari Politici, 1931–1945, Francia, b. 50, Telegramma n°40919, "Visita Ammiraglio Darlan a Nizza," 18 ottobre 1941.

40. Panicacci, *Les Alpes-Maritimes,* 112. The Italian irredentist newspaper *Il Nizzardo* mocked the steady stream of Vichy dignitaries by christening Nice "The Mecca of the National Revolution." See *Il Nizzardo,* Anno IX, n°3, 23 marzo 1942, 3.

41. ASMAE, Affari Politici, 1931–1945, Francia, b. 50, Nota Ministero Affari Esteri, Rome, 31 ottobre 1941.

42. AUSSME, D7, b. 15, CIAF Notiziario quindicinale n°11, 1–15 maggio 1941, 13.

43. ADAM 104 W 2, Note de Renseignements n°12, suite à lettre n°3148 du 31 mai 1941 de la CIAF relative à l'affaire Angèle P. à Levens.

44. *L'Éclaireur du Sud-Est,* 10 mai 1941.

45. ASMAE, Serie Armistizio Pace, b. 8, Rapporto n°2678 Vice-Console Giorgio Fragnito, Nice, 11 maggio 1941.

46. ASMAE, Serie Armistizio Pace, b. 8, Rapporto n°16144/Pr. Presidenza CIAF allo Stato Maggiore Regio Esercito, Turin, 18 maggio 1941.

47. ADAM 26 W 6, Rapport n°1,656 du Diréceur de la Police de Nice, Nice, 18 avril 1941.

48. ASMAE, Serie Armistizio Pace, b. 3, Lettera n°856 CIAF, Sottocommissione per l'Esercito, Chambery, 21 febbraio 1941.

49. Complete lyrics of the song are available in ADAM 166 W 26, n°444 R. Ufficio di P.S. di Confine Ponte dell'Unione, Mentone, 25 février 1941. See also ADAM 616 W 241, Rapport n°155/4 du Capitaine Brodard, Commandant de la séction de Roquebrune-Cap-Martin, Roquebrune, 15 mars 1941. It is worth noting that the song also became popular in the Hautes-Alpes department. ASMAE, Serie Armistizio Pace, b. 1, n°209 del delegato CIAF a Gap Eugenio Mazzarini, "Situazione politica nella zona delle Alte Alpi," 27 febbraio 1941.

50. ADAM 616 W 223, Rapport du Commissaire Spécial au Préfect des Alpes-Maritimes, Breil, 9 février 1941.

51. For example, the popular children's song from the French Revolution "*Cadet Rousselle*" became a popular anti-Italian song. ASMAE, Serie Armistizio Pace, b. 20, Rapporto n°5989 Presidente della Sottocommissione Affari Generali, Turin, 2 aprile 1941.

52. ADAM 104 W 2, Lettera n°3276 CIAF, 1ma Sezione di Controllo al Prefetto delle Alpes-Maritimes, Nice, 3 giugno 1941. See ADAM 104 W 2, Note de renseignements n°13, 24 juin 1941.

53. Ronald C. Rossbottom, *When Paris Went Dark: The City of Light under German Occupation, 1940–1944* (New York: Little, Brown, 2014), 215–23.

54. ASMAE, Serie Armistizio Pace, b. 3, Nota n°1117 Presidente della Sottocommissione Affari Generali alla Sottocommissione per l'Esercito, Turin, 12 gennaio 1941.

55. Castor oil became an emblem of Fascist violence. Starting in the 1920s, the Blackshirts forced their political opponents to drink great quantities of this laxative. The victims, whose trousers had been tied, inevitably soiled their clothes and were thus publicly humiliated.

56. ASMAE, Serie Armistizio Pace, b. 3, Rapporto n°1354 di prot. I "Scritte anti-Italiane sui fusti di carburanti provenienti dalla Francia," Generale di Brigata Fernando Gelich, Segretario Generale della CIAF, Turin, 18 marzo 1941.

57. After the formal CIAF complaint, the factory was closed for one day and the factory worker received a six-month suspended sentence. A detailed dossier on the incident can be found in ADAM 104 W 2.

58. ADAHP 42 W 80, Rapport au Ministère de l'Intérieur sur un incident à la cathédrale de Digne le 6 avril entre Français et membres du détachement italien de Contrôle, 15 avril 1941.

59. ADAHP 42 W 80, Rapport du Ministère de l'Intérieur sur un incident avec Chef du détachement italien de Contrôle à Digne, 22 avril 1941.

60. The writer was alluding to the St. Bartholomew's Day massacre in 1572, when thousands of Protestants perished in widespread massacres across France. ASMAE, Serie Armistizio Pace, b. 3, Telegramma n°54/33 Vice-console d'Italia a Ajaccio, 25 agosto 1940.

61. ACS, CIAF, Commissariato civile di Mentone ed Ufficio informazioni (1940–1943), b. 1, n°3872 Commissario Civile di Mentone Virgilio Magris, Mentone, 20 marzo 1941.

62. ADAM 616 W 241, Rapport n°127/2 Sergent-chef Guillermet, "Incident entre jeunes français et italiens survenu à Monaco," Cap d'Ail, 30 octobre 1940.

63. ADAM 616 W 241, Rapport n°2877 Commissaire Spécial Beausoleil au Préfet des Alpes-Maritimes, 5 novembre 1940.

64. ASMAE, Serie Armistizio Pace, b. 20, Rapporto n°3193/624 Console Italiano in Monaco Sanfelice, 31 dicembre 1940.

65. ASMAE, Serie Armistizio Pace, b. 8, Rapporto n°1343 R delegato CIAF Quinto su caso Giov. Battista B., David B., Ranuzzi, Nice, 26 maggio 1942, 2; emphasis mine.

66. In fact, to a certain extent French who had quarrels with Italians were denounced and taken into custody by the Italian army after November 1942. See chapter 8.

67. Simon Kitson, *The Hunt for Nazi Spies: Fighting Espionage in Vichy France* (Chicago: University of Chicago Press, 2008), 101–102. For an example of French surveillance of CIAF commissions, see ADAHP 42 W 80, Circulaire n°106/S/2-SR/SCA, "Instruction particulière n°4, Renseignements sur les incidents eventuels avec les autorités des commissions de contrôle d'armistice," 18 avril 1941.

68. ADAHP 42 W 80, Rapport n° S4/2 du Chef d'Escadron Ogier, "sur les personnes en relations avec des Commissions d'Armistice ou Membres de celles-ci," 2 mai 1942.

69. ASMAE, Affari Politici, 1931–1945, Francia, b. 68, Relazione Console Italiano Mazzolini sulla sua attività a Nizza, 20 marzo 1943, Part III, I Gruppi d'Azione Nizzarda, 8.

CHAPTER 4. A PRELUDE TO FULL OCCUPATION

1. The full text of the "Proclamation Concerning the Administration and the Judicial Organization of the Occupied Territories" is available in Rainero, *La Commission italienne d'armistice,* 407–413.

2. Proclamation Articles 2 and 3.

3. Proclamation Article 5.

4. Nicole Dombrowski Risser, *France under Fire: German Invasion, Civilian Flight, and Family Survival during World War II* (Cambridge: Cambridge University Press, 2012), 194–95.

5. Molinari and Panicacci, *Menton dans la Tourmente,* 47.

6. ADAM 616 W 260, "Conférence pour l'étude des problèmes posés par l'occupation et la propagande italiennes tenue à Vichy le 16 décembre 1940," 8–9. The only exception was the firefighters in some Savoy territories, who were allowed to return.

7. The Renseignements Géneraux was a branch of the police created in 1911 whose role consisted of obtaining information on people or organizations who could undermine the state's security.

8. Fearing that the massing of three Italian divisions near the border was a harbinger of a military invasion, French local authorities launched the complete evacuation of Menton, Carnolès, and Cap-Martin on the evening of 3 June under the code name "Exécutez Mandrin." More than thirteen thousand people, with minimal luggage, were transferred in convoys of buses and trucks at first to Cannes and Antibes and, after a few days, on 7 June, farther west in the Pyrénées-Orientales department. See Molinari and Panicacci, *Menton dans la Tourmente,* 19–21. A firsthand description of the difficult living conditions of the refugees in the Pyrénées-Orientales can be found in ADAM, Fonds privés, 1 J 236; Lefebure, *Récit manuscrit de l'évacuation de Menton,* 22–103.

9. Most of the villas were occupied or given to Italian units or civilians. By impounding properties of citizens of hostile countries, the 31 August 1941 decree of the Duce de facto formalized these expropriations. Administrators were nominated by army commanders to manage the properties. See ADAHP 42 W 81, Rapport n°852/Int présenté par le Maitre des Requêtes au Conseil d'État Theis, Président de la Sous-Délégation pour les Affaires Administratives, à l'Amiral Duplat, Président de la D.F.C.I.A., 11 juillet 1942, 2–3.

10. The Vanguardist organization was a Fascist youth organization, part of the Balilla movement, that grouped youths from fourteen to seventeen years old as a

way to indoctrinate them and to prepare them for becoming the warriors of the new future Fascist army.

11. "W" in slang means *Viva* (Hurray). The slogans therefore translate as "Hurray for the king," "Hurray for the Duce," "Hurray for the dead," "Hurray for the [Division] Cosseria." In some houses, soldiers with a wicked sense of humor tagged the walls with "*Grazie, era buono*" (Thank you, it was good). ADAM 397 W 59, Procès verbal de constat CR46558, 5 novembre 1943.

12. ADAM 616 W 161, procès-verbal 4 juillet 1941, interview with Mme Francine C.

13. Proclamation Articles 9 and 12.

14. Proclamation Article 13.

15. Proclamation Articles 21–23.

16. Proclamation Article 25.

17. ACS, CIAF, Commissariato civile di Mentone ed Ufficio informazioni (1940–1943), b. 2, Rapporto 511/R6/gab Commissario Civile Mentone Giuseppe Frediani a G. B. Marziali, Prefetto CIAF dei Amministrazione Territori Francesi Occupati, 1 giugno 1942, 2.

18. For more on the creation of nations and the harnessing of nationalism by modern states, see Benedict Anderson, *Imagined Communities: Reflections on the Origin and Spread of Nationalism* (London: Verso, 1983). On how the French public school system in the nineteenth century created a national consciousness in France, see Eugen Weber, *Peasants into Frenchmen* (Stanford, CA: Stanford University Press, 1976), 303–338.

19. Jean-Louis Panicacci, *L'Occupation Italienne, Sud-Est de la France, Juin 1940–Septembre 1943* (Rennes: Presses Universitaires de Rennes, 2010), 46.

20. Gray, *Le terre nostre ritornano*, 108.

21. ACS, CIAF, Commissariato civile di Mentone ed Ufficio informazioni (1940–1943), b. 1, Rapporto Renato Freschi, Direttore delle Scuole di Mentone al Commissario Civile di Mentone, 2 aprile 1943; Molinari and Panicacci, *Menton dans la Tourmente*, 58.

22. Claude Barneaud, *Les Mentonnais et la Résistance* (Menton: Société d'Art et d'Histoire du Mentonnais, 1992), 34.

23. ACS, CIAF, Commissariato civile di Mentone ed Ufficio informazioni (1940–1943), b. 2, fasc. 21, Rapporto n°8/269 Giuseppe Valenti, comandante della 21sima Compagna Speciale CC. RR. al Commissario Civile di Mentone, 15 ottobre 1942.

24. ACS, CIAF, Commissariato civile di Mentone ed Ufficio informazioni (1940–1943), b. 2, fasc. 21, Rapporto 784/gab/R6 Commissario Civile di Mentone Giuseppe Frediani alla CIAF, Amministrazione dei Territori Francesi Occupati, 19 novembre 1942.

25. 618 W 161, Rapport n°2022 de l'Inspecteur de Police Mirlicourtois, Breil, 28 juin 1941. See also Mirlicourtois's Rapport n°3634, 15 décembre 1941, and Rapport n°309 de l'Inspecteur Principal Bonneau, Breil, 2 février 1942.

26. Panicacci, *Les Alpes-Maritimes*, 140.

27. Milza, *Voyage en Ritalie*, 403–404.

28. ADAHP 42 W 81, Rapport n°852/Int présenté par le Maitre des Requêtes au Conseil d'Etat Theis, Président de la Sous-Délégation pour les Affaires Administratives, à l'Amiral Duplat, Président de la D.F.C.I.A., 11 juillet 1942, 11.

29. Ibid.

30. ADAM 618 W 161, Rapport n°2022 de l'Inspecteur de Police Mirlicourtois, Breil, 28 juin 1941, Rapport n°1365 du Commissaire, Chef du Service des Renseignement Généraux à Monsieur le Conseiller d'Etat, Préfet Régional, Intendance de Police (Service des Renseignement Généraux), Breil, 13 mai 1942.

31. ADAM 618 W 161, Rapport n°309 de l'Inspecteur Provincial Bonneaux, Breil, 12 février 1942.

32. Louis Caperan-Moreno, *Histoire de Menton* (Menton: Annales de la Société d'Art et d'Histoire du Mentonnais, 1993), 116.

33. *Mare Nostrum* (Latin for "Our Sea") was a rallying cry for Italian colonialist expansion in the 1880s, later revamped by the Italian irredentist poet Gabriele D'Annunzio, and finally used by the Fascist propaganda as an equivalent to "the place in the sun."

34. Italo Balbo was an Italian Fascist leader since the early 1920s who later became one of the major aces of the Italian air force. He died on 28 June 1940 when his plane was shot down by friendly fire in North Africa.

35. Molinari and Panicacci, *Menton dans la Tourmente,* 56.

36. AN, F 1 C III 1137, Rapport du 4 janvier 1941, cited in Molinari and Panicacci, *Menton dans la Tourmente,* 52.

37. ACS, CIAF, Commissariato civile di Mentone ed Ufficio informazioni (1940–1943), b. 2, Rapporto 511/R6/gab Commissario Civile Mentone Giuseppe Frediani a G. B. Marziali, Prefetto CIAF dei Amministrazione Territori Francesi Occupati, 1 giugno 1942, 12.

38. ACS, CIAF, Commissariato civile di Mentone ed Ufficio informazioni (1940–1943), b. 3, Rapporto Commissario Civile Mentone Giuseppe Frediani a G. B. Marziali, Prefetto CIAF dei Amministrazione Territori Francesi Occupati, "Barneaud, Marcello, Segretario Municipale di Mentone", CIAF, 9 febbraio 1942. Marcel Barneaud later joined the *Combat* Resistance group and was arrested by the Italians in the 7 May 1943 roundup in Nice. He eventually returned to France in 1944. See Barneaud, *Les Mentonnais et la Résistance,* 42. Marcel Barneaud was registered as "Barnaud [*sic*], Marcel Charles, number 455," in the comprehensive list of French citizens arrested by the Italians in the Alpes-Maritimes from November 1942 to September 1943 available for consultation in ADAM 166 W 9.

39. ACS, CIAF, Commissariato civile di Mentone ed Ufficio informazioni (1940–1943), b. 3, Lettera di Mrs Barneaud al Commissario Civile di Mentone, 26 aprile 1942.

40. *Il Nizzardo,* Anno IX, n°26, 6 settembre 1942.

41. A copy of the letter can be found in AUSSME, M3, b. 34, Lettera di Jean Durandy al Commissario Civile di Mentone, 7 settembre 1942.

42. Molinari and Panicacci, *Menton dans la Tourmente,* 63–64.

43. *Il Nizzardo,* Anno IX, n°34, 1 novembre 1942. It is worth noting that from the perspective of the French state, Durandy remained the mayor of Menton on the grounds that a small part of the municipal territory of Menton was still in the French free zone. See ACS, CIAF, Commissariato civile di Mentone ed Ufficio informazioni (1940–1943), b. 1, fasc. 14, Rapporto n°748/gab/R4 Rapporto Commissario Civile Mentone Giuseppe Frediani ad Amministrazione Territori Francesi Occupati, CIAF, 31 ottobre 1942.

44. In my opinion the Mentonese dialect seems much more related to the Ligurian one than to the Provençal. The Italian authorities also sought to stir up local separatism in Corsica with the dual effort to demarcate the Corsican population from France and to stress the cultural ties with Italy. See Karine Varley, "Between Vichy France and Fascist Italy: Redefining Identity and the Enemy in Corsica during the Second World War," *Journal of Contemporary History* 47, no. 3 (2012): 515.

45. The Comité des Traditions Mentonnaises was partly financed with a one-time payment of fifty thousand lire by the Italian authorities. See AUSSME, M3, b. 34, Amministrazione dei territori francesi occupati, "Pro-memoria concernenti le irregolarita' esistenti nell'amministrazione del Commissariato Civile di Mentone e proposte sul modo di sanarle," Torino, 21 settembre 1942, 8.

46. A detailed dossier on Marcel Firpo is available in the Dossiers de Procédure, Cour de Justice, Section Nice, ADAM 318 W 63. Furthermore, a few Italian reports on Firpo can be found in ACS, CIAF, Commissariato civile di Mentone ed Ufficio informazioni (1940–1943), b. 2. Firpo was sentenced to seven years in prison after the war.

47. *Giornale di Genova,* 17 marzo 1942. A French translation of the article is available in ADAM 166 W 10, Rapport n°1072 du Commissariat spécial de Menton, replié sur Cap-Martin au Préfet Régional des Alpes-Maritimes, 18 mars 1942.

48. Dossiers of some of these grants can be examined in ADAM 560 W 215.

49. Dombrowski Risser, *France under Fire,* 175–76.

50. For more on the *a bras ouverts* campaign, see Torrie, *"For Their Own Good,"* 76–78.

51. ASMAE, Serie Armistizio Pace b. 20, Rapporto n°18795 Presidente CIAF Vacca Maggiolini, "Mentone, situazione politica ed economica," Torino, 28 giugno 1941, 4. The Italian state spent eight hundred thousand lire to pay war damages for lost goods. Rapporto n°15800 Sottocommissione Affari Generali, Torino, 1 settembre 1941.

52. ACS, CIAF, Commissariato civile di Mentone ed Ufficio informazioni (1940–1943), b. 1, Rapporto 571/R5/gab Commissario Civile Mentone Giuseppe Frediani a G. B. Marziali, Prefetto CIAF dei Amministrazione Territori Francesi Occupati, 1 giugno 1942, 3.

53. Proclamation Article 8.

54. Giampaolo Guzzi, *L'Occupazione italiana di Mentone (1940–1943): storia postale* (Self-published, 2003), 12–31.

55. ADAHP 42 W 81, Rapport n°852/Int présenté par le Maitre des Requêtes au Conseil d'Etat Theis, Président de la Sous-Délégation pour les Affaires Administratives, à l'Amiral Duplat, Président de la D.F.C.I.A., 11 juillet 1942, 9.

56. From the 1870s until recently, Italian male citizens in their eighteenth year received a pink call-up postcard ordering them to have a medical examination at the military district of their region. If deemed fit for military service, they would be enlisted for a period of time (normally a year and a half in peacetime, longer at a time of war) between the ages of twenty and fifty-five. See Virgilio Ilari, *Storia del servizio militare in Italia*, vol. 3, *"Nazione Militare" e "Fronte del Lavoro" (1919–1943)* (Roma: Rivista Militare, Centro Militare di Studi Strategici, 1990), 307–313. Occasionally, youths would be drafted in Menton from January 1942 onward.

57. ACS, CIAF, Commissariato civile di Mentone ed Ufficio informazioni (1940–1943), b. 1, fasc. 14, Lettera del Commissario Civile di Mentone Virgilio Magris al comandante dei Carabinieri di Mentone, 1 maggio1941; Lettera n°2570 f C. Vittorelli, Prefetto per l'Amministrazione dei Territori Occupati; Rapporto A.85 Commissario Civile di Mentone, Virgilio Magris all'Amministrazione dei Territori Occupati, 30 maggio 1941.

58. ADAHP 42 W 81, Rapport n°852/Int présenté par le Maitre des Requêtes au Conseil d'Etat Theis, Président de la Sous-Délégation pour les Affaires Administratives, à l'Amiral Duplat, Président de la D.F.C.I.A., 11 juillet 1942, 14.

59. ADAHP 42 W 81, Compte-rendu de la Conférence interministérielle ayant pour l'objet l'étude des problèmes posés par l'occupation et la propagande italienne tenue le jeudi 10 décembre 1941 à l'Hôtel Thermal à Vichy, 21.

60. ACS, CIAF, Commissariato civile di Mentone ed Ufficio informazioni (1940–1943), b. 1, fasc. 1, Commissario Civile di Mentone, amministrazione municipale, Rapporto "Evoluzione demografica della città di Mentone."

61. June–November 1940: Aldo Leoni; November 1940–September 1941: Virgilio Magris; September 1941–November 1942: Giuseppe Frediani; November 1942–August 1943: Gino Berri; August 1943–September 1943: Alberto Castaldi.

62. Molinari and Panicacci, *Menton dans la Tourmente*, 44.

63. A display of the leaflets and the postcard can be found in Guzzi, *L'Occupazione italiana di Mentone*, 51–53.

64. ADAM 616 W 260, "Conférence pour l'étude des problèmes posés par l'occupation et la propagande italiennes tenue à Vichy le 16 décembre 1940," 25–26.

65. Molinari and Panicacci, *Menton dans la Tourmente*, 48.

66. The documentation on the negotiations regarding the electricity network is available in ACS, CIAF, Commissariato civile di Mentone ed Ufficio informazioni (1940–1943), b. 2. For water and gas, see ACS, CIAF, Commissariato civile di Mentone ed Ufficio informazioni (1940–1943), b. 3.

67. Barneaud, *Les Mentonnais et la Résistance*, 37.

68. ADAM 166 W 26, Segnalazioni 463/gab/R3, 8 aprile 1942 and 301 gab/R3, 27 aprile 1942, del Commissario Civile Dott. Giuseppe Frediani alla CIAF, Amministrazione Territori Occupati, Torino.

69. ACS, CIAF, Commissariato civile di Mentone ed Ufficio informazioni (1940–1943), b. 2, Rapporto 511/R6/gab Commissario Civile Mentone Giuseppe Frediani al G. B. Marziali, Prefetto CIAF dei Amministrazione Territori Francesi Occupati, 1 giugno 1942, 3.

70. 618 W 161, Rapport n°2247 du Commissaire Spécial de Breil, Chef de Service, au Préfet des Alpes-Maritimes, 5 août 1941.

71. 618 W 161, Rapport n°924 du Commissaire, Chef du Service des Renseignement Généraux au Préfet Régional, Intendant de Police, 2 avril 1942.

72. 618 W 161, Rapport n°211 du Commissaire, Chef du Service des Renseignement Généraux au Préfet Régional, Intendant de Police, 23 janvier 1942. The *Befana* is an Italian tradition tied to the Epiphany that has no equivalent in Anglo-Saxon and French cultures. She can be described as an ugly old witch riding a broomstick, who is supposed to deliver charcoal to mischievous children and candies to obedient ones. The tradition, still widely celebrated, was enmeshed in the Fascist discourse and thus transformed into the *Befana fascista,* or the Epiphany of the Duce. See Victoria de Grazia, *How Fascism Ruled Women: Fascism, 1922–1945* (Berkeley: University of California Press, 1992), 111.

73. Molinari and Panicacci, *Menton dans la Tourmente,* 62.

74. ADAM 166 W 26 holds a few dossiers of people expelled from Menton.

75. ASMAE, Serie Armistizio Pace, b. 20, Rapporto n°15800 Sottocommissione Affari Generali, Torino, 1 settembre 1941; Rapporto n°5327 T.O. Prefetto dei Territori Occupati G. B. Marziali, Torino, 2 settembre 1941.

76. ACS, CIAF, Commissariato civile di Mentone ed Ufficio informazioni (1940–1943), b. 2, Lettera n°4584 del Prefetto dei Territori Occupati al Commissario Civile di Mentone Giuseppe Frediani, 3 luglio 1942. Frediani issued two successive instructions to his subordinates that echoed the words of Marziali.

77. ACS, CIAF, Commissariato civile di Mentone ed Ufficio informazioni (1940–1943), b. 2, Rapporto 511/R6/gab Commissario Civile Mentone Giuseppe Frediani a G. B. Marziali, Prefetto CIAF dei Amministrazione Territori Francesi Occupati, 1 giugno 1942, 61–62.

78. Giuseppe Frediani, *La Pace separata di Ciano* (Roma: Bonacci Editore, 1990), 122–23. For more on the history of the Comité des Traditions Mentonnaises, see ACS, CIAF, Commissariato civile di Mentone ed Ufficio informazioni (1940–1943), b. 2, Rapporto 511/R6/gab Commissario Civile Mentone Giuseppe Frediani a G. B. Marziali, Prefetto CIAF dei Amministrazione Territori Francesi Occupati, 1 giugno 1942.

79. Barranco would later play an important role in Nice during the Italian occupation from November 1942 to September 1943; see chapter 7.

80. Frediani, *La Pace separata di Ciano,* 105.

81. ACS, CIAF, Commissariato civile di Mentone ed Ufficio informazioni (1940–1943), b. 1, Rapporto 571/R5/gab Commissario Civile Mentone Giuseppe Frediani a G. B. Marziali, Prefetto CIAF dei Amministrazione Territori Francesi Occupati, 1 giugno 1942, 11.

82. ACS, CIAF, Commissariato civile di Mentone ed Ufficio informazioni (1940–1943), b. 2, fasc. 48, Lettera Commissario Civile Mentone Giuseppe Frediani, 18 aprile 1942.

83. ACS, CIAF, Commissariato civile di Mentone ed Ufficio informazioni (1940–1943), b. 1, Rapporto Commissario Civile di Mentone Gino Berri "Attività del Commissariato Civile di Mentone, 1 giugno 1942–31 gennaio 1943," 33.

84. ACS, Provincia d'Imperia, Affari di Gabinetto, II, 11, 6, rapporto riservato del 22.3.1943, cited by Panicacci, *L'Occupation Italienne*, 64.

85. *La Gazzetta del Popolo*, 27 ottobre 1941, cited by Panicacci, *L'Occupation Italienne*, 72.

86. A summary of the units in the occupied zone can be found in Domenico Schipsi, *L'occupazione italiana dei territori metropolitani francesi (1940–1943)* (Roma: Stato Maggiore dell'Esercito, Ufficio Storico, 2007), 17.

87. The Guardia alla Frontiera (Frontier Guards, or GaF) was made official by king's decree on 28 April 1937. For more on the Guardia alla Frontiera, see Ascoli, *La Guardia alla Frontiera*; Alessandro Bernasconi and Daniela Collavo, *Dei Sacri Confini Guardia Sicura: la Guardia alla Frontiera, 1934–1943* (Trento: Temi, 2002).

88. In six months Italian casualties in the Greek campaign amounted to 13,755 dead; more than 63,000 wounded, including 12,368 with frozen limbs; and more than 25,000 missing. For more on the appalling Italian campaign in Greece, see Rochat, *Le Guerre Italiane*, 259–84.

89. ADAHP 42 W 81, Rapport n°2779 du Commissaire Spécial Sangla du Chef de Service à Monsieur le Préfet des Basses-Alpes, 30 mai 1942.

90. ADAHP 42 W 81, Préfecture des Basses-Alpes, Note de Renseignements, 14 mars 1941.

91. Service Historique de l'Armée de Terre (hereafter, SHAT) 1P78, Dossier 2, Rapport de Sarraz-Bournet, General Inspector of the Ministry of Interior of Vichy and member of the CIAF French Delegation in Torino, 23 July 1941, cited in Schipsi, *L'occupazione italiana*, 29.

92. ADAHP 42 W 80, Rapport du Préfet des Basses-Alpes au Ministre Secrétaire d'État à l'Intérieur, 8 janvier 1941; ADAHP 42 W 81 Rapport du Préfet des Basses-Alpes au Ministre Secrétaire d'État à l'Intérieur, 5 février 1941.

93. ADAHP 42 W 80, Rapport du Préfet Des Basses-Alpes au Ministre de l'Intérieur, 26 octobre 1940.

94. ADAHP 42 W 81, Compte-rendu de la Conférence interministérielle ayant pour l'objet l'étude des problèmes posés par l'occupation et la propagande italienne tenue le jeudi 10 décembre 1941 à l'Hôtel Thermal à Vichy, 14.

95. No doctor lived in Larche, so local inhabitants called the doctor of the town of Jausiers, twelve and a half kilometers away, but the French doctor was not available. Larche, on the other hand, was only two kilometers from the Italian garrison of Maison-Méane. The boy thus received medical assistance from the local Italian military doctor. ADAHP 42 W 82, Rapport n°295/S du Lieutenant Colonel Bertrand, Commandant le District Militaire de Barcelonnette à Monsieur le Colonel, Commandant militaire du département des Hautes-Alpes, 29 juillet 1942.

96. ADAHP 42 W 82, Rapport n°609-HA/I du Colonel Colas, Commandant militaire du département des Hautes-Alpes, Gap, 15 juillet 1942.

97. Jackson, *France: The Dark Years,* 328. For more on the role of women in Vichy propaganda, see Miranda Pollard, *Reign of Virtue: Mobilizing Gender in Vichy France* (Chicago: University of Chicago Press, 1998).

98. French public opinion barely tolerated casinos, which were seen as places of debauchery at a time when the majority of the population was suffering. The Alpes-Maritimes prefect, under direct orders from Vichy, shut down casinos on the French Riviera on 11 November 1942. This decision was severely criticized by some, not only because it left hundreds of people jobless but also because it merely displaced the issue. Players moved to the Monaco casino, which, of course, was outside of Vichy's jurisdiction. Many documents on the casinos can be found in ADAM 616 W 166.

99. ADAHP 42 W 81, Rapport AN.3028 du Sous-prefet de Barcelonnette à Monsieur le Prefet des Basses-Alpes, 3 décembre 1941.

100. ADAHP 42 W 80, Rapport n°2915 du Commissaire Principal Sangla, Chef de Service à Monsieur le Préfet des Basses-Alpes, 4 juin 1942; Rapport n°35/4 de l'Adjudant Doux sur les fréquentations de militaires italiens par des jeunes filles de Larche, 13 juin 1942.

101. ADAHP 42 W 41, Rapport n°374/4 du Chef d'Escadron Ogier sur la physionomie du département, Digne, 6 janvier 1943, 8.

102. ADAHP 42 W 81, Rapport n°852/Int présenté par le Maitre des Requêtes au Conseil d'Etat Theis, Président de la Sous-Délégation pour les Affaires Administratives, à l'Amiral Duplat, Président de la D.F.C.I.A., 11 juillet 1942, 9; 618 W 161, Rapport n°388 de l'Inspecteur Principal Bonneau à Monsieur le Commissaire, Chef des Renseignements Generaux, Breil, 9 février 1942.

103. ADAM 616 W 260, "Conférence pour l'étude des problèmes posés par l'occupation et la propagande italiennes tenue à Vichy le 16 décembre 1940," 33.

104. ADAHP 42 W 81, Compte-rendu de la Conférence interministérielle ayant pour l'objet l'étude des problèmes posés par l'occupation et la propagande italienne tenue le jeudi 10 décembre 1941 à l'Hôtel Thermal à Vichy, 24.

105. More information on the Basque provinces can be found in Sandra Ott, *War, Judgment, and Memory in the Basque Borderlands, 1914–1945* (Reno: University of Nevada Press, 2008).

106. *Passeurs* were smugglers or guides who passed goods and people across the border.

107. The STO was implemented with the law of 16 February 1943 that required all males over twenty to be drafted to Germany as forced labor. The law is widely acknowledged as one of the main instigators for the development of the rural Resistance movement, the *Maquis.* For more on the topic, see H. R. Kedward, *In Search of the Maquis: Rural Resistance in Southern France, 1942–1944* (Oxford: Oxford University Press, 1995).

108. ASMAE, Serie Armistizio Pace b. 20, Rapporto n°18795 Presidente CIAF Vacca Maggiolini "Mentone, situazione politica ed economica," Torino, 28 giugno 1941, 1–2.

CHAPTER 5. THE NOVEMBER 1942 INVASION

1. Cited by Frederic Spotts, *The Shameful Peace: How French Artists and Intellectuals Survived the Nazi Occupation* (New Haven, CT: Yale University Press, 2008), 158–59.

2. AUSSME, D7, b. 20, CIAF Notiziario quindicinale n°33, 1–15 aprile 1942, 33.

3. AUSSME, D7, b. 20, CIAF Notiziario quindicinale n°34, 16–31 aprile 1942, 27; Ermanno Amicucci, *Nizza Italiana* (Milano: Mondadori, 1942). It is interesting to note that the first five editions of the book, printed between 1939 and 1942, were published under the title of *Nizza e l'Italia* (Nice and Italy). Significantly, Amicucci changed the title to *Nizza Italiana* (The Italian Nice) in the sixth edition, published in August 1942.

4. AUSSME, D7, b. 21, CIAF Notiziario quindicinale n°36, 15–31 maggio 1942, 35.

5. *Il Nizzardo*, Anno IX, n°8, 3 maggio 1942, 1.

6. Rainero, *La Commission italienne d'armistice*, 295–96.

7. Costa Bona, *Dalla guerra alla pace*, 125–27.

8. Schipsi, *L'occupazione italiana*, 72–73.

9. AUSSME, N1–11, DS 2119, Direttiva n°13788 di prot., "Secondo fronte" dal Stato Maggiore R. Esercito al Capo di S.M., Diario Storico SMRE, Allegato 38, 19 agosto 1942.

10. Jackson, *France: The Dark Years*, 221–23.

11. Costa Bona, *Dalla guerra alla pace*, 128–29.

12. AUSSME, N1–11, DS 1099, Telegramma n°19355 Superesercito al Comando Quarta Armata, 22.55, Diario Storico Comando Quarta Armata, Allegato 12, 10 novembre 1942.

13. Schipsi, *L'occupazione italiana*, 114.

14. AUSSME, N1–11, DS 1101, Telegramma n°3830/02 Comando XXII CA, Diario Storico XXII CA, Allegato 18, 10 novembre 1942.

15. AUSSME, N1–11, DS 1099, Rapporto n°7777/op. Generale Vercellino, "Rapporto situazione per il periodo 20 Settembre–20 Ottobre 1942," Diario Storico Comando 4° Armata, Allegato 9, 4 novembre 1942. AUSSME, N1–11, DS 987, "Stralcio della relazione mensile sul servizio 'P' (Propaganda) del mese di ottobre," Diario Storico I CA, Allegato 32, 31 ottobre 1942.

16. Schipsi, *L'occupazione italiana*, 106–107.

17. AUSSME, N1–11, DS 1101, Telegramma n°8007/op. Generale Vercellino, Diario Storico XXII CA, Allegato 17.

18. AUSSME, N1–11, DS 1101, Telegramma n°8053/op. Generale Vercellino, Diario Storico XXII CA, Allegato 21.

19. AUSSME, N1–11, DS 1016, Chiamata Comando Quarta Armata (Generale Trabucchi) at 1 A.M., 11 novembre, Diario Storico XV CA, Allegato 27. For Tabellini's absence, see AUSSME, N1–11, DS 1099 Diario Storico Quarta Armata, 11 novembre 1942.

20. AUSSME, N1–11, DS 1099, Diario Storico Quarta Armata, 11 novembre 1942; Fonogramma Capo Ufficio Operazioni, General Gerlier, al Comando Quarta Armata, 8.100/op., Diario Storico Comando Quarta Armata, Allegato 14.

21. Two out of the three army corps met the goals set by the Esigenza O, the I CA units by reaching Modane and the Orelle valley, while the XV CA met even fewer problems as motorized Piave units, followed closely by Legnano units, entered Nice at 3:30 P.M. Only the XXII CA did not reach its objective: the Mescla Bridge on the Var River. AUSSME, N1–11, DS 1099, Diario Storico Quarta Armata, 11 novembre 1942.

22. Gen. Ugo Cavallero was made field marshal on 1 July 1942, a few months before the invasion of France.

23. Ugo Cavallero, *Diario, 1940–1943*(Roma: Ciarrapico, 1984), 563–66. For the official directive received on 12 November at 2:30 P.M. by the Comando Quarta Armata, see AUSSME, N1–11, DS 1099, Telegramma SMRE (Superesercito), Diario Storico Comando 4° Armata, Allegato 19.

24. Schipsi, *L'occupazione italiana,* 121.

25. Ibid., 136.

26. ARC, T-821, Roll 270, IT 3131, Lettera n°04/3832 di prot. Comando XV CA "Contegno delle truppe," 19 novembre 1942.

27. For instance, the Genova Cavalleria (an Italian regiment) arrived in Grasse only on 21 November. See AUSSME, N1–11, DS 1099 Diario Storico Quarta Armata, 20 novembre.

28. Schipsi, *L'occupazione italiana,* 135.

29. AUSSME, N1–11, DS 1099 Diario Storico 4° Armata, 14 novembre; Rapporto n°10294/op. Comando Quarta Armata al SMRE, Diario Storico Quarta Armata, Allegato 41, 17 dicembre 1942.

30. AUSSME, D7, b. 51, I, Documento 41, Rapporto conversazione Vacca Maggiolini e Ammiraglio Duplat, 14 novembre 1942.

31. Rainero, *La Commission italienne d'armistice,* 310.

32. AUSSME, N1–11, DS 1099, Telegramma n°12711/op. SMRE al Comando Quarta Armata, Diario Storico Comando Quarta Armata, Allegato 30, 14 novembre 1942.

33. ACS, CIAF, Commissariato civile di Mentone ed Ufficio informazioni (1940–1943), b. 1, Rapporto n°7728 T.O. del Prefetto CIAF Marziali, "Atteggiamento da assumere nei riguardi della parte francese," 14 novembre 1942.

34. AUSSME, N1–11, DS 1099, Fonogramma Capo Ufficio Operazioni, Generale Gerlier, al Comando Quarta Armata, 8.100/op., Diario Storico Comando Quarta Armata, Allegato 14.

35. Full text is available in Panicacci, *Les Alpes-Maritimes,* 169. One original leaflet can be found in AUSSME, N1–11, DS 1099, Diario Storico Comando Quarta Armata in the Allegati folder.

36. ASMAE, Affari Politici, 1931–1945, Francia, b. 54, Lettera n°24693 CIAF Sottocommissione Affari Generali al Marchese Don Blasco D'Ajeta, Capo Segreteria del Ministro degli Esteri, Torino, 12 novembre 1942.

37. AUSSME, N1–11, DS 1099, Fonogramma Capo Ufficio Operazioni, Generale Gerlier, al Comando Quarta Armata, 8.100/op., Diario Storico Comando Quarta Armata, Allegato 14.

38. See, for instance, General Vercellino's 20 November report on the occupation of France. AUSSME, N1–11, DS 1099, Telegramma n°8772/op. "Occupazione territorio francese," Direttiva 60.100/op., Diario Storico Comando Quarta Armata.

39. See, for instance, the alarming report of one CIAF official in Gap, Eugenio Mazzarini, who wrote of a great number of volunteers flocking to the Armée d'Armistice recruitment centers. ASMAE, Serie Armistizio Pace, b. 1, Rapporto n°209 Delegato CIAF a Gap Eugenio Mazzarini, "Situazione politica nella zona delle Alte Alpi," 27 febbraio 1941, 4–5. The report was challenged a few weeks later by Mazzarini's superior, Gen. Paolo Micheletti, who claimed the French army was nowhere near ready to undertake a war campaign. ASMAE, Serie Armistizio Pace, b. 1, Rapporto n°8023 Presidente CIAF Affari Generali "Situazione politica nella zona delle Alte Alpi," Turin, 17 marzo 1941.

40. Olivier Wieviorka, *Histoire de la Résistance, 1940–1945* (Paris: Perrin, 2013), 196.

41. Henri Amoroux, *La vie Française sous l'Occupation* (Paris: Fayard, 1961), 279–90.

42. Schipsi, *L'occupazione italiana,* 145–46.

43. ADAM 616 W 241, Fichier 23, Note du Sous-Préfet, Dirécteur du Cabinet du Commandant Blanc, 25 novembre 1942. According to the different reports, border guards and gendarmes were disarmed at Saint-Étienne-de-Tinée, Isola, Breil, Saorge, Castellar, Castillon, Carnolès, and Roquebrune. All firearms were subsequently handed back, except in Roquebrune.

44. ADAM 616 W 133, Rapport n°3974 du Commissaire Spécial de Menton à Roquebrune au Préfet des Alpes-Maritimes, Roquebrune-Cap-Martin, 16 novembre 1942; ADAM 616 W 134, Rapport du Chef d'Escadron Soymie, Commandant de la Gendarmerie dans les Alpes-Maritimes, Nice, 2 décembre 1942, 2. It is interesting to note that the Menton civil commissar Frediani minimized the friction with the French authorities in his report, mentioning only "some episodes of passive resistance in the handover of weapons [by French border guards]." ACS, CIAF, Commissariato civile di Mentone ed Ufficio informazioni (1940–1943), b. 2, Rapporto 766/gab/R a G.B. Marziali, Menton, 11 novembre 1942.

45. ADAHP 42 W 82, unsigned police report, 13 novembre 1942.

46. ADAM 616 W 241, Fichier 19, Lettre du Maire de Castillon au Préfet des Alpes-Maritimes, 12 novembre 1942; Fichier 13, Lettre du maître d'école de Castillon, 13 novembre 1942; Lettre du Maire de La Bollène-Vésubie au Préfet des Alpes-Maritimes, 16 novembre 1942.

47. Several statements to the police in Roquebrune can be found in ADAM 560 W 217.

48. For instance, troops of the Taro Division broke down the door of a garage in Roquesteron to steal staples, such as potatoes and cabbage, as well as gas. See ADAM 159 W 49, procès-verbal n°200, Roquesteron, 14 novembre 1942.

49. ADAM 616 W 241, Fichier 20, Rapport n°3955 du Commissaire Quilici, Roquebrune-Cap-Martin, 14 novembre 1942.

50. ARC, T-821, Roll 270, IT 3131, Lettera n°04/3832 "Contegno delle truppe," Comando XV CA, 19 novembre 1942.

51. ADAM 616 W 47, télégramme officiel, 12 novembre 1942, 12:15 P.M.

52. ADAM 616 W 241, Fichier 16, Lettre n°23 du Préfet des Alpes-Maritimes, Nice, 16 novembre 1942, 1. The prefect went as far as to chastise the head of the Nice Censorship Office for having failed to scratch the word "Occupation" from a *Petit Niçois* (a local newspaper) column title on 16 novembre 1942. ADAM 616 W 242, Fichier 47, Note du Préfet des Alpes-Maritimes au chef de Censure de Nice, 18 novembre 1942.

53. ADAM 616 W 133, Rapport n°3287 du Breil Police Commissaire, 11 novembre 1942.

54. ADAM 616 W 133, Rapport n°3293 du Breil Police Commissaire, 12 novembre 1942.

55. Maurice Blanchard, "Historique de la prise de contact," unpublished, 6, Musée de la Résistance, Nice, cited by Panicacci, *Les Alpes-Maritimes,* 169.

56. ADAM 616 W 186, Commission de Contrôle Postal de Nice, Rapport n°3311, Rapport Mensuel n°12, Année 1942, 31 décembre 1942.

57. ADAHP 42 W 85, Rapport du Commissaire de la Ville de Digne au Préfet des Basses-Alpes, 30 novembre 1942.

58. ADAM 616 W 133, Rapport n°3974 du Commissaire Spécial de Menton à Roquebrune au Préfet des Alpes-Maritimes, Roquebrune-Cap-Martin, 16 novembre 1942. It should be noted that in the postwar trials this friendly attitude toward the Italian troops was harshly punished by the Comités d'Épuration; see chapter 9.

59. ADAM 616 W 134, Rapport du Chef d'Escadron Soymie, Commandant de la Gendarmerie dans les Alpes-Maritimes, Nice, 2 décembre 1942, 3.

60. ADAM 616 W 133, Rapport n°3974 du Commissaire Spécial de Menton à Roquebrune au Préfet des Alpes-Maritimes, Roquebrune-Cap-Martin, 16 novembre 1942.

61. ADAM 616 W 134, Rapport n°X/2 du Captain Bidet sur des inscriptions anti-italiennes à Cap d'Ail, Roquebrune, 17 novembre 1942.

62. ASMAE, Affari Politici, 1931–1945, Francia, b. 54, Telespresso n°330/R.857 dal Delegato CIAF a Cannes Eugenio (Plaja Occupazione della zona da parte delle truppe italiane), Cannes, 12 novembre 1942, 3.

63. For a concise history of Monaco, see Julian Hale, *The French Riviera: A Cultural History* (Oxford: Oxford University Press, 2009), 33–49.

64. W. Somerset Maugham, *Strictly Personal* (Garden City, NY: Doubleday, Doran and Co., 1941), 156. Ironically, unbeknownst to Maugham, his Italian chambermaid would work for both the Italian and the German occupation forces and would be sentenced after the war to three years in prison. ADAM 318 W 55, Cours de Justice des Alpes-Maritimes, Dossier Catherine G.

65. ASMAE, Affari Politici, 1931–1945, Francia, b. 55, Lettera n°168923 di prot. del Presidente per gli Affari Economici e Finanziari, CIAF, 26 marzo 1942. See also Abramovici, *Un Rocher bien occupé,* 94–99.

66. AUSSME, N1–11, DS 1016, n°60.000/op. di prot., Attuazione Emergenza O, 10 novembre 1942, Diario Storico XV CA, Allegato 24, 2.

67. ADAM 616 W 241, Rapport sur des A/S. d'incidents qui se sont produits en Principauté de Monaco à l'occasion du passage des troupes italiennes du Commissaire Principal de Beausoleil au Préfet des Alpes-Maritimes, 14 novembre 1942; Abramovici, *Un Rocher bien occupé,* 158.

68. Abramovici, *Un Rocher bien occupé,* 159.

69. Walter Oberaugh and Carol Jose, *Guerilla in Striped Pants: A US Diplomat Joins the Italian Resistance* (New York: Praeger, 1992), 4.

70. The consul Oberaugh was arrested by the Italians on 2 December, deported to Italy, and later ended up in the Italian Resistance.

71. Abramovici, *Un Rocher bien occupé,* 160.

72. ADAM 616 W 241, Rapport du Commissaire Principal de Beausoleil sur des manifestations de fidelité de la population monégasque à S.A.S. le Prince Louis II de Monaco, Beausoleil, 16 novembre 1942.

73. ADAM 616 W 241, Rapport du Commissaire Principal de Beausoleil sur des incidents en Principauté de Monaco, Beausoleil, 18 novembre 1942. According to Oberaugh, the invasion of the consulate happened on 20 November. For a firsthand account of the episode, see Oberaugh and Jose, *Guerilla in Striped Pants,* 8–12.

74. AUSSME, N1–11, DS 1099, n°3142 di prot. "I" "Occupazione del Principato di Monaco," Diario Storico Quarta Armata, Allegato 36, 17 novembre 1942.

75. ADAM 616 W 241, Rapport du Commissaire Principal de Beausoleil sur des incidents en Principauté de Monaco, Beausoleil, 18 novembre 1942.

76. Exhaustive lists of individuals arrested in the Italian military occupation in the Alpes-Maritimes, sorted by nationalities chronologically and by alphabetical order, can be found in ADAM 166 W 9.

77. A detailed report on Bava's arrest is available in ADAM 166 W 9.

78. ADAM 616 W 242, Fichier 25, Lettre du Préfet des Alpes-Maritimes au Commandant de la Division Legnano, 19 novembre 1942.

79. ADAM 616 W 242, Fichier 25, Lettre du Général Bancale au Préfet des Alpes-Maritimes, 20 novembre 1942.

80. AUSSME, N1–11, DS 1099, Telescritto n°3225 di prot. "I" Comando 4 Armata al SMRE, Ufficio Operazioni I, Diario Storico Quarta Armata, Allegato 39, 20 novembre 1942. The order was relayed down to the commanders of all three army corps. See AUSSME, N1–11, DS 1101, Fonogramma a mano n°3226 di prot. "I" Comando Quarta Armata ai Comandi I, XV, XXII Corpi D'Armata, Diario Storico XXII CA, Allegato 55, 20 novembre 1942.

81. AUSSME, N1–11, DS 1101, Telegramma n°3366 "I" di prot. Azione degli organi di polizia italiani nei territori occupati, Diario Storico XXII CA, Allegato 69, 25 novembre 1942.

82. A detailed account of the two arrests and the motivations behind them can be found in ADAM 166 W 9.

CHAPTER 6. THE ITALIANS SETTLE IN

1. AUSSME, N-1–11, DS 1016, Telegramma n°8772/op. di prot. Comando Quarta Armata, Diario Storico XV CA.

2. Rainero, *La Commission italienne d'armistice*, 68–70.

3. Schipsi, *L'occupazione italiana*, 166–67.

4. AUSSME, N-1–11, DS 2078, Telegramma n°20299 dal SMRE, Diario Storico SMRE, Allegato 111, 24 novembre 1942.

5. AUSSME, N-1–11, DS 1101, Telegramma n°8843/op. di prot., "Linea di demarcazione tra forze italiane e germaniche nel territorio francese," Diario Storico XXII CA, Allegato 40, 21 novembre 1942.

6. AUSSME, N-1–11, DS 1101, Lettera n°4078/02 di prot., Comando XXII CA, Diario Storico XXII CA, Allegato 76, 27 novembre 1942. The XXII CA received a communication from the Felber headquarters at 6 A.M. on 27 November. The German attack on Toulon began at 3 A.M.

7. Schipsi, *L'occupazione italiana*, 312–13.

8. AUSSME, N-1–11, DS 987, Fonogramma a mano n°9157/op. di prot., Comando Quarta Armata, Diario Storico I CA, Allegato 122, 27 novembre 1942, 11 a.m.; Telegramma n°4839/op. di prot., "Provvedimenti di sicurezza," Diario Storico I CA, Allegato 123, 28 novembre 1942.

9. AUSSME, N-1–11, DS 987, Lettera n°4877/op. di prot., Comando I CA, Diario Storico I CA, Allegato 126, 29 novembre 1942.

10. AUSSME N-1–11, DS 987, Lettera n°6157/serv. di prot., "Disarmo delle forze francesi, Depositi di protezione," Comando I CA, Diario Storico I CA, Allegato 138, 5 dicembre 1942; AUSSME, L-13, b. 225, Lettera A. Gr. Felber. 1814/42, 14 dicembre 1942, cited by Schipsi, *L'occupazione italiana*, 208.

11. AUSSME, N-1–11, DS 1101, Lettera n°9856/op. di prot., Comando Quarta Armata, Diario Storico XXII CA, Allegato 121, 9 dicembre 1942.

12. AUSSME, N-1–11, DS SMRE 2079, Lettera n°21260, Allegato 22, 7 dicembre 1942.

13. Massimo Borgogni, *Italia e Francia durante la crisi militare dell'Asse* (Siena: Nuova Immagine, 1994), 162.

14. AUSSME, N-1–11, DS 2079, Telescritto SMRE al Comando Quarta Armata, Diario Storico SMRE, Allegato 52, 30 dicembre 1943.

15. Burrin, *France under the Germans*, 166–69.

16. ARC, T-821, Roll 270, IT 3131, Lettera n°1582/dg., "Territori occupati della Francia," Commissione Consultiva per il Diritto di Guerra presso il Consiglio dei Ministri al Comando Supremo, 30 dicembre 1942.

17. ARC, T-821, Roll 265, IT 3099, Lettera, "Regime Giuridico del territorio occupato e delle Forze di Occupazione," non datata; Schipsi, *L'occupazione italiana*, 274. The *Relève* was the forced labor program instituted by Vichy in September 1942.

18. ASMAE, Affari Politici, 1931–1945, Francia, b. 54, Appunto Ministero degli Affari Esteri, 26 dicembre 1942.

19. ASMAE, Affari Politici, 1931–1945, Francia, b. 59, Rapporto n°2432 R, "Manifestazioni Italiane a Nizza," 14 novembre 1942. Calisse reiterated his annoyance with the overweening attitude of Gen. Amedeo De Cia, commander of the Legnano Division, in another letter to the Ministry of Foreign Affairs. ASMAE, Affari Politici, 1931–1945, Francia, b. 54, Rapporto n°2358 R, "Collaborazione con il Comando delle Truppe Italiane," 17 novembre 1942. In the same letter, Calisse also emphasized the positive disposition of the XV CA commander, General Bancale, who graciously accepted the help of the CIAF delegation.

20. Calisse had found out about the episode only because Prefect Ribière had reported Marciani's query to him, as Ribière had insisted that any talks on the matter had to be done via CIAF officials. ASMAE, Affari Politici, 1931–1945, Francia, b. 54, Rapporto n°2479 R, "Occupazione militare italiana," 2 dicembre 1942.

21. ASMAE, Affari Politici, 1931–1945, Francia, b. 54, Rapporto n°2549 R, "Occupazione militare italiana: protezione connazionali e relazioni con le autorità locali," 24 dicembre 1942.

22. ASMAE, Affari Politici, 1931–1945, Francia, b. 54, Telespresso n°31061 MAE-Confalonieri "Francia 1–2 Occupazione Italiana," 17 dicembre 1942; stessa busta, Telespresso n°31118.

23. ASMAE, Affari Politici, 1931–1945, Francia, b. 54, Lettera n°80 da Bonarelli a Vitetti (MAE), 22 dicembre 1942.

24. Schipsi, *L'occupazione italiana,* 276–77.

25. AUSSME, D7, b. 119, Documento 51, Memorandum per il Generale Vercellino, 31 dicembre 1942.

26. Rainero, *La Commission italienne d'armistice,* 322.

27. Ibid., 323.

28. ASMAE, Affari Politici, 1931–1945, Francia, b. 69, Telegramma n°165 "I" di prot. dal comando Quarta Armata "Tutela di connazionali," 6 gennaio 1943.

29. ARC, T-821, Roll 345, IT 4356, Telegramma n°41 /R. di prot. dal Console Italiano a Nizza Calisse, Nice, 16 gennaio 1943.

30. A complete roster of the Fourth Army can be found in the Quarta Armata's *Diari Storici,* AUSSME, N 1–11, DS 1099 (Oct.-Dec. 1942), DS 1127 (Jan.-Feb. 1943), DS 1218 (March-Apr. 1943), DS 1320 (May-June 1943). Unfortunately, diaries of the Fourth Army past June 1943 could not be found.

31. The Pusteria controlled the northern half of the Alpine border (Savoy, Haute-Alpes, and Basses-Alpes), and the Argens Tactic Group was created in January 1943 as a reserve strategically placed to shore up the coastline defenses between Toulon and Saint Tropez, deemed by the Italian General Staff the weakest point of the Italian front line in the event of a prospective Allied attack. AUSSME, N 1–11, DS 1099, Rapporto n°10822/op., "Nuovo ordinamento dell'Armata, Comando Quarta Armata," Diario Storico Quarta Armata, Allegato 64, 27 dicembre 1942. A map

locating the Italian forces in France from December 1942 to June 1943 is available in Schipsi, *L'occupazione italiana,* 770.

32. See map 2.

33. ARC, T-821, Roll 266, IT 3099, Rapporto n°561/am/1, "Collegio nazionale di Fort Carré ad Antibes," Comando EFTF, 20 gennaio 1943.

34. The telegram 19/op. of 10 January 1943 from the I CA Comando has not been found, but a good résumé is included in ARC, T-821, Roll 261, IT 3078, Rapporto n°3229, "Sbarramento della zona costiera mediterranea," Comando I CA, 22 aprile 1943.

35. ARC, T-821, Roll 265, IT 3099, Rapporto n°1238/inf., "Informazioni varie circa frequentatori del porto di Antibes," Comando Divisione Legnano, 12 dicembre 1942; ADAM 616 W 133, Rapport n°25.816 du Commissaire Central de Cannes "sur l'état d'esprit de la population et la situation économique de la ville," 14 décembre1942.

36. ARC, T-821, Roll 266, IT 3099, Rapporto n°822/inf., "Pesca sul littorale francese," Comando I CA, 1 febbraio 1943. As time went by, Italian local commanders loosened the requirement in exchange for 10 percent of the daily catch. See ARC, T-821, Roll 266, IT 3099, Rapporto n°275/22, "Percentuale pescato a disposizione truppe di operazione," R. Capitaneria di Porto Nizza, 31 marzo 1943. For the full regulations in Provence, see Rapporto n°5503/inf., "Regolamento per la pesca sulla costa della Provenza," Comando I CA, 26 giugno 1943.

37. A detailed pattern of a *caposaldo,* along with drawings of its construction, can be found in ARC, T-821, Roll 262, IT 3081.

38. The Forbidden Coastal Zone should not be confused with the Forbidden Zone, created in the summer of 1940, an area that included the Nord and Pas-de-Calais departments, even though the northern part of the Forbidden Coastal Zone was itself already in the Forbidden Zone.

39. Alary, *La ligne de démarcation,* 40–41; Claude Malon, *Occupation, Épuration, Reconstruction, le monde de l'entreprise au Havre (1940–1950)* (Saint-Aignan: Publications des Universités de Rouen et du Havre, 2012), 61.

40. ARC, T-821, Roll 262, IT 3081, Rapporto n°6300/op., "Organizzazione costiera– Secondo tempo," Comando Quarta Armata, 18 aprile 1943; see also ARC, T-821, Roll 265, IT 3095, Rapporto n°4940/op., "Potenziamento della organizzazione difensiva," Comando Quarta Armata, 19 marzo 1943.

41. AUSSME, N1–11, DS 988, Rapporto n°6521/op., "Schieramento–unità di manovra–lavori," Comando Divisione Legnano, Diario Storico Divisione Legnano, Allegato 38, 16 dicembre 1942.

42. AUSSME, N1–11, DS 1219, Rapporto n°3337/op., "Riserve di settore e di divisione," Comando Divisione Legnano, Diario Storico Divisione Legnano, Allegato 51, 30 marzo 1943.

43. ARC, T-821, Roll 262, IT 3080, Rapporto n°1901/op., "Difesa antiparacadusti del territorio francese occupato," Comando I CA, 12 marzo 1943; Rapporto n°203770/1, "Militari per i nuclei antiparacadutisti," SMRE, 20 maggio 1943. It did

not help that NAP units sometimes even lacked trucks or cars needed to patrol. See AUSSME, N1–11, DS 1263, Rapporto n°5480/op., "Materiali per il N.A.P. n°13," Comando Divisione Legnano, Diario Storico Divisione Legnano, Allegato 55, 20 maggio 1943.

44. AUSSME, N1–11, DS 1263, Rapporto n°2872/op., "Esercitazione di due N.A.P. con termine del 2 giugno c.a.," Comando Divisione Legnano, Diario Storico Divisione Legnano, Allegato 113, 4 giugno 1943.

45. AUSSME, N1–11, DS 988, Rapporto n°6827/op., "Sistemazione difensiva," Comando Divisione Legnano, Diario Storico Divisione Legnano, Allegato 62, 25 dicembre 1942.

46. AUSSME, N1–11, DS 1016, Rapporto n°9939/op., "Ispezione dei reparti delle g.u. dipendenti," Comando Quarta Armata, 10 dicembre 1942, in Rapporto n°02/2988, "Ispezione," Comando XV CA, Diario Storico XV CA, Allegato 81, 14 dicembre 1942.

47. AUSSME N1–11, DS 1320, Direttiva n°10.200/op., "Agi e sicurezza," Comando Quarta Armata, Diario Storico Quarta Armata, Allegato 33, 12 giugno 1943.

48. AUSSME, N1–11, DS 1102, Rapporto n°242/op., "Ispezioni ai lavori di fortificazioni," Comando Quarta Armata, Diario Storico XXII CA, Allegato 44, 5 gennaio 1943.

49. AUSSME, M3, b. 476, Divisione Legnano (occupazione Francia), Rapporto n°1946/inf., "Festa del lavoro in Francia," Comando Divisione Legnano, 6 maggio 1943.

50. ARC, T-821, Roll 269, IT 3105, n°1217/inf., "Misure protettive da eventuali azioni terroristiche," Comando 67° Reggimento Legnano, 10 maggio 1943.

51. AUSSME, M3, b. 476, Divisione Legnano (occupazione Francia), Rapporto n°1239/inf., "Fotografie della costa ed uso della spiaggia," Comando Divisione Legnano, 8 maggio 1943.

52. AUSSME, Giustizia militare. Sentenze, carteggio, F19, b. 82, n°3039 del processo, 23 marzo 1943; AUSSME, Giustizia militare. Sentenze, carteggio, F19, b. 84, n°3062 del processo, 2 marzo 1943.

53. AUSSME, Giustizia militare. Sentenze, carteggio, F19, b. 84, n°3127 del processo, 2 maggio 1943.

54. AUSSME, Giustizia militare. Sentenze, carteggio, F19, b. 82, n°2878 del processo, 29 gennaio1943.

55. AUSSME, M3, b. 476, Divisione Legnano (occupazione Francia), Rapporto n°7306, "Difesa di segreto militare," 12 maggio 1943.

56. ARC, T-821, Roll 261, IT 3077, Rapporto n°e/53/rp, "Contegno degli ufficiali in rapporto alle relazioni femminili," Comando Aeronautica Italiano in Provenza, 6 settembre 1943.

57. Mimmo Franzinelli, *Il riarmo dello spirito, i cappellani militari nella seconda guerra mondiale* (Paese: Pagus Edizioni, 1991) 141.

58. For a list of the brothels in Nice, see ARC, T-821, Roll 265, IT 3095, Rapporto n°4842, "Riepilogo delle norme disciplinari in vigore nel Presidio di Nizza,"

Comando Presidio militare di Nizza, 11 agosto 1943. Sometimes the brothels were shared with the French populace, but in those instances in order to avoid dangerous confrontations, certain time slots would be reserved for the Italians. For instance, in Digne, the capital of the Basses-Alpes department, the brothel was reserved for the Italians from 5 P.M. to 8 P.M.. See ADAHP 42 W 82, Extraits du registre des arrêtés du maire, 18 janvier 1943.

59. ADAHP 42 W 82, Rapport du Commissaire de Police de la ville de Digne, "Enquêtes de moralité et de moeurs," 1 mars 1943.

60. Rodogno, *Fascism's European Empire,* 159–61. It is unlikely that Italian doctors bothered to test prostitutes for venereal diseases.

61. ARC, T-821, Roll 269, IT 3105, Rapporto n°3/60, "Elementi sospetti residenti a Cannes," Comando CC.RR. Divisione Legnano, 7 maggio 1943.

62. ARC, T-821, Roll 269, IT 3105, Rapporto n°8/71, "Segnalazione su persone sospette residenti a Cannes e relative proposte," Comando 39° Sezione CC.RR. Divisione, Legnano, 5 maggio 1943.

63. ARC, T-821, Roll 369, IT 4804, Rapporto n°32/7-Seg, "Aggressione subita dal caporal maggiore R. Pier Luigi del 78° Reggimento Fanteria Lupi di Toscana," Comando Divisione Lupi di Toscana, 20 dicembre 1942.

64. AUSSME, M3, b. 476, Divisione Legnano (occupazione Francia), Rapporto n°6629/inf., "Difesa del segreto militare," Comando I CA, 26 luglio 1943.

65. AUSSME, M3, b. 476, Divisione Legnano (occupazione Francia), Rapporto n°2749/I, "Tutela del segreto militare," Comando Quarta Armata, 27 febbraio 1943.

66. AUSSME, M3, b. 476, Divisione Legnano (occupazione Francia), Rapporto n°3104/inf., "Intercettazione conversazioni telefoniche," Comando Divisione Legnano, 23 maggio 1943.

67. AUSSME, N1–11, DS 988, Rapporto n°162260, "Riservatezza," Diario Storico Divisione Legnano, Allegato 65, 16 dicembre 1942.

68. AUSSME, Giustizia militare. Sentenze, carteggio, F19, b. 82, n°2919 del processo, 12 marzo 1943.

69. AUSSME, M3, b. 476, Divisione Legnano (occupazione Francia), Rapporto n°1193/inf., "Posti controllo autoveicoli," Comando Divisione Legnano, 23 marzo 1943.

70. AUSSME, M3, b. 476, Divisione Legnano (occupazione Francia), Rapporto n°7026/op., "Servizio ai posti di blocco e controlli," Comando Divisione Legnano, 27 giugno1943.

71. AUSSME, M3, b. 476, Divisione Legnano (occupazione Francia), Rapporto n°15445/inf., "Posto controllo autoveicoli n°3," Comando Settore 68° Reggimento, 12 aprile 1943.

72. AUSSME, M3, b. 476, Divisione Legnano (occupazione Francia), Rapporto n°5353/inf., "Controllo traffico automezzi," Comando Divisione Legnano, 12 giugno 1943.

73. ARC, T-821, Roll 269, IT 3105, Rapporto n°286/I, Comando Quarta Armata, 8 gennaio 1943.

74. AUSSME, M3, b. 476, Divisione Legnano (occupazione Francia), Rapporto n°92/inf., "Tutela del segreto militare," Comando Divisione Legnano, 12 gennaio 1943.

75. AUSSME, M3, b. 476, Divisione Legnano (occupazione Francia), Rapporto n°142/inf., "Tutela del segreto militare," Comando I CA, 15 gennaio 1943.

76. AUSSME, M3, b. 476, Divisione Legnano (occupazione Francia), Rapporto n°3882/inf., "Tutela del segreto militare," Comando Quarta Armata, 18 marzo 1943.

77. AUSSME, N1–11, DS 1127, Circolare Comando Quarta Armata, Diario Storico Quarta Armata, Allegato 32, 25 gennaio 1943.

78. ARC, T-821, Roll 395, IT 5024, Direttiva n°146760/prot., "Convivenza degli ufficiali al rancio della truppa," Rome, 26 luglio 1941.

79. All quotes are from ARC, T-821, Roll 395, IT 5024, Rapporto n°05/1504/prot., "Convivenza degli ufficiali al rancio truppa," Comando Corpo D'Armata Celere, 29 agosto 1941; Rapporto n°02/7520 Comando XI CA, 26 agosto 1941; Rapporto n°51 R.P. del Comandante II CA, Generale Ambrosio, 27 agosto 1941; Rapporto n°44 R.P. del Comandante V CA, Generale Balocco, 24 agosto 1941. The experiment was permanently canceled a few months later. Rapporto n°5731/29760, "Ufficiali conviventi al rancio," Ministero della Guerra, 12 dicembre 1941.

80. The Bourbon army was a pre-unification army. Modern Italy was unified in 1861. The Bourbon were a Spanish dynasty ruling over southern Italy.

81. John A. English, *On Infantry* (New York: Praeger, 1984), 68.

82. ARC, T-821, Roll 266, IT 3099, "Relazione sulle unità tedesche in transito nel territorio del corpo d'armata," 20 agosto 1943. The ten-page report bears the seal of the I CA and was probably edited by a commander of one the last units that stayed in France until the 8 September Italian armistice with the Allies.

83. AUSSME, Giustizia militare. Sentenze, carteggio, F19, b. 83, n°2932 del processo, 1 aprile 1943.

84. See, for instance, the case of Luigi M. of the Legnano Division, who on Christmas Day threatened to kill his unit commander with hand grenades. AUSSME, Giustizia militare. Sentenze, carteggio, F19, b. 83, n°2863 del processo, 2 aprile 1943.

85. AUSSME, Giustizia militare. Sentenze, carteggio, F19, b. 83, n°3561 del processo, 28 febbraio 1943.

86. AUSSME, Giustizia militare. Sentenze, carteggio, F19, b. 84, no number, processo Angelo M., 19 maggio 1943.

87. AUSSME, Giustizia militare. Sentenze, carteggio, F19, b. 84, n°3543 del processo, 27 maggio, 1943.

88. The soldier was sentenced to three years and three months in prison for the insult, seven more months because it was committed in wartime, one more month for being in service, and finally an additional month for committing the act in the presence of other soldiers. AUSSME, Giustizia militare. Sentenze, carteggio, F19, b. 82, n°2549 del processo, 4 febbraio 1943.

89. AUSSME, Giustizia militare. Sentenze, carteggio, F19, b. 84, n°3671 del processo, 25 maggio 1943.

90. The captain was formally prosecuted by his commander because business with civilians was strictly forbidden unless authorized by division commanders. However, upon discovering that the captain did not intend to speculate with the goods but, on the contrary, redistributed the proceeds fairly, the 223rd Coastal Division commander decided to drop any disciplinary measures. ARC, T-821, Roll 268, IT 3102, Rapporto n°31 R.U., "Inchiesta disciplinare a carico del Capitano D. del 512° Bt Territoriale Mobile," 4 aprile 1943.

91. ARC, T-821, Roll 268, IT 3102, Rapporto n°386 R.U., "Sottotenente L. Gaetano," 28 luglio1943. The episode occurred in an Alpine unit, and it is well known that Alpini soldiers and officers bonded more than any other unit in the Regio Esercito.

92. AUSSME, N1–11, DS 1102, Rapporto n°1245/07, "Mentalità combattiva integrale," Comando XXII CA, Diario Storico XXII CA, Allegato 164, 29 febbraio 1943.

93. AUSSME, N1–11, DS 989, Ordine del Giorno Comando Divisione Legnano, Diario Storico Divisione Fanteria Legnano, Allegato 11, 22 novembre 1942. Marciani also cited the 1896 Battle of Adwa, which was one of the most shameful military disasters of the Italian army. The Battle of Adwa ended the disastrous Italian campaign against Abyssinia and was one of the first defeats inflicted on a European state by an African one. See Raymond Jonas, *The Battle of Adwa: African Victory in the Age of the Empire* (Cambridge, MA: Belknap Press of Harvard University Press, 2011).

94. The number of autocinemas was inadequate for such a vast army, and thus units, especially the most isolated ones, had to get by with makeshift arrangements. AUSSME, N1–11, DS 1312, Rapporto n°1027/SA., "Relazione mensile sul servizio A," Comando I CA, Diario Storico I CA, Allegato 25, 1 giugno1943.

95. AUSSME, N1–11, DS 1219, Rapporto n°951/A, "Relazione mensile sul servizio A," Comando Divisione Legnano, Diario Storico Divisione Legnano, Allegato 156, 22 aprile 1943.

96. AUSSME, N1–11, DS 987, "Relazione mensile sul servizio A," Comando I CA, Diario Storico I CA, Allegato 117; AUSSME, N1–11, DS 1100, Rapporto n°240/SA, "Relazione mensile sul servizio A," Comando I CA, Diario Storico I CA, Allegato 26, 1 febbraio 1943.

97. AUSSME, N1–11, DS 1218, Rapporto n°1106 dal Comando Quarta Armata, "Relazione del servizio 'A' del mese di febbraio 1943," Diario Storico Quarta Armata, Allegato 62, 13 marzo1943; AUSSME, N1–11, DS 1217, Rapporto n°1330/02, "Situazione mensile (21 gennaio–20 febbraio 1943)," Comando XXII CA, Diario Storico XXII CA, Allegato 20, 1 marzo 1943.

98. Giorgio Rochat, "La giustizia militare dal 10 giugno 1940 all'8 settembre 1943," in *Fonti e problemi per la storia della giustizia militare*, ed. Nicola Labanca and Pier Paolo Rivello (Giappichelli: Torino, 2004), 231–32.

99. Ibid., 232. See, for instance, AUSSME Giustizia militare. Sentenze, carteggio, F19, b. 84, n°3125 del processo Giuseppe V., 16 giugno 1943. The soldier was sentenced to six years and six months.

100. AUSSME, N1–11, DS 1218, Rapporto n°1106, "Relazione del servizio 'A' del mese di febbraio 1943," Comando Quarta Armata Diario Storico Quarta Armata, Allegato 62, 13 marzo1943, 6 "Conclusione."

101. AUSSME, N1–11, DS 1218, Rapporto n°1106, "Relazione del servizio 'A' del mese di febbraio 1943," Comando Quarta Armata, Diario Storico Quarta Armata, Allegato 62, 13 marzo1943.

102. AUSSME, N1–11, DS 1127, Rapporto n°4427/op., "Rapporto situazione mensile per il periodo 20 gennaio–20 Febbraio," Stato Maggiore, Ufficio Operazioni, Diario Storico Quarta Armata, Allegato 64, 28 febbraio, 1943, 4.

103. AUSSME, N1–11, DS 1217, Rapporto n°1330/02, "Rapporto situazione mensile (21 gennaio–20 febbraio 1943)," Comando XXII CA, Diario Storico XXII CA, Allegato 6, 1 marzo1943. Eventually the protests paid off, but only to a degree. Fourth Army soldiers were granted extra money in June 1943, but to their dismay, the decision was not retroactive, and the soldiers were paid in the devalued French currency. See AUSSME, N1–11, DS 1312, Rapporto n°1027/SA, "Relazione mensile sul servizio A," Comando I CA, Diario Storico I CA, Allegato 25, 1 giugno1943.

104. AUSSME, N1–11, DS 1016, Rapporto n°9939/op., "Ispezione dei reparti delle g.u. dipendenti," Comando Quarta Armata 10 dicembre 1942, in Rapporto n°02/2988, "Ispezione," Comando XV CA, Diario Storico XV CA, Allegato 81, 14 dicembre 1942.

105. AUSSME, N1–11, DS 1100, Rapporto n°7281/SM, "Rifornimenti alle truppe," Diario Storico I CA, Allegato 35, 11 dicembre 1942.

106. AUSSME, N1–11, DS 989, Rapporto n°251/am1, "Rapporto situazione 20 Dicembre–20 Gennaio 1943," Diario Storico Divisione Celere EFTF, Allegato 77, 23 gennaio 1943.

107. ADAM 616 W 133, Bulletin Hébdomadaire de Renseignement n°3915, Semaine 7–13 décembre 1942. L'Istituto Luce was a state-owned company created in 1924 and used by the Fascist regime to spread its propaganda via movies and newsreels.

108. ARC, T-821, Roll 266, IT 3099, Rapporto n°191/inf., "Bollettino Informazioni n°2," Comando 224° Divisione Costiera, 15 marzo 1943.

109. ADAHP 42 W 42, Rapport n°57/4 du Chef d'Escadron Ogier, juin 1943.

CHAPTER 7. LIFE UNDER THE OCCUPATION

1. ADAM 616 W 99, "Synthèse des rapports des Préfets de la Zone Libre pour le mois de mars 1943," 15 avril 1943; "Synthèse des rapports des Préfets de la Zone Libre pour le mois d'avril 1943," 18 mai 1943; "Synthèse des rapports des Préfets de la Zone Libre pour le mois de juillet 1943," 17 août 1943.

2. ADAM 616 W 249, Rapport mensuel du mois d'avril 1943 du Ravitaillement Général des Alpes-Maritimes.

3. ADAM 616 W 134, Rapport du Chef d'Escadron Soymie, Commandant de la compagnie de Gendarmerie dans les Alpes-Maritimes, Nice, 9 mars 1943.

4. A summary of the 1942 frauds is in ADAM 157 W 29.

5. ADAM 616 W 50, Lettre d' Emile G. au préfet, Nice, 22 juin 1943.

6. Monthly reports of the prefect are available in ADAHP 42 W 40.

7. ADAM 616 W 306, Circulaire envoyée aux familles, Collège classique des garçons de Cannes, 22 janvier 1943.

8. ARC, T-821, Roll 266, IT 3099, Rapporto n°2888/inf., "Notiziario n°12," Comando I CA, 12 aprile 1943.

9. ARC, T-821, Roll 266, IT 3099, Rapporto n°3307/inf., "Notiziario n°14," Comando I CA, 15 aprile 1943.

10. ADAM 616 W 134, Rapport du Chef d'Escadron Soymie, Commandant de la compagnie de Gendarmerie dans les Alpes-Maritimes, Nice, 2 décembre 1942.

11. AUSSME, N1–11, DS 987, "Relazione sull'attività svolta nel trimestre ottobre-novembre-dicembre dalla direzione di commissariato," Diario Storico I CA, Allegato 173, senza data.

12. ADAHP 42 W 42, Rapporto n°2.700 du Commissaire de police de la ville de Digne, 20 mai 1943.

13. Between the Italian occupation (November 1942–September 1943) and the German occupation (September 1943–August 1944), foreign armies consumed between two to seven tons of fresh staples each day. Panicacci, "Le temps des pénuries dans les Alpes-Maritimes," 192–97.

14. AUSSME, N1–11, DS 1217, Rapporto n°1772/02, " Situazione mensile (21 febbraio–20 marzo 1943)," Diario Storico XXII CA, 24 marzo 1943.

15. ADAM 159 W 46, Rapport n°1214, "Traffic de denrées contigentées, affaire Léopold G.," 22 novembre 1942. The civilian asserted that he had bought the beef from another Italian unit, but his explanation made no sense and was probably given to excuse himself and the beef wholesaler.

16. AUSSME, Giustizia militare. Sentenze, carteggio, F19, b. 84, n°3465 del processo, senza data (1943).

17. ADAHP 42 W 83, Lettre Cab/358, "Arrestation d'une française par les autorités italiennes" du Préfet des Basses-Alpes au Colonel Pansini, Commandant des troupes italiennes à Digne, 18 janvier 1943. The sentence can be found in AUSSME, Giustizia militare. Sentenze, carteggio, F19 b. 82, n°2867 del processo, 20 marzo 1943.

18. AUSSME, Giustizia militare. Sentenze, carteggio, F19 b. 82, n°2930 del processo, 18 marzo 1943.

19. ADAHP 42 W 82, Rapport n°9/4 du Commandant de la Gendarmerie d'Annot, 4 mars 1943.

20. AUSSME, Giustizia militare. Sentenze, carteggio, F19 b. 82, n°2887 del processo, 22 marzo 1943.

21. AUSSME, Giustizia militare. Sentenze, carteggio, F19 n. 84, n°3242 del processo, 8 juin 1943.

22. ACS, Tribunali militari di guerra e tribunali militari territoriali di guerra: Seconda Guerra Mondiale (1939–1945), Tribunale Militare XV Corpo d'Armata, Volume XIV, processo n°91/16, 5 aprile 1943; ACS, Tribunali militari di guerra e

tribunali militari territoriali di guerra: Seconda Guerra Mondiale (1939–1945), Tribunale Militare XV Corpo d'Armata, volume XV, processo n°1039/42, 1 maggio 1943; processo n°250 Matteo F., Lorenzo A., Filippo B., 6 maggio 1943.

23. ACS, Tribunali militari di guerra e tribunali militari territoriali di guerra: Seconda Guerra Mondiale (1939–1945), Tribunale Militare XV Corpo d'Armata, Volume XIV, processo n°251, 29 maggio 1943.

24. AUSSME, Giustizia militare. Sentenze, carteggio, F19 b. 83, n°3312 del processo, 18 aprile 1943.

25. Boxes of military court trial transcripts include several cases of theft from wagons; see, for instance, AUSSME, Giustizia militare. Sentenze, carteggio, F19 b. 84, n°3400 del processo, 1 maggio 1943; n°3072/2091, 1 maggio 1943; n°3127, 2 maggio 1943; n°3637, 27 maggio 1943; n°3834, 30 giugno 1943.

26. ADAHP 42 W 85, Lettre Cab.6174, "Vols commis par des militaires italiens," Préfet des Basses-Alpes, 17 décembre 1942.

27. AUSSME, N 1–11, DS 989, Rapporto n°906/M, "Relazione riassuntiva bimestrale–Diario Storico," Delegazione Trasporti Militari n°613, 1 marzo 1943.

28. AUSSME, Giustizia militare. Sentenze, carteggio, F19 b. 84, n°3011 del processo, 3 maggio 1943.

29. ADAM 28 W 75, Rapport n°7036 du Commissariat central de police de Cannes, 20 avril 1943.

30. AUSSME, Giustizia militare. Sentenze, carteggio, F19 b. 82, n°2641 del processo, 4 marzo 1943.

31. ADAM 28 W 75, Lettre du Maire de Mandelieu à Monsieur le Colonel, Commandant la place de Mandelieu, 23 février 1943.

32. ADAM 616 W 241, Fichier 23, Incidents Occupation Italienne, Gendarmerie Nationale, Section de Cannes, "Rapport sur des incidents dûs à la présence des troupes étrangères en opérations," 9 janvier 1943.

33. This is a rough estimate based on the data found in the *Diari Storici* (logbooks) of the different units. The Fourth Army Diari Storici seldom went into detail and noted only the total number of soldiers arrested each month.

34. Rochat, "La giustizia militare," 239–40.

35. AUSSME, Giustizia militare. Sentenze, carteggio, F19 b. 83, n°3230 del processo, 14 aprile 1943.

36. See, for instance, AUSSME, Giustizia militare. Sentenze, carteggio, F19 b. 84, n°3310 del processo, 6 maggio 1943.

37. AUSSME, Giustizia militare. Sentenze, carteggio, F19 b. 82, n°2635 del processo, 10 marzo 1943.

38. AUSSME, Giustizia militare. Sentenze, carteggio, F19 b. 84, n°3622 del processo, 2 giugno 1943.

39. AUSSME, Giustizia militare. Sentenze, carteggio, F19 b. 83, n°3461 del processo, 22 aprile 1943.

40. AUSSME, Giustizia militare. Sentenze, carteggio, F19 b. 82, n°2735 del processo, 25 febbraio 1943; n°2675, 25 febbraio 1943; n°2628, 12 marzo 1943; n°2919, 12 marzo 1943.

41. AUSSME, Giustizia militare. Sentenze, carteggio, F19 b. 83, n°2848 del processo, 6 maggio 1943; n°3304, 26 aprile 1943; n°3108, 6 aprile 1943; ACS, Tribunali militari di guerra e tribunali militari territoriali di guerra: Seconda Guerra Mondiale (1939–1945), Tribunale Militare XV Corpo d'Armata, volume XIV, processo n°120, 10 aprile 1943.

42. ADAM 616 W 241, Fichier 23, Incidents occupation italienne, Lettre n°2431 du Directeur du Bureau d'Hygiène à Monsieur le Médecin-Inspecteur de la Santé, Nice, 21 novembre 1942.

43. ADAM 616 W 242, Fichier 47, occupation yachts et aérodromes, Lettre n°3991 de la Mairie de Villefranche-sur-Mer, 22 décembre 1942.

44. ADAHP 42 W 83, Rapport de l'Adjundant Giraud sur des incidents provoqués par des troupes italiennes de passage à Castellane, 16 janvier 1943.

45. ADAM 616 W 241, Fichier 23, Incidents occupation italienne, Lettre du Lieutenant Jomotte sur des incidents dûs à la présence des troupes italiennes en opérations, 5 janvier 1943.

46. AUSSME, Giustizia militare. Sentenze, carteggio, F19 b. 83, n°3325 del processo, 19 aprile 1943.

47. ADAM 616 W 261, Rapport n°541 de l'Inspecteur Caubel, Ministère de l'Agriculture et du Ravitaillement, 9 août 1943.

48. AUSSME, Giustizia militare. Sentenze, carteggio, F19 b. 84, n°3124 del processo, senza data.

49. ADAHP 42 W 83, Lettre de Monsieur le Maire de Sisteron à Monsieur le Préfet des Basses Alpes, 23 août 1943.

50. ADAHP 42 W 83, Lettre n°36 RG/C, "Incidents avec les troupes d'occupation italiennes" du Préfet des Basses-Alpes, 3 mai 1943, and the attached reply, note n°118.

51. AUSSME, Giustizia militare. Sentenze, carteggio, F19 b. 83, n°3398 del processo, 19 aprile 1943.

52. ADAM 616 W 242, Fichier 6, Lettre du Préfet des Alpes-Maritimes au Général Commandant la XVème Division des troupes italiennes Legnano, 14 décembre 1942.

53. ADAM 616 W 241, Fichier 23, Incidents occupation italienne, Rapport du Gardien de la Paix Dussert, "Intervention au sujet d'un double incident, entre soldats civils italiens et civils français," 27 décembre 1942. For irredentist support of Italian soldiers, see ADAM 166 W 10, Fichier Incidents provoqués par les troupes italiennes, Rapport des gardiens cyclistes Durand et Chiodi sur incident place Garibaldi entre soldat italien et public, 9 décembre 1942.

54. ADAM 616 W 215, Procès-verbal n°189, "Incident entre un officier italien et le sieur C. Edouard," 25 janvier 1943.

55. ADAM 166 W 10, Fichier Incidents provoqués par les troupes italiennes, Rapport n°710/2 du Lieutenant Jomotte, sur un incident à Gattières, et dû à la présence des troupes étrangères en opérations, 14 décembre 1942.

56. ADAM 166 W 10, Fichier Incidents provoqués par les troupes italiennes, Commissaire central à Nice, rapport journalier 16 janvier 1943.

57. ADAM 166 W 10, Fichier Incidents provoqués par les troupes italiennes, Rapport n°702/2 du Lieutenant Jomotte, sur des incidents dûs à la présence des troupes étrangères en opérations, 14 décembre 1942.

58. ADAM 166 W 11, Fichier Incidents divers, Rapport n°8684/S.P.-2 du Commissaire Divisionnaire de Nice, 21 juin 1943.

59. ADAM 166 W 10, Fichier Incidents provoqués par les troupes italiennes, Rapport n°6/4 di Lieutenant Jomotte, 14 janvier 1943.

60. ADAM 166 W 10, Fichier Incidents provoqués par les troupes italiennes, Rapport n°26.511 du Commissariat de police de Cannes, 26 décembre 1942.

61. ADAHP 42 W 83, Rapport n°5/4 du Maréchal des Logis Chef Dagorne sur un incident provoqué par des militaires des troupes italiennes d'opérations, 31 mars 1943.

62. ADAHP 42 W 83, Rapport n°3034/Q.7 du Commissaire principal Sangla, 28 aprile 1943.

63. Vinen, *Unfree French*, 219–20.

64. Paul Sanders, *Histoire du marché noir: 1940–1946* (Paris: Perrin, 2001), 74–93.

65. ADAM 166 W 3, Rapport n°1464, "Vol de colis de prisonniers sur le trajet Puget–Theniers–Digne," 18 mai 1943.

66. ADAM 616 W 312, Préfecture des Alpes-Maritimes, Bureau des Affaires Économiques, Communiqué Officiel 77/MI/LM, 15 décembre 1942.

67. Police daily reports for the year 1942 can be found in ADAM 166 W 1.

68. ADAM 166 W 3, Lettre du PDG de Guichard-Perrachon et Cie au Préfet des Alpes-Maritimes, 27 janvier 1943.

69. AN, 72AJ 1927, "Vols en cours d'expédition part fer," 11 mars 1943, and Directeur du Service Central du Mouvement au M. le Baron d'André, mars 1943, cited by Mouré, "Réalités cruelles," 179.

70. Mouré, "Réalités cruelles," 175.

CHAPTER 8. MILITARY REPRESSION, CIVILIAN RESISTANCE

1. Rossbottom, *When Paris Went Dark*, 160–62.

2. Unfortunately, any historian studying the Italian security agencies is often confronted with the scarcity of documents, many of which had been destroyed in the first days after the September 1943 armistice. Upon precipitously leaving the French territory on 8 September 1943, Italian security officials burned confidential documents such as arrest reports and interrogation summaries. For instance, the destruction of the papers of the Italian counterespionage operations in Nice is confirmed by one member of the SIM quartered there: the CCRR Pietro Speranza, ACS, Ministero Interno, Direzione Generale P.S., Divisione personale P.S. (1890–1966), Versamento 1973, Dossier Rosario Barranco, Dichiarazione Speranza, 20 June 1945. The official reason was the fear that the Gestapo and the Abwehr, the German military intelligence service, could use the security archives to track down Jews and

other dissidents. However, it is plausible that the Italians also wanted to destroy any proof of their own misdeeds as the tide of war was turning. After all, having arrested resisters and anti-Axis partisans would have negatively affected any security agent who might be investigated by purging committees in the aftermath of the conflict.

3. A voluminous box on Rosario Barranco is available in ACS, Ministero Interno, Direzione Generale P.S., Divisione personale P.S. (1890–1966), Versamento 1973, Dossier Rosario Barranco.

4. Joseph Girard, "Contribution à l'étude de l'épuration dans les Alpes-Maritimes," *Recherches régionales, Alpes-Maritimes et Contrées limitrophes* 59 (July–September 1976): 4–6; Mauro Canali, *Le Spie del Regime* (Bologna: Il Mulino, 2004), 473–75.

5. An undated memorandum written by Barranco called "Promemoria per l'ecc. il Capo della Polizia" deliberately embellished his deeds by boasting about the arrest of Gallo. Actually, Gallo was in the Vernet prison camp as of 1939 as one of the leaders of the International Brigades who had fought in the Spanish Civil War. In 1941 Gallo was extradited to Italy and confined to Ventotene. After the ousting of Mussolini in July 1943, Gallo took command of the Garibaldi Brigades, the communist partisan forces. After the war, Luigi Longo would become one of the leaders of the Italian Communist Party. The memorandum is not reliable, as Barranco wrote it at the end of 1943 to ingratiate himself with the Germans, who were demanding his removal from the Italian police because of his pro-Jewish policy in the first half of 1943. For the full explanation, see ACS, Ministero Interno, Direzione Generale P.S., Divisione personale P.S. (1890–1966), Versamento 1973, Dossier Rosario Barranco, "Copia della dichiarazione resa dal dott. Eugenio Appollonio, gia' capo della segreteria di S.E. Tamburini, capo della Polizia," Roma, 30 maggio 1946. It is revealing, on the other hand, that Barranco did not hesitate to arrest Sarni, the head of the Monaco Fascio, as well as a few other local Fascist dignitaries for minor offenses.

6. ACS, Ministero Interno, Direzione Generale P.S., Divisione personale P.S. (1890–1966), Versamento 1973, Dossier Rosario Barranco, Lettera prot. n°224/50649 from the head of the Italian police, "Dr. Rosario Barranco, Commissario di P.S. ed altri presunti criminali di guerra, richiesti dalla Francia," 8 marzo 1947. In truth it seems that a SIM agent had already been brought to Nice at the beginning of 1942 under the cover of a welfare program to supervise an information-gathering network. See ASMAE, Affari Politici, 1931–1945, Francia, b. 68, Memorandum del Delegato CIAF Quinto Mazzolini al Ministero degli Affari Esteri, Direzione Affari Generali, Rome, 20 marzo 1943, Parte II, "Sulla Situazione Generale."

7. ARC, T-821, Roll 369, IT 4807, Rapporto n°6/04 di prot., "Notizie 'I' nel territorio occupato," Comando XXII CA, Ufficio Informazioni, 13 novembre 1942. The Ufficio "I" was sometimes called Servizio "I" or Sezione "I."

8. ARC, T-821, Roll 266, IT 3099, Rapporto n°2220 "I" di prot., "Servizio informazioni sulla tradotta Mentone-Genova," Comando Quarta Armata, Ufficio Informazioni, 16 febbraio 1943.

9. ARC, T-821, Roll 266, IT 3099, Rapporto n°792/inf. di prot., "Fondi per azioni informativa," Comando I CA, Ufficio Informazioni, 1 febbraio 1943.

10. ARC, T-821, Roll 268, IT 3102, Rapporto n°3455/inf. di prot., "Fondi per azione informativa," Comando I CA, Ufficio Informazioni, 28 aprile 1943. The document contains receipt forms for the rewards that were completed by the Ufficio "I" officer.

11. ARC, T-821, Roll 266, IT 3099, Rapporto n°616 di prot., Segr.-All.4, "Attività informativa," Comando Reggimento Genova Cavalleria, 15 dicembre 1942.

12. ARC, T-821, Roll 266, IT 3099, Rapporto n°1082/inf., "Richiesta Informazioni," Comando Divisione Legnano, Sezione Informazioni, 3 dicembre 1942, and the CIAF reply, Rapporto n°2550R, "Richiesta informazioni: V. Alfredo-C. Henry," Delegazione CIAF a Nizza, 28 dicembre 1942. See also ARC, T-821, Roll 265, IT 3099, Rapporto n°5516/op., "Informazioni," Comando 68° Reggimento Fanteria Legnano, 5 dicembre 1942. According to French reports, the ring of informers was much wider. ADAM 616 W 242 Fichier 25, Arréstations civils, Rapport "Individus arrêtés et internés à la caserne Dugommier à Antibes," Commissariat de Police de Antibes, 5 janvier 1943.

13. ARC, T-821, Roll 268, IT 3102, Rapporto n°3510/inf. di prot., "Assunzione agenti," Comando I CA, 30 aprile 1943.

14. Schipsi, *L'occupazione italiana*, 394–95.

15. ARC, T-821, Roll 265, IT 3099, Rapporto n°103/inf. di prot., "Territorio francese metropolitano. Arresto di sudditi di stati nemici ed internamento di civili," Comando I CA, Ufficio Informazioni, 9 gennaio 1943.

16. ACS, Ministero Interno, Direzione Generale P.S., Divisione personale P.S. (1890–1966), Versamento 1973, Dossier Rosario Barranco, "Promemoria per l'Ecc. il Capo della Polizia," senza data.

17. AUSSME, N1–11, DS 1099, Direttiva n°3657 "I" di prot., "Sicurezza delle truppe di occupazione," Diario Storico Quarta Armata, Allegato 52, 4 dicembre 1942. The number of hostages escalated depending on the severity of the attack, ranging from three for an attack that had no consequences for Italian property and soldiers to twenty for every Italian victim, double if the target was an officer.

18. ARC, T-821, Roll 265, IT 3099, Rapporto n°258/inf., "Ostaggi," Comando I CA, Ufficio Informazioni, 12 gennaio 1943.

19. ARC, T-821, Roll 269, IT 3105, Rapporto n°430/inf. di prot., "Sicurezza delle truppe d'occupazione," Comando Divisione Legnano, Sezione Informazioni, 19 gennaio 1943; underlined in original.

20. ARC, T-821, Roll 265, IT 3099, Rapporto n°452/P.1 di prot., "Direttive per la salvaguardia delle FF.AA. italiane e per la tutela del rispetto al prestigio italiano," Comando Quarta Armata, Ufficio Politico, 28 gennaio 1943.

21. ADAM 166 W 9, Rapport n°9512, "Incident du 26 Décembre, rue Châteauneuf," Inspecteur Wasilieff, 31 décembre 1942; Rapport B.S.E. 291 E, Inspécteur Carrere, 12 janvier 1943. Box 166 W 9 contains an exhaustive list, compiled by French postwar authorities, of persons arrested in the Italian occupation period in the Alpes-Maritimes, divided by nationality, as well as one complete list in alphabetical order.

22. ADAM 166 W 9, Rapport n°185, "Arrestation du Consul de Pologne à Monaco par les Autorités Militaires Italiennes," Commissariat de Beausoileil, 19 janvier 1943.

23. ADAM 166 W 9, Rapport n°2651, "Arrestations effectuées en Principauté de Monaco et dans mon secteur par les Autorités Militaires Italiennes," Commissariat de Beausoleil, 28 décembre 1942. In the 26 January sweep ten Belgians were also arrested.

24. ADAM 616 W 233, Rapport n°7008, "Personnalités fascistes, Commandant Valente, dit Salerno et Capitaine Tisani," 27 juin 1945.

25. Panicacci, L'Occupation Italienne, 231–32.

26. ADAM 318 W 31, Cours de Justice des Alpes-Maritimes, Dossier Guillaume P., Procès-verbal n°2176, déclaration de Mr. Vaizman, 2 décembre 1942.

27. ARC, T-821, Roll 265, IT 3099, Rapporto n°1065, "I" di prot., "Repressione reati in danno delle truppe di occupazione," Comando Quarta Armata, Ufficio Informazioni, 30 gennaio 1943; Rapporto n°1173/inf. di prot., "Custodia di arrestati nel campo di Sospello," Comando I CA, Ufficio Informazioni, 13 febbraio 1943. The orders were reiterated because apparently some prisoners with specific charges were still erroneously sent to the Sospel camp. See AUSSME, M3, b. 476, Divisione Legnano (occupazione Francia), Rapporto n°1155/inf., "Custodia di arrestati nel campo di Sospello," Comando Divisione Legnano, Sezione Informazioni, 17 febbraio 1943.

28. ARC, T-821, Roll 265, IT 3099, Rapporto n°4471/inf. di prot., "Trasferimento campo di concentramento," Comando I CA, Ufficio Informazioni, 30 maggio 1943.

29. ARC, T-821, Roll 265, IT 3099, Rapporto n°3925/inf. di prot., "Internati civili," Comando I CA, Ufficio Informazioni, 14 maggio 1943. The camp also hosted some non-communist resisters, such as one branch of the Alsace-Lorraine resistance network captured in Cannes on 25 May 1943. See ADAM 616 W 182, Liste "État nominatif des personnes résident [sic] à Cannes internées à Modane pour le motif figurant en face de chaque nom."

30. ADAM 104 W 4, O.D. n°517, "Doléances sur le sort des internés au camp de Sospel," 13 février 1943.

31. ADAM 104 W 4, W.I. n°330, "Libération prochaine des internés civils de Sospel," 10 mars 1943.

32. ARC, T-821, Roll 265, IT 3099, Rapporto n°6623, "I" di prot., "Internati civili ed assegnati a residenza forzata," Comando Quarta Armata, 28 aprile 1943.

33. ADAM 104 W 5, Bulletin d'Information n°239, Police Régionale de Nice, 15 juillet 1943.

34. A summarized history of the tribunal from the French perspective can be found in ADAM 618 W 162, Rapport n°343, "A/S de M. Blanc René," 21 juin 1956.

35. ADAM 616 W 261, Note, "Renseignements fournis par M. Jean," pas de date.

36. Panicacci, L'Occupation Italienne, 224–25.

37. ADAM 616 W 182 has a lot of individual records of arrests in the Italian occupation period.

38. ARC, T-821, Roll 270, IT 3131, Rapporto n°1085, "I" di prot., "Rapporti dei militari con l'Azione Nizzarda," Comando Quarta Armata, Ufficio Informazioni, 29 gennaio 1943.

39. Panicacci, *L'Occupation Italienne*, 226.

40. ADAM 616 W 242 Fichier 24, Arréstations civils français, Lettre au Commandant XVème Corps d'Armée Italienne, 11 décembre 1942; Panicacci, *Les Alpes-Maritimes*, 173.

41. ADAM 616 W 242, Fichier 24, Arréstations civils français, Rapport n°96/4 de la Gendarmerie Nationale, Brigade de Beausoleil, 20 décembre 1942.

42. ADAM 616 W 242, Fichier 18, Rapport n°193 du Commissaire Eveno, 26 janvier 1943. The folder does not contain Ribière's letter of protest, but does include the official, icy reply from Vercellino in response to the prefect's query about his subordinate. Lettre n°1174 S, "Fonctionnaire de la Préfecture: M. Galli," 26 janvier 1943.

43. See chapter 11.

44. Dossiers for Ribière and Chaigneau can be found in ADAM 86 W 7. One should also recognize that the Alpes-Maritimes prefect apparently enjoyed little popularity among the local French population, for he was accused of not being able to stop the black-marketeering. Thus, his departure may have been demanded by higher civil servants in Vichy. In fact, the new prefect, Jean Chaigneau, proved to be more flexible in his relations with Italian authorities and more successful in the administration of food distribution within the department.

45. AUSSME, D7, b. 18, Notiziario quindicinale n°24, 20 novembre 1941, 24.

46. ASMAE, Affari Politici, 1931–1945, Francia, b. 42, Telespresso n°597 R., "Amministrazione di Nizza," 19 marzo 1942.

47. Significantly, the document has been found in an Italian archive. ASMAE, Affari Politici, 1931–1945, Francia, b. 68, Mairie de Nice, Cabinet du Maire, Rapport établi le 15 mai 1943.

48. ARC, T-821, Roll 266, IT 3099, Notiziario n°30, Comando I CA, Ufficio "I," 6 giugno 1943.

49. I could not find the newspaper issue, but the attack was so virulent that even the Italian consulate in Nice complained the article was untimely. ASMAE, Affari Politici, 1931–1945, Francia, b. 68, Telegramma n°20932, "Giornale il Nizzardo," Gino Augusto Spechel, 18 luglio 1943.

50. Panicacci, *Les Alpes-Maritimes*, 178.

51. ARC, T-821, Roll 266, IT 3099, Rapporto n°2043/inf., "Notiziario n°1," Comando I CA, Ufficio Informazioni, 18 marzo 1943.

52. ARC, T-821, Roll 266, IT 3099, Rapporto n°1047 di prot. sm/1, "Attività informativa," Comando EFTF, 8 febbraio 1943.

53. ADAM 104 W 4, Rapport n°317 A.A. "s/s/arrestations pratiquées à Cannes et région par les Autorités Italiennes," Intendance de Police de Nice, 10 février 1943.

54. Panicacci, *Les Alpes-Maritimes*, 115.

55. It was not unusual until 1942 for a resister to also be Pétainist.

56. Wieviorka, *Histoire de la Résistance*, 74–86.

57. Some examples of Gaullist leaflets can be found in ADAM 159 W 43. Some examples of youth rebelliousness, such as the scratching of Pétain's portrait, can be found in ADAM 616 W 306.

58. H. R. Kedward, *Resistance in Vichy France: A Study of Ideas and Motivation in the Southern Zone, 1940–1942* (Oxford: Oxford University Press, 1978), 223–24.

59. Jean-Louis Panicacci, "Les Communistes italiens dans les Alpes-Maritimes (1939–45)," *Annali della Fondazione Giangiacomo Feltrinelli* 24 (1985): 155–80.

60. The Italian army was also wary not to support any French collaborationist parties, even though it appears they occasionally used their informers. In fact, both the PPF and the Parti Franciste vied for official endorsement as the Fascist Party in France, but the Italians dismissed their claims, especially in light of their marked unpopularity among the French population. For a report on the PPF, see ARC, T-821, Roll 265, IT 3099, Rapporto n°5235/inf. di prot., "Collaborazione del P.P.F.," Comando I CA, 19 giugno 1943. For a report on the Parti Franciste, see ARC, T-821, Roll 266, IT 3099, n°4647/inf. di prot., "Notiziario n°28," Comando I CA, 1 giugno 1943.

61. ADAM 166 W 1, Rapport n°130/4 du Capitaine André sur des incidents à caractère anti-nationaux, 8 septembre 1942.

62. ADAM 166 W 1, Rapport n°153/4 de l'Adjudant-Chef Tourre sur des attentats commis à Nice, 12 octobre 1942.

63. ADAM 166 W 1, Rapport n°11.750/09 de l'Inspécteur Moschetti, 27 octobre 1942.

64. ADAM 166 W 1, Rapport n°6.024/PS, "Attentat par engin explosif à l'hôtel de la préfecture," Inspécteur de police Langlais, 5 mai 1943.

65. Sereni became a leading figure of the PCI (Partito Comunista Italiano) in postwar Italy until his death in 1977. He was arrested in June 1943 by the Italian police.

66. ARC, T-821, Roll 266, IT 3099, Rapporto n°3786/inf., "Propaganda comunista presso i militari a Nizza," Comando I CA, 8 maggio 1943.

67. AUSSME, M3 476, Divisione Legnano (occupazione Francia), Rapporto n°1390/inf. di prot., "Contegno passivo di nostri militari di fronte alla subdola propaganda nemica," 25 febbraio 1943. Allegedly, Italian soldiers who denounced French civilians were automatically granted fifteen days of leave; see ADAM 104 W 4, unsigned note, "Au sujet des arréstations opérées par les autorités italiennes," 6 avril 1943.

68. ARC, T-821, Roll 266, IT 3099, Rapporto n°3705 "I" di prot., "Arresti operai in seguito denuncia di militari delle nostre truppe d'occupazione," Comando Quarta Armata, Ufficio Informazioni, 18 marzo 1943.

69. AUSSME, Giustizia militare. Sentenze, carteggio, F19, b. 84, n°3016 del processo, 26 mai 1943.

70. *La Parola del Soldato*, n°7, 15 May 1943. The issue can be found in ARC, T-821, Roll 266, IT 3099, or in AUSSME, M3, b. 476, Divisione Legnano (occu-

pazione Francia), Rapporto n°1860 di prot., "Manifestino propaganda," Comando III Battaglione, 68° Reggimento Fanteria Legnano, 1 luglio 1943.

71. ARC, T-821, Roll 266, IT 3099, Rapporto n°1146/inf. di prot., "Segnalazione," Comando 223° Divisione costiera, 1 agosto 1943.

72. AUSSME, Giustizia militare. Sentenze, carteggio, F19, b. 84, senza numero, 22 agosto 1943.

73. ARC, T-821, Roll 261, IT 3077, Rapporto n°13805/S.P., "Procedura d'eccezione," 14 agosto 1943.

74. ADAM 166 W 1, Rapport n°3050/PS, "Attentat par explosif contre divers commerçants Italiens d'Antibes," 24 février 1943. Four Italian anti-Fascists were arrested by Italian troops shortly thereafter. At least one of the informers had been responsible for arrests on 4 January 1943 in Antibes. See ADAM 166 W 11, Fichier Attentats contre les troupes italiennes, *Bulletin Journalier,* 9 février 1943.

75. ASMAE, Affari Politici, 1931–1945, Francia, b. 80, fasc. 1, Attività comunista, Rapporto n°14836, "Movimento Comunista in Francia," CIAF Ufficio "I," 8 gennaio 1943.

76. Wieviorka, *Histoire de la Résistance,* 240–42.

77. For an example of boulders being thrown onto tracks, see ADAM 166 W 1, Rapport n°9/4 de l'Adjudant Diana, sur un attentat commis sur la voie ferrée dans la nuit de 7 au 8 mars 1943 entre les gares d'Èze et Cap d'Ail. For an example of the sabotage of a bridge, see Procès-verbal n°114, "Dégats par engin explosif à un poteau télégraphique sur le pont de l'avenue Saint-Laurent et découverte à ce même endroit d'un engin explosif non éclaté," 17 janvier 1943.

78. ADAM 616 W 114, Lettre du Sous-Préfet de Grasse à Monsieur le Préfet des Alpes-Maritimes, 8 mars 1943.

79. ADAM 166 W 1 contains several reports of incidents involving the destruction of railway lines before September 1943. For examples of sabotage of telephone lines, see ADAM 166 W 10, Fichier Incidents provoqués par les troupes italiennes, 1942–1943, Rapport n°443/2 du Chef d'Escadron Soymie, 3 mars 1943. Several reports of sabotage can also be found in 166 W 11, Fichier Attentats contre les troupes italiennes. Telephone lines were also wrecked in the Basses-Alpes, ADAHP 43 W 83, Rapport n°28/2 du gendarme Combe sur un acte de sabotage commis à Mirabeau, sur la ligne téléphonique, 29 avril 1943.

80. ADAM 166 W 11, Fichier Attentats contre les troupes italiennes, Rapport n°58 du Commissariat de Cagnes-sur-Mer "a/s de ratés de moteurs, explosions et coups de fusil entendus le 4.1.43," 5 janvier 1943.

81. ADAM 166 W 11, Fichier Attentats contre les troupes italiennes, procès-verbal n°17 du 11 janvier 1943, "Affaire tentative meutre Maggio," 13 janvier 1943. Notwithstanding the flimsy evidence, the local Italian commander decided to arrest the notables of the village of Saint-Laurent-du-Var the day after the incident. ADAM 616 W 242, Fichier 24, Arrestations civils français, Lettre du maire de St-Laurent du Var, 12 janvier 1942. The mayor stressed that the officer was courteous but firm, warning the notables that they would be held responsible for other incidents in the area. They were released shortly thereafter.

82. ADAM 166 W 11, Fichier Attentats contre les troupes italiennes, Rapport n°3351/PS, "Attentat par explosif contre les baraquements situés dans l'enceinte de la gare en bordure de l'avenue Thiers," Préfecture Régionale de Nice, 4 mars 1943.

83. AUSSME, N1–11, DS 1127, n°4427 op. Rapporto "Situazione mensile per il periodo 20 gennaio–20 febbraio 1943," Diario Storico Quarta Armata, Allegato 64.

84. ADAM 166 W 11, Fichier Attentats contre les troupes italiennes, Rapport n°3.472/PS, Préfecture Régionale de Nice, 7 mars 1943.

85. ADAM 166 W 11, Fichier Attentats contre les troupes italiennes, Rapport n°3029, "Explosion de bombe dans la caserne Dugommier," Commissariat de Police d'Antibes, 13 mars 1943.

86. ADAM 166 W 11, Fichier Attentats contre les troupes italiennes, Rapport n°25/4, "Sur l'explosion d'un pétard à la porte d'entrée du garage Burlando à Cannes," Gendarmerie de Cannes, 11 avril 1943.

87. ARC, T-821, Roll 268, IT 3102, Rapporto n°10248 di prot. Segreto "Situazione mediterranea," Stato Maggiore Regio Esercito, 29 marzo 1943.

88. ARC, T-821, Roll 270, IT 3115, Rapporto n°3188/op. Comando Divisione Legnano, "Presumibile attività nemica sul litorale mediterranea," 26 marzo 1943.

89. AUSSME, N1–11, DS 1186, n°3229/inf., "Sbarramento della zona costiera mediterranea," Diario Storico I CA, Allegato 67, 22 aprile 1943. Safe-conducts were given to doctors, priests, members of the French police, and a few other limited categories.

90. ASMAE, Affari Politici, 1931–1945, Francia, b. 71, Rapporto n°678, "Attentato a Nizza," Ufficiale collegamento Ministero Affari Esteri presso la Quarta Armata, Conte Bonarelli, 2 maggio 1943; ADAM 166 W 11, Fichier Attentats contre les troupes italiennes, Rapport "Attentats contre trois officiers de l'armée d'operation," Commissaire central de la police de Nice, 27 avril 1943.

91. Prefect Ribière was fired shortly after the attack. Durrafour, on the other hand, while identified as "hostile to the Axis" in a February 1943 report, apparently kept his position as the head of the Nice police. In May 1943 the Italian authorities did not believe his removal was necessary. ARC, T-821, Roll 266, IT 3099, Rapporto n°1047 di prot. sm/1, "Attività informativa," Comando Divisione Celere EFTF, 8 febbraio 1943, and 616 W 125, Lettre du Préfet des Alpes-Maritimes au Secrétaire Géneral de la Police, 24 mai 1943.

92. ADAM 616 W 242, Fichier 8 Zone côtière attentat 27 avril, Lettre du Commandant de la place maritime de Nice au Préfet des Alpes-Maritimes, "Attentat du 27 avril 1943," sans date.

93. ARC, T-821, Roll 266, IT 3099, Notiziario n°18, I CA Comando, 27 aprile 1943.

94. L'Éclaireur du Sud-Est, 30 avril 1943.

95. ARC, T-821, Roll 266, IT 3099, Rapporto n°3499/inf. di prot., "Misure protettive da eventuali azione terroristiche," Comando I CA, 29 aprile 1943.

96. ARC, T-821, Roll 266, IT 3099, Rapporto n°3502/inf. di prot., "Orario spettacoli cinematografici per le truppe," Comando I CA, 29 aprile 1943.

97. ARC, T-821, Roll 266, IT 3099, Rapporto n°3091 di prot. sm/1, "Misure di sicurezza," Comando EFTF, 28 aprile 1943.

98. AUSSME, N1–11, DS 1320, Rapporto n°6824/I di prot., "Epurazione della città di Nizza," Diario Storico Quarta Armata, Allegato 7, 1 maggio 1943; ARC, T-821, Roll 265, IT 3099, Rapporto n°1244/op. di prot., "Epurazione della città di Nizza," Comando 223° Divisione Costiera, 6 mai 1943; AUSSME, N1–11, DS 1320, Rapporto n°4833/op. di prot., "Operazione di polizia, Campo provvisorio di Le Cais," Comando Divisione Legnano, Diario Storico Divisione Legnano, Allegato 4, 2 maggio 1943.

99. Gregor Joseph Kranjc, *To Walk with the Devil: Slovene Collaboration and Axis Occupation, 1941–1945* (Toronto: University of Toronto Press, 2013), 80.

100. Osti Guerrazzi, *L'Esercito italiano in Slovenia*, 82–92.

101. AUSSME, N1–11, DS 1320, Telescritto cifrato n°7125/I. di prot., Diario Storico Quarta Armata, Allegato 9c, 8 maggio 1943.

102. AUSSME, Giustizia militare. Sentenze, carteggio, F19, b. 84, non numerato, 22 agosto 1943.

103. ADAM 104 W 5, Rapport n°69/4 sur des arrestations operées dans la ville de Nice par les troupes italiennes d'opérations dans la nuit du 6 au 7 mai 1943, Gendarmerie Nationale, Séction de Nice, 9 mai 1943.

104. See, for example, ADAM 318 W, Dossier Joseph C., procès-verbal n°3042, "Déclarations du sieur Veroni Adolphe," 5 octobre 1944.

105. AUSSME, N1–11, DS 1218, Rapporto n°3962 di prot. op., "Piazza Militare di Nizza," Diario Storico Quarta Armata, Allegato 13, 28 febbraio 1943.

106. ADAM 104 W 5, Note de renseignements, 28 mai 1943. The reunion was held on 10 May.

107. ACS, Ministero degli Interni, Direzione Generale P.S., Serie H2, B. 201, Anno 1943, Dossier n°168, "Attentati contro truppe d'occupazione in Francia, 1943," Appunto n°500-13403, Ispettore Barranco, 1 giugno 1943. The report mentions that eighteen persons were freed after a few weeks.

108. ADAM 166 W 11, Fichier Attentat contre troupes italiennes janvier-juillet 1943, Rapporto n°148/2, sur un incident à l'égard des troupes italiennes, 8 mai 1943.

109. ASMAE, Affari Politici, 1931–1945, Francia, b. 71, Rapporto n°7124/I., "Attentati contro le truppe d'operazione," Comando Quarta Armata, 9 maggio 1943.

110. ADAM 166 W 11, Fichier Attentat contre troupes italiennes janvier-juillet 1943, Rapport n°74/4 sur les répercussions de l'attentat commis à Laghet contre les troupes d'opérations italiennes, Gendarmerie Nationale, Section de Nice, 13 mai 1943. The Italians retaliated by arresting ten individuals living in Trinité-Victor, including the mayor of the town. Some of those arrested were released a few days later.

111. ADAM 166 W 11, Fichier Attentat contre troupes italiennes janvier-juillet 1943, Rapport n°6643/PS, "Attentat commis à Nice," Intendance de Police de Nice, 12 mai 1943.

112. ASMAE, Affari Politici, 1931–1945, Francia, b. 71, Telegramma n°3147 R., "Attentato contro soldati italiani," Ambasciata italiana a Parigi, 14 maggio 1943.

113. ASMAE, Affari Politici, 1931–1945, Francia, b. 71, Telespresso n°129/2, "Attentato terroristico contro truppe occupazione a Cannes," Delegato CIAF a Cannes, 17 maggio 1943.

114. For the latest Cannes attack, see ADAM 28 W 75, Rapport n°1316, "Attentat par explosifs dans la cour d'un immeuble occupé par des services italiens à Cannes," Renseignements Généraux de Cannes, 17 mai 1943; ADAM 166 W 11, Fichier Attentat contre troupes italiennes janvier–juillet 1943, Rapport n°223/SAP, "Recherches des auteurs de l'attentat par explosifs commis à Cannes dans la soirée du 16 mai 1943," 21 mai 1943.

115. ADAM 166 W 11, Fichier Attentat contre troupes italiennes janvier–juillet 1943, Rapport n°3751, Renseignements Généraux à Nice, 12 juin 1943.

116. ADAM 166 W 11, Fichier Attentats contre les troupes italiennes, Rapport n°7768/PS, "Assassinat des époux Moraglia. Affaire contre B. Césare et G. Philippe," 5 juin 1943. Moraglia's informer status was also confirmed by the Italian consul in Nice, Spechel. ASMAE, Affari Politici, 1931–1945, Francia, b. 69, "Rapporto mensile per il mese di giugno 1943," 26 giugno 1943. The two resisters were later prosecuted by the Italian military court in August 1943 as part of the trial of the Italian communist cell in the Alpes-Maritimes.

117. ASMAE, Affari Politici, 1931–1945, Francia, b. 71, Rapporto n°619, "Rapporto mensile per il mese di giugno 1943," Console italiano a Nizza Spechel, 26 giugno 1943; ADAM 166 W 11, Fichier Attentat contre troupes italiennes janvier-juillet 1943, Rapport n°1629, "Evénements et incidents survenus au cour de la journée du 5.6.1943," Commissariat central de Nice, 6 juin 1943.

118. Information on railway sabotage and bombing attacks on French collaborationists and Vichy organizations can be found in ADAM 166 W 1.

119. ADAM 616 W 134, Rapport n°64/4, "Sur un attentat commis sur la voie ferrée," Gendarmerie Nationale, Séction de Cannes, 21 juillet 1943.

120. ADAM 104 W 5, Rapport n°3866, "Arrestations operées à Cagnes-sur-Mer par les troupes d'opérations le 21 courant," Commissariat de Police Cagnes-sur-Mer, 22 juillet 1943.

121. ADAM 166 W 11, Fichier Attentat contre troupes italiennes janvier-juillet 1943, Rapport n°66/V, Inspécteur Abraham, 20 juillet 1943.

122. Apparently no member of the SIM was hurt. ASMAE, Affari Politici, 1931–1945, Francia, b. 68, Telegramma n°4687 R., "Attentato a Nizza," Console italiano a Nizza Spechel, 21 luglio 1943.

123. ASMAE, Affari Politici, 1931–1945, Francia, b. 68, Telegramma n°21564 P.R., "Attentato terroristico al ristorante Davico," Console italiano a Nizza Spechel, 23 luglio 1943.

124. ADAM 166 W 11, Fichier Attentat contre troupes italiennes janvier–juillet 1943, O.D. n°2188, 2178, 2732, 2735.

125. In the case of the American citizen who died in the Sospel camp, it is unclear if the death was linked to the living conditions within the camp. The report states only that the detainee died of "natural causes" without further details. ADAM 166 W 9, Rapport n°145, "Décès d'un américain interné au camp de concentration italien de

Sospel," Commissaire de Breil, 16 janvier 1943. An Italian directive for the planning of the 6 May massive roundup emphasized that military doctors should check the health of the persons arrested to prevent anyone with a condition incompatible with incarceration from being detained. AUSSME, N1–11, DS 1320, Rapporto n°6824/I di prot., "Epurazione della città di Nizza," Diario Storico Quarta Armata, Allegato 7, 1 maggio 1943. On the other hand, Becchi died shortly after being released from custody. ASMAE, Affari Politici, 1931–1945, Francia, b. 68, Telegramma n°239 R, "Sig. Francesco Becchi: morte," Console italiano a Nizza Calisse, 19 marzo 1943. Calisse seemed to criticize the SIM in his report, as he underlined the fact that Becchi was seventy-seven years old and his health might have been incompatible with detention. Jean-Louis Panicacci also cites the case of a fuoriuscito, Luigi Rosso, who had been tortured and killed in the Dugommier barracks. However, no archival document, either French or Italian, has been found to corroborate the alleged murder, and Panicacci's assumption seems solely based on the oral testimony of another resister, Louis Pietri. Panicacci, L'Occupation Italienne, 233.

126. AUSSME, Giustizia militare. Sentenze, carteggio, F19, b. 82, n°3052 del processo, 13 febbraio 1943. The culprit was sentenced to thirty years in prison. He escaped the death penalty only because previously he had been decorated for heroic deeds.

127. Reports on the incident can be found in ADAHP 42 W 82.

128. AUSSME, N1–11, DS 1100, Rapporto n°1348/inf. di prot., "Intempestività di sentinelle o vedette nel fare uso delle armi," Diario Storico Divisione Legnano, Allegato 68, 20 febbraio 1943; ARC, T-821, Roll 269, IT 3105, Rapporto n°640/inf., "Sabotaggio linee telefoniche," Comando Divisione Legnano, 25 gennaio 1943.

129. Unfortunately, in a few instances edgy sentinels did fire on French bystanders who had been mistaken in the night for resisters. See ADAM 166 W 10, Fichier Incidents provoqués par les troupes italiennes, 1942–1943, Rapport "Coup de feu tiré par une sentinelle italienne sur Mme Mortier," 25 avril 1943. The woman was immediately rushed to the hospital by Italian soldiers. To my knowledge, no one was killed in such incidents.

130. Burgwyn, Mussolini Warlord, 162.

131. ASMAE, Affari Politici, 1931–1945, Francia, b. 55, "Studio preliminare per lo studio di un programma di penetrazione nella zona delle rivendicazioni italiane ed in quella limitrofa, in provincia di Nizza," 23 settembre 1941.

132. Information on Lamboglia can be gleaned in his Dossier d'Étranger, ADAM 123 W 12.

133. Archives Municipales de Nice (hereafter, AMN), AM 3H 65, Lettre du conservateur du Musée Massena, 4 juin 1943.

134. The memorandum can be found in ASMAE, Affari Politici, 1931–1945, Francia, b. 80, Lettera n°40 Div. II "Istituti di Studi Liguri–Programma di studi provenzali," Ministero dell'Educazione Nazionale, 23 gennaio 1943.

135. Rainero, La Commission italienne d'armistice, 336. See also the report of the conference "Il Trofeo della Turbia nella latinità" on the ramifications of the Ro-

man heritage in the Alpes-Maritimes organized by Lamboglia, *Il Nizzardo,* Anno X, n°25, 27 giugno 1943, 2.

136. For the official order of the restructuring, see AUSSME, N1–11, DS 4A, Telegramma n°11390/op., Diario Storico Comando Supremo, 1218–15, 10 marzo 1943; for further details in the CIAF restructuring, see ARC, T-821, Roll 345, IT 4356, Telegramma n°16172/I, 15 aprile 1943.

137. ASMAE, Affari Politici, 1931–1945, Francia, b. 69, Rapporto n°55751, "Rapporti della Commissione di Armistizio colla Francia col Comando 4° Armata," 20 maggio 1943.

138. See, for instance, the case of Captain Marzovilla, member of the navy under-commission in Nice, who lost his position due to "interference of informants working for different organizations." ARC, T-821, Roll 345, IT 4356, Telegramma n°33 R.P. di prot., Sottocommissione per la Marina al presidente della CIAF, 7 aprile 1943, and the reply, Telegramma n°883 /Ma di prot. Sottocommissione Forze Armate, Ufficio Marina, 19 giugno 1943.

139. ARC, T-821, Roll 345, IT 4356, Telegramma n°16367/I "Attivita' informativa," Vacca Maggiolini, 11 maggio 1943.

140. Rainero suggests that Vacca Maggiolini emerged from the duel with Vercellino victorious. Rainero, *La Commission italienne d'armistice,* 324–25. I concur with Schipsi's interpretation that the CIAF president came out as the underdog of the contest. Schipsi, *L'occupazione italiana,* 289–91.

141. Rainero, *La Commission italienne d'armistice,* 336.

142. AUSSME, N1–11, DS 1100, Rapporto n°451/SA., Comando I CA, Diario Storico I CA, Allegato 51, 3 marzo 1943.

143. For instance, three CIAF civilians were intercepted at the French-Italian border with wristwatches, jewelry, and other expensive trinkets to be imported illegally into France. ACS, Tribunali militari di guerra e tribunali militari territoriali di guerra: Seconda Guerra Mondiale (1939–1945), Tribunale Militare XV Corpo D'Armata, Volume XIV, processo n°251, Gastone S., Giuseppe B. e Secondo L, 29 maggio 1943. The French were also aware of these shady activities. ADAM 166 W 26, Lettre "Membres des Commissions Etrangères d'Armistice," Préfet des Alpes-Maritimes au Ministre de l'Interieur, 4 mars 1942.

144. Rainero, *La Commission italienne d'armistice,* 337.

145. ASMAE, Affari Politici, 1931–1945, Francia, b. 69, Rapporto n°5713/1140, "Campi di concentramento," Console Gloria, 23 luglio 1943.

146. ASMAE, Affari Politici, 1931–1945, Francia, b. 68, Telegramma n°23856 P.R., Ministro degli Esteri Guariglia al Ministero della Guerra e Stato Maggiore Esercito, 1 agosto 1943.

147. AUSSME, D7, b. 5, Rapporto n°14276 di prot., "Coprifuoco a Nizza," 11 agosto 1943. See also Rapporto n°16421/op., "Coprifuoco a Nizza," 30 agosto 1943.

148. ARC, T-821, Roll 9, IT 19, Rapporto n°1/2893, "Appunto per l'Eccellenza il Generale Ambrosio," 28 maggio 1943. See also AUSSME, N1–11, DS 1218, Rap-

porto n°11119 di prot., "Situazione nei territori francesi occupati," Diario Storico Quarta Armata, Allegato 56, 12 giugno 1943.

149. ARC, T-821, Roll 9, IT 19, Telegramma n°3532/R. R. Consolato Bastia, 2 giugno 1943. The second document is unsigned and has only a date and location ("*Roma, lì 28 Giugno XXI*"), but someone scribbled at the end of the document "Autore = Turcato!" and it is plausible that the Italian CIAF delegate in Bastia was behind the report.

150. ACS, Ministero della Cultura Popolare (1922–1945), b. 14, Rapporto 126, sottofascicolo 2, "Il R. Console d'Italia in Corsica Ugo Turcato al Ministero degli Affari Esteri," Ajaccio, 6 giugno 1942, cited by Marco Cuzzi, "La rivendicazione fascista della Corsica (1938–1943)," Recherches Regionales–Alpes-Maritimes et contrées limitrophes 187 (juillet–septembre 2007): 68.

151. Turcato's criticism was tersely rebuffed by the army. See ARC, T-821, Roll 9, IT 19, Comando Supremo, Ufficio Operazioni Esercito Scacchiere Occidentale, "Situazione in Corsica," 14 giugno 1943, and ARC, T-821, Roll 9, IT 19, Comando Supremo, Ufficio Operazioni Esercito Scacchiere Occidentale, "Rapporti del Comm. Turcato sulla Corsica," 5 luglio 1943.

CHAPTER 9. COLLABORATION AND ACCOMMODATION

1. A holistic and comparative analysis of German occupation policies in the Second World War can be found in Mark Mazower, *Hitler's Empire: How the Nazis Ruled Europe* (New York: Penguin Press, 2008).

2. Robert Paxton, *Vichy France, Old Guard and New Order, 1940–1944* (New York: Columbia University Press, 1972). For more on the historiographical debate about the question of collaboration in France, see Alain Michel, "Collaboration and Collaborators in Vichy France, an Unfinished Debate," in *Collaboration with the Nazis: Public Discourse after the Holocaust,* ed. Roni Stauber (London: Routledge, 2011), 169–85.

3. Burrin, *France under the Germans,* 461–62.

4. Werner Rings, *Life with the Enemy: Collaboration and Resistance in Hitler's Europe, 1939–1945* (Garden City, NY: Doubleday, 1982), 73–85 and 278.

5. The two units enjoy a rich bibliography, ranging from apologetic accounts of veterans to fictional narratives written by sympathizers in postwar France. See Philippe Carrard, *The French Who Fought for Hitler: Memories from the Outcasts* (New York: Cambridge University Press, 2010). For a general history on the topic, see Pierre Giolitto, *Volontaires français sous l'uniforme allemand* (Paris: Perrin, 1999).

6. Peter Novick, *L'Épuration française, 1944–1949* (Paris: Balland, 1985), 242.

7. Vinen, *Unfree French,* 342–43.

8. Philippe Bourdrel, *L'Épuration sauvage* (Paris: Perrin, 2002), 199–214.

9. Megan Koreman, *The Expectation of Justice: France, 1944–1946* (Durham, NC: Duke University Press, 1999), 97–98.

10. The Cours of Justice boxes can be found in ADAM 318 W.

11. ADAM 318 W 39, Cours de Justice des Alpes-Maritimes, Dossier Marius F.

12. ADAM 318 W 28, Cours de Justice des Alpes-Maritimes, Dossier Avelino F.; ADAM 318 W 32, Cours de Justice des Alpes-Maritimes, Dossier Leopold B.

13. ADAM 318 W 85, Cours de Justice des Alpes-Maritimes, Dossier Louis T.

14. ADAM 318 W 51, Cours de Justice des Alpes-Maritimes, Dossier Ambroise A.

15. ADAM 318 W 31, Cours de Justice des Alpes-Maritimes, Dossier Guillaume Paolini.

16. A list of Italians (roughly 150 people) tried in absentia is available in ADAM 318 W 10.

17. ADAM 618 W 165. The list is sorted by alphabetical order. Each entry was classified into different categories: 17/37 (old militants), MSVN (Fascist Milice), AN (GAN adherents), MN (March to Nice), FFR (Fascist Republican Party), W.SS (Waffen SS). The list is a catchall in that it included people who were later acquitted of any ties, as well as anyone who had been even remotely associated with the Italian state from as early as the 1920s. Another unofficial list compiled by the French police totaled 540 individuals in the Alpes-Maritimes, 330 of whom lived in Nice and had signed up for the March to Nice, acted as informers, or espoused annexationist ideas. See ADAM 104 W 17. The other irredentist hubs apart from Nice were Monaco (50 people) and Antibes (28). No date is provided for either list, but they were presumably compiled after the war.

18. ADAM 318 W 24, Cours de Justice des Alpes-Maritimes, Dossier Flaminio C.

19. ADAM 318 W 110, Cours de Justice des Alpes-Maritimes, Dossier Juste P.

20. ADAM 318 W 110, Cours de Justice des Alpes-Maritimes, Dossier Vincent R.

21. ADAM 318 W 51, Cours de Justice des Alpes-Maritimes, Dossier Joseph T.

22. ADAM 318 W 86, Cours de Justice des Alpes-Maritimes, Dossier Cesare G.

23. ADAM 318 W 34, Cours de Justice des Alpes-Maritimes, Dossier Jean F.

24. For an example of the manure business, see ADAM 318 W 18, Cours de Justice des Alpes-Maritimes, Dossier Joseph V.

25. ADAM 318 W 118, Cours de Justice des Alpes-Maritimes, Dossier Joseph C.

26. This particular business was a marked success and enabled him to live an expensive lifestyle, according to the French police search in 1944, which uncovered a large quantity of foodstuffs, including white bread, an extreme rarity at the end of the war. ADAM 318 W 22, Cours de Justice des Alpes-Maritimes, Dossier Jean-Baptiste B.

27. An appropriate name indeed, as "*bagarre*" in French means brawl, or street fight.

28. ADAM 318 W 34, Cours de Justice des Alpes-Maritimes, Dossier Ezio C. It is interesting to note that in order to further compromise Ezio C's position, Bagarre mentioned his alleged affair with his secretary.

29. ADAM 318 W 54, Cours de Justice des Alpes-Maritimes, Dossier Albert O. Some additional documents, a letter of the mayor of Saint-Laurent-du-Var and a

letter by one of the prisoners' wives to Italian local authorities, can be found in ARC, T-821, Roll 265, IT 3099.

30. ADAM 318 W 111, Cours de Justice des Alpes-Maritimes, Dossier Barthelemy G.

31. For instance, a tailor in Monaco demanded substantial reparations from the CIAF declaring that after his detention in June 1940 in French internment camps, his store had been shunned by the French population and the pro-French Monegasques, presumably affecting his bottom line dramatically. ADAM 318 W 35, Cours de Justice des Alpes-Maritimes, Dossier Blaise A., translation n°544 of the 16 September 1940 letter sent to the CIAF.

32. ADAM 318 W 54, Cours de Justice des Alpes-Maritimes, Dossier Albert O. and Ida R. Albert O. was sentenced to twenty years, not so much for his ties with the Italian engineers, but for having allegedly denounced two civilians to the CIAF.

33. The expression stems from the fact that many Italians viewed themselves as inhabitants of a region or even a village before considering themselves Italians. Thus, the symbol of this fierce parochialism (*campanilismo*) was the bell tower, the powerful symbol of Italian Catholic piety, which soared in the center of nearly every village or city in Italy.

34. ADAM 318 W 32, Cours de Justice des Alpes-Maritimes, Dossier Antoine C.

35. ADAM 318 W 20, Cours de Justice des Alpes-Maritimes, Dossier Marie M., Arthur G., and others, procès-verbal n°2872/18 Richard P., 28 septembre 1944.

36. ADAM 318 W 124, Cours de Justice des Alpes-Maritimes, Dossier Enrico A.

37. ADAM 318 W 62, Cours de Justice des Alpes-Maritimes, Dossier Gino and Hélène C.

38. ADAM 318 W 25, Cours de Justice des Alpes-Maritimes, Dossier Charles S.

39. ADAHP 42 W 42, Rapport n°4041/Q.7-2 du Commissaire Sangla, 31 mai 1943.

40. ADAHP 42 W 42, Rapport n°3074 du Commissariat de police de Digne, 4 juin 1943.

41. ADAHP 42 W 42, Rapport du Commissariat de police de Digne, 24 juin 1943.

42. ADAHP 42 W 42, Rapport d'Information du Commissaire Principal, Chef du District de Police des Basses-Alpes, 29 janvier 1943.

43. ADAM 28 W 75, Lettre du Sous-Préfet de Grasse au colonel Mariani, chef d'Etat Major du Géneral Commandant le Ier Corps d'Armée, 6 juillet 1943.

44. ADAM 166 W 21, Contrôle télephonique n°2006, 15 mars 1943.

45. ADAM 159 W 46, Rapport n°2851, Police régionale d'État de Nice, 29 décembre 1942.

46. AUSSME, Giustizia militare. Sentenze, carteggio, F19, b. 83, n°3137 del processo, 14 aprile 1943.

47. AUSSME, Giustizia militare. Sentenze, carteggio, F19, b. 84, n°2883–3258 del processo, 4 maggio 1943.

48. For more on these relationships, see Vinen, *Unfree French,* 157–81.

49. The teenager was eventually sentenced to four years, not a surprising sentence if we remember the chauvinism of 1940s France and the fact that the teacher was

also the local president of the Comité d'Épuration. ADAM 318 W 115, Cours de Justice des Alpes-Maritimes, Dossier Christiane O., Déposition de Étienne P.

50. The Italian nurse was ultimately acquitted of any crime, as both the rich aristocratic widow and the bishop of Nice, Monseigneur Rémond, vouched for her. ADAM 318 W 134, Cours de Justice des Alpes-Maritimes, Dossier Lucia C.

51. ADAM 318 W 26, Cours de Justice des Alpes-Maritimes, Dossier Antoinette R. The woman was acquitted, as supposedly the French judges understood her reasons for engaging in an innocent relationship with an Italian soldier. It does, however, exemplify the chauvinist and xenophobic attitude of part of the population that her case was brought to the attention of the Comité d'Épuration.

52. ADAM 318 W 29, Cours de Justice des Alpes-Maritimes, Dossier Hélène M.

53. See the comparative essay of Anette Warring, "Intimate and Sexual Relations," in *Surviving Hitler and Mussolini: Daily Life in Occupied Europe*, ed. Robert Gildea, Olivier Wieviorka, and Anette Warring (New York: Berg, 2006), 88–128.

54. Fabrice Virgili, *Shorn Women: Gender and Punishment in Liberation France* (New York: Berg, 2002).

55. Finally, their names were whitewashed after the war. See ADAM 318 W 54, Cours de Justice des Alpes-Maritimes, Dossier Joseph F. and Dossier Lucie G., and ADAM 318 W 30, Cours de Justice des Alpes-Maritimes, Dossier Menardo/Barberis.

56. ADAM 318 W 24, Cours de Justice des Alpes-Maritimes, Dossier Jean G.

57. ADAM 318 W 39, Cours de Justice des Alpes-Maritimes, Dossier Edouard, Rose et Marie P.

58. ADAM 318 W 27, Cours de Justice des Alpes-Maritimes, Dossier Adalgisio and Egidio L., Note n°432 de l'Inspecteur Max Martin.

59. ADAM 318 W 27, Cours de Justice des Alpes-Maritimes, Dossier Charles P.

60. Vinen, *Unfree French*, 217.

CHAPTER 10. THE ITALIAN JEWISH POLICY IN FRANCE

1. Léon Poliakov, *La condition des Juifs en France sous l'occupation italienne* (Paris: CDJC, 1946). Later the CDJC published an English version: Léon Poliakov and Jacques Sabille, *Jews under the Italian Occupation* (New York: Howard Fertig, 1983).

2. For books following Poliakov's footsteps, see Jonathan Steinberg, *All or Nothing: The Axis and the Holocaust, 1941–1943*, 2nd ed. (New York: Routledge, 2002); Carpi, *Between Mussolini and Hitler*. This view has been partially criticized by Davide Rodogno, especially in his "La politique des occupants italiens à l'égard des Juifs en France métropolitaine, Humanisme ou pragmatisme?" *Vingtième Siècle, Revue d'histoire* 93, no. 1 (2007): 63–77.

3. For more on the roots of anti-Semitism in France, see Michael Marrus and Robert Paxton, *Vichy France and the Jews* (New York: Basic Publishers, 1981), 25–45. For a good picture of the Dreyfus Affair, see Piers Paul Read, *The Dreyfus Affair: The Scandal That Tore France in Two* (New York: Bloomsbury Press, 2012).

4. André Kaspi, *Les Juifs pendant l'Occupation* (Paris: Seuil, 1997), 38–40.

5. For a detailed account of the introduction of anti-Semitic laws into Vichy's legal framework, see Richard H. Weisberg, *Vichy Law and the Holocaust in France* (Newark, NJ: Harwood Academic Publishers, 1997), 37–81.

6. Renée Poznanski, *Jews in France during the Second World War* (Hanover, NH: Brandeis University Press, 2001), 251–62.

7. For an overview on the Vél d'Hiver roundup, see Maurice Rajsfus, *La Rafle du Vél d'Hiv* (Rennes: Presses Universitaires de France, 2002).

8. Darquier de Pellepoix's role in Vichy's anti-Semitic campaigns is well illustrated in Carmen Callil, *Bad Faith: A Forgotten History of Family, Fatherland, and Vichy France* (London: Vintage, 2007).

9. Cited by Hale, *French Riviera*, 26. The joke is referring to the fact that "Cannes" and "Kahn" are homophones. Cannes is the city in the Cote d'Azur where many Jews fled; Kahn is a typical Jewish German family name. It is difficult to estimate the total number of Jews in the Alpes-Maritimes. In August 1941, the names of 5,554 Jews were officially recorded, but the number of Jews increased threefold in the subsequent months, especially after November 1942. See Jean Kleinmann, "Pérégrinations des Juifs étrangers dans les Alpes-Maritimes (1938–1944)," in *Le Refuge et le Piège: Les Juifs et les Alpes (1938–1945)*, ed. Jean-William Dereymez (Paris: L'Harmattan, 2008), 200.

10. Scores of anti-Semitic letters can be found in ADAM 616 W 188.

11. Cited by Hale, *French Riviera*, 26. Tristan Bernard here alludes to the fact that Bloch is a common Jewish family name, as in the case of Kahn.

12. Kleinmann, "Pérégrinations des Juifs étrangers," 207–208.

13. ADAM 166 W 16, Lettre n°3258, Préfet des Alpes-Maritimes au Commissaire divisionnaire, Chef du service régional aux Renseignements Géneraux, 1 septembre 1942. In theory, children under the age of eighteen were not targeted unless their parents chose to bring the children with them. Other categories were excluded, such as individuals older than sixty, the seriously ill, and pregnant women. In fact, these exceptions were rarely applied.

14. ADAM 166 W 16, Rapport n°3874, "Compte rendu d'ensemble des opérations effectuées le 26 août 1942," Commissaire divisionnaire, Chef du service régional aux Renseignements Géneraux au Préfet des Alpes-Maritimes, Nice, 27 août 1942, 3. Out of thirty-three conversations taped by the Contrôles Techniques on 27 August, nineteen disapproved of the measures, nine approved, and five were neutral. See also the R.G. *Bulletin Journalier*, 27 août 1942.

15. Poznanski, *Jews in France*, 292–302.

16. For more on the evolution of the attitude of the Catholic Church with regard to the Jewish population in France, see W. D. Halls, *Politics, Society and Christianity in Vichy France* (Oxford: Berg, 1995), "Part III: The Scapegoats."

17. ADAM 166 W 16, Lettre de l'évêque de Montauban sur le respect de la personne humaine, 26 août 1942.

18. ADAM 166 W 16, Communiqué de son Eminence le Cardinal Gerlier, à lire en chaire, 6 septembre 1942.

19. ADAM 616 W 242, Fichier 17, Mesure Israélites et étrangers, Extrait du Journal Officiel, 12 décembre 1942, Loi n°1077 du 11 décembre 1942.

20. ADAM 30 W 101, Correspondance Express n°18743 Ministère de l'Intérieur aux Préfets Régionaux, 6 décembre 1942. Fourteen hundred Jews in the Alpes-Maritimes were officially singled out to be deported inland. ADAM 616 W 242, Fichier 17, Mesure Israélites et étrangers, Lettre du Préfet des Alpes-Maritimes au Préfet régional du Rhône, 18 décembre 1942.

21. ADAM 616 W 242, Fichier 17, Mesure Israélites et étrangers, Lettre n°2522 secret, 14 décembre 1942; Télégramme n°499, 11 janvier 1943, Lettre au Préfet, 12 janvier 1943.

22. ARC, T-821, Roll 265, IT 3095, n°4849/I. di prot., "Provvedimenti a carico di personale di razza ebraica nei territori occupati dalle forze armate italiane," 30 dicembre 1942. (The original document put a question mark instead of the date, but it appears that was due to a transcription error; see Carpi, *Between Mussolini and Hitler,* 277–78n24.)

23. ASMAE, Affari Politici, 1931–1945, Francia, b. 80, Lettera n°027 al Console Calisse, 6 gennaio 1943.

24. For some examples of foreign Jews who caught wind of the Italian soft policy, see Susan Zuccotti, *Holocaust Odysseys: The Jews of Saint-Martin-Vésubie and Their Flight through France and Italy* (New Haven, CT: Yale University Press, 2007), 71–81.

25. ASMAE, Affari Politici, 1931–1945, Francia, b. 68, Telegramma n°159 R, "Assegnazione a residenza forzata," Console Italiano a Nizza Calisse, 23 febbraio 1943.

26. More information on the committee and on Angelo Donati can be found in Carpi, *Between Mussolini and Hitler,* 94–97.

27. For Camerani's views, see ASMAE, Serie Armistizio Pace b. 8, n°1628 Segreto Nice, 29 marzo 1941.

28. For a more detailed view on Donati, see Carpi, *Between Mussolini and Hitler,* 97–98. Carpi had access, via French Shoah specialist Serge Klarsfeld, to the Donati documents, a collection of Donati's memoirs, along with his interview in 1944. Mazzolini's personal friendship with Donati could explain why Mazzolini was already favorable in February 1942 to the idea of taking the Jews under the CIAF delegation's wing. ASMAE, Serie Armistizio Pace b. 8, Lettera n°333 R, Delegato CIAF Mazzolini alla Sottocommissione Affari Giuridici CIAF, 21 febbraio 1942.

29. For instance, in his book on the Jewish refuge of Saint-Martin-Vésubie, Alberto Cavaglion credits Donati not only for financing the stay of destitute Jews in the Alpine resorts but also for lobbying for a policy of protection against the Jews. See Alberto Cavaglion, *Les Juifs de Saint-Martin-Vésubie, Septembre–Novembre 1943* (Nice: Serre, 1995), 22–27. The same argument is found in Kaspi, *Les Juifs pendant l'Occupation,* 294–95. Daniel Carpi, on the other hand, thinks that Donati's importance has been widely exaggerated, as even one man as rich and influential as Donati could not have much weight to change the Italian state's policy on such an important matter. See Carpi, *Between Mussolini and Hitler,* 98.

30. ADAM 166 W 10, Fichier Assignations à résidence, Note 6 avril 1943.

31. One copy of the unsigned document written in June 1943 and titled "Note sur les effets de la protection accordée par l'Italie aux Juifs de Nice" can be found in 318 W 79, Cours de Justice des Alpes-Maritimes, Dossier Antoine Gabriel D.

32. Steinberg, *All or Nothing,* 109.

33. Carpi, *Between Mussolini and Hitler,* 102–103.

34. Ibid., 112.

35. AUSSME, N1–11, DS 1100, Rapporto n°1165/inf., "Assegnazione a residenza forzata," Diario Storico I CA, Allegato 39, 14 febbraio 1943.

36. AUSSME, N1–11, DS 1218, Rapporto n°1772/02 Telegramma 81/135, Diario Storico Comando Quarta Armata, Allegato 3, 1 marzo 1943; see also ASMAE, Affari Politici, 1931–1945, Francia, b. 80, Lettera n°306/C. di prot., "Arresto degli Ebrei da parte delle autorità francesi," Conte Bonarelli, 5 marzo 1943.

37. Carpi, *Between Mussolini and Hitler,* 125–26.

38. ARC, T-821, Roll 265, IT 3095, n°5550 di prot., "Ebrei dimoranti in territori francesi occupati dalle forze armata italiane," Stato Maggiore Regio Esercito al Comando della 4° Armata, 30 aprile 1940. In fact, it seems the document was a confirmation of a directive already sent on 26 March (n°4514 "I"). See also n°2528/inf. di prot., "Afflusso di ebrei nel dipartimento delle Alpi Marittime," Comando I CA, 1 aprile 1943.

39. The CIAF officially communicated the nomination of Lospinoso only at the end of May. See ADAM 171 W 3, n°7302/02, "Opérations d'internements de Juifs," Délégation militaire de contrôle pour le dispositif alpin, 20 mai 1943.

40. Panicacci, *L'Occupation Italienne,* 201–203.

41. Carpi, *Between Mussolini and Hitler,* 135–36.

42. Apart from Saint-Martin-Vésubie, Jews were housed in eight other Alpine villages (Megève, Saint-Gervais, Castellane, Barcelonnette, Vence, Moutiers, Sainte-Marie, Venanson). Zuccotti, *Holocaust Odysseys,* 90.

43. Cavaglion, *Les Juifs de Saint-Martin-Vésubie,* 40.

44. Ibid., 44.

45. ADAM 166 W 10, Fichier Assignations à résidence, Contrôle Postal XH n°127, 13 avril 1943; Contrôle Postal WI n°524, 8 avril 1943.

46. ADAM 166 W 10, Fichier Assignations à résidence, Rapport n°2/4 de la Brigade de Saint-Martin-Vésubie, 7 avril 1943.

47. ARC, T-821, Roll 265, IT 3095, n°4276/inf., "Afflusso ebrei," Comando I CA, 24 maggio 1943.

48. ADAM 616 W 51, Note de renseignements pour le rapport du 25 juillet 1943, Mesures administratives prises à l'encontre des français et étrangers.

49. ASMAE, Affari Politici, 1931–1945, Francia, b. 80, Telegramma n°5000 R., "Comunicazione per Ministro Vidau," Console italiano a Nizza Spechel, 31 luglio 1943.

50. ASMAE, Affari Politici, 1931–1945, Francia, b. 80, Telegramma n°25012/P.R. daVidau, 2 agosto 1943; Telegramma n°24335/C. da Vidau, 6 agosto 1943.

51. ASMAE, Affari Politici, 1931–1945, Francia, b. 80, Telegramma n°24348/P.R., "Ebrei nella zona di occupazione italiana: lavoro obbligatorio," Ambasciata Italiana a Parigi, 28 agosto 1943.

52. ARC, T-821, Roll 265, IT 3095, n°7967/inf., "Trasferimento ebrei in residenza forzata," Comando I CA, 3 settembre 1943; Panicacci, Les Alpes-Maritimes, 278–80.

53. ADAM 616 W 233, Note from the Légion Française des Combattants, Alpes-Maritimes "Juifs indésirables," 8 septembre 1943.

54. Panicacci, Les Alpes-Maritimes, 198–201; Kaspi, Les Juifs pendant l'Occupation, 296–98.

55. For more on the hasty Italian withdrawal, see chapter 11.

56. Almost all of the arrested Jews were deported to the east to extermination camps. The exodus has been admirably recounted in vivid detail by Cavaglion in Les Juifs de Saint-Martin-Vésubie.

57. Focardi, Il cattivo tedesco ed il bravo italiano, 113–21.

58. Poliakov and Sabille, Jews under the Italian Occupation; Hannah Arendt, Eichmann in Jerusalem: A Report on the Banality of Evil (New York: Viking Press, 1963).

59. Steinberg, All or Nothing, 220–41.

60. Carpi, Between Mussolini and Hitler, 248–49.

61. The sovereignty thesis also has been put forth by Eric Gobetti to explain the Italian protection of Jews in the Balkans. See Gobetti, Alleati del nemico, 131–32.

62. This idea was exposed in a Vichy police report. See ADAM 166 W 10, RG Note 6 avril 1943.

63. Rodogno, "La politique des occupants italiens," 66–67.

64. As an example, only one Fourth Army document of the thousands perused for this work was tainted by a dose of anti-Semitism. Colonel Ulisse Bonfigli, head of the Comando Settore Cannes, complained in one of his reports of "a terrorist cell in Cannes financed by the enemy propaganda and by international Judaism" (giudaismo internazionale). ARC, T-821, Roll 269, IT 3105, n°1324/inf. di prot., "Atto terroristico," Comando Divisione Fanteria "Legnano," 17 maggio 1943.

65. Carpi, Between Mussolini and Hitler, 106–107.

Chapter 11. Drawing the Curtain on the Occupation

1. Philip Morgan, The Fall of Mussolini (Oxford: Oxford University Press, 2007), 11–33.

2. AN, F1, cIII 1137, rapport périodique du 3 août 1943, n°126 C.B., cited by Panicacci, L'Occupation Italienne, 252. The same page contains other examples and testimonies of the Italian state of mind at the end of July 1943.

3. ARC, T-821, Roll 338, IT 4296, n°12620 di prot. S.P., "Contegno," 27 luglio 1943.

4. ARC, T-821, Roll 267, IT 3100, n°211210 di prot., "Commento alla truppa sulla situazione attuale," 1 agosto 1943.

5. ARC, T-821, Roll 338, IT 4296, n°2075/C.I/Ris. di prot., "Astensione dei militari da qualsiasi attività politica," Comando Generale MSVN, 28 luglio 1943.

6. ARC, T-821, Roll 338, IT 4296, n°9477/T., "Abolizione del saluto romano e cancellazione di emblemi," 29 luglio 1943. These changes were not limited to the Italian army but also touched the other services. The air force, for instance, asked its officers to remove the Fascio on their uniforms. ARC, T-821, Roll 261, IT 3077, n°324/O, "Variante al regolamento sull'Uniforme," 15 agosto 1943.

7. ARC, T-821, Roll 270, IT 3124, n°758/P.D., "Contegno dei militari in rapporto alle relazioni femminili," 12 agosto 1943. See also ARC, T-821, Roll 261, IT 3077, n°E/53/R.P., "Contegno degli ufficiali in rapporto alle relazioni femminili," Comando Aeronautica della Provenza, 6 settembre 1943.

8. ARC, T-821, Roll 267, IT 3100, n°14068/op. di prot., "Incapacità di comando," 8 agosto 1943.

9. ARC, T-821, Roll 261, IT 3077, n°13805/S.P., "Procedura d'eccezione," Comando Quarta Armata, 14 agosto 1943.

10. ARC, T-821, Roll 266, IT 3099, n°27279/SIM/R. di prot., "Italiani fuoriusciti e sovversivi in Francia," 14 agosto 1943. See also n°1351/inf. di prot., "Trasmissione manifestini propaganda sovversiva," Comando 223° Divisione Costiera, 21 agosto 1943.

11. For more details, see Panicacci, *L'Occupation Italienne*, 262–63.

12. ARC, T-821, Roll 265, IT 3099, n°7217/inf. di prot., "Competenza in fatto di reati e contravvenzioni ai nostri danni da parte di cittadini francesi," Comando I CA, 12 agosto 1943.

13. *L'Éclaireur de Nice et du Sud-Est,* 17 August 1943.

14. Panicacci, *L'Occupation Italienne,* 264–65.

15. ARC, T-821, Roll 267, IT 3099, n°76/12/inf. di prot., "Consegna armi da parte di civili," Comando I CA, 22 agosto 1943.

16. For the Italian communist organization, see AUSSME, Giustizia militare. Sentenze, carteggio, F19, b. 84, senza numero, 22 agosto 1943. For the Armée Secrète, see AUSSME, Giustizia militare. Sentenze, carteggio, F19, b. 84, n°1548 del processo, 15 luglio 1943. The smashing of the Armée Secrète was an extremely hard blow for the local Resistance movement, as it was an umbrella organization for important Resistance movements such as Combat, Libération, and Franc-Tireur. A document found in the Alpes-Maritimes confirms the arrest in June 1943 of its main leaders: André Comboul, Jean Allègre, and Albert Bardi de Fortour. See ADAM 169 W 3, "Organisation officielle des Mouvements de Résistance dans les Alpes-Maritimes et la Zone Sud en 1942/1943," no date.

17. Schipsi, *L'occupazione italiana,* 466–70.

18. Ibid., 454.

19. ARC, T-821, Roll 249, IT 2295, n°16973/I. di prot., "Notizie dalla Francia," Presidenza CIAF, 15 agosto 1943.

20. ARC, T-821, Roll 354, IT 4527, Promemoria Comando Supremo, I Reparto Ufficio Operazioni Esercito, Scacchiere Occidentale, per il sottocapo di S.M Generale "Notizie dalla Francia," 19 agosto 1943.

21. ARC, T-821, Roll 249, IT 2295, Trascrizione dell'incontro a Villa Federzoni (Bologna), 15 agosto 1943, 1.

22. One German army corps, the 87th, was deployed in mid-August 1943 in Liguria, just across the French-Italian border, but not without meeting some hostile reactions from local Italian commanders. See Schipsi, *L'occupazione italiana*, 471–76.

23. ARC, T-821, Roll 261, IT 3077, Rapporto n°14289/S.P., "Incidenti con militari germanici," Comando Quarta Armata, 20 agosto 1943.

24. ARC, T-821, Roll 270, IT 3115, Rapporto n°1868/prot., "Coprifuoco a Golfe Juan," Comando 167° Reggimento Alpino Costiero, 16 agosto 1943.

25. Schipsi, *L'occupazione italiana*, 474.

26. Mario Torsiello, *Le operazioni delle unità italiane nel settembre–ottobre 1943* (Roma: Stato Maggiore dell'Esercito, Ufficio Storico, 1975), 146–47.

27. Among the wide literature on the 1943 armistice, Elena Aga-Rossi's *Una nazione allo sbando. L'armistizio italiano del settembre 1943 e le sue conseguenze* (Bologna: Il Mulino, 2003) stands out as one of the best books.

28. Torsiello, *Le operazioni delle unità italiane*, 151–52.

29. Panicacci, *L'Occupation Italienne*, 287.

30. Ibid., 291–92; Torsiello, *Le operazioni delle unità italiane*, 162–64.

31. See, for instance, ADAM 616 W 215, Fichier 9, Capitulation Italienne, Rapport n°832/2, Gendarmerie Roquebrune/Cap-Martin sur les évènements consécutifs à l'occupation allemande, 12 septembre 1943.

32. The directive can be found in Torsiello, *Le operazioni delle unità italiane*, 170. For having given the order to disband, Vercellino was prosecuted in the aftermath of the war for desertion, but was later acquitted.

33. ADAM 616 W 215, Fichier 9, Capitulation Italienne, Rapport n°14/4, sur un incident crée par un Lieutenant des troupes italiennes de passage, Brigade de Saorge, 10 septembre 1943.

34. ADAM 616 W 215, Fichier 9, Capitulation Italienne, Rapport 29A, Gendarmerie de Breil-sur-Roya, 11 septembre 1943.

35. ADAM 616 W 215, Fichier 6, Rapport n°472/2, sur un incident à l'occasion d'un enlèvement de matériel abandonné par les troupes italiennes à St-Vallier de Thiez, Gendarmerie de Grasse, 12 septembre 1943.

36. See, for instance, ADAM 616 W 114, Rapport Bureau de liaison 994, Gendarmerie de campagne, Lieutenant Commandant Scheieler, 16 octobre 1943.

37. ADAM 616 W 114, Rapport n°262/2 Brigade de Lantosque, 24 décembre 1943; ADAHP 42 W 82, Rapport n°6380, "Accident occasioné par l'éclatement de grenade," RG Basses-Alpes, 11 septembre 1943, and ADAM 616 W 215, Fichier 6, Lettre du maire de Trinité-Victor au Préfet des Alpes-Maritimes, "Explosion ayant entrainé blessures à des enfants," 25 septembre 1943.

38. For an overview of the data, see Panicacci, *L'Occupation Italienne*, 306–307.

39. ADAM 616 W 215, Fichier 9, Capitulation Italienne, Rapport n°12011 CAB, Préfet des Basses-Alpes, 9 septembre 1943.

40. ADAM 616 W 215, Fichier 9, Capitulation Italienne, Procès-verbal n°152/4 sur la découverte d'un cadavre de militaire italien au Mont-Agel, Brigade de la Turbie, 10 septembre 1943.

41. ADAM 159 W 49, Procès-verbal n°4/74 Brigade de Isola, 15 septembre 1943.

42. ADAM 616 W 215, Fichier Nice Communications émanant du Commandement allemand, Verbindungsstab 994 Abt. Ic, Az. 63 a, tgb 2317/43, Asile aux soldats italiens, 16 septembre 1943.

43. AN, F1, cIII 11194, rapport périodique du 1er octobre 1943, cited by Panicacci, *L'Occupation Italienne*, 311. It is interesting to note that the report underlined that the sympathy was stronger "on the coastline, where the population was heavily mixed [between Italians and French]."

44. Emmanuel Volpi, *L'Occupation italienne dans le département du Var (Novembre 1942-Septembre 1943)*, Master 2 d'Histoire préparé sous la direction de Jean-Louis Panicacci (Nice: UFR LASH, 2007), 99–100, cited by Panicacci, *L'Occupation Italienne*, 312–13.

45. Panicacci, *L'Occupation Italienne*, 312.

46. ADAM 169 W 7, réponse de la Ville de Fontan au quéstionnaire du CHOL sur l'occupation et la Libération, cited by Panicacci, *L'Occupation Italienne*, 310.

47. ADAM 616 W 97, Rapport d'information sur les mois de septembre et octobre 1943, 6bis–8.

48. ADAM 616 W 97, Rapport d'information sur les mois de novembre et décembre 1943, 10 janvier 1943.

49. Rick Atkinson, *The Guns at Last Light: The War in Western Europe, 1944–1945* (New York: Henry Holt, 2013), 188–205.

CONCLUSION

1. Pierre Rigoulot, *L'Alsace-Lorraine pendant la guerre, 1939–1945* (Paris: Presses Universitaires de France, 1997), 23–24.

2. Dieter Wolfanger, *Nazification de la Lorraine mosellane* (Sarreguemines: Editions Pierron, 1982), 83–84.

3. Christophe Nagyos, *Guerres et paix en Alsace-Moselle: de l'annexion à la fin du nazisme; histoire de trois départements de l'Est, 1870–1945* (Strasbourg: La nuée bleue, 2005), 32–35; Rigoulot, *L'Alsace-Lorraine pendant la guerre*, 53–60.

4. A Gauleiter headed each Reichsgau (territories annexed by the Germans in the Second World War, akin to an English shire).

5. ADAM 169 W 3, "Occupation et Libération de la Commune de Nice, Guerre 1939–1945," Mairie de Nice, 7 mai 1949.

6. Panicacci, *L'Occupation Italienne*, 327. The Italians in total killed 40 civilians, the Germans 159 only in the Alpes-Maritimes. In total the Germans executed more than 1,000 people in southeastern France and deported 4,000 resisters and more than 3,000 Jews, most of whom did not return alive.

7. AN, AJ41, 329, "Statistique Générale," 27 février 1944, cited in Alan Mitchell, *Nazi Paris: The History of an Occupation, 1940–1944* (New York: Berghahn, 2008), 107–108. As Mitchell warns the reader, data should be taken with a grain of salt. However, the difference in numbers is evident to the point that Mitchell asserts that "by far the most executions occurred in the former Occupied Zone, the least in the Italian zone" (108).

8. For more on the liberation of Corsica, see Panicacci, *L'Occupation Italienne*, 314–23. It should be noted that the Germans did not occupy Corsica, as the island would be freed in September by a surprising alliance between Italian units quartered on the island and the local Resistance movement. The Italians lost more than six hundred men fighting the Germans.

9. AUSSME, M3, b. 53, Circolare Ufficio "I," Seconda Armata, 12 maggio 1941.

10. Osti Guerrazzi, *L'Esercito italiano*, 19.

11. A similar process could have occurred on the eastern front with the Wehrmacht. Indeed, some historians posit that both the harsh environment of partisan attacks and peer pressure might explain how ordinary men became perpetrators of vicious atrocities. See Christopher Browning, *Ordinary Men: Reserve Police Battalion 101 and the Final Solution in Poland* (New York: HarperCollins, 1992).

12. Osti Guerrazzi, *Non non sappiamo odiare*, 63.

13. Gobetti, *L'occupazione allegra*, 180–81.

14. See ARC, T-821, Roll 265, IT 3099, Rapporto n°4687/inf. di prot., "Direttive delle forze sovversive in Francia," Comando I CA, 3 giugno 1943.

15. Even in the Savoy region, where the Italians were confronted by groups of Maquis (bands of Resistance fighters in rural areas, whose ranks swelled because of draft dodgers), the situation did not escalate tremendously. See Christian Villermet, *A Noi Savoia, Histoire de l'occupation italienne en Savoie, novembre 1942–septembre 1943* (Les Marches: La Fontaine de Siloé, 1991); see especially part 3, "Les Réactions des Savoyards." The Savoy was the only French region, aside from Corsica, where a resister, Henri Lanier, was executed for having participated in a deadly ambush against Italian troops in Grenoble. See Panicacci, *L'Occupation Italienne*, 226–27.

16. See, for instance, ADAM 616 W 135, Rapport bi-mensuel n°6095/SP, Commissariat de police d'Antibes, 14 avril 1943.

17. Doumanis refers to the relationships between Italian soldiers and the local Greek population in the Dodecanese archipelago and notes, "The Italians were seen to share similar views regarding marriage, family and honour, as well as cultural tastes, including music, singing and even romantic love." Nicholas Doumanis, *Myth and Memory in the Mediterranean: Remembering Fascism's Empire* (Houndmills, Hampshire: Macmillan, 1997), 166.

18. Varley, "Between Vichy France and Fascist Italy," 524.

19. Mazower, *Hitler's Empire*, 236–37.

20. AUSSME, D7, b. 5, Rapporto n°14276 di prot., "Coprifuoco a Nizza," 11 agosto 1943.

21. ASMAE, Affari Politici, 1931–1945, Francia, b. 68, Lettera C. De Constantin a Guariglia, untitled, 14 agosto 1943. The latter point is somewhat surprising and perhaps hints at the extent to which some Fascist civil servants had no clue of the dire military situation in Italy.

22. Thomas Johnston Laub, *After the Fall: German Policy in Occupied France, 1940–1944* (New York: Oxford University Press, 2010), 18–19.

BIBLIOGRAPHY

Primary Sources

Archives Départementales des Alpes-de-Haute-Provence (ADAHP)

Série 042 W Préfecture–Cabinet
Miscellaneous

Archives Départementales des Alpes-Maritimes (ADAM)

Série 616 W Cabinet du préfet–1er Bureau
Série 166 W Intendance de Police de la région de Nice
Série 104 W Contrôle de la situation administrative, politique et économique et
 morale du département
Série 318 W Cour de Justice et Chambre civique, Séction de Nice
Miscellaneous

Archives Municipales de la ville de Nice (AMVN)

Archivio Centrale dello Stato (ACS)

Fondo CIAF, Commissariato di civile di Mentone e Ufficio Informazioni
Miscellaneous

*Archivio dell'Ufficio Storico dello Stato Maggiore dell'Esercito
(AUSSME)*

Fondo D7, Commissione Italiana per l'Armistizio con la Francia (CIAF)
Fondo N1–11, Diari Storici della Seconda Guerra Mondiale
Fondo F19, Tribunale Militare Quarta Armata
Miscellaneous

Archivio Storico Diplomatico del Ministero degli Affari Esteri (ASMAE)

Gabinetto Armistizio-Pace, Francia

Affari Politici, 1931–1945, Francia

Washington National Archives, Archival Research Catalog (ARC)

Collection of Italian Military Records 1935–1943, National Archives Microfilm T-821

Selected Secondary Sources

Abramovici, Pierre. *Un Rocher bien occupé, Monaco pendant la guerre, 1939–1945.* Paris: Éditions du Seuil, 2001.

Aga-Rossi, Elena. *Una nazione allo sbando. L'armistizio italiano del settembre 1943 e le sue conseguenze.* Bologna: Il Mulino, 2003.

Alary, Eric. *La ligne de démarcation.* Paris: Perrin, 2003.

Amicucci, Ermanno. *Nizza Italiana.* Milano: Mondadori, 1942.

Amoroux, Henri. *La vie Française sous l'Occupation.* Paris: Fayard, 1961.

Anderson, Benedict. *Imagined Communities: Reflections on the Origin and Spread of Nationalism.* London: Verso, 1983.

Andújar, Manuel. *Saint-Cyprien, plage . . . : camp de concentration.* Clermont-Ferrand, France: Presses Universitaires Blaise Pascal, 2003.

Anglade, Jean. *La vie quotidienne des immigrés en France de 1919 à nos jours.* Paris: Hachette, 1976.

Arendt, Hannah. *Eichmann in Jerusalem: A Report on the Banality of Evil.* New York: Viking Press, 1963.

Ascoli, Massimo. *La Guardia alla Frontiera.* Roma: Stato Maggiore Esercito, Ufficio Storico, 2003.

Atkinson, Rick. *The Guns at Last Light: The War in Western Europe, 1944–1945.* New York: Henry Holt, 2013.

Azeau, Henri. *La Guerre Franco-Italienne, Juin 1940.* Paris: Presses de la Cité, 1967.

Azzi, Stephen Corrado. "The Historiography of Fascist Foreign Policy." *Historical Journal* 36, no. 1 (1993): 187–209.

Badoglio, Pietro. *Italy in the Second World War: Memories and Documents.* Westport, CT: Greenwood Press, 1976.

Barneaud, Claude. *Les Mentonnais et la Résistance.* Menton: Société d'Art et d'Histoire du Mentonnais, 1992.

Bechelloni, Antonio, Michel Dreyfus, and Pierre Milza, eds. *L'intégration italienne en France, un siècle de présence italienne dans trois régions françaises (1880–1980).* Paris: Editions Complexe, 1995.

Bernasconi, Alessandro, and Daniela Collavo. *Dei Sacri Confini Guardia Sicura: la Guardia alla Frontiera, 1934–1943.* Trento: Temi, 2002.

Bervoets-Tragholz, Marcel. *La liste de Saint-Cyprien.* Bruxelles: Alice Éditions, 2006.

Borgogni, Massimo. *Italia e Francia durante la crisi militare dell'Asse*. Siena: Nuova Immagine, 1994.

———. *Mussolini e la Francia di Vichy: dalla dichiarazione di guerra al fallimento del riavvicinamento italo-francese (giugno 1940–aprile 1942)*. Siena: Nuova immagine, 1991.

Bosworth, Richard. "Italian Foreign Policy and Its Historiography." In *Altro Polo: Intellectuals and Their Ideas in Contemporary Italy*, edited by Richard Bosworth and Gino Rizzo, 65–85. Sydney: Sydney University Press, 1983.

Botti, Ferruccio, and Virgilio Ilari. *Il Pensiero Militare dal Primo al Secondo Dopoguerra (1919–1949)*. Roma: Ufficio Storico SME, 1985.

Bourdrel, Philippe. *L'Épuration sauvage*. Paris: Perrin, 2002.

Browning, Christopher. *Ordinary Men: Reserve Police Battalion 101 and the Final Solution in Poland*. New York: HarperCollins, 1992.

Burgwyn, James H. *Empire on the Adriatic: Mussolini's Conquest of Yugoslavia, 1941–1943*. New York: Enigma, 2005.

———. "General's Roatta War against the Partisans in Yugoslavia: 1942." *Journal of Modern Italian Studies* 9, no. 3 (2004): 314–29.

———. *Mussolini Warlord: Failed Dreams of Empire, 1940–1943*. New York: Enigma, 2012.

Burrin, Philippe. *France under the Germans: Collaboration and Compromise*. New York: New Press, 1996.

———. "Writing the History of Military Occupation." In *France at War: Vichy and the Historians*, edited by Sarah Fishman, Laura Lee Downs, Ioannis Sinagoglou, Leonard V. Smith, and Robert Zarestky, 77–90. Oxford: Berg, 2000.

Callil, Carmen. *A Forgotten History of Family, Fatherland, and Vichy France*. London: Vintage, 2007.

Calvino, Italo. *L'entrata in Guerra*. Torino: Einaudi, 1954.

Canali, Mauro. *Le Spie del Regime*. Bologna: Il Mulino, 2004.

Caperan-Moreno, Louis. *Histoire de Menton*. Menton: Annales de la Societe d'Art et d'Histoire du Mentonnais, 1993.

Carpi, Daniel. *Between Mussolini and Hitler: The Jews and the Italian Authorities in France and Tunisia*. Hanover, NH: University Press of New England, 1994.

Carrard, Philippe. *The French Who Fought for Hitler: Memories from the Outcasts*. New York: Cambridge University Press, 2010.

Carrier, Richard. "Réflexions sur l'efficacité militaire de l'armée des Alpes, 10–25 juin 1940." *Revue historique des armées* 250 (2008): 85–93.

Cattaruzza, Marina. *L'Italia ed il confine orientale, 1866–2006*. Bologna: Il Mulino, 2006.

Cavaglion, Alberto. *Les Juifs de Saint-Martin-Vésubie, Septembre-Novembre 1943*. Nice: Editions Serre, 1995.

Cavallero, Ugo. *Diario, 1940–1943*. Roma: Ciarrapico, 1984.

Cima Bernard, Raymond Cima, and Michel Truttman. *La glorieuse défense du Pont Saint-Louis: Juin 1940*. Menton: Cima, 1995.

Cointet, Jean-Paul. *La Légion française des combattants*. Paris: Albin Michel, 1995.

Collingham, Lizzie. *The Taste of War: World War II and the Battle for Food*. New York: Penguin, 2012.

Collotti, Enzo. "Sulla politica di repressione nei Balcani." In *La memoria del nazismo nell'Europa di oggi*, edited by Leonardo Paggi, 181–211. Firenze: Nuova Italia, 1997.

Costa Bona, Enrica. *Dalla guerra alla pace, Italia-Francia, 1940–1947*. Milano: Franco Angeli, 1995.

Cros, Pierre. *Saint-Cyprien, 1939–1945, le village, le camp, la guerre*. Canet: Éditions Trabucaire, 2001.

Cuzzi, Marco. "La rivendicazione fascista della Corsica (1938–1943)." *Recherches Regionales–Alpes-Maritimes et contrées limitrophes* 187 (juillet–septembre 2007): 58–71.

David, Daniel. "Les fortifications alpines françaises." *Revue historique des armées* 250 (2008): 4–15.

De Caprariis, Luca. "'Fascism for Export'? The Rise and Eclipse of the Fasci Italiani all'Estero." *Journal of Contemporary History* 35, no. 2 (2000): 151–83.

De Felice, Renzo. *Mussolini il duce*. Vol. II. Torino: Einaudi, 1981.

De Grazia, Victoria. *The Culture of Consent: Mass Organisation of Leisure in Fascist Italy*. Cambridge: Cambridge University Press, 1981

———. *How Fascism Ruled Women: Fascism, 1922–1945*. Berkeley: University of California Press, 1992.

Del Boca, Angelo. *I gas di Mussolini. Il fascismo e la guerra d'Etiopia*. Roma: ed. Riuniti, 2007.

Delperrié de Bayac, Jacques. *Histoire de la Milice, 1918–1945*. Paris: Fayard, 1969.

Di Nolfo, Ennio. "Mussolini e la decisione italiana di entrare nella seconda guerra mondiale." In *L'Italia e la politica di potenza in Europa (1938–1940)*, edited by Ennio Di Nolfo, Romain H. Rainero, and Brunello Vigezzi, 19–38. Milano: Marzorati, 1986.

Diamond, Hannah. *Fleeing Hitler, France 1940*. Oxford: Oxford University Press, 2007.

Dombrowski Risser, Nicole. *France under Fire: German Invasion, Civilian Flight, and Family Survival during World War II*. Cambridge: Cambridge University Press, 2012.

Doumanis, Nicholas. *Myth and Memory in the Mediterranean: Remembering Fascism's Empire*. Houndmills, Hampshire: Macmillan, 1997.

English, John A. *On Infantry*. New York: Praeger, 1984.

Faidutti-Rudolph, Anne Marie. *L'Immigration italienne dans le sud-est de la France*. Gap, France: Ophrys, 1964.

Ferenc, Tone. *There Is Not Enough Killing: Condemned to Death, Hostages, Shot in the Ljubljana Province, 1941–1943*. Ljubljana, Slovenia: Institute for Contemporary History, Society of the Writers of the History of the Liberation War, 1999.

Fette, Julie. *Exclusions: Practicing Prejudice in French Law and Medicine, 1920–1945*. Ithaca, NY: Cornell University Press, 2012.

Focardi, Filippo. *Il cattivo italiano e il bravo italiano. la rimozione delle colpe della seconda guerra mondiale*. Bari: Laterza, 2013.

Fogg, Shannon L. *The Politics of Everyday Life in Vichy France: Foreigners, Undesirables, and Strangers*. Cambridge: Cambridge University Press, 2009.

Fogu, Claudio. "Italiani brava gente: The Legacy of Fascist Historical Culture on Italian Politics of Memory." In *The Politics of Memory in Postwar Europe*, edited by Richard Ned Below, Wulf Kansteiner, and Claudio Fogu, 147–76. Durham, NC: Duke University Press, 2006.

Franzina, Emilio, and Matteo Sanfilippo. Introduzione to *Il fascismo e gli emigrati, la parabola dei Fasci italiani all'estero (1920–1943)*, edited by Emilio Franzina and Matteo Sanfilippo, v–xxxi. Bari: Laterza, 2003.

Franzinelli, Mimmo. *Il riarmo dello spirito, i cappellani militari nella seconda guerra mondiale*. Paese: Pagus Edizioni, 1991.

———. *I tentacoli dell'Ovra, Agenti, collaboratori e vittime della polizia politica fascista*. Torino: Bollati Boringhieri, 1999.

Frediani, Giuseppe. *La Pace separata di Ciano*. Roma: Bonacci Editore, 1990.

Gabaccia, Donna R. *Italy's Many Diasporas*. Seattle: University of Washington Press, 2000.

Gallinari, Vincenzo. *Le Operazioni del giugno 1940 sulle Alpi Occidentali*. Roma: Ufficio Storico SME, 1981.

Gariglio, Dario. *Popolo italiano, corri alle armi! 10–25 giugno 1940, l'attacco alla Francia*. Peveragno: Blue Edizioni, 2001.

Gildea, Robert. *Marianne in Chains: Daily Life in the Heart of France during the German Occupation*. New York: Metropolitan Books, 2003.

Giolitto, Pierre. *Histoire de la Milice*. Paris: Perrin, 1997.

———. *Volontaires français sous l'uniforme allemand*. Paris: Perrin, 1999.

Girard, Joseph. "Contribution à l'étude de l'épuration dans les Alpes-Maritimes." *Recherches régionales, Alpes-Maritimes et Contrées limitrophes* 59 (July–September 1976).

Gobetti, Eric. *Alleati del nemico, l'occupazione italiana in Jugoslavia (1941–1943)*. Roma: Laterza, 2013.

———. *L'occupazione allegra. Gli Italiani in Jugoslavia (1941–1943)*. Roma: Carocci, 2007.

Gooch, John. *Mussolini and His Generals: The Armed Forces and Fascist Foreign Policy, 1922–1940*. Cambridge: Cambridge University Press, 2007.

Gray, Ezio Maria. *Le terre nostre ritornano . . . Malta–Corsica–Nizza*. Novara: Istituto Geografico De Agostini, 1941.

Grynberg, Anne. *Les camps de la honte, les internés juifs des camps français (1939–1944)*. Paris: Éditions la Découverte, 1991.

Guillon, Jean-Marie. *Le Var, la guerre, la Résistance, 1939–1945*. Toulon: CDDP, 1994.

Guzzi, Giampaolo. *L'Occupazione italiana di Mentone (1940–1943): storia postale*. Self-published, 2003.

Hale, Julian. *The French Riviera: A Cultural History*. New York: Oxford University Press, 2009.

Halls, W. D. *Politics, Society, and Christianity in Vichy France*. Oxford: Berg, 1995.

Heyriès, Hubert. *Les Garibaldiens de 14, splendeurs et misères des Chemises Rouges en France de la Grande Guerre à la Seconde Guerre Mondiale*. Nice: Editions Serre, 2005.

Ilari, Virgilio. *Storia del servizio militare in Italia*. Vol. 3, *"Nazione Militare" e "Fronte del Lavoro" (1919–1943)*. Roma: Rivista Militare, Centro Militare di Studi Strategici, 1990.

Isoard, Paul. "Le 11 Novembre 1942." *Cahiers de la Méditerranée* 62 (June 2001): 187–98.

Istituto storico della resistenza in Cuneo e provincia. *8 settembre: lo sfacelo della Quarta armata*. Torino: Book store, 1979.

Jackson, Julian. *The Fall of France: The Nazi Invasion of 1940*. Oxford: Oxford University Press, 2004.

———. *France: The Dark Years, 1940–1944*. Oxford: Oxford University Press, 2003.

Jonas, Raymond. *The Battle of Adwa: African Victory in the Age of the Empire*. Cambridge, MA: Belknap Press of Harvard University Press, 2011.

Kallis, Aristotle A. *Fascist Ideology: Territory and Expansionism in Italy and Germany, 1922–1945*. London: Routledge, 2000.

Kaspi, André. *Les Juifs pendant l'Occupation*. Paris: Seuil, 1997.

Kaufmann, J. E., and H. W. Kaufmann. *The Maginot Line: None Shall Pass*. Westport, CT: Praeger, 1997.

Kedward, H. R. *In Search of the Maquis: Rural Resistance in Southern France, 1942–1944*. Oxford: Oxford University Press, 1995.

———. *Resistance in Vichy France: A Study of Ideas and Motivation in the Southern Zone, 1940–1942*. Oxford: Oxford University Press, 1978.

Kitson, Simon. "French Police, German Troops, and the Destruction of the Old District of Marseille, 1943." In *Policing and War in Europe*, edited by Louis A. Knalfa, 133–44. Westport, CT: Greenwood Press, 2002.

———. *The Hunt for Nazi Spies: Fighting Espionage in Vichy France*. Chicago: University of Chicago Press, 2008.

Kleinmann, Jean. "Pérégrinations des Juifs étrangers dans les Alpes-Maritimes (1938–1944)." In *Le Refuge et le Piège: Les Juifs et les Alpes (1938–1945)*, edited by Jean-William Dereymez, 189–222. Paris: L'Harmattan, 2008.

Knox, MacGregor. "Il Fascismo e la politica estera italiana." In *La Politica estera italiana (1860–1985)*, edited by Richard Bosworth and Sergio Romano, 287–330. Bologna: Il Mulino, 1991.

———. *Hitler's Italian Allies: Royal Armed Forces, Fascist Regime, and the War of 1940–1943*. Cambridge: Cambridge University Press, 2000.

———. "The Sources of Italy's Defeat in 1940: Bluff or Institutionalized Incompetence." In *German Nationalism and the European Response, 1890–1945*, edited by Carole Fink, Isabel V. Hull, and MacGregor Knox, 247–66. Norman: University of Oklahoma Press, 1985.

Koestler, Arthur. *Schiuma della terra*. Bologna: Il Mulino, 1985.

———. *The Scum of the Earth*. London: Hutchinson, 1968.

Koreman, Megan. *The Expectation of Justice: France, 1944–1946*. Durham, NC: Duke University Press, 1999.

Kranjc, Gregor Joseph. *To Walk with the Devil: Slovene Collaboration and Axis Occupation, 1941–1945*. Toronto: University of Toronto Press, 2013.

Krumeich, Gerd. "The Cult of Joan of Arc under the New Regime." In *Politics and Culture during the Nazi Occupation, 1940–1944*, edited by Gerhard Hirschfeld and Patrick Marsh, 92–102. New York: Berg, 1989.

Labanca, Nicola, and Pier Paolo Rivello, eds. *Fonti e problemi per la storia della giustizia militare*. Giappichelli: Torino, 2004.

Laub, Thomas Johnston. *After the Fall: German Policy in Occupied France, 1940–1944*. New York: Oxford University Press, 2010.

Le Crom, Jean-Pierre. *Au Secours Maréchal!* Paris: Presses Universitaires de France, 2013.

Lefebure, Victor. "Récit manuscrit de l'évacuation de Menton et de la vie à menton pendant la seconde guerre mondiale." Unpublished. Cahiers n°1 L'histoire des évacués de Menton en juin 1940.

Lembo, Daniele. *La Carne Contro l'Acciaio, Il Regio Esercito Italiano alla vigilia della seconda guerra mondiale*. Copiano: Grafica MA.RO, 2003.

Lewis, Mary Dewhurst. *The Boundaries of the Republic: Migrant Rights and the Limits of Universalism in France, 1918–1940*. Stanford, CA: Stanford University Press, 2007.

Loi, Salvatore. *Jugoslavia 1941*. Torino: Il Nastro Azzurro, 1953.

———. *Le operazioni delle unità italiane in Jugoslavia (1941–1943)*. Roma: Ufficio Storico, Stato Maggiore dell'Esercito, 1978.

Mallett, Robert. *Mussolini and the Origins of the Second World War, 1933–1940*. New York: Palgrave, 2003.

Malon, Claude. *Occupation, Épuration, Reconstruction, le monde de l'entreprise au Havre (1940–1950)*. Saint-Aignan: Publications des Universités de Rouen et du Havre, 2012.

Marchini, Ugo. *La battaglia delle Alpi occidentali, giugno 1940, narrazione, documenti*. Roma: Stato Maggiore dell'Esercito, Ufficio Storico, 1947.

Marrus, Michael, and Robert Paxton. *Vichy France and the Jews*. New York: Basic Publishers, 1981.

Mastellone, Salvo. "L'Idea di Latinità (1914–1922)." In *Italia e Francia dal 1919 al 1939*, edited by Jean-Baptiste Duroselle and Enrico Serra. Milano: Istituto per gli studi di politica internazionale, 1981.

Maugham, W. Somerset. *Strictly Personal*. Garden City, NY: Doubleday, Doran and Co., 1941.

Mazower, Mark. *Hitler's Empire: How the Nazis Ruled Europe*. New York: Penguin Press, 2008.

Melograni, Piero. *La Guerra Degli italiani, 1940–1945*. Roma: Istituto Luce, 2003.

Michel, Alain. "Collaboration and Collaborators in Vichy France, an Unfinished Debate." In *Collaboration with the Nazis, Public Discourse after the Holocaust*, edited by Roni Stauber, 169–85. London: Routledge, 2011.

Milza, Pierre. "L'image de l'Italie Fasciste dans la France des années 1936–1939." In *Italia e Francia dal 1919 al 1939,* edited by Jean Baptiste Duroselle and Enrico Serra, 271–302. Milano: Istituto per gli studi di politica internazionale, 1981.

———. "L'immigration italienne en France d'une guerre à l'autre: interrogations, directions de recherche et bilans." In *Les Italiens en France de 1914 à 1940,* edited by Pierre Milza, 1–42. Rome: École française de Rome, 1986.

———. *Voyage en Ritalie.* Paris: Payot, 2004.

Milza, Pierre, and Denis Peschanski, eds. *Exils et Migration, Italiens et Espagnols en France, 1938–1946.* Paris: L'Harmattan, 1994.

MINCULPOP. *Gli Italiani nei campi di concentramento in Francia; documenti e testimonianze.* Rome: Società Editrice del Libro Italiano, 1940.

Mitchell, Alan. *Nazi Paris: The History of an Occupation, 1940–1944.* New York: Berghahn, 2008.

Molinari, Pascal, and Jean-Louis Panicacci. *Menton dans la Tourmente, 1939–1945.* Menton: Société d'art et d'histoire du mentonnais, 1984.

Montanari, Mario. *L'Esercito Italiano alla vigilia della seconda guerra mondiale.* Roma: Ufficio Storico SME, 1993.

Morgan, Philip. *The Fall of Mussolini.* Oxford: Oxford University Press, 2007.

Mouré, Kenneth. "Réalités cruelles: State Controls and the Black Market for Food in Occupied France." In *Food and War in Twentieth-Century Europe,* ed. Ina Zweiniger-Bargielowska, Rachel Duffett, and Alain Drouard, 169–82. Burlington, VT: Ashgate, 2011.

Nagyos, Christophe. *Guerres et paix en Alsace-Moselle: de l'annexion à la fin du nazisme; histoire de trois départements de l'Est, 1870–1945.* Strasbourg: La nuée bleue, 2005.

Novick, Peter. *L'Épuration française, 1944–1949.* Paris: Balland, 1985.

Oberaugh, Walter, and Carol Jose. *Guerrilla in Striped Pants: A US Diplomat Joins the Italian Resistance.* Westport, CT: Praeger, 1992.

Oliva, Gianni. *"Si Ammazza troppo poco," I crimini di guerra italiani, 1940–1943.* Milano: Mondadori, 2006.

Ostenc, Michel. "La Non-Belligérance italienne, 4 septembre 1939–10 juin 1940." *Guerres mondiales et conflits contemporains* 194 (1999): 79–99.

Osti Guerrazzi, Amedeo. *L'Esercito italiano in Slovenia, 1941–1943, Strategie di repressione antipartigiana.* Roma: Viella, 2011.

———. *The Italian Army in Slovenia: Strategies of Antipartisan Repression, 1941–1943.* Basingstoke: Palgrave Macmillan, 2013.

———. *Non non sappiamo odiare, L'esercito italiano tra fascismo e democrazia.* Torino: UTET, 2010.

Ott, Sandra. *War, Judgment, and Memory in the Basque Borderlands, 1914–1945.* Reno: University of Nevada Press, 2008.

Pane, Caroline. "Le Case d'Italia in Francia. Organizzazione, attività e rappresentazione del fascismo all'estero." *Memoria e Ricerca* 41 (2012): 161–80.

Panicacci, Jean-Louis. *Les Alpes-Maritimes, 1939–1945, un département dans la tourmente.* Nice: Editions Serre, 1989.

———. "Les Communistes italiens dans les Alpes-Maritimes (1939–45)." *Annali della Fondazione Giangiacomo Feltrinelli*. Vol. 24. Milano, 1985, 155–80.

———. "Un Journal Irrédentiste sous l'Occupation: *Il Nizzardo.*" *Cahiers de la Méditerranée* 33/34 (December 1986–June 1987): 143–58.

———. *L'Occupation Italienne, Sud-Est de la France, Juin 1940–Septembre 1943.* Rennes: Presses Universitaires de Rennes, 2010.

———. "Le temps des pénuries dans les Alpes-Maritimes (1939–1949)." *Cahiers de la Méditerranée* 48 (Juin 1994): 191–209.

Paoletti, Ciro. *A Military History of Italy.* Westport, CT: Praeger, 2008.

Paxton, Robert. *Vichy France, Old Guard and New Order, 1940–1944.* New York: Columbia University Press, 1972.

Poliakov, Léon. *La condition des Juifs en France sous l'occupation italienne.* Paris: CDJC, 1946.

Poliakov, Léon, and Jacques Sabille. *Jews under the Italian Occupation.* New York: Howard Fertig, 1983.

Pollard, Miranda. *Reign of Virtue: Mobilizing Gender in Vichy France.* Chicago: University of Chicago Press, 1998.

Poznanski, Renée. *Jews in France during the Second World War.* Hanover, NH: Brandeis University Press, 2001.

Rainero, Romain. *La Commission italienne d'armistice avec la France, les rapports entre la France de Vichy et l'Italie de Mussolini, 10 juin 1940–8 septembre 1943.* Vincennes: Service Historique de l'Armée, 1985.

Rainero, Romain H. *Les Piémontais en Provence, Aspect d'une émigration oubliée.* Nice: Editions Serre, 2001.

Rajsfus, Maurice. *La Rafle du Vél d'Hiv.* Rennes: Presses Universitaires de France, 2002.

Rapone, Leonardo. "Les Italiens en France comme problème de la politique étrangère italienne, entre guerre fasciste et retour à la démocratie." In *Exils et Migration, Italiens et Espagnols en France, 1938–1946,* edited by Pierre Milza and Denis Peschanski, 175–98. Paris: L'Harmattan, 1994.

Read, Piers Paul. *The Dreyfus Affair: The Scandal That Tore France in Two.* New York: Bloomsbury Press, 2012.

Rigoulot, Pierre. *L'Alsace-Lorraine pendant la guerre, 1939–1945.* Paris: Presses Universitaires de France, 1997.

Rings, Werner. *Life with the Enemy: Collaboration and Resistance in Hitler's Europe, 1939–1945.* Garden City, NY: Doubleday, 1982.

Roatta, Mario. *Otto milioni di baionette.* Milano: Mondadori, 1946.

Rochat, Giorgio. "La giustizia militare dal 10 giugno 1940 all'8 settembre 1943." In *Fonti e problemi per la storia della giustizia militare,* edited by Nicola Labanca and Pier Paolo Rivello, 231–32. Giappichelli: Torino, 2004.

———. *Le Guerre Italiane, 1935–1943.* Torino: Einaudi, 2005.

———. "Les Italiens dans la deuxième Marne." In *Les batailles de la Marne, de l'Ourcq à Verdun (1914 et 1918),* edited by François Cochet, 223–36. Paris: Soteca, 14–18 éditions, 2004.

Rochat, Giorgio, and Giulio Massobrio. *Breve Storia dell'Esercito Italiano dal 1861 al 1943*. Torino: Einaudi, 1978.

Rodogno, Davide. *Fascism's European Empire: Italian Occupation during the Second World War*. Cambridge: Cambridge University Press, 2006.

———. "La politique des occupants italiens à l'égard des Juifs en France métropolitaine, Humanisme ou pragmatisme?" *Vingtième Siècle, Revue d'histoire* 93, no. 1 (2007): 63–77.

Rossbottom, Ronald C. *When Paris Went Dark: The City of Light under German Occupation, 1940–1944*. New York: Little, Brown, 2014.

Ruggiero, Alain. "Comment prouver que Nice est bien Française?" *Cahiers de la Méditerranée* 33–34 (December 1986–June 1987): 127–39.

Sanders, Paul. *Histoire du marché noir: 1940–1946*. Paris: Perrin, 2001.

Sarraz-Bournet, Marius. *Témoignage d'un silencieux*. Paris: Éditions Self, 1948.

Schipsi, Domenico. *L'occupazione italiana dei territori metropolitani francesi (1940–1943)*. Roma: Stato Maggiore dell'Esercito, Ufficio Storico, 2007.

Schor, Ralph. *Un évêque dans le siècle: Monseigneur Paul Rémond (1873–1963)*. Nice: Editions Serre, 1984.

———. "Le fascisme italien dans les Alpes-Maritimes, 1922–1939." *Cahiers de la Méditerranée* 42 (June 1991).

———. *Français et immigrés en temps de crise (1930–1980)*. Paris: L'Harmattan, 2004.

———. "Les Italiens dans les Alpes-Maritimes, 1919–1939." In Milza, *Les Italiens en France*, 576–607.

Serra, Enrico. "L'emigrazione italiana in Francia durante il secondo governo Crispi (1893–1896)." In *L'emigrazione italiana in Francia prima del 1914*, edited by Jean Baptiste Duroselle and Enrico Serra, 145–70. Milano: Franco Angeli, 1978.

Sica, Emanuele. "The Italian Army and the Battle of the Alps." *Canadian Journal of History* 47, no. 2 (2012): 355–78.

Spotts, Frederic. *The Shameful Peace: How French Artists and Intellectuals Survived the Nazi Occupation*. New Haven, CT: Yale University Press, 2008.

Steinberg, Jonathan. *All or Nothing: The Axis and the Holocaust, 1941–1943*, 2nd ed. New York: Routledge, 2002.

Strang, G. Bruce. *On the Fiery March: Mussolini Prepares for War*. Westport, CT: Praeger, 2003.

Sullivan, Brian R. "Fascist Italy's Military Involvement in the Spanish Civil War." *Journal of Military History* 59, no. 4 (2007): 697–727.

Taravella, Luigi. "La pratique religieuse comme facteur d'intégration." In *L'intégration italienne en France, un siècle de présence italienne dans trois régions françaises (1880–1980)*, edited by Antonio Bechelloni, Michel Dreyfus, and Pierre Milza, 71–84. Paris: Editions Complexe, 1995.

Taylor, Lynne. *Between Resistance and Collaboration: Popular Protest in Northern France, 1940–1945*. London: Macmillan, 2000.

Torrie, Julie. *"For Their Own Good": Civilian Evacuations in Germany and France, 1939–1945*. New York: Berghahn, 2010.

Torsiello, Mario. *Le operazioni delle unità italiane nel settembre–ottobre 1943.* Roma: Stato Maggiore dell'Esercito, Ufficio Storico, 1975.

Trabucchi, Alessandro. *I vinti hanno sempre torto.* Torino: F. de Silva, 1947.

Turinetti di Priero, Alberto. *La battaglia delle Alpi, 10–25 giugno 1940, La Divisione Superga e gli Alpini nell'Alta Valle di Susa.* S. Ambrogio, Italy: Susalibri, 1990.

Valota Cavallotti, Bianca. "L'immagine Fascista dell'Impero." In *L'Italia e la politica di potenza in Europa (1938–1940),* edited by Ennio di Nolfo, Romain H. Rainero and Brunello Vigezzi, 121–44. Milano: Marzorati, 1986.

Varley, Karine. "Between Vichy France and Fascist Italy: Redefining Identity and the Enemy in Corsica during the Second World War." *Journal of Contemporary History* 47, no. 3 (2012): 505–527.

———. "Entangled Enemies: Vichy, Italy, and Collaboration." In *France in an Era of Global War, 1914–1945,* edited by Ludivine Broch and Allison Carrol, 152–70. Houndmills, Basingstoke, Hampshire: Palgrave Macmillan, 2014.

Veillon, Dominique. *Vivre et Survivre en France, 1939–1947.* Paris: Payot, 1995.

Vial, Éric. "I Fasci in Francia." In *Il fascismo e gli emigrati, la parabola dei Fasci italiani all'estero (1920–1943),* edited by Emilio Franzina and Matteo Sanfilippo, 27–42. Bari: Laterza, 2003.

Villermet, Christian. *A Noi Savoia, Histoire de l'occupation italienne en Savoie, novembre 1942–septembre 1943.* Les Marches: La Fontaine de Siloé, 1991.

Vinen, Richard. *The Unfree French: Life under the Occupation.* New Haven, CT: Yale University Press, 2006.

Virgili, Fabrice. *Shorn Women: Gender and Punishment in Liberation France.* New York: Berg, 2002.

Warring, Anette. "Intimate and Sexual Relations." In *Surviving Hitler and Mussolini: Daily Life in Occupied Europe,* edited by Robert Gildea, Olivier Wieviorka, and Anette Warring, 88–128. New York: Berg, 2006.

Weber, Eugen. *Peasants into Frenchmen.* Stanford, CA: Stanford University Press, 1976.

Weil, Patrick. "Espagnols et Italiens en France: la politique de la France." In Milza and Peschanski, *Exils et Migration,* 87–110.

Weisberg, Richard H. *Vichy Law and the Holocaust in France.* Newark, NJ: Harwood Academic Publishers, 1997.

Whittam, John. *The Politics of the Italian Army, 1861–1918.* London: Croom Helm, 1977.

Wiegandt-Sakoun, Caroline. "Le Fascisme Italien en France." In *Les Italiens en France de 1914 à 1940,* edited by Pierre Milza, 432–69. Rome: École française de Rome, 1986.

Wieviorka, Olivier. *Histoire de la Résistance, 1940–1945.* Paris: Perrin, 2013.

Wolfanger, Dieter. *Nazification de la Lorraine mosellane.* Sarreguemines: Editions Pierron, 1982.

Zuccotti, Susan. *Holocaust Odysseys: The Jews of Saint-Martin-Vésubie and Their Flight through France and Italy.* New Haven, CT: Yale University Press, 2007.

INDEX

Abwehr, 124, 232
Aigues-Mortes, 44
Ajaccio, 29, 52
Alfieri, Dino, 173
Allied landings 7, 79, 181
Alsace-Lorraine 11, 235; evacuation of 22; Germanization, 183–84
Ambrosio, Vittorio 79, 147, 148, 173
Amè, Cesare, 129
Amicucci, Ermanno, 78
Andreoli, Giuseppe, 142
Antibes (Alpes-Maritimes), 22, 51, 86, 100, 117, 128–29, 137, 245
antisemitism: in Côte d'Azur 164–67; Italian 166, 173, 251; Vichy xii, xiii, 36, 133, 162–65, 167–70
anti-Fascism. *See* fuoriusciti
anti-italianism 19–21, 36, 38, 50, 86, 160; towards CIAF officials, 51–52; coup de poignard dans le dos June 1940 (backstabbing), 20, 24, 47, 156, 187; denaturalization, xii, 36; xenophobic slurs, 35, 50–51, 86
Ardèche, 165
Armée des Alpes, 21, 23
Armée Secrète, 135–36, 176
Armellini, Quirino, 175,
armistice: Franco-German (Compiègne, 22 June 1940), xi, 27–28, 37, 81, 96, 183; Franco-Italian (Villa Incisa, 22 June 1940), xi, 28–32, 53, 70, 77, 93, 96, 98–99, 183; Italian with the Allies (Cassibile, 3 September 1943), 6, 159, 170, 174, 178–79

assimilation, 163; of Italian emigrants, 18, 20
Atlantic Wall, 101
Avanguardisti (Vanguardists), 18, 58, 66

Badoglio, Pietro, 15–16, 175, 178–79
Balilla, 18, 66, 154
Balocco, Riccardo, 108
Bancale, Emilio, 89
Bando Vercellino (Vercellino Proclamation), 176
Barcelonnette, 180
Barneaud, Marcel, 62
Barranco, Rosario, 69, 127–29, 166, 231–32
Basque borderlands, 72–73
Basses-Alpes, 19, 28, 52, 59, 70–74, 80, 84, 124, 132, 143–44, 157, 166; and black market 117–19; and farmers 38
Bastianini, Giuseppe, 148
Battle of the Alps, 22–24
Beausoleil (Alpes-Maritimes), 17, 42, 154,
Befana, 67
Belin, René, 49
Berthelot, Henry, 4
Bessans (Savoie), 28
Beziers (Languedoc), 20
bicycle, 92, 141; theft of, 125
Bizerte (Tunisia), 29
black market, xiv, 10–11, 21, 39, 117, 125–26, 236; Germans and, 124; Italian soldiers and, 12, 115, 118–19; Jews and, 164; prevention of, 125; smuggling across the border, 72, 119, 147

Blackshirts, 45, 149, 175, 207
Bonarelli di Castelbompiano, Vittorio
  Emanuele, 98, 146
Bordighera (Liguria), 145
Bottai, Giuseppe, 145
Botto, Guido, 59
Bourg-Saint-Maurice (Savoie), 80, 84
Bousquet, René, xiii, 164, 167
Bramans (Savoie), 28
Brandl, Hermann "Otto," 124
Breil-sur-Roya (Alpes-Maritimes), 50, 58,
  85, 180; Italian military tribunal in, 58,
  132
Bridoux, Eugène, 84
Brückel, Joseph, 184
Buti, Gino, xiii, 34

Cagnes-sur-Mer (Alpes-Maritimes), 138
Calisse, Alberto, 97–99, 165–66, 173
Calvino, Italo, 57–58
Camerani, Silvio, 43, 46, 166
Cannes (Alpes-Maritimes), xiv, 17, 22, 33,
  38, 46, 80, 82, 104–5, 120, 128, 131,
  138–39, 142, 157, 164
Cap d'Ail (Alpes-Maritimes), 86
capisaldi (strongholds), 101
Cappatti, Louis, 48
carabinieri (Italian military police), 106,
  120–21, 123, 140, 169; and the SIM 128,
  132
Case d'Italia, 17, 85, 153, 155
Caserne Dugommier, 138, 141, 242
Castellane, 84, 250
Castellar (Alpes-Maritimes), 85, 218
Castillon (Alpes-Maritimes), 84, 157, 218
church, 43, 48, 59, 84, 165; conflict be-
  tween Italian and French clergy, 60–61.
  See also Rémond, Paul
Cavallero, Ugo, 15, 81, 99
Četniks, 185
Chantiers de la Jeunesse, 65, 100
children 7, 18, 40, 50, 66–67, 71, 104, 154,
  157, 159, 180, 185, 203, 248
CIAF. See Commissione di Armistizio con
  la Francia
Ciano, Galeazzo, 5, 15, 30, 79, 174
Circular 3 C, 6
collaboration/accommodation, 7, 10, 153–
  61; with the CIAF 153; with the Italian

army, 70–72, 153–57; forms of, 151–52;
  state collaboration (with Germany),
  30–31, 78; and women 71–72, 158–59
Comando Supremo. See Stato Maggiore
  dell'Esercito
Combat (Resistance group), 62, 135, 210,
  252. See also Resistance
combat zone, 100–101, 127, 139
Comité d'Aide aux Réfugiés (Refugees' Aid
  Committee), 166
Comité des Traditions Mentonnaises, 62
Comité Dubouchage. See Comité d'Aide
  aux Réfugiés
Comité d'Épuration, 246–47
Commissariat General aux Questions Juives
  (Office for Jewish Affairs, or CGQJ), 164
Commissione Consultiva per il Diritto di
  Guerra presso il Consiglio dei Ministri
  (War Law Advisory Committee of the
  Council of Ministers), 96–97
Commissione di Armistizio con la Francia
  (Italian Armistice Commission with
  France, or CIAF) 29–30, 78, 83, 138–39,
  165–69, 172–73, 177; Amministrazione
  dei Territori Occupati (Administration
  of Occupied Territories Bureau), xii, 56,
  62, 68; Delegati per l'Assistenza ed il
  Rimpatrio (Delegates for the Assistance
  and Repatriation), xii, xiv, 34–35, 37, 40,
  50–54, 97, 119, 127, 133–34; and Italian
  army 56, 68–69, 74, 77, 92, 97–99, 128,
  144–50, 189; and Italian immigrants
  and irredentists 36–41, 42–43, 45–46,
  83, 153, 155; and Vichy officials 32–33,
  36–37, 39, 46–48, 53–57, 61–62, 64–65,
  129, 146
Compagnons de France, 50
Contrôle Postal (Postal Control), 143, 169,
  219, 250
Côte d'Azur. See French Riviera
Cours of Justice, 152. See also postwar
  trials
Cros-de-Cagnes (Alpes-Maritimes), 138

D'Annunzio, Gabriele, 204, 210
Daladier, Édouard, 19, 39
Darlan, François, xii, 49, 79, 93
Darnand, Joseph, xii, 47, 49
de Laborde, Jean, 47

de Lattre de Tassigny, Jean, 84
de Pellepoix, Louis Darquier, 164
de Revel, Thaon, 145
Delpeyrou, Marcel, 117
demarcation line, 28
denunciation, 35–36, 129, 131, 136, 141,
    152, 155, 158–60, 166–67
Deuxième Bureau, 54
di Gualtieri, Gen. Avarna, 97, 167
Digne-les-Bains, 19, 52, 86, 94, 114, 120,
    122, 143–44, 180
Donati, Angelo Mordechai, 13, 166–70, 173
Doriot, Jacques, 49
drôle de guerre (Phoney War), 19, 38
Drôme, 165
Duce. *See* Mussolini, Benito
Duplat, André, 30
Duraffour, Paul, 139, 164. *See also* police
    (French)
Durandy, Jean, 57, 61; dismissal by Italian
    authorities, 62

education 17–18, 20, 35, 58, 117, 135, 142,
    158, 169, 175, 183; closing of French
    schools 59, 61, 84–85; National Revolu-
    tion and, 48
Emanuele III, Vittorio, xv, 4, 68, 174, 178
Esigenza Ovest (Plan West, Esigenza O),
    79, 87
evacuations 21–22

farmers, 38; black market 116–18; France
    Éternelle, 38
Fasci all'Estero (branches in France), 17, 88,
    128, 233
Fascism. *See* irredentism and Fascism
Fascist Grand Council, 174
Felber Hans-Gustav, 67
Filles aux Boches (Girls for Krauts), 158.
    See also women
Firpo, Marcel, 62–63, 66, 211. *See also*
    Comité des Traditions Mentonnaises
First World War, 4
Flandin, Pierre-Etienne, 47
Fontan (Alpes-Maritimes), 28, 59, 60, 66,
    181
Forbidden Coastal Zone (zone côtière
    interdite), 101
Forces Unies de la Jeunesse Patriotique, 51

foreigners 8, 27, 36, 86, 131, 163, 201, 247
Fort Carré (Antibes), 100
Fort La Malgue (Toulon), 94
Fourth Army (Italian occupation army). *See*
    Italian army
Franc-Tireur, 135, 252
Frediani, Giuseppe, 61–63, 68–69
free zone, xii, xiv, 12, 28, 50, 54- 55, 60, 64,
    66–67, 71–72, 77, 128, 134–37, 163–65,
    172, 174; sovereignty in, 85, 89–90, 97;
    cinematographic activities (Victorine
    Studios), 48; Italian sphere of influence,
    29, 33; occupation of, 79–90, 100
Frenay, Henri, xiv, 137
French Army, xiii, 4, 17, 19–22, 29–30,
    47–48, 55, 69, 84–85, 89, 124, 138, 162,
    218; Armée des Alpes, 22–24; demobi-
    lization of, 28, 83–84; and depots, 84,
    95–96, 99, 146
French Riviera: evacuation of, 22; Jewish
    refugees in, 164–66, 170–71; politics
    of, 46–49, 85, 133–34; Resistance in,
    134–39, 141–43
fuoriusciti. *See* Resistance

Gallo, Luigi. *See* Longo, Luigi
Garibaldi, Ezio, xii, 43–44, 83. *See also* ir-
    redentism and Fascism
Garibaldi, Sante, 43
Garibaldiens de l'Argonne, 4, 155
Gattières (Alpes-Maritimes), 123
Gaullist propaganda, 46, 132, 237
Gerlier, Pierre-Marie, 165
German Armistice Commission (CTA), 29,
    78, 98
German army, 81, 93–94; German Army
    Command in the West (Oberbefehlshaber
    West, or ObW), 98, 167
Gestapo, 13, 56, 168, 232
Giornale di Genova, 63
Giornata D'Azione Nizzarda (Day of
    Nicean Action), 44–45
Giustizia e Libertà, 18
Grasse (Alpes-Maritimes), 47, 80, 82, 85,
    158
Gray, Ezio Maria, 31
Green Line, 28, 50, 57, 60–61, 71
Grossi, Camillo, 29
Groupements de Travailleurs Étrangers, 165

Gruppi d'Azione Nizzarda (Nice Action Groups) (GAN), 44–45, 141–42, 153–54. *See also* irredentism
Guardia alla Frontiera (GaF), 70, 197, 214
Guariglia, Raffaele, 195

Hautes-Alpes, 28–29, 70, 79, 174–75, 206
Haute-Savoie, xi, 3, 6, 17, 22, 28–29, 31, 50, 176, 143, 189
Henriot, Philippe, 49
Hitler, Adolf, 5, 16, 24, 30–31, 73, 79, 95–96
Hyères (Var), 94

Il Nizzardo, 44–46, 62, 78, 134
International Brigades, 21, 33, 233
internment camps (Italian), xiv, 132; Embrun, 134; Modane, 140; Sospel, 235, 241
internment camps (French): Vernet, 20–21, 33, 43, 98, 147, 196, 200, 233; Saint-Cyprien, 20–21, 196
irredentism and Fascism, 3–5, 31, 66–67, 70, 95, 117, 134, 153–56, 159–60, 173, 18; Fascist regime, 68–69, 173–74; informers, 89, 128–31, 133, 137, 140–42, 161; in Monaco, 42–43, 52–54, 87–90; propaganda, 8–9, 16–18, 44–46, 59, 61, 65, 73–74, 77–78, 82, 110–11, 144–46; targeted by Resistance, 50, 86, 137, 142–43, 152. *See also* Commissione di Armistizio con la Francia; Gruppi d'Azione Nizzarda; Italian occupation army
Isola (Alpes-Maritimes), 59, 157, 218
Istituto di Studi Liguri, 145
Italian army (before November 1942), 16, 20, 22–24, 30, 37, 49, 54–56, 64
Italian occupation army (Fourth Army), 7–8, 10–13, 29, 77, 79–90, 100–102, 115, 117–19, 142–44, 174, 185–89; and CIAF (before and after November 1942), 56, 68–69, 74, 77, 92, 97–99, 144–50, 189; and Germans, 94–96, 112, 177–79; and irredentist movement, 88–89, 141–42; and Jews, 166–73; and local civilians, 69–72, 101, 118, 120–26, 154–58, 180–81; morale, 85–86, 104–14, 175–76, 187; occupation policy, 77, 82–83, 89–92, 129–30, 139, 185–89; and Resistance, 31, 130–33, 136–41; and Vichy, 91, 93–94, 96–97, 133–34

Italian political police, 89, 127–29, 131–32, 166
Italiani Brava Gente, 6, 171, 189

Jews, xii, xiii, xiv, xv, 7, 13, 27, 73, 155, 181, 185, 205, 232; in Côte d'Azur, 164–67; and the Italian protection, 133, 166–73; Vichy's Jewish policy, 36, 162–65
Jodl, Alfred, 177

L'Action Française, 163
L'Éclaireur de Nice et du Sud-est, 46, 48
La Gazzetta del Popolo, 46
La Parola del Soldato (The Word of the Soldier), 136
La Vallée du Maréchal, 47
Lamboglia, Nino, xv, 143, 145–46, 242–43
Lanslebourg (Savoie), 28
Lanslevillard (Savoie), 28
Larche (Basses-Alpes), 71–72, 214
Laval, Pierre, 27, 78–79, 97, 151–52, 164–65, 167, 170
Le Bourghet (Alpes-Maritimes), 61
Le Petit Niçois, 46
Le Pontet (Vaucluse), 94
Légion des Volontaires Français contre le Bolchevisme (LVF), 135
Légion Française des Combattants (LFC), xii, 47–48, 135, 143
Lepri Stanislao, 88
Libération-Sud, 135
Ligne Maginot Alpine, 23
Longo, Luigi, 128, 135, 233
Lospinoso, Guido, xiv, 168–70

Maison-Méane (Basses-Alpes), 70–72
Mandelieu (Alpes-Maritimes), 120
Manosque (Basses-Alpes), 124
"March to the Ocean," 16
Marcia Su Nizza (March on Nice), 44, 86, 153
Marciani, Giovanni, 98, 110, 222, 227
Mare Nostrum, 61, 77, 210
Marenco, Giovanni, 62
Marion, Paul, 49
Marquis, André, 93
Marziali, G. B., 62, 68
Maurras, Charles, 49, 163
Mazzarini, Eugenio, 218

Mazzolini, Quinto, 40, 45–46, 53–54, 133–34, 166
Méailles (Basses-Alpes), 119
Médecin, Jean, xv, 39, 47, 133–34
Menton (Alpes-Maritimes), xiii, 17, 22, 28, 39, 44, 51, 56–57, 69–70, 82–84, 87, 113, 132, 147, 159, 183–84; embezzlement in, 67–68; Italianization of, 55, 58–62, 64, 73–74, 77; occupation and looting of, xi, 6, 11–12, 24, 57–58; repatriation, 63, 65; tensions between Italians and French, 66–67; Ufficio Assistenza per il Rimpatrio dei Mentonaschi (Office for the Repatriation of the Mentonese Population), xiii, 62–63
Mers-el-Kébir (Algeria), 31, 93, 199
Micheletti, Paolo, 197, 218
Milice Française, 138, 142, 184, 205
Modane (Savoie), xiv, 79, 82, 132, 140
Monaco (Principality of), 42–45, 50, 52–53, 87–89, 131, 133, 153–54
Montauban (Tarn-et-Garonne), 165
Montgenèvre (Hautes-Alpes), 28, 70
Montoire (Loir-et-Cher), 31
Montvalezan (Savoie), 28
Moresco, Mattia, 145
MUR (Mouvement Unis de la Résistance), xiv, 137
Mussolini, Benito, xii, 44, 52, 56, 58, 65, 83, 87, 89, 111–12, 129, 160, 191 i; foreign policy, 5, 7, 11, 15–17, 24, 30–31, 78, 185; and Jews, 167–68; July 1943 dismissal, xv, 13, 170, 174–75; slogans against, 35–36, 51, 113–14, 159; speeches, x

National Socialist People's Welfare Organization, or NSV, 202
Nazi-Soviet Pact, 135
Nice (Alpes-Maritimes), xi–xv, 3, 19, 50–51, 60, 64, 94, 123, 125, 135, 140–41, 152–56, 158–60, 179, 181, 184; irredentist claims of, 5, 11, 16–17, 30–31, 34–35, 38, 42, 44–46, 54, 59, 65–66, 73–74, 77, 97, 145–46, 154, 189; Italian personnel in, 18, 29, 43, 53, 127–28, 148–49, 153, 156, 165–66, 168; Jews in, 164–66, 168, 170, 181; November 1942 occupation of, 78–79, 81, 83, 85–89; ousting of Vichy officials, 133–34; rationing and black market in, 38–40, 116–19; and Monument des Morts (Monument for the Fallen Soldiers), 48; Resistance attacks, 138–39, 142–43; Vichy propaganda of 46–49; and Vieux Nice, 47, 205; wave of arrests, 130–31
nucleo antiparacadutisti (anti-paratrooper units) (NAP), 102–3

Oberaugh, Walter, 88
Oberg, Carl xiii, 164, 167
Olmi, Roberto, 136
Olry, René, 21
Opera Nazionale Dopolavoro, 18
Operation Alaric, 177
Operation Anton, 81–82
Operation Dragoon, 181
Operation Husky, xiv, 176
Operation Lila, 93
Operation Torch, 110
Operti, Raffaello, 113
Organisation de Résistance de l'Armée (Resistance Organization of the Army), 84
Organisation Todt, 101, 112
Organizzazione per la Vigilanza e la Repressione dell'Antifascismo (Organization for Vigilance and Repression of Anti-Fascism) (OVRA), 18
Orlando, Taddeo, 193

Pact of Steel, xi, 6, 15
Paris, xi, 4; 1919 peace conference, 9; Italian community in, 40
Parti Franciste, 135, 237
Parti Populaire Français (PPF), 49, 135; antisemitism, 164
Partito Nazionale Fascista (National Fascist Party) (PNF), 42–44, 68, 69, 153–54
Pétain, Philippe, 23, 27, 31, 49, 71, 79, 84, 93, 134–35, 151; and propaganda 39, 47–48
Piedmont, 60, 70, 82, 157
Piedmont-Sardinia (Kingdom of), 3, 46
Pintor, Pietro, 29
police (French), xii, 19, 30, 35, 47, 105, 124, 187, 208; and Italian army, 106, 120, 124, 138–39, 176; and Italians, 20, 43, 89, 97, 133, 145, 153, 160; and Jews, xiii, 164–70; ousted from Menton, 22, 57, 63; reports, 38, 85, 141, 157; and Resistance, 128, 142

Polizia Politica. *See* Italian political police
Pont de l'Union (Menton), 51, 84
postwar trials, 153
Prince Louis II, 87–88
prisoners of war, xiii, 28, 37, 71
Purple Line, 28

Rafle du Vél d'Hiver (Vel d'Hiver
    Roundup), xiii, 164
rationing, xii, 12, 38–39, 45, 53, 63, 72,
    100–101, 113, 115–18, 135, 155, 157,
    159–60, 174, 180; in Italy, 50, 65, 70;
    in the Italian army, 107–9, 154; ration
    cards, xiv, 37, 41, 85, 97, 125, 165
rear zone, 100
Red Line, 28
refugees, 22; Jewish, xiv, 164–73; Menton-
    ese, 22, 62–65, 197
Relève, xiii, 97
Rémond, Paul, 39, 46–49, 60, 117, 134
Renseignements Généraux, 57, 113, 208
requisitions, 85, 100, 112, 119, 124,
    141–42, 156
Resistance, 10, 83–84, 88, 91, 123, 148,
    155, 184–86; arrests of, 92, 128, 131–32,
    140–41, 144, 176; attacks against Italian
    irredentists, army, and CIAF, 12–13,
    51–52, 128, 137–39, 141–43, 154, 176;
    attacks against Vichy 135–36, 143, 181;
    early period (pre November 1942), 73,
    134–35; fuorisciti, xiii, xiv, 18–19, 21,
    33, 42–43, 89, 135–37, 168, 142, 176,
    197; propaganda and, 136–37, 176;
    sabotage, 105, 138, 142–43, 176, 181
roundups, xiii, xiv, 10, 20, 129–31, 134,
    140–42, 153, 164–65, 168, 190, 210, 242
Rhône, 29, 77, 94
Ribière, Marcel, xiv, 46–47, 49, 61, 85, 117,
    133–34, 139, 164, 222, 236, 239
Ristolas (Hautes-Alpes), 28
Roatta, Mario, 6, 144, 177–78
Roblot, Emile, 88
Robotti, Mario, 185
Rome-Berlin Axis, 5
Roquebrune-Cap-Martin (Alpes-Mari-
    times), 57, 85–86, 218

Sainte-Foy (Savoie), 28
Saint-Étienne de Tinée (Alpes-Maritimes),
    61, 218

Saint-Laurent-du-Var (Alpes-Maritimes),
    17, 47, 121, 238, 245
Saint-Louis Bridge, 24, 44, 65
Saint-Martin-Vésubie (Alpes-Maritimes), xv,
    169–70. *See also* Jews
Saint Raphaël (Var), 93
Saint Tropez (Var), 93, 222
Sanfelice, Antonio, 52–53
Sarraut, Albert, 19
Savona (Liguria), xii, 44–45
SBM (Société des Bains de Mers et des
    Étrangers), 87
Schaeffer, Carl, 87
schools, 17–18, 20, 35, 48, 58–59, 61, 68,
    84–85, 117, 135, 142, 158, 169, 175,
    183, 209
Scramble for Africa, 3
Secours National, 39, 63, 202
Séez (Savoie), 28
Sereni, Emilio, 136, 237
Service d'Ordre Légionnaire (SOL), xii, 48,
    135
Service du Travail Obligatoire (STO), xiv,
    73, 154, 170
Servizio Informazioni Militare (SIM), 18,
    128–32, 143
Società Dante Alighieri, 20
Sollières (Savoie), 28
Sorice, Antonio, 147
Spanish Civil War, 5, 21, 33, 63, 196, 233
Stato Maggiore Italiano (Italian General
    Staff) (SMG), 23, 29–30, 81, 99, 111,
    139, 174, 176–77
Stato Maggiore dell'Esercito (Italian Gen-
    eral Staff Army) (SMRE), 80–83, 89, 95
Strobino, Federico, 170–71
Système D, 39

Tabellini, Ugo, 80
Tallarigo, Marcello, 69
Témoignage chrétien au sud, 135
Termignon (Savoie), 28
theft 10, 12, 45, 85, 115, 119–22, 125, 157,
    190
Third Republic, 11, 27, 71, 135
Thoard (Basses-Alpes), 124
Toulon, 29, 81, 92–95, 129, 179–81
Trabucchi, Alessandro, 133, 165, 178
Traglia, Gustavo, 44
Trinité-Victor (Nice), 142, 240

Tur, Vittorio, 94
Turcato, Ugo 148–49, 244

Unione Popolare Italiana (UPI), 135
Ustaša, 185

Vacca Maggiolini, Arturo, 29, 78, 83, 98–99, 147
Valentin, François, 49–50
Vallat, Xavier, 164
Vence (Alpes-Maritimes), 17, 124, 250
Ventimiglia, 60, 65
Vercellino, Mario, xiii–xv, 81, 89, 97–98, 113, 138, 141, 176, 179, 188; conflict with CIAF, 146–48; criticism of Fourth Army, 101–4, 107, 137, 175; occupation policy, 80, 89, 91–92, 99, 129–30, 144
Verneau, Jean-Édouard, 84
Vichy regime, xii–xiv, 7, 9, 11–13, 19, 29–31, 38, 40–41, 105, 115–17, 120, 151; and Alsace, 183–84; and CIAF, 32–33, 36–37, 39, 46–48, 53–57, 61–62, 64–65, 129, 146; and francité, 47–50; and Germans, 27–28, 79; and Italian occupation army, 82–85, 91, 93–97, 123–25, 133–35; and Jews, 36, 162–72; and National Revolution, 27, 39, 47–49, 71–72, 206
Villeneuve-Loubet (Alpes-Maritimes), 47, 49
Viscardi, Ercole, 52
Vogl, Oskar, 78
von Mackensen, Hans Georg, 168
von Neubronn, Alexander, 96
von Ribbentrop, Joachim, 30, 168
von Rundstedt, Gerd, 98
von Stülpnagel, Otto, 101

Wehrmacht. See German army
Wiesbaden accords, 29
women, 7, 40–41, 49, 51, 64, 71, 103–5, 107, 114–15, 142, 157–60, 167, 169, 180, 185

Zoppi, Vittorio, xiii, 34

Emanuele Sica is professor of history at the Royal Military College of Canada.

The University of Illinois Press
is a founding member of the
Association of American University Presses.

_____

Composed in 10/13 Sabon
by Lisa Connery
at the University of Illinois Press
Designed by Dennis Roberts
Manufactured by Sheridan Books, Inc.

University of Illinois Press
1325 South Oak Street
Champaign, IL 61820-6903
www.press.uillinois.edu